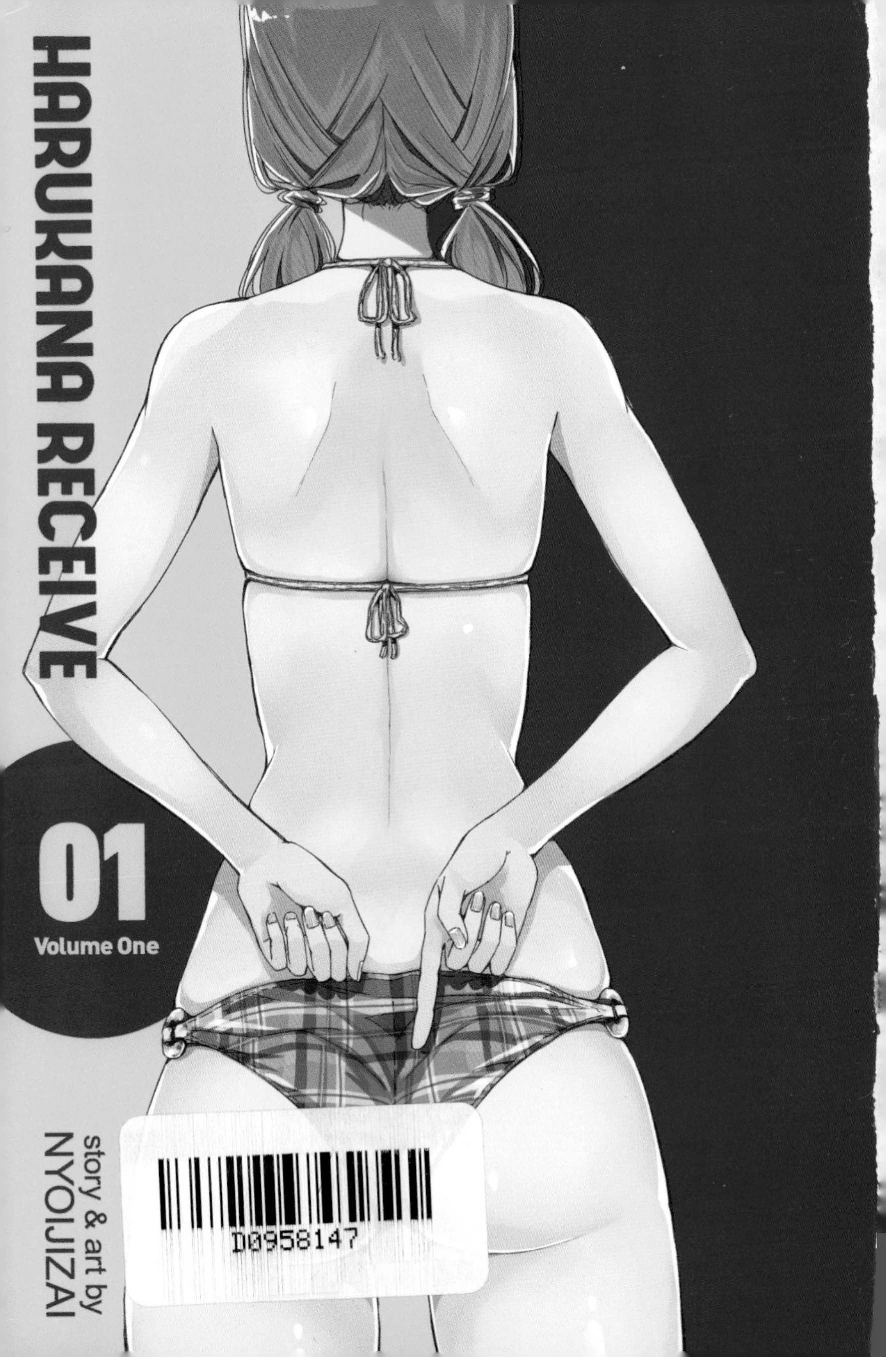
HARUKANA RECEIVE
01
Volume One
story & art by
NYOIJIZAI

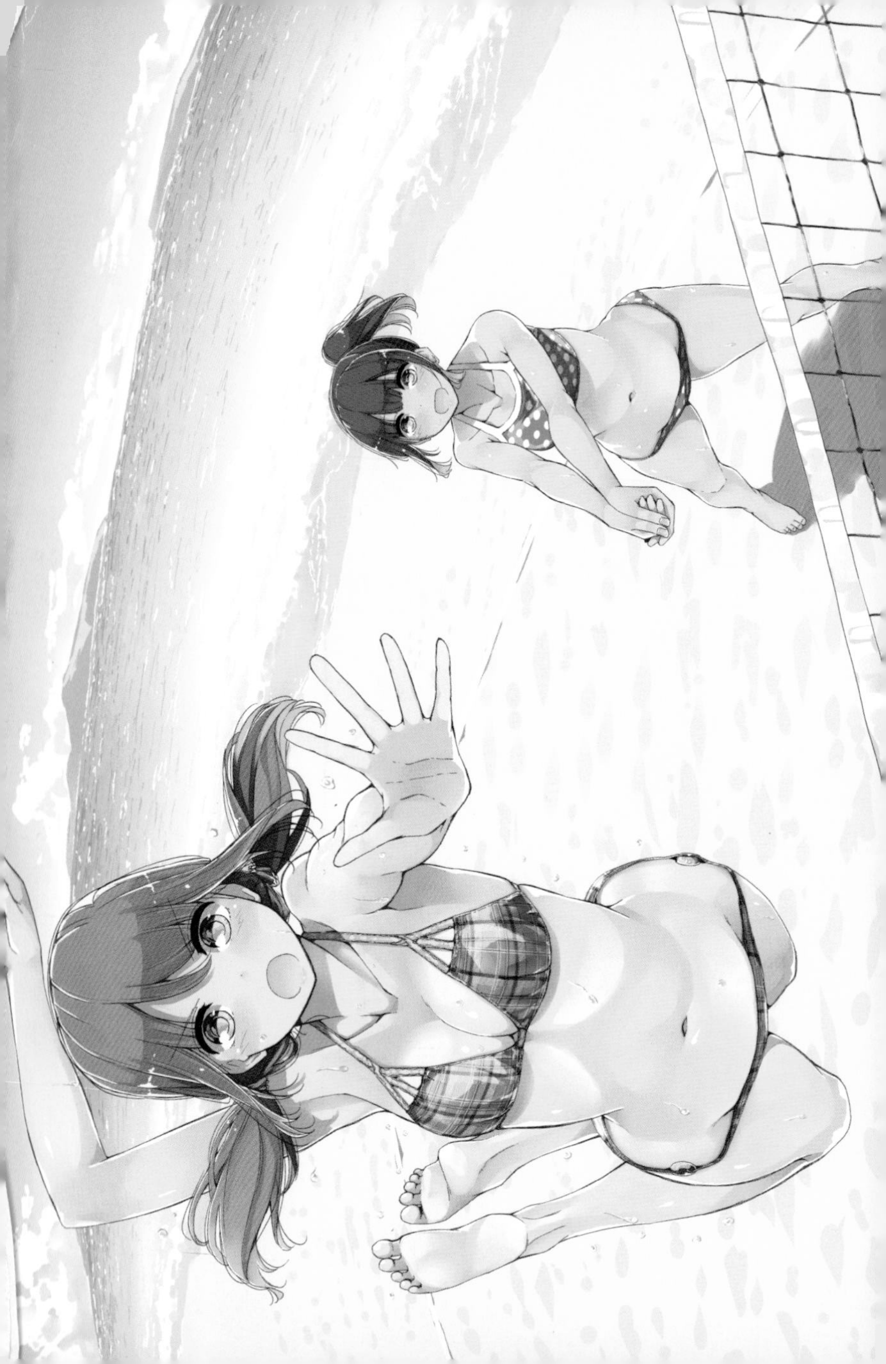

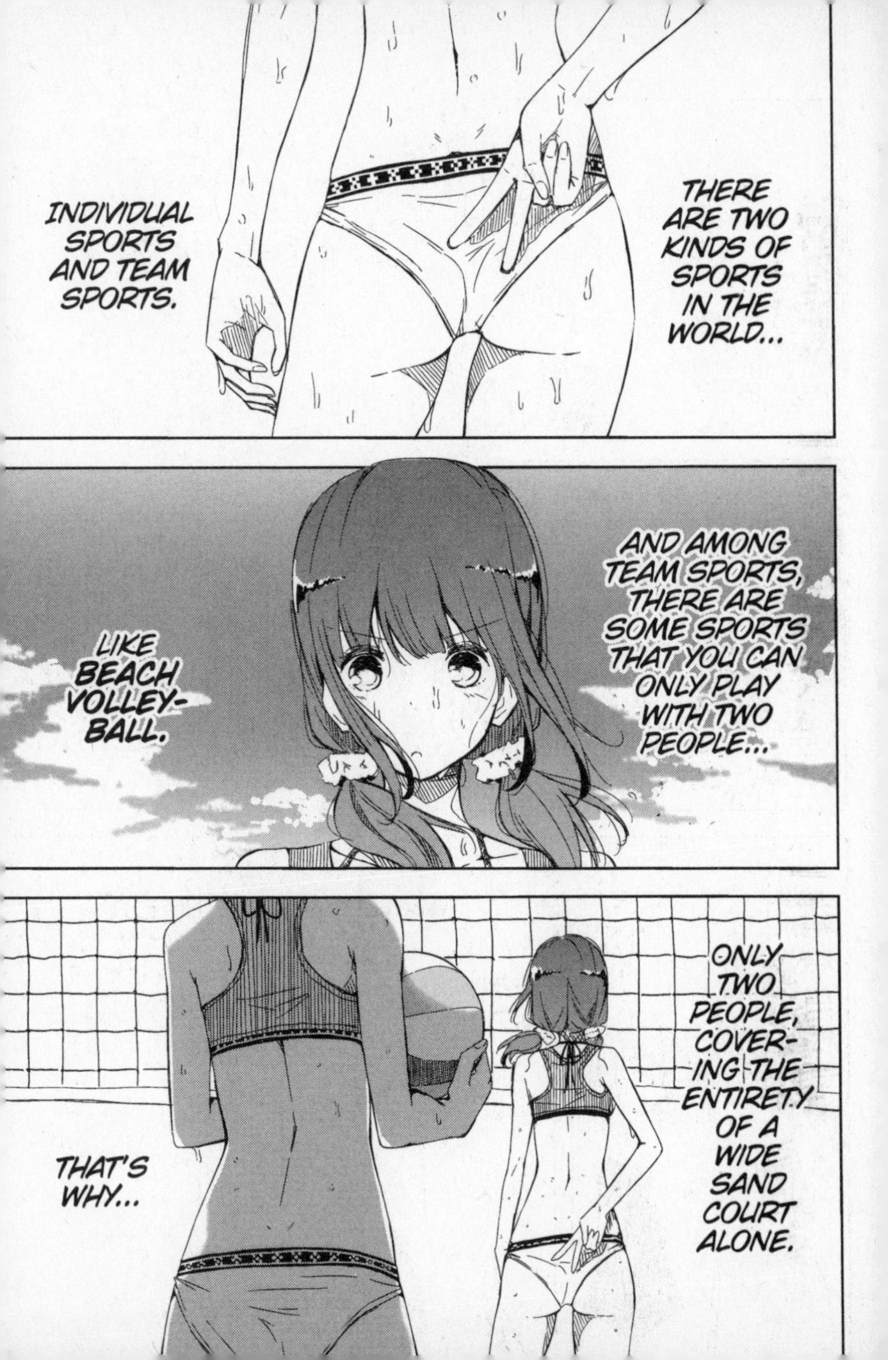
THERE ARE TWO KINDS OF SPORTS IN THE WORLD...
INDIVIDUAL SPORTS AND TEAM SPORTS.
AND AMONG TEAM SPORTS, THERE ARE SOME SPORTS THAT YOU CAN ONLY PLAY WITH TWO PEOPLE...
LIKE BEACH VOLLEYBALL.
ONLY TWO PEOPLE, COVERING THE ENTIRETY OF A WIDE SAND COURT ALONE.
THAT'S WHY...

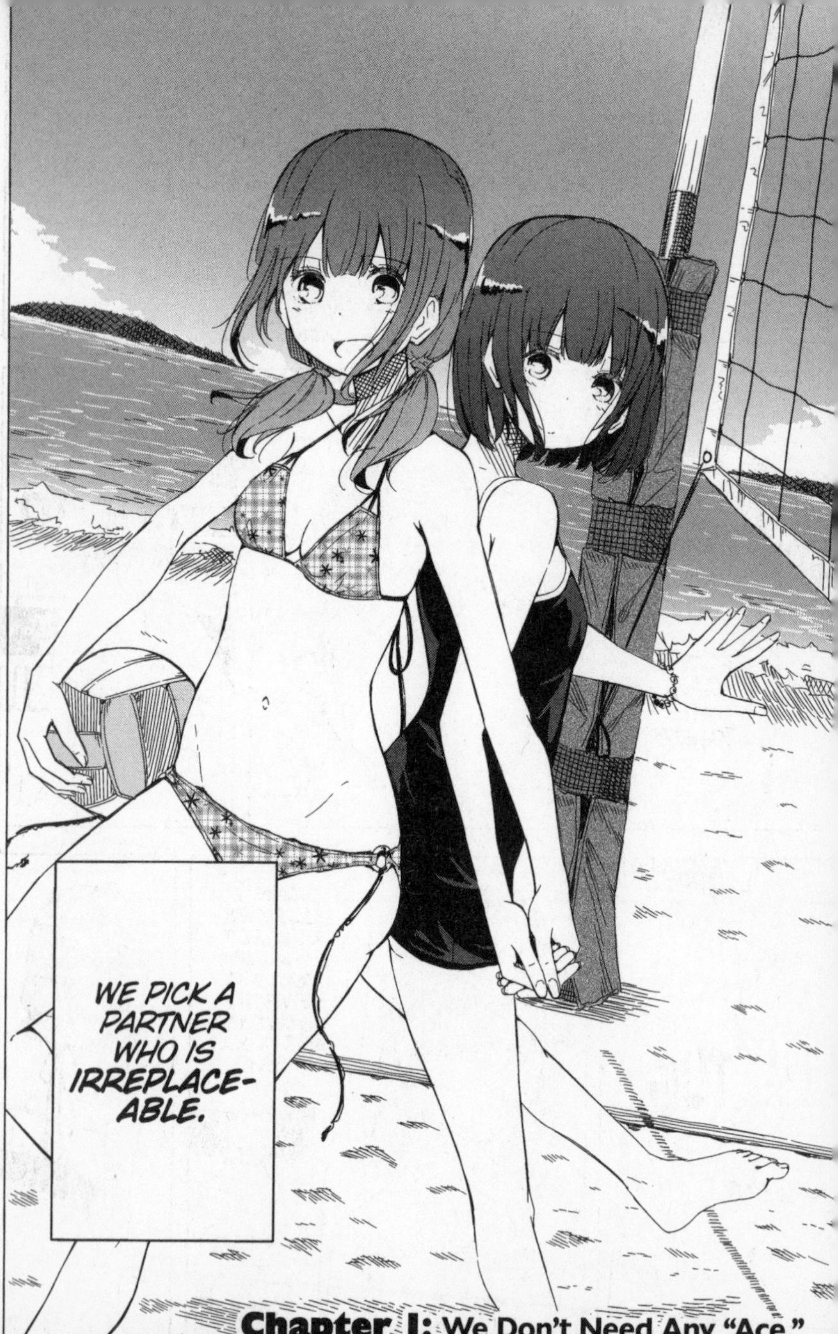
WE PICK A PARTNER WHO IS IRREPLACE-ABLE.

Chapter 1: We Don't Need Any "Ace."

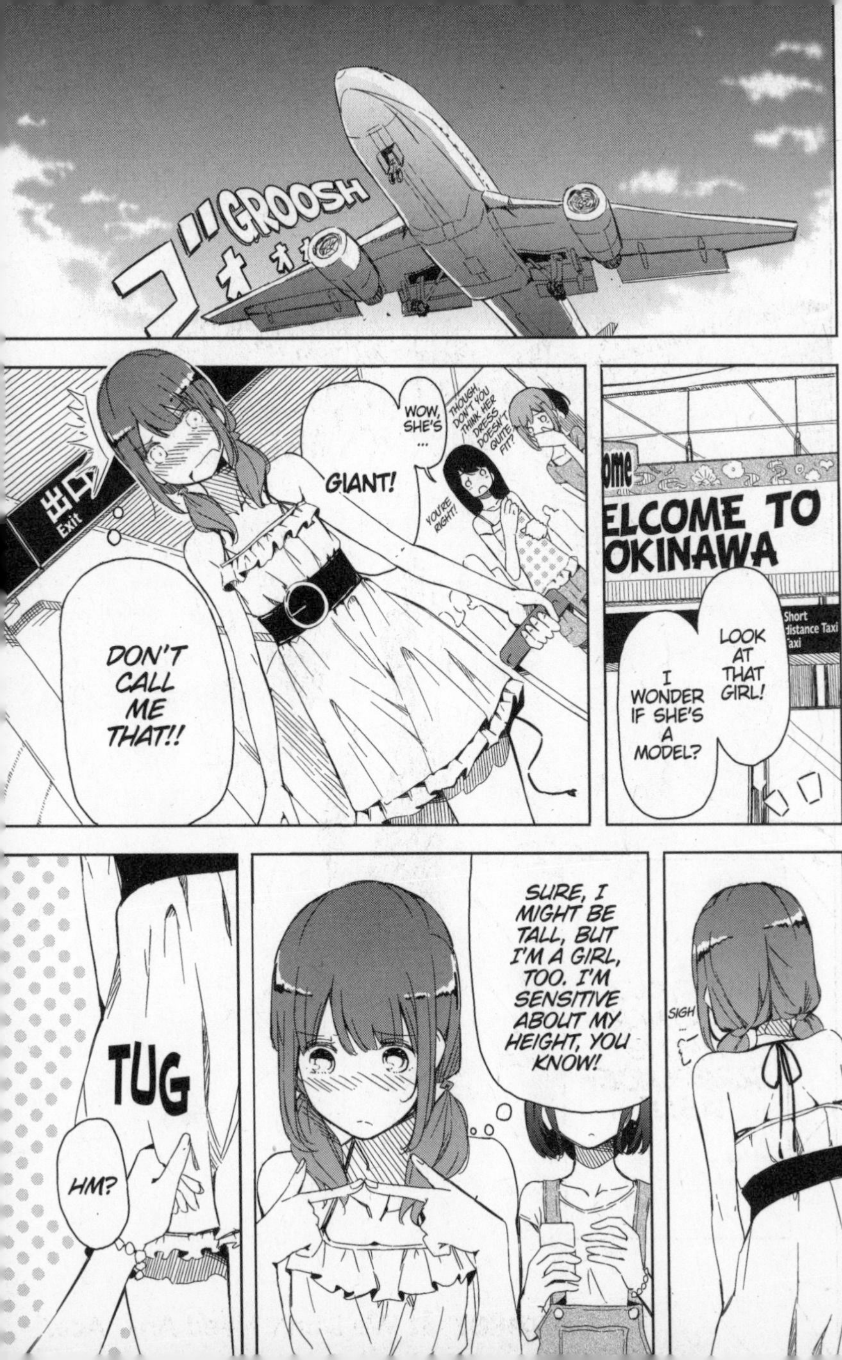
GROOSH
ome
ELCOME TO
OKINAWA
Short
distance Taxi
Taxi
LOOK AT THAT GIRL!
I WONDER IF SHE'S A MODEL?
WOW, SHE'S ...
GIANT!
THOUGH, DON'T YOU THINK HER DRESS DOESN'T QUITE FIT?
YOU'RE RIGHT!
出口
Exit
DON'T CALL ME THAT!!
SIGH ...
SURE, I MIGHT BE TALL, BUT I'M A GIRL, TOO. I'M SENSITIVE ABOUT MY HEIGHT, YOU KNOW!
TUG
HM?

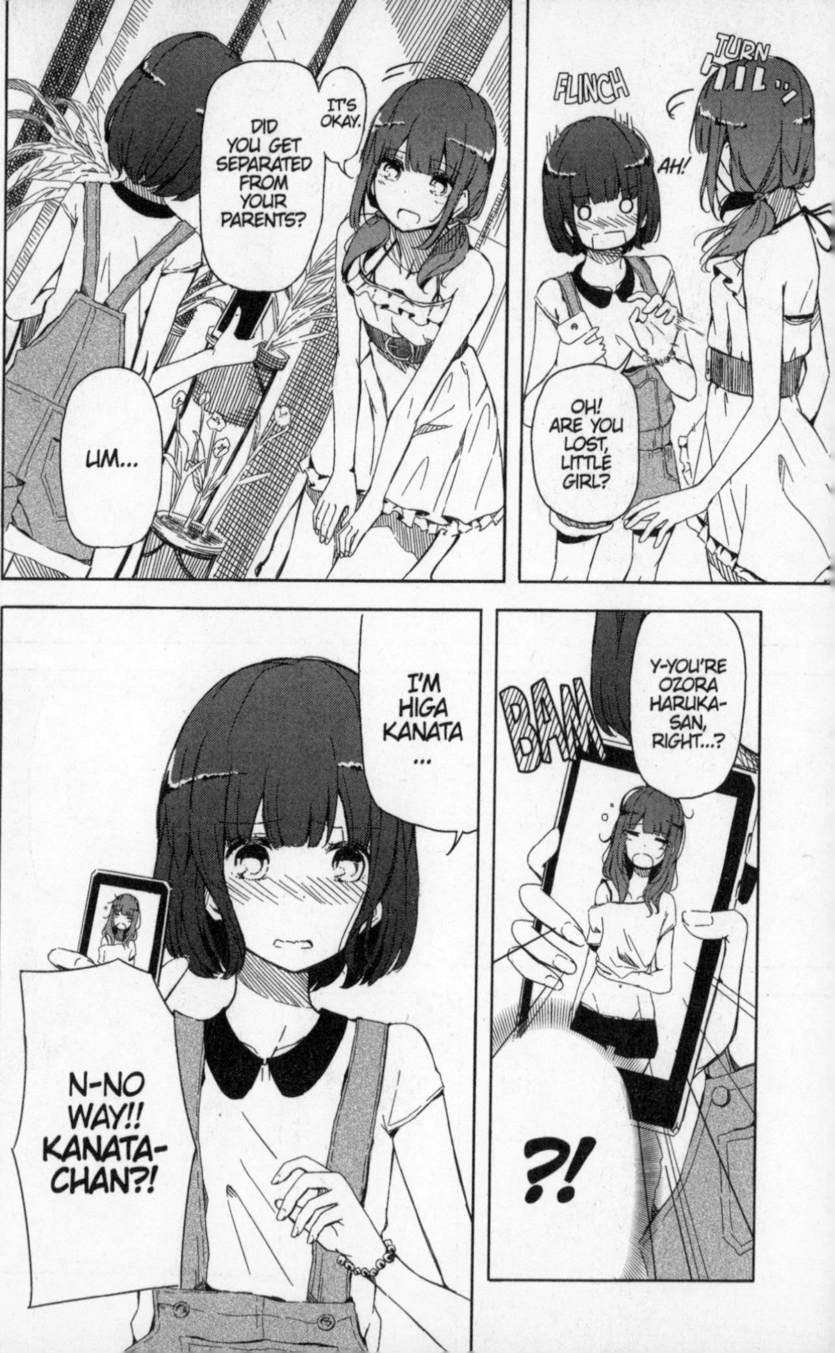
TURN
FLINCH
AH!
OH! ARE YOU LOST, LITTLE GIRL?
DID YOU GET SEPARATED FROM YOUR PARENTS?
IT'S OKAY.
UM...
Y-YOU'RE OZORA HARUKA-SAN, RIGHT...?
BAM
?!
I'M HIGA KANATA ...
N-NO WAY!! KANATA-CHAN?!

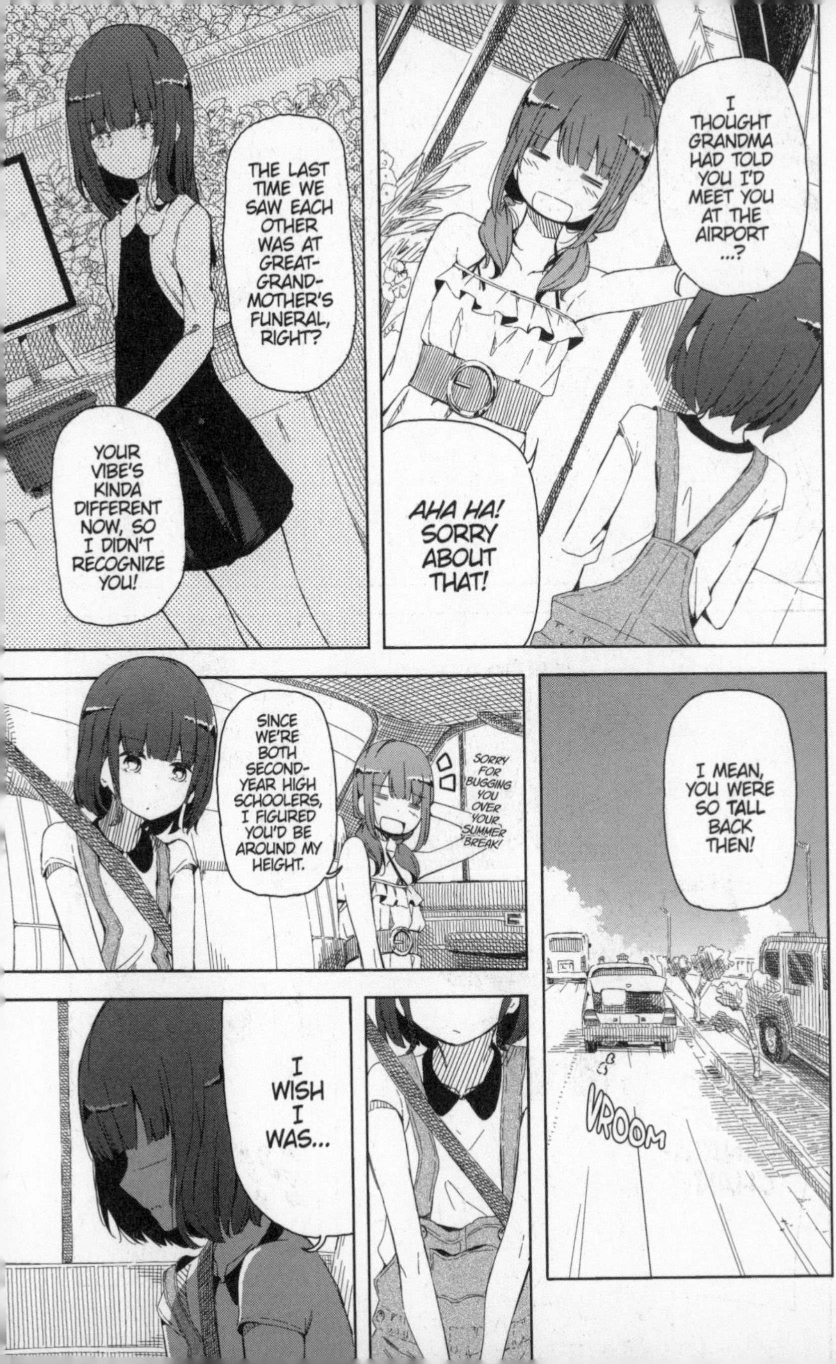
I THOUGHT GRANDMA HAD TOLD YOU I'D MEET YOU AT THE AIRPORT ...?
AHA HA! SORRY ABOUT THAT!
THE LAST TIME WE SAW EACH OTHER WAS AT GREAT-GRANDMOTHER'S FUNERAL, RIGHT?
YOUR VIBE'S KINDA DIFFERENT NOW, SO I DIDN'T RECOGNIZE YOU!
I MEAN, YOU WERE SO TALL BACK THEN!
VROOM
SORRY FOR BUGGING YOU OVER YOUR SUMMER BREAK!
SINCE WE'RE BOTH SECOND-YEAR HIGH SCHOOLERS, I FIGURED YOU'D BE AROUND MY HEIGHT.
I WISH I WAS...

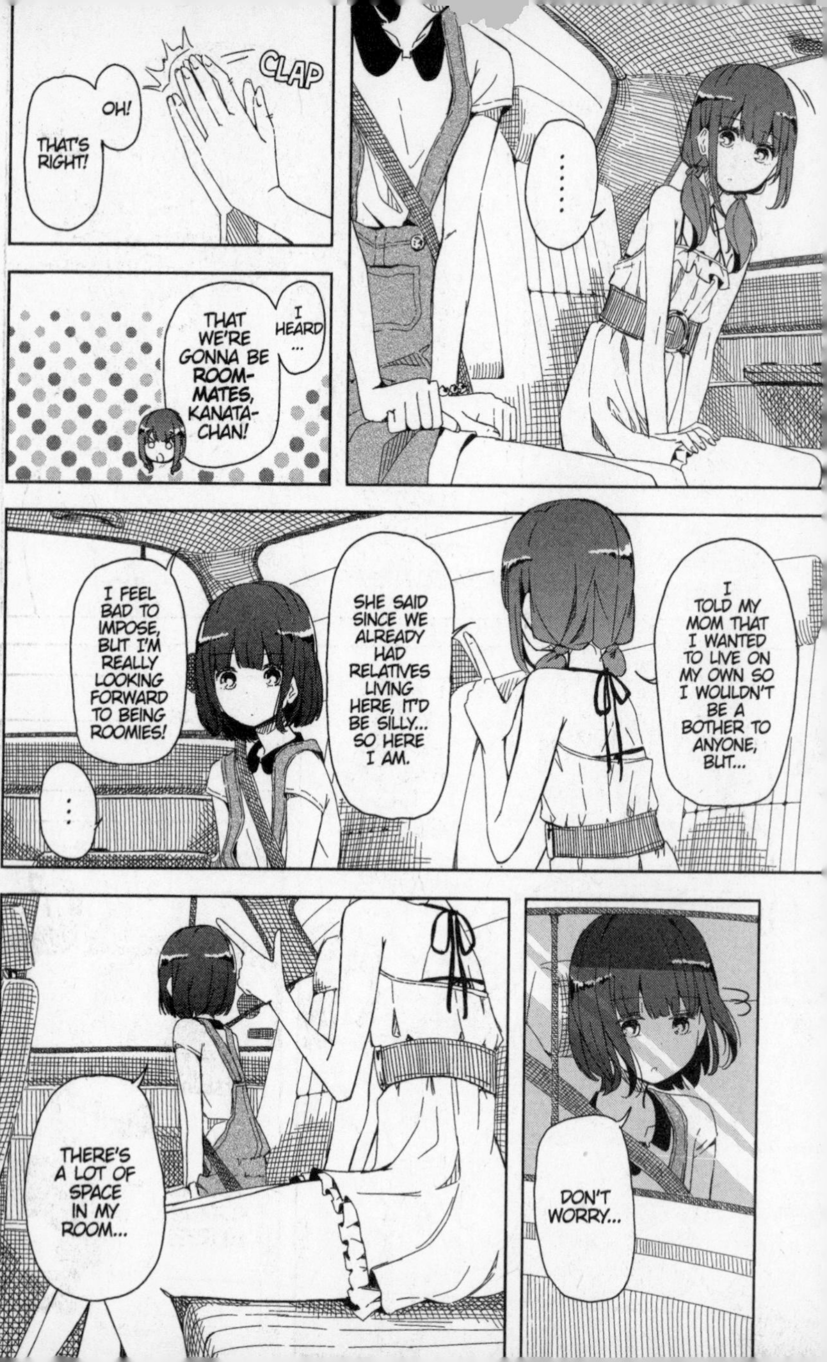
......
OH! THAT'S RIGHT!
CLAP
I HEARD...
THAT WE'RE GONNA BE ROOMMATES, KANATA-CHAN!
I TOLD MY MOM THAT I WANTED TO LIVE ON MY OWN SO I WOULDN'T BE A BOTHER TO ANYONE, BUT...
SHE SAID SINCE WE ALREADY HAD RELATIVES LIVING HERE, IT'D BE SILLY... SO HERE I AM.
I FEEL BAD TO IMPOSE, BUT I'M REALLY LOOKING FORWARD TO BEING ROOMIES!
...
DON'T WORRY...
THERE'S A LOT OF SPACE IN MY ROOM...

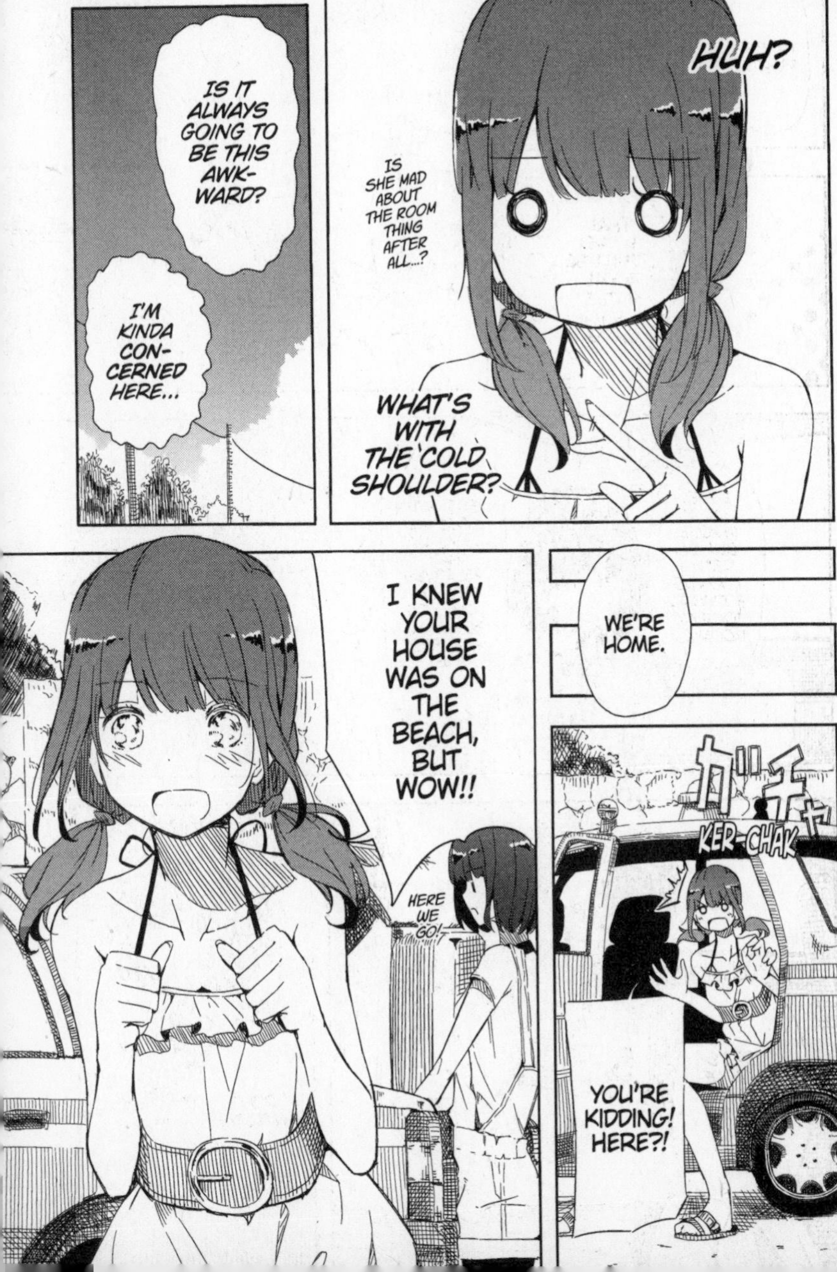
HUH?
IS SHE MAD ABOUT THE ROOM THING AFTER ALL...?
WHAT'S WITH THE COLD SHOULDER?
IS IT ALWAYS GOING TO BE THIS AWK-WARD?
I'M KINDA CON-CERNED HERE...
WE'RE HOME.
カチャ
KER-CHAK
YOU'RE KIDDING! HERE?!
I KNEW YOUR HOUSE WAS ON THE BEACH, BUT WOW!!
HERE WE GO!

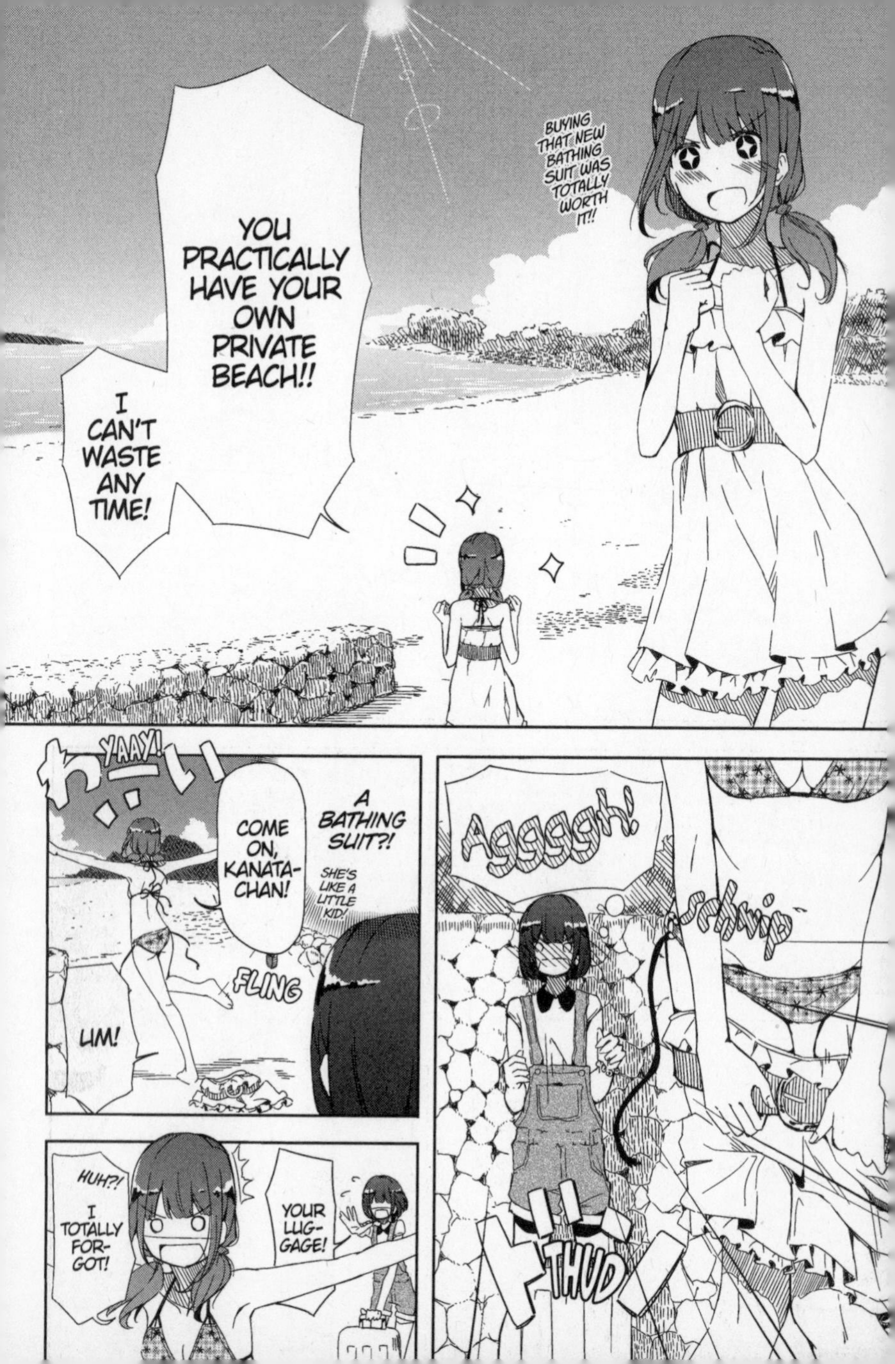
BUYING THAT NEW BATHING SUIT WAS TOTALLY WORTH IT!!
YOU PRACTICALLY HAVE YOUR OWN PRIVATE BEACH!!
I CAN'T WASTE ANY TIME!
Aggggh!
schwip
THUD
YAAY!
A BATHING SUIT?!
SHE'S LIKE A LITTLE KID!
COME ON, KANATA-CHAN!
FLING
UM!
YOUR LUG-GAGE!
HUH?!
I TOTALLY FOR-GOT!

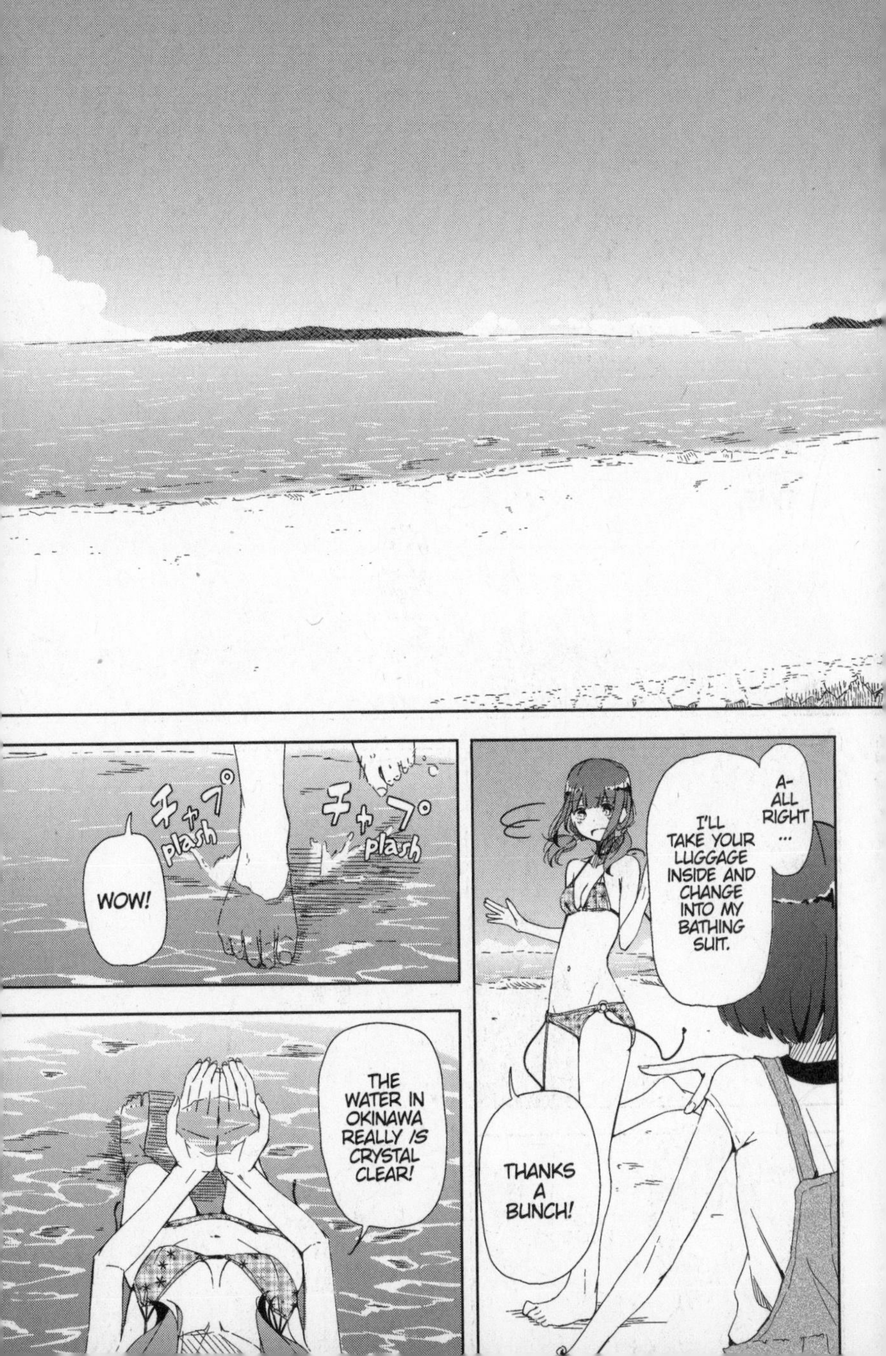
A-ALL RIGHT ...
I'LL TAKE YOUR LUGGAGE INSIDE AND CHANGE INTO MY BATHING SUIT.
THANKS A BUNCH!
チャプ
plash
チャプ
plash
WOW!
THE WATER IN OKINAWA REALLY IS CRYSTAL CLEAR!

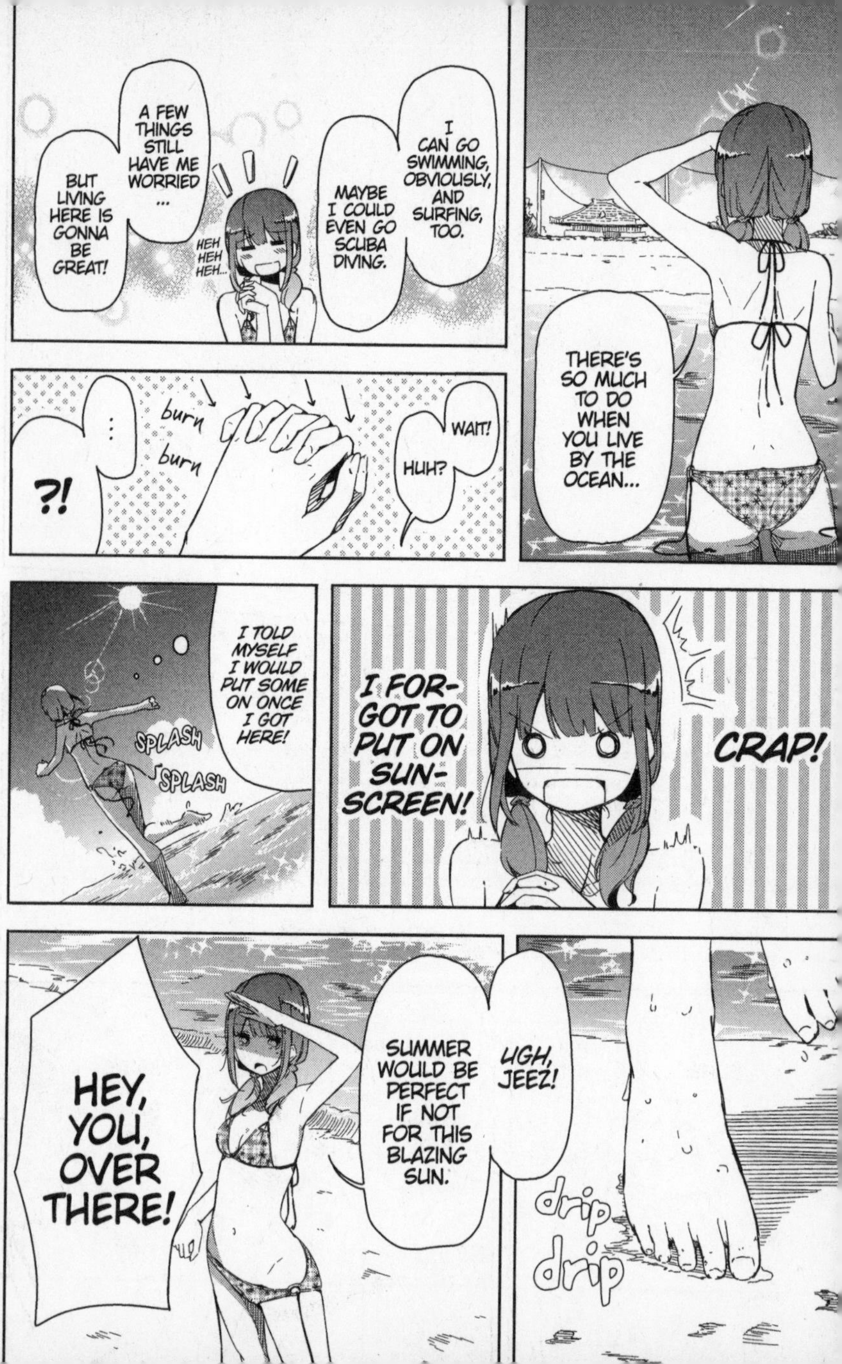
THERE'S SO MUCH TO DO WHEN YOU LIVE BY THE OCEAN...
I CAN GO SWIMMING, OBVIOUSLY, AND SURFING, TOO.
MAYBE I COULD EVEN GO SCUBA DIVING.
HEH HEH HEH...
A FEW THINGS STILL HAVE ME WORRIED...
BUT LIVING HERE IS GONNA BE GREAT!
WAIT!
HUH?
burn
burn
...
?!
CRAP!
I FOR-GOT TO PUT ON SUN-SCREEN!
I TOLD MYSELF I WOULD PUT SOME ON ONCE I GOT HERE!
SPLASH
SPLASH
UGH, JEEZ!
drip
drip
SUMMER WOULD BE PERFECT IF NOT FOR THIS BLAZING SUN.
HEY, YOU, OVER THERE!

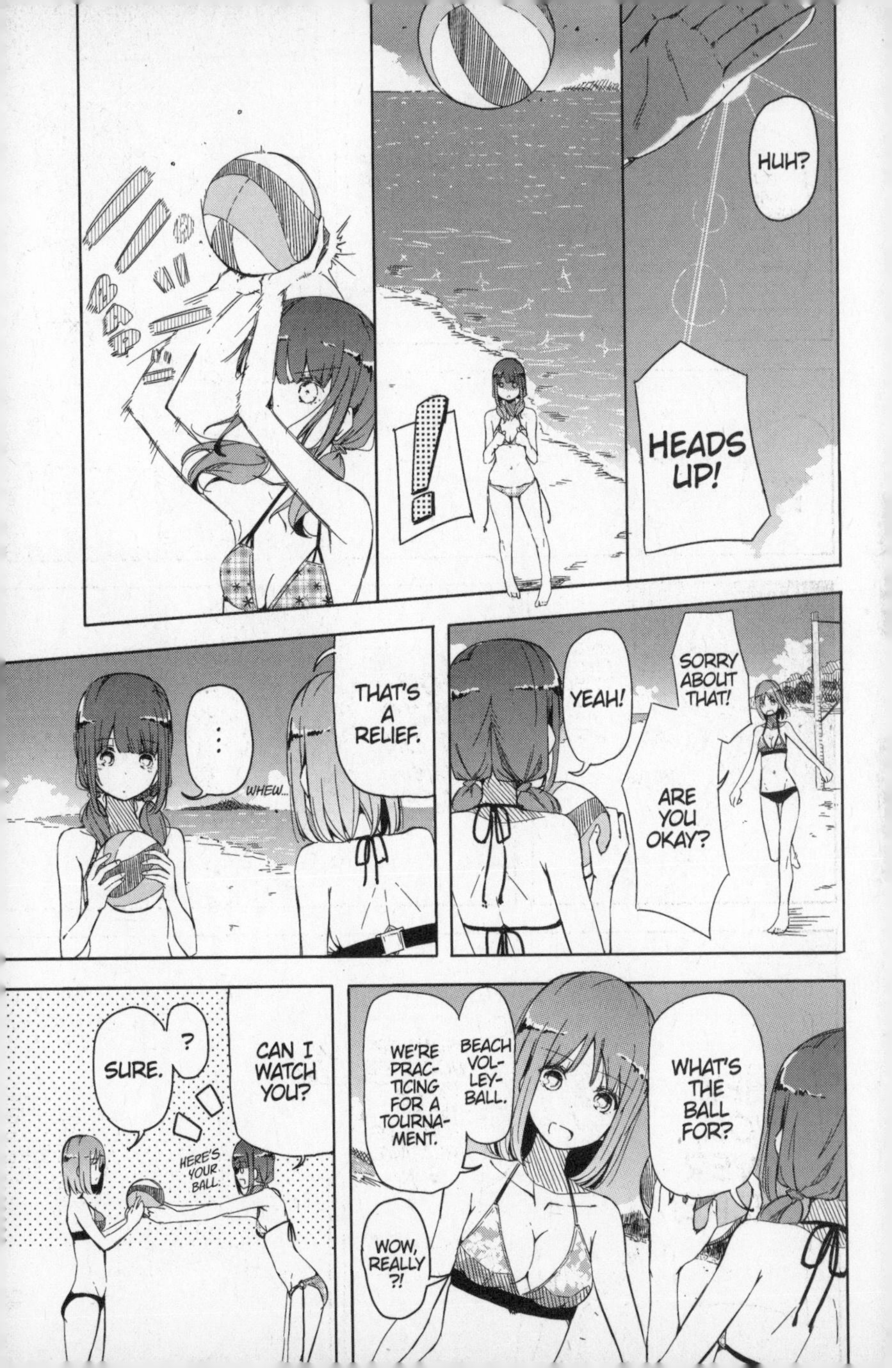
HUH?
HEADS UP!
!
SORRY ABOUT THAT!
ARE YOU OKAY?
YEAH!
THAT'S A RELIEF.
WHEW...
...
WHAT'S THE BALL FOR?
BEACH VOL-LEY-BALL.
WE'RE PRAC-TICING FOR A TOURNA-MENT.
WOW, REALLY ?!
CAN I WATCH YOU?
?
SURE.
HERE'S YOUR BALL.

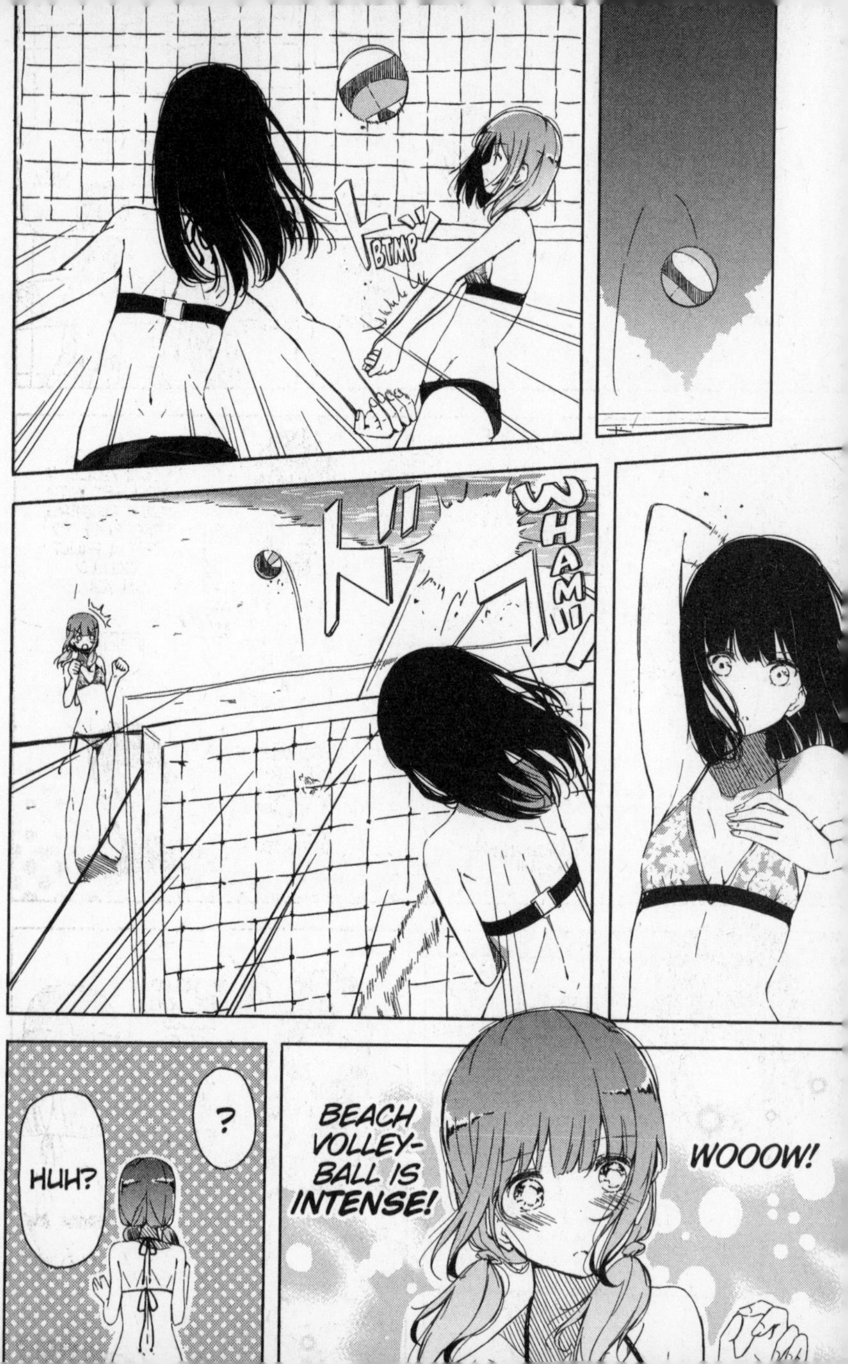
BTIMP
WHAM!!
WOOOW!
BEACH VOLLEY-BALL IS INTENSE!
?
HUH?

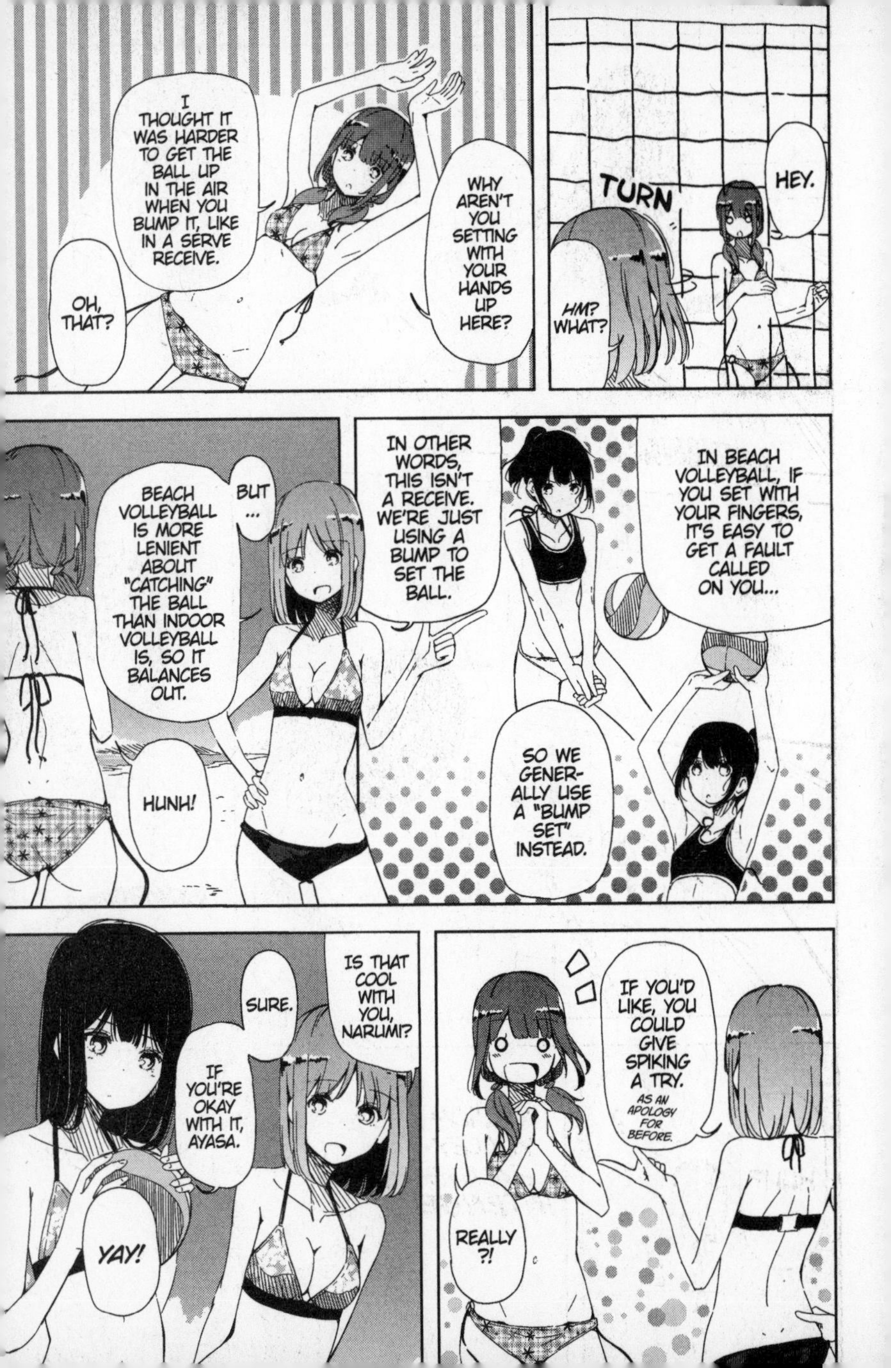
HEY.
TURN
HM? WHAT?
WHY AREN'T YOU SETTING WITH YOUR HANDS UP HERE?
I THOUGHT IT WAS HARDER TO GET THE BALL UP IN THE AIR WHEN YOU BUMP IT, LIKE IN A SERVE RECEIVE.
OH, THAT?
IN BEACH VOLLEYBALL, IF YOU SET WITH YOUR FINGERS, IT'S EASY TO GET A FAULT CALLED ON YOU...
SO WE GENERALLY USE A "BUMP SET" INSTEAD.
IN OTHER WORDS, THIS ISN'T A RECEIVE. WE'RE JUST USING A BUMP TO SET THE BALL.
BUT ...
BEACH VOLLEYBALL IS MORE LENIENT ABOUT "CATCHING" THE BALL THAN INDOOR VOLLEYBALL IS, SO IT BALANCES OUT.
HUNH!
IF YOU'D LIKE, YOU COULD GIVE SPIKING A TRY.
AS AN APOLOGY FOR BEFORE.
REALLY ?!
IS THAT COOL WITH YOU, NARUMI?
SURE.
IF YOU'RE OKAY WITH IT, AYASA.
YAY!

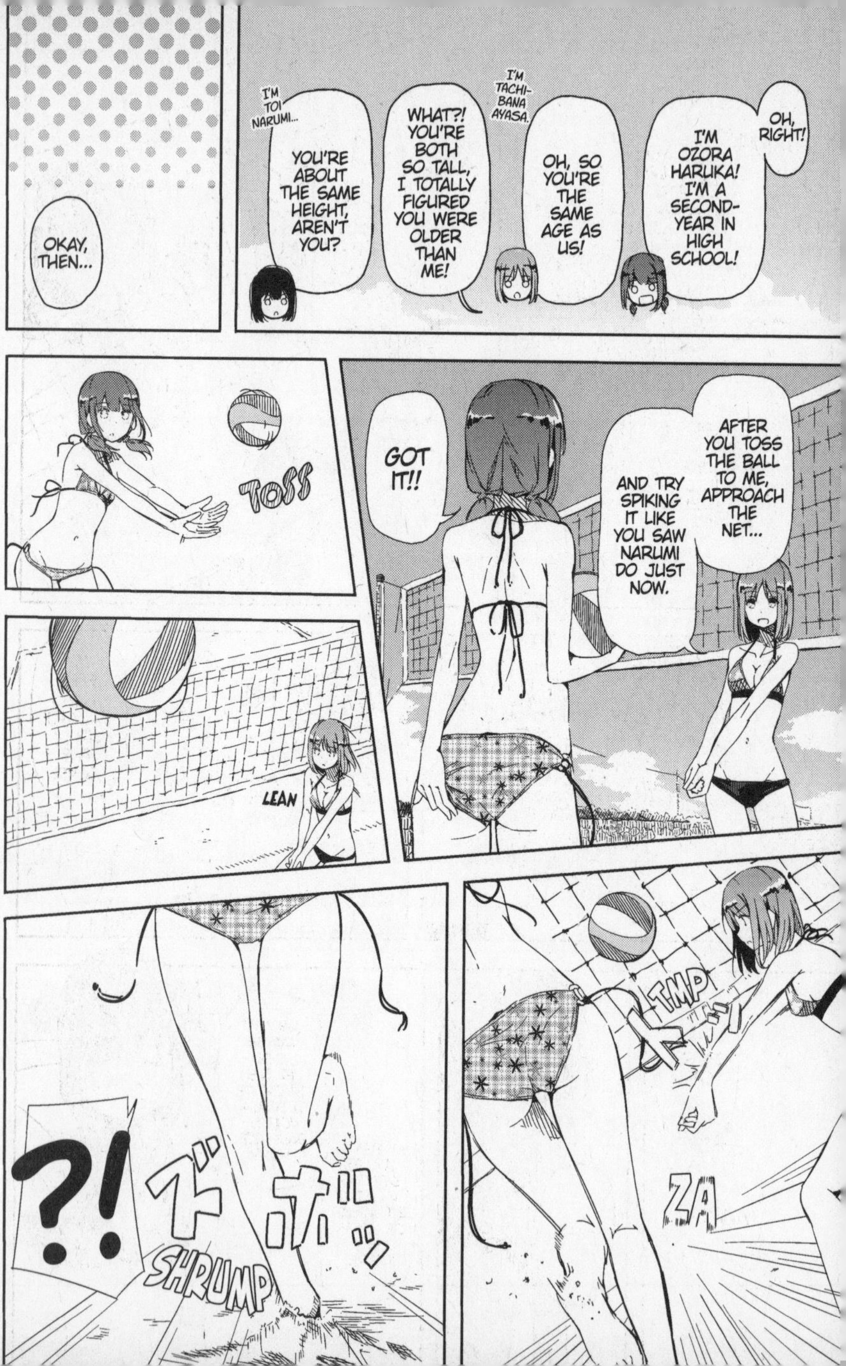
OH, RIGHT!
I'M OZORA HARUKA! I'M A SECOND-YEAR IN HIGH SCHOOL!
I'M TACHIBANA AYASA.
OH, SO YOU'RE THE SAME AGE AS US!
WHAT?! YOU'RE BOTH SO TALL, I TOTALLY FIGURED YOU WERE OLDER THAN ME!
I'M TOI NARUMI...
YOU'RE ABOUT THE SAME HEIGHT, AREN'T YOU?
OKAY, THEN...
AFTER YOU TOSS THE BALL TO ME, APPROACH THE NET...
AND TRY SPIKING IT LIKE YOU SAW NARUMI DO JUST NOW.
GOT IT!!
TOSS
LEAN
TMP
ZA
?!
ズザッ
SHRUMP

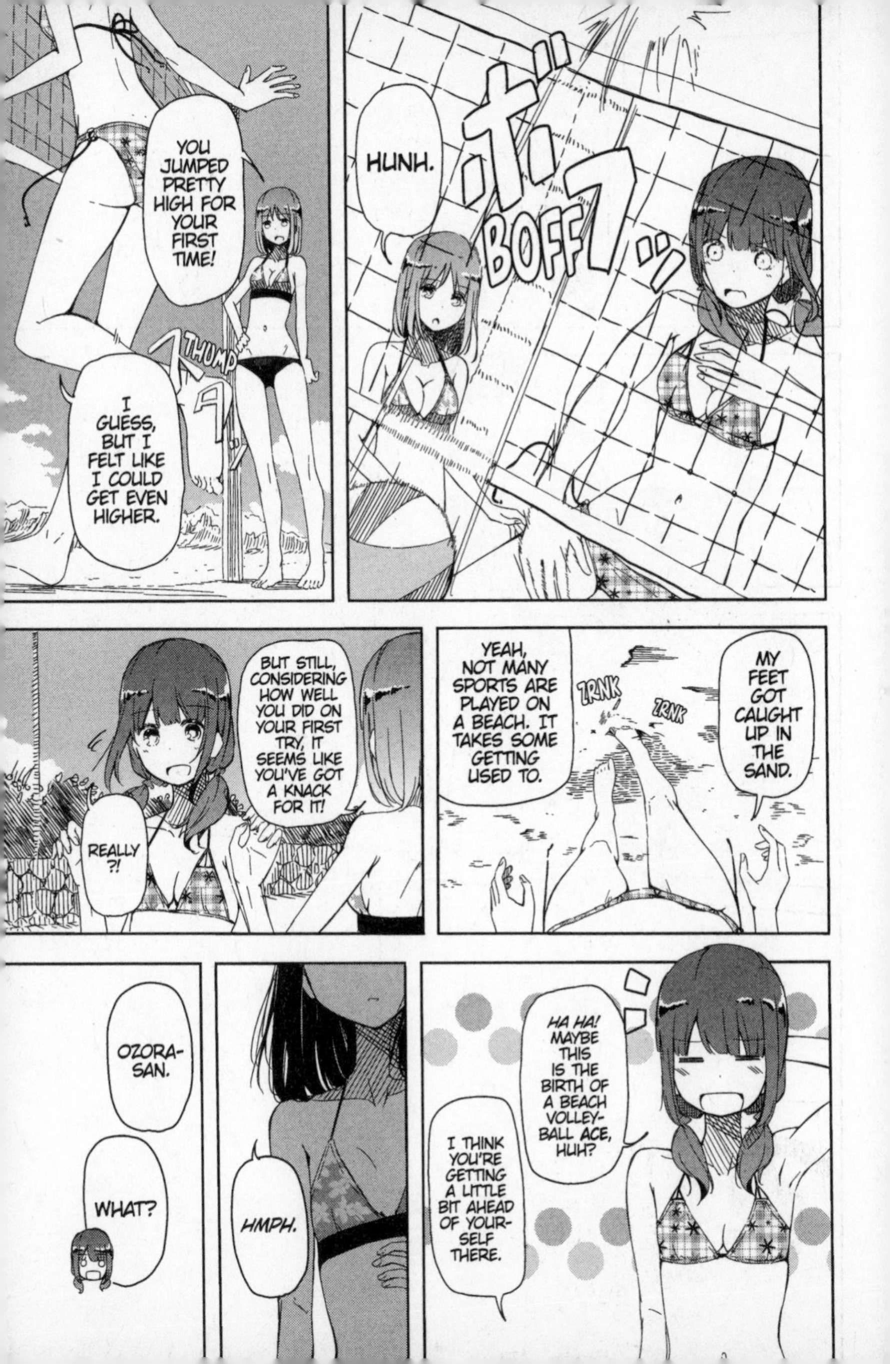
HUNH.
BOFF
YOU JUMPED PRETTY HIGH FOR YOUR FIRST TIME!
THUMP
I GUESS, BUT I FELT LIKE I COULD GET EVEN HIGHER.
MY FEET GOT CAUGHT UP IN THE SAND.
ZRNK
ZRNK
YEAH, NOT MANY SPORTS ARE PLAYED ON A BEACH. IT TAKES SOME GETTING USED TO.
BUT STILL, CONSIDERING HOW WELL YOU DID ON YOUR FIRST TRY, IT SEEMS LIKE YOU'VE GOT A KNACK FOR IT!
REALLY ?!
HA HA! MAYBE THIS IS THE BIRTH OF A BEACH VOLLEY-BALL ACE, HUH?
I THINK YOU'RE GETTING A LITTLE BIT AHEAD OF YOUR-SELF THERE.
HMPH.
OZORA-SAN.
WHAT?

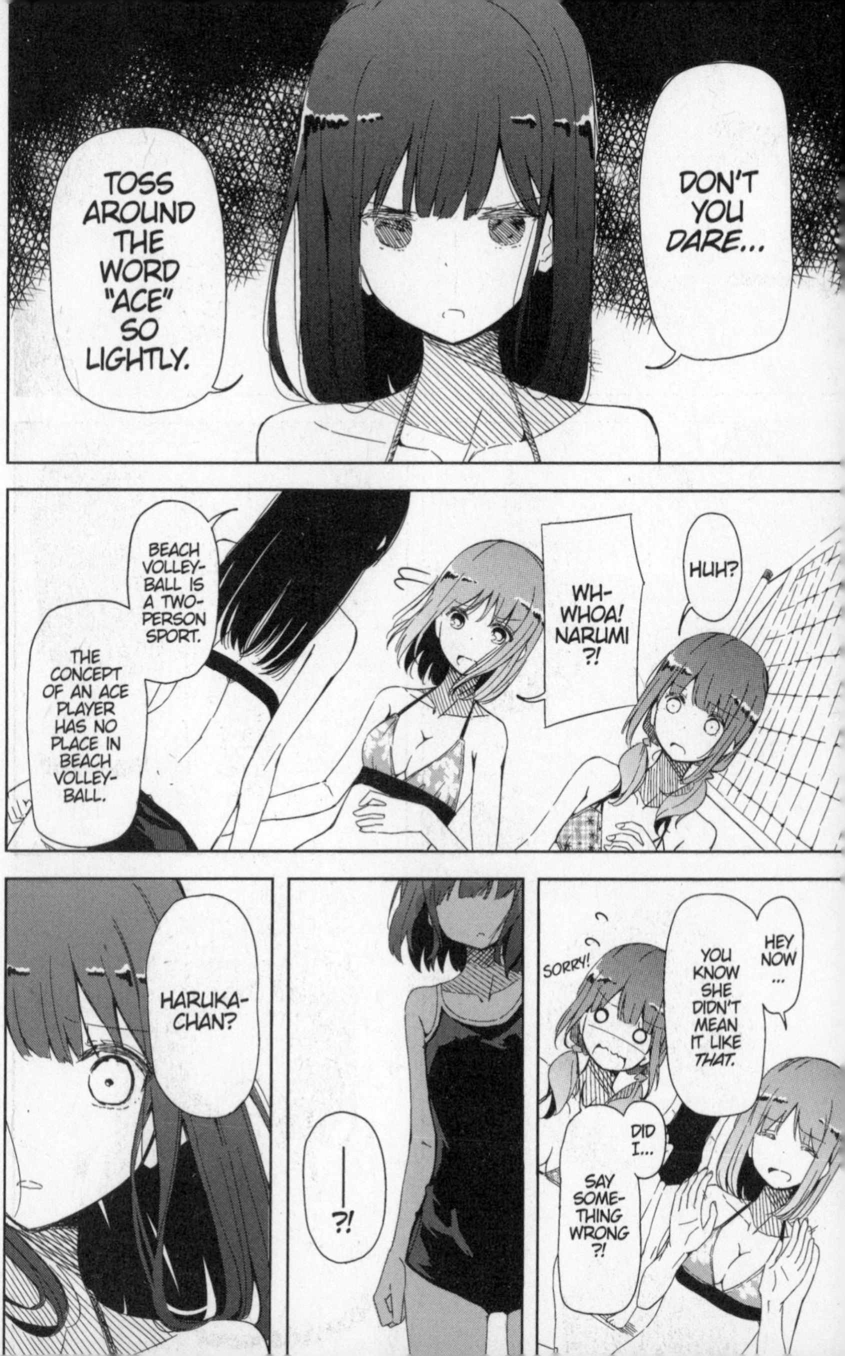
DON'T YOU DARE...
TOSS AROUND THE WORD "ACE" SO LIGHTLY.
HUH?
WH-WHOA! NARUMI?!
BEACH VOLLEYBALL IS A TWO-PERSON SPORT.
THE CONCEPT OF AN ACE PLAYER HAS NO PLACE IN BEACH VOLLEYBALL.
HEY NOW...
YOU KNOW SHE DIDN'T MEAN IT LIKE *THAT.*
SORRY!
DID I...
SAY SOMETHING WRONG?!
—?!
HARUKA-CHAN?

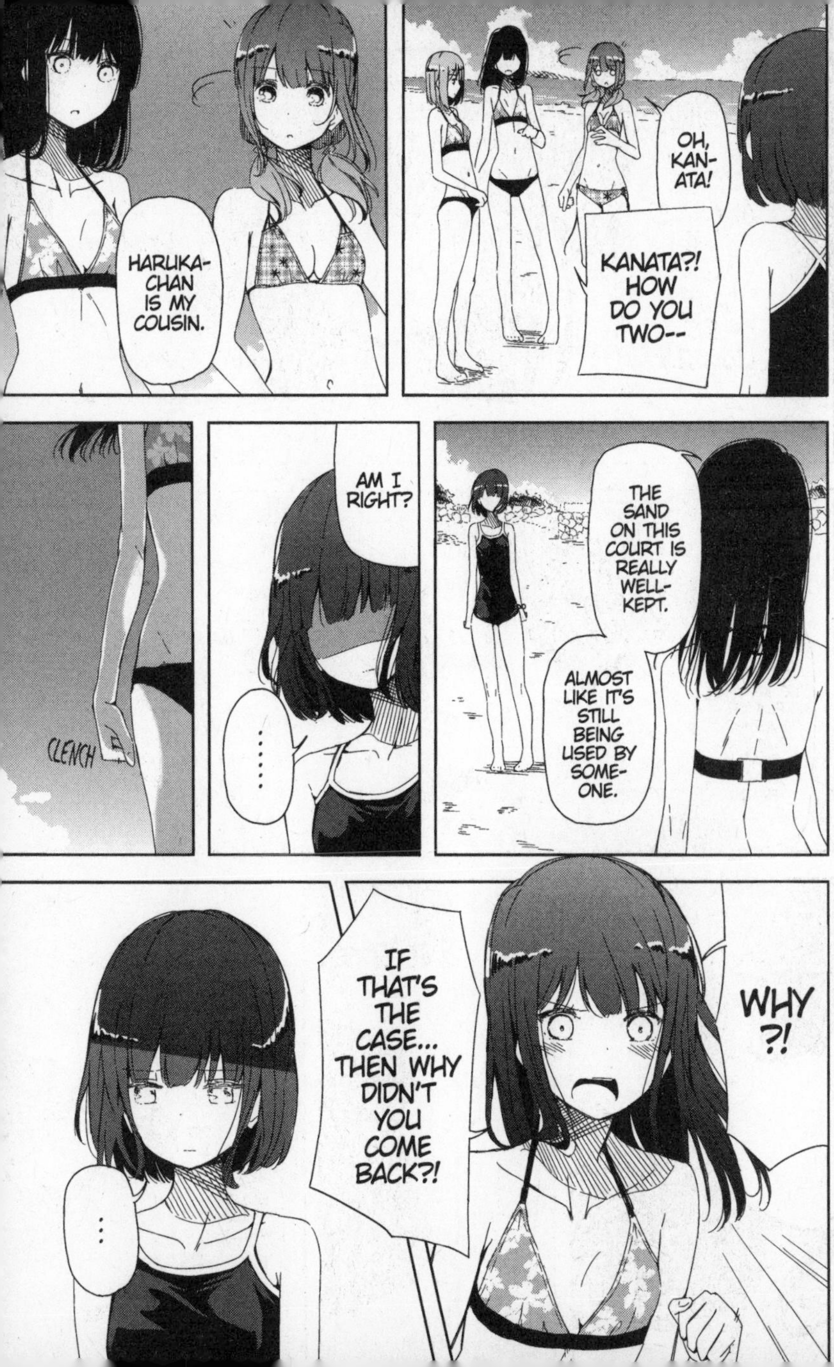
OH, KANATA!
KANATA?! HOW DO YOU TWO--
HARUKA-CHAN IS MY COUSIN.
THE SAND ON THIS COURT IS REALLY WELL-KEPT.
ALMOST LIKE IT'S STILL BEING USED BY SOME-ONE.
AM I RIGHT?
......
CLENCH
WHY?!
IF THAT'S THE CASE... THEN WHY DIDN'T YOU COME BACK?!
...

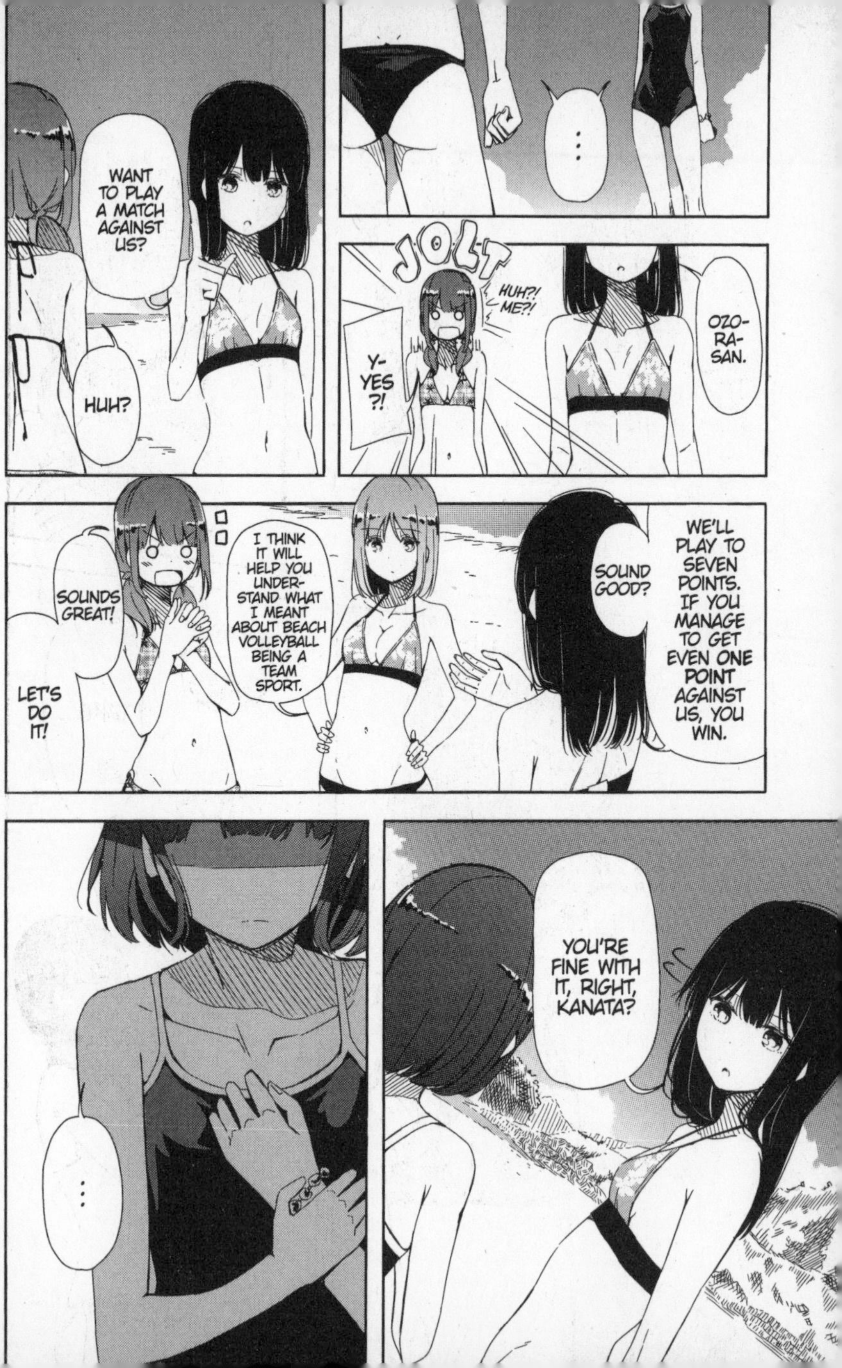
…
OZO-RA-SAN.
JOLT
HUH?! ME?!
Y-YES?!
WANT TO PLAY A MATCH AGAINST US?
HUH?
WE'LL PLAY TO SEVEN POINTS. IF YOU MANAGE TO GET EVEN ONE POINT AGAINST US, YOU WIN.
SOUND GOOD?
I THINK IT WILL HELP YOU UNDER-STAND WHAT I MEANT ABOUT BEACH VOLLEYBALL BEING A TEAM SPORT.
SOUNDS GREAT!
LET'S DO IT!
YOU'RE FINE WITH IT, RIGHT, KANATA?
…

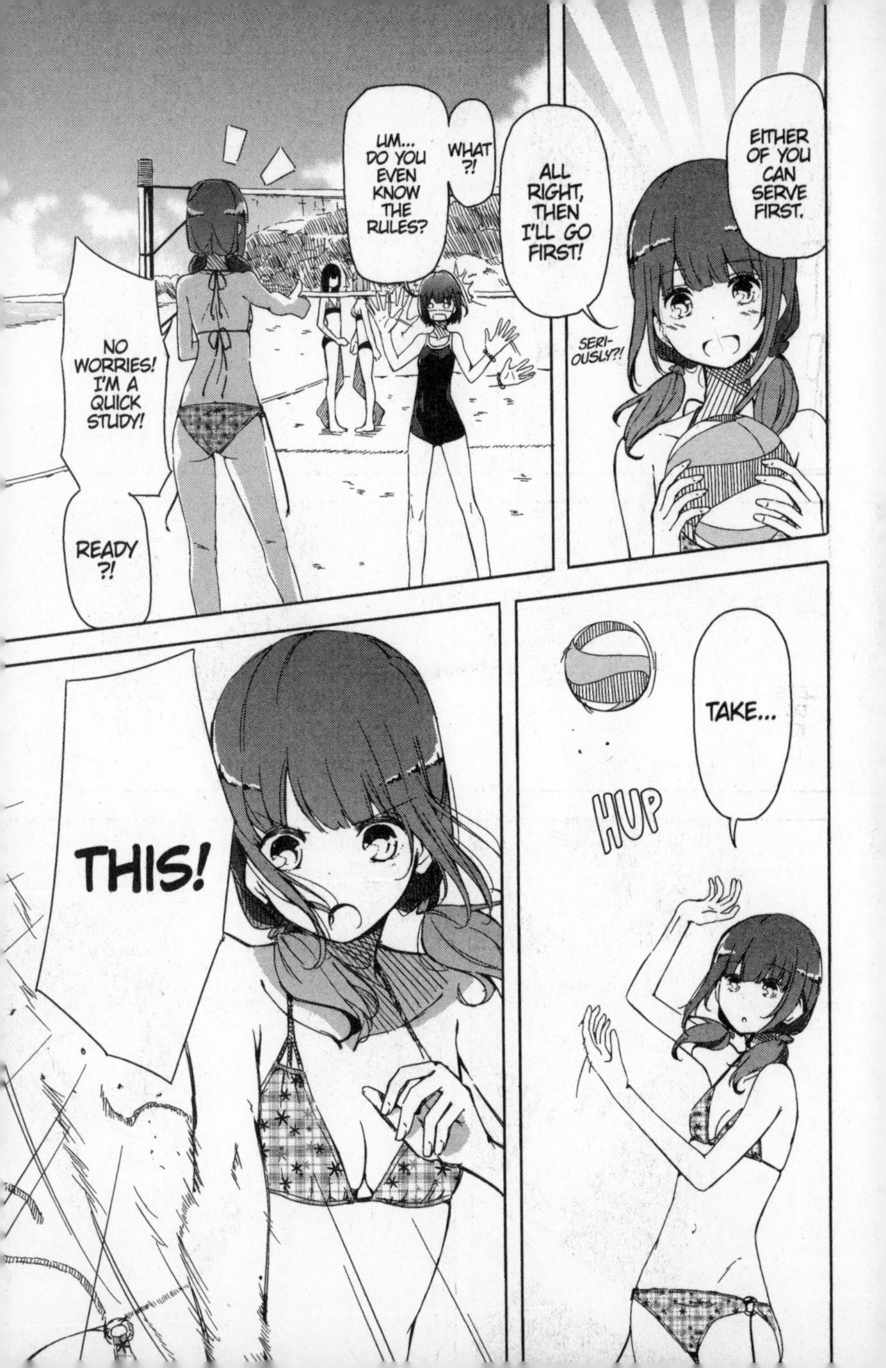
EITHER OF YOU CAN SERVE FIRST.
ALL RIGHT, THEN I'LL GO FIRST!
SERI-OUSLY?!
WHAT?!
UM... DO YOU EVEN KNOW THE RULES?
NO WORRIES! I'M A QUICK STUDY!
READY?!
TAKE...
HUP
THIS!

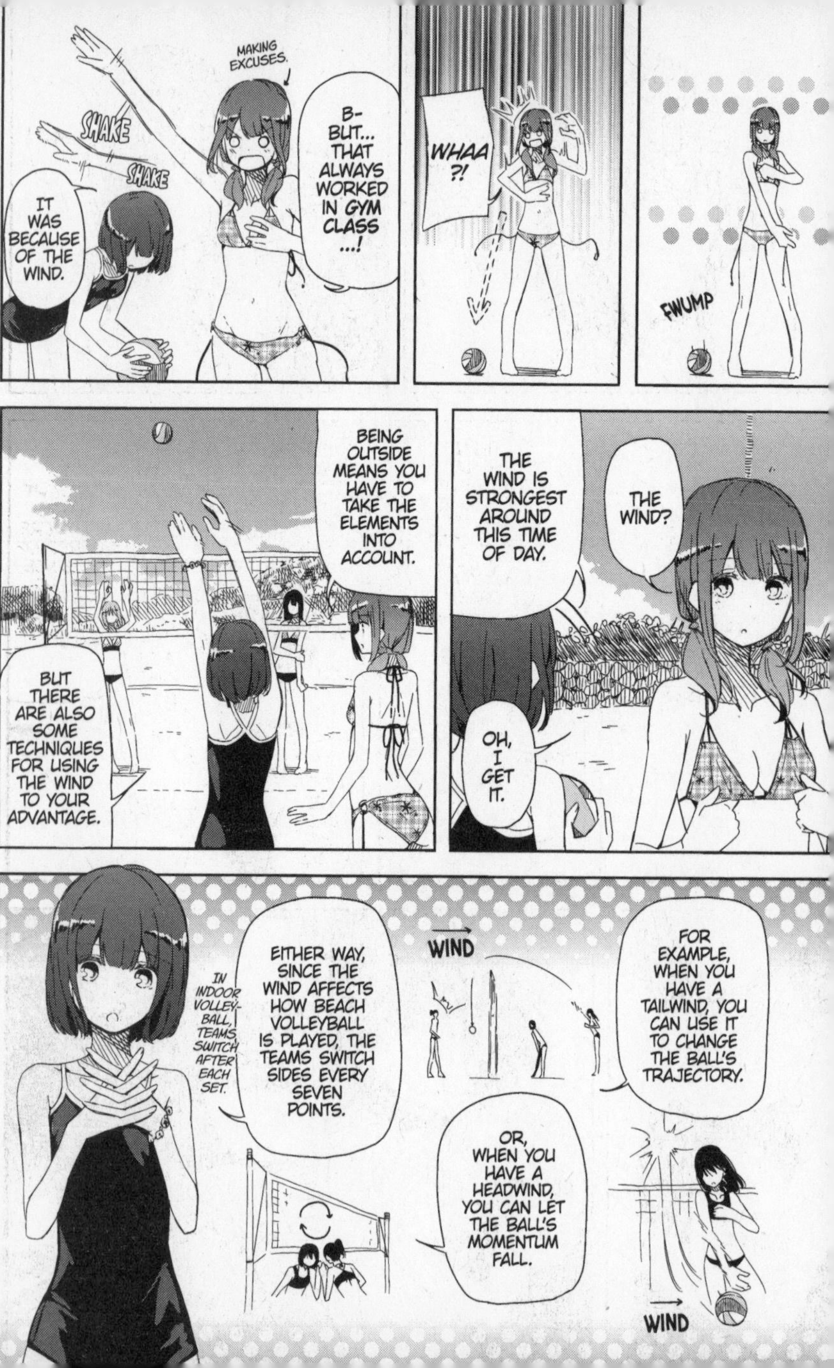
FWUMP
WHAA?!
MAKING EXCUSES.
B-BUT... THAT ALWAYS WORKED IN GYM CLASS...!
SHAKE
SHAKE
IT WAS BECAUSE OF THE WIND.
THE WIND?
THE WIND IS STRONGEST AROUND THIS TIME OF DAY.
OH, I GET IT.
BEING OUTSIDE MEANS YOU HAVE TO TAKE THE ELEMENTS INTO ACCOUNT.
BUT THERE ARE ALSO SOME TECHNIQUES FOR USING THE WIND TO YOUR ADVANTAGE.
FOR EXAMPLE, WHEN YOU HAVE A TAILWIND, YOU CAN USE IT TO CHANGE THE BALL'S TRAJECTORY.
WIND
OR, WHEN YOU HAVE A HEADWIND, YOU CAN LET THE BALL'S MOMENTUM FALL.
WIND
EITHER WAY, SINCE THE WIND AFFECTS HOW BEACH VOLLEYBALL IS PLAYED, THE TEAMS SWITCH SIDES EVERY SEVEN POINTS.
IN INDOOR VOLLEYBALL, TEAMS SWITCH AFTER EACH SET.

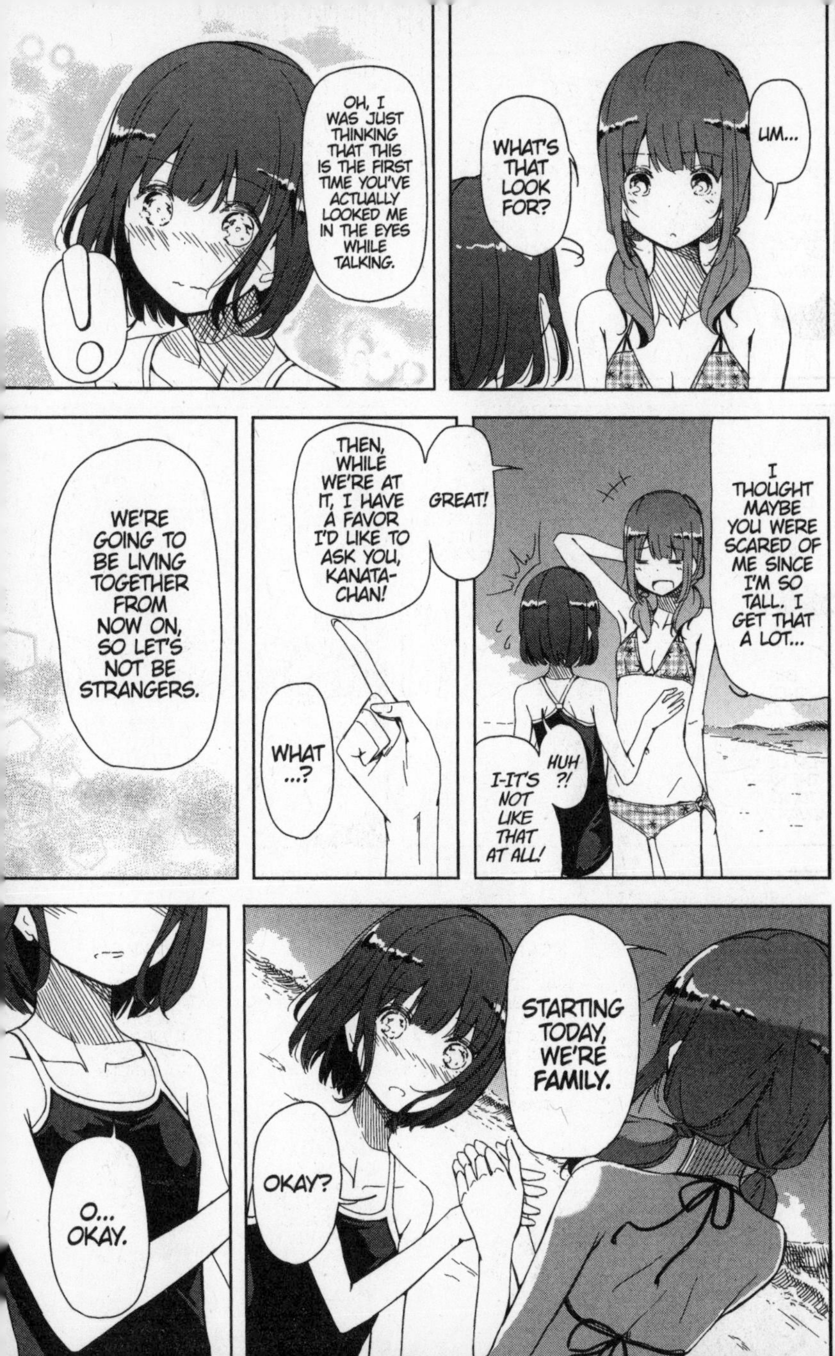
UM...
WHAT'S THAT LOOK FOR?
OH, I WAS JUST THINKING THAT THIS IS THE FIRST TIME YOU'VE ACTUALLY LOOKED ME IN THE EYES WHILE TALKING.
!
I THOUGHT MAYBE YOU WERE SCARED OF ME SINCE I'M SO TALL. I GET THAT A LOT...
HUH?!
I-IT'S NOT LIKE THAT AT ALL!
GREAT!
THEN, WHILE WE'RE AT IT, I HAVE A FAVOR I'D LIKE TO ASK YOU, KANATA-CHAN!
WHAT...?
WE'RE GOING TO BE LIVING TOGETHER FROM NOW ON, SO LET'S NOT BE STRANGERS.
STARTING TODAY, WE'RE FAMILY.
OKAY?
O... OKAY.

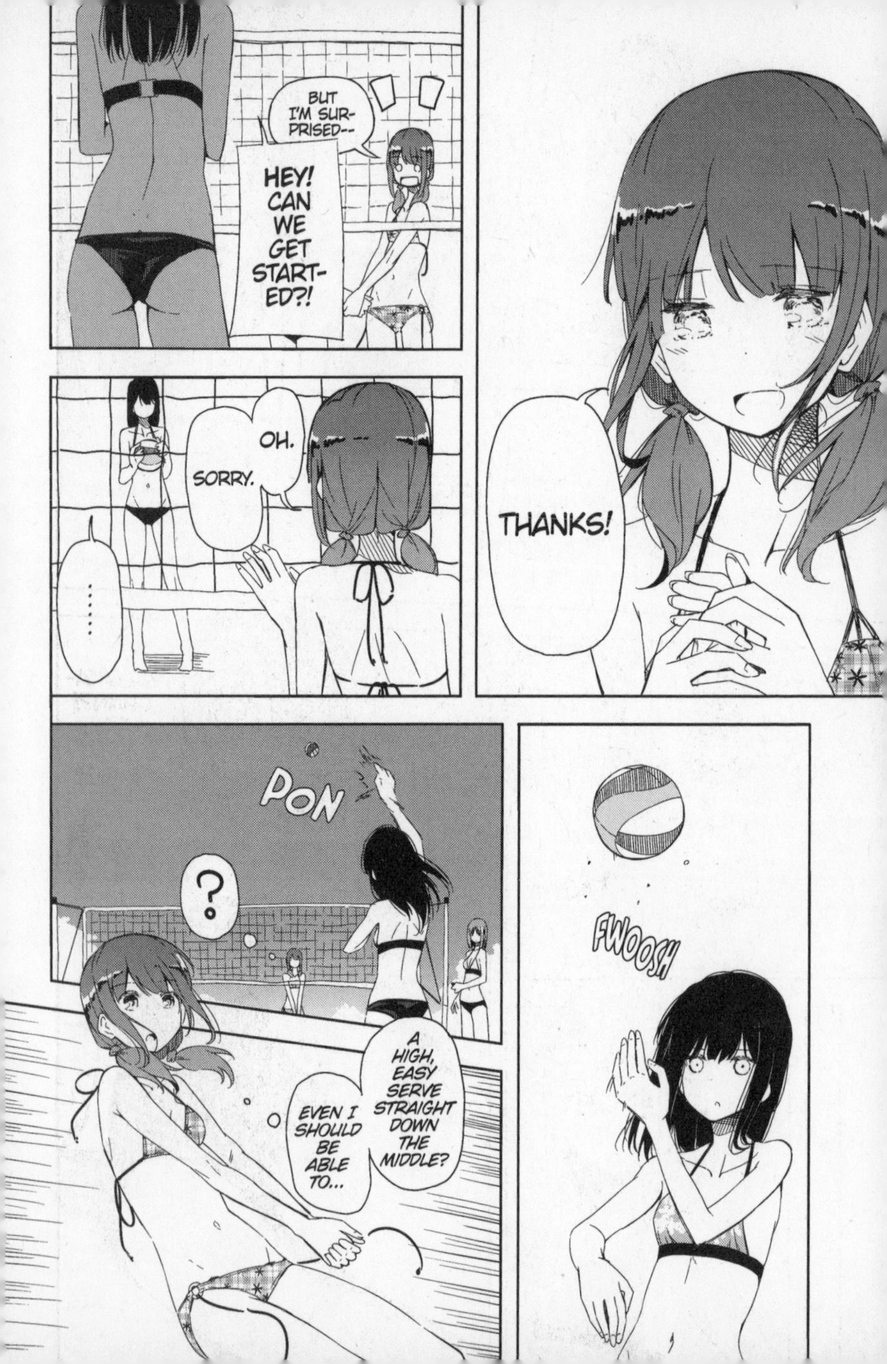
THANKS!
BUT I'M SUR-PRISED--
HEY! CAN WE GET START-ED?!
OH. SORRY.
......
FWOOSH
PON
?
A HIGH, EASY SERVE STRAIGHT DOWN THE MIDDLE?
EVEN I SHOULD BE ABLE TO...

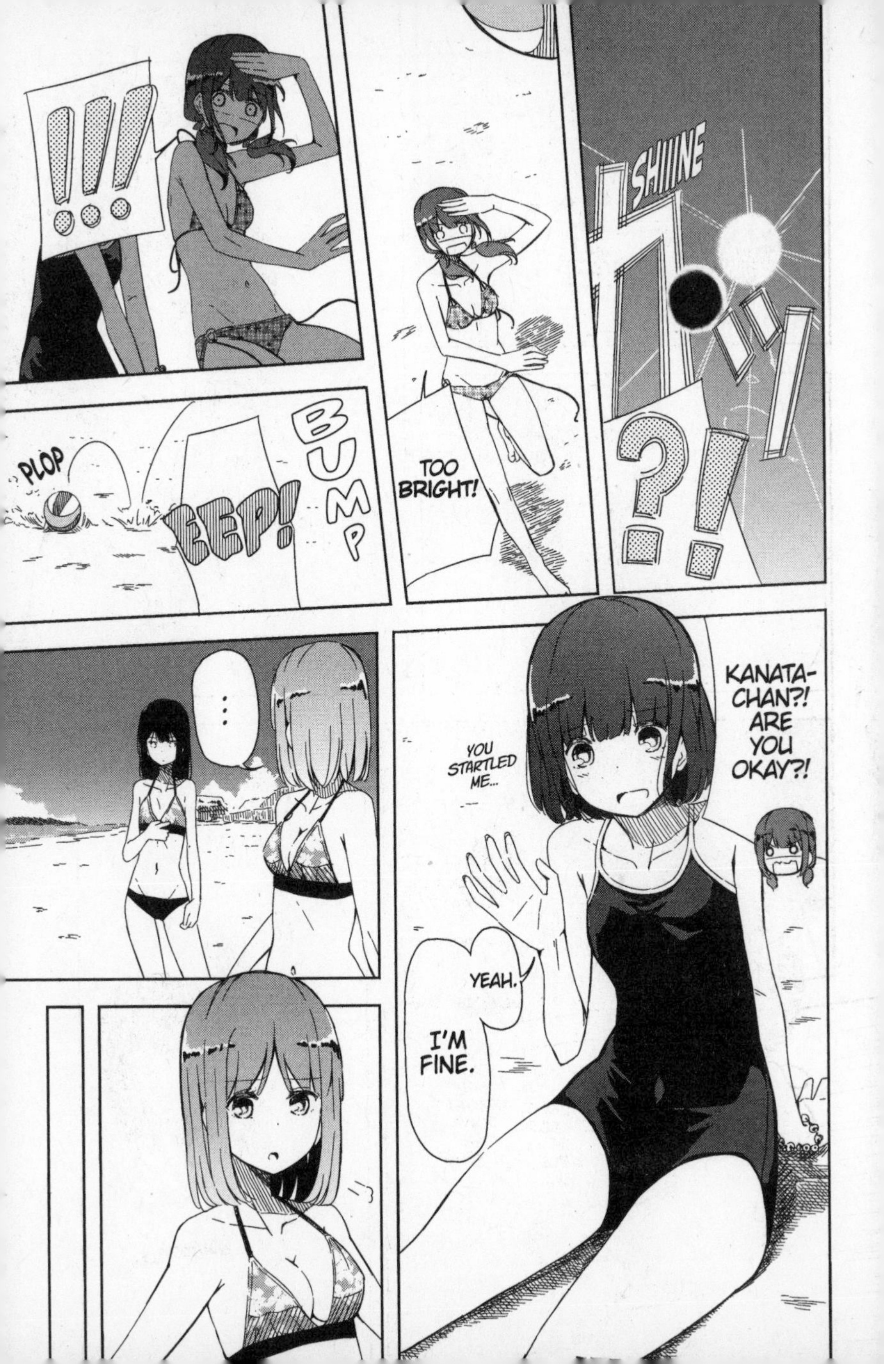

SHIINE
?!
TOO BRIGHT!
!!!
BUMP
EEP!
PLOP
KANATA-CHAN?! ARE YOU OKAY?!
YOU STARTLED ME...
YEAH.
I'M FINE.
...

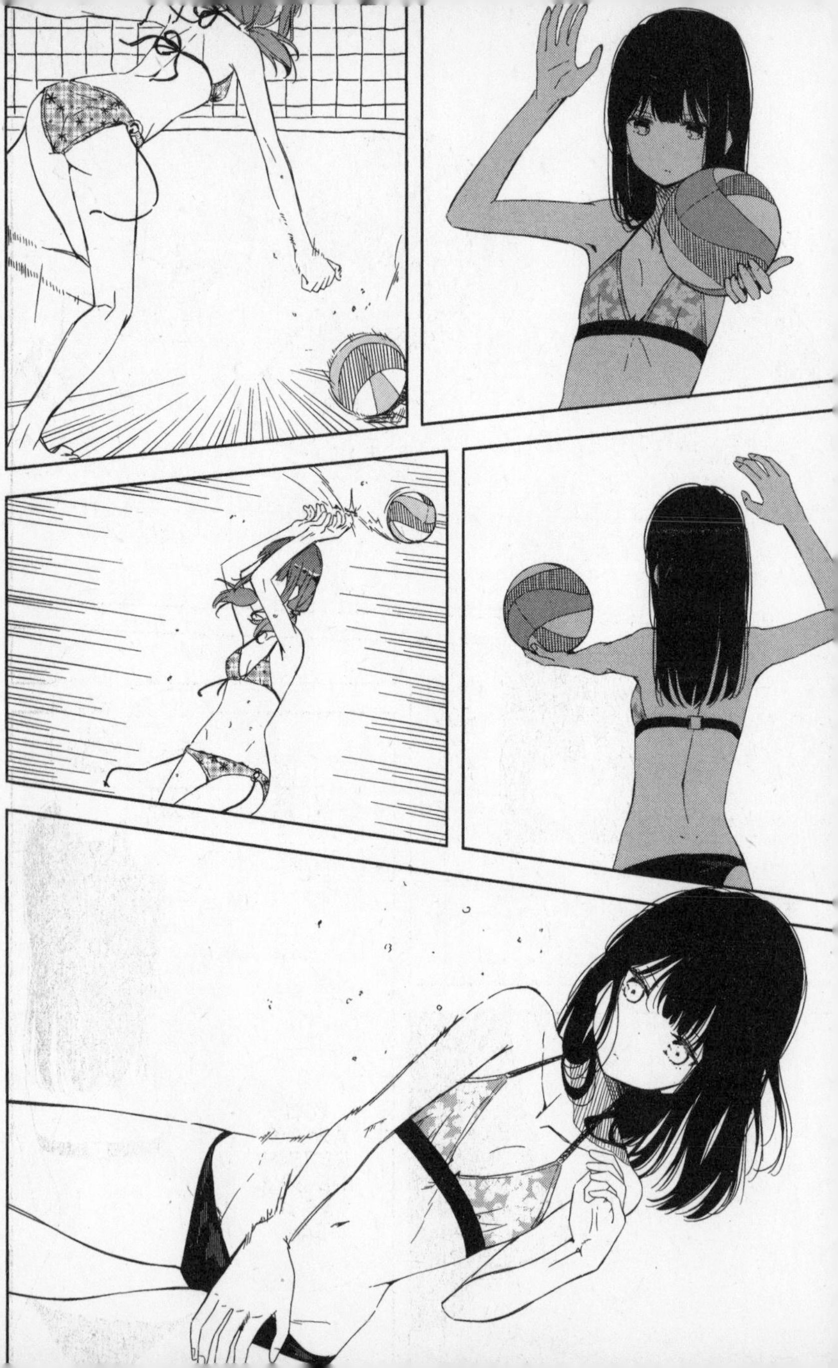

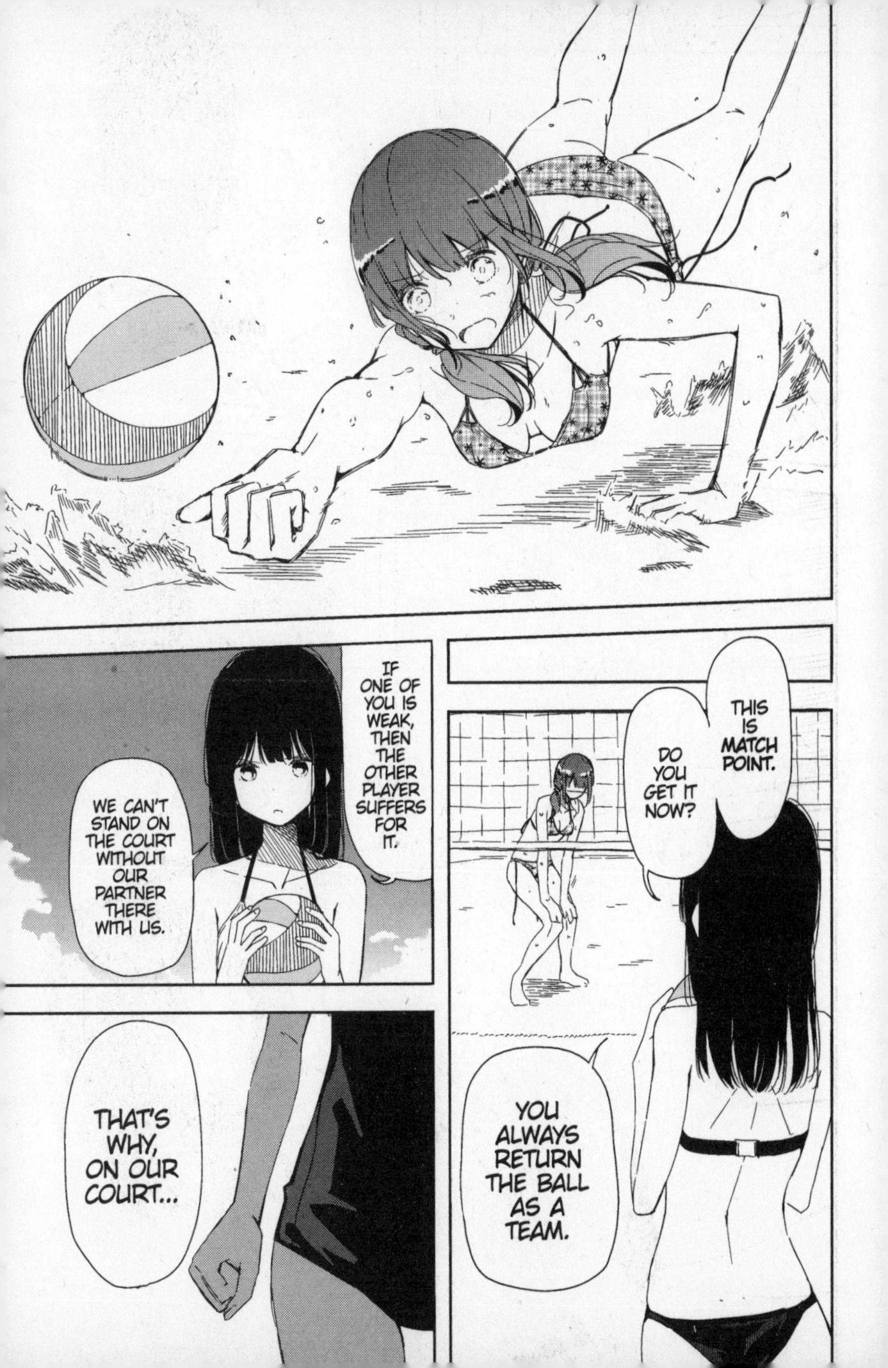
THIS IS MATCH POINT.
DO YOU GET IT NOW?
IF ONE OF YOU IS WEAK, THEN THE OTHER PLAYER SUFFERS FOR IT.
WE CAN'T STAND ON THE COURT WITHOUT OUR PARTNER THERE WITH US.
THAT'S WHY, ON OUR COURT...
YOU ALWAYS RETURN THE BALL AS A TEAM.

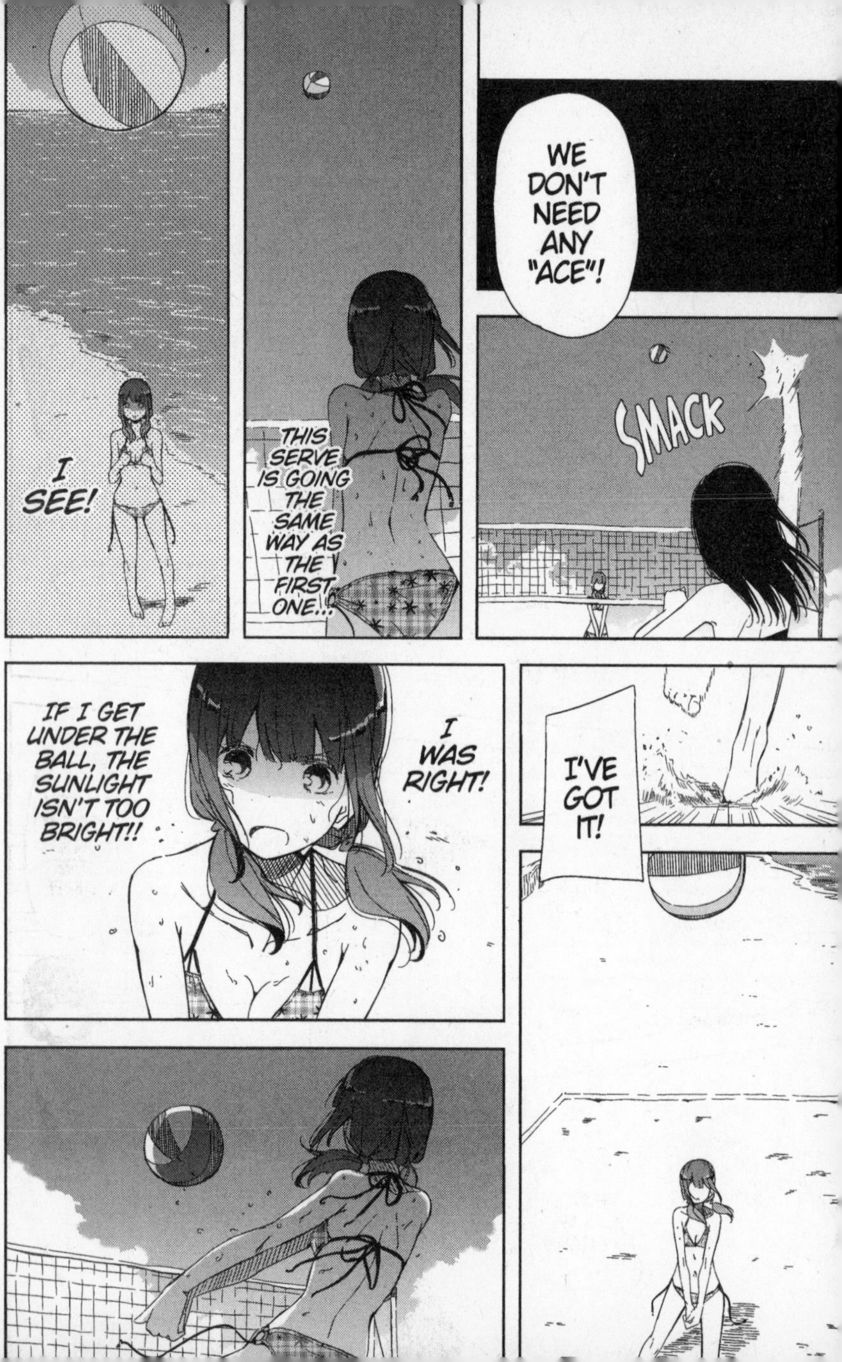
WE DON'T NEED ANY "ACE"!
SMACK
THIS SERVE IS GOING THE SAME WAY AS THE FIRST ONE..!
I SEE!
I'VE GOT IT!
I WAS RIGHT!
IF I GET UNDER THE BALL, THE SUNLIGHT ISN'T TOO BRIGHT!!

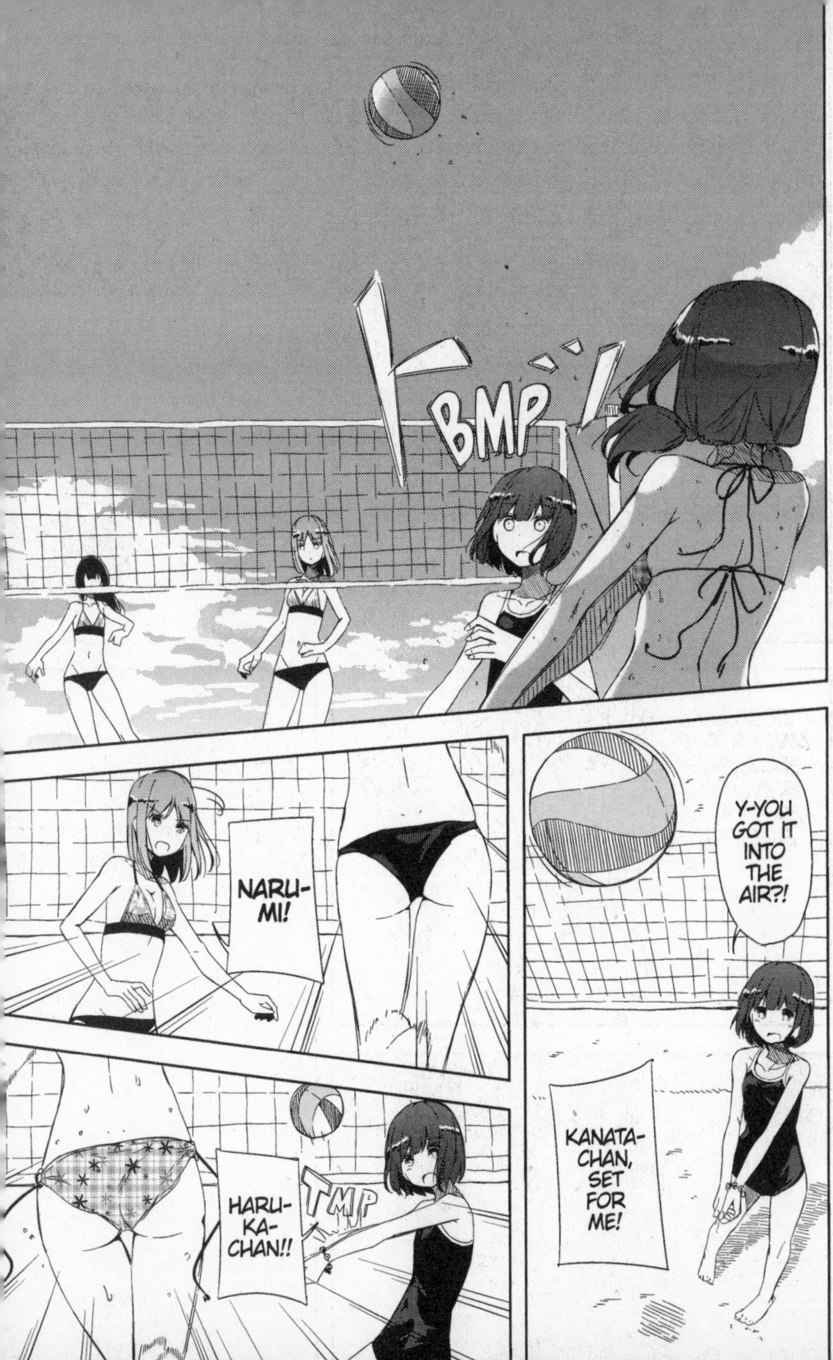
BMP
Y-YOU GOT IT INTO THE AIR?!
NARU-MI!
KANATA-CHAN, SET FOR ME!
HARU-KA-CHAN!!
TMP

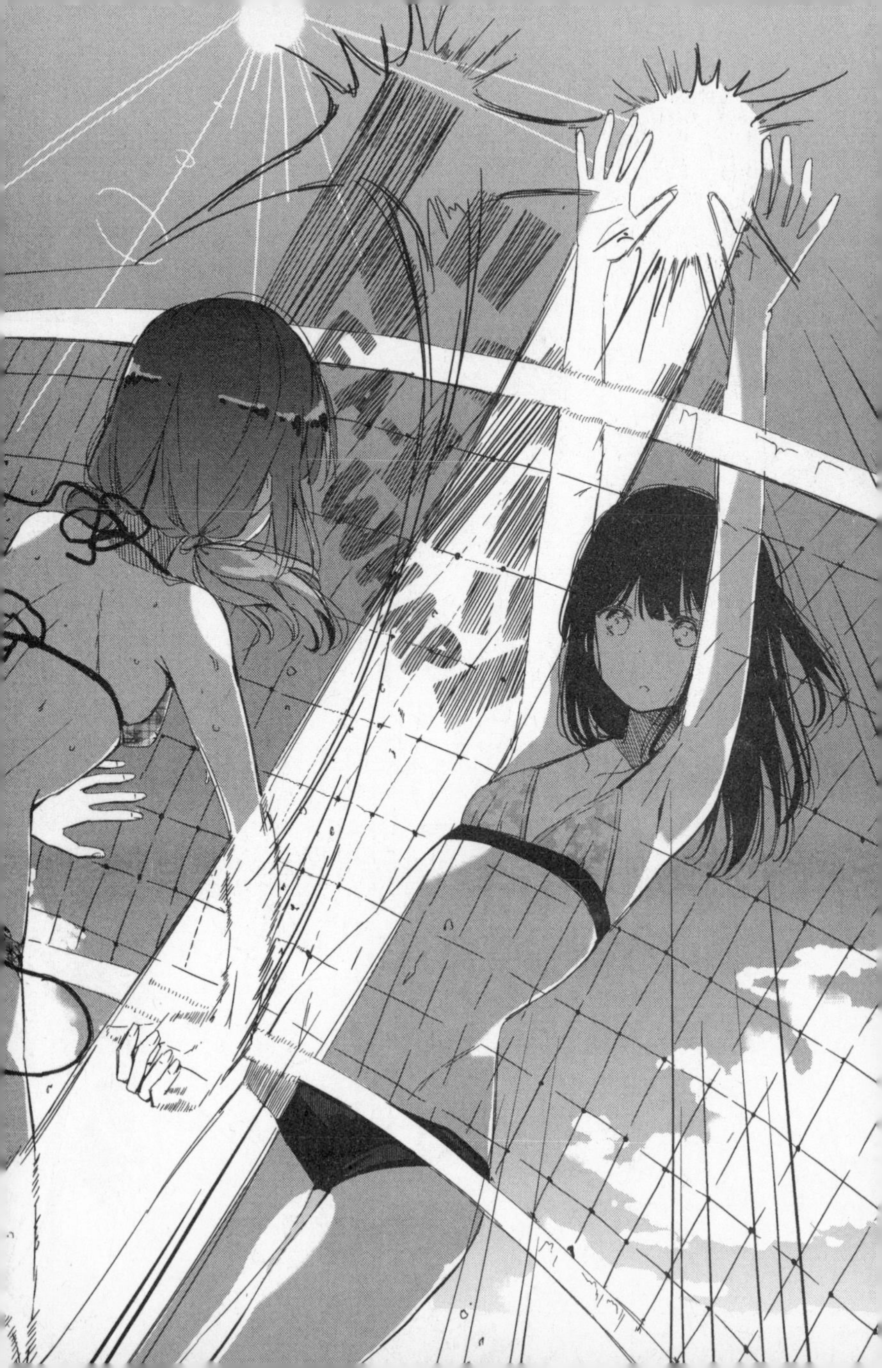

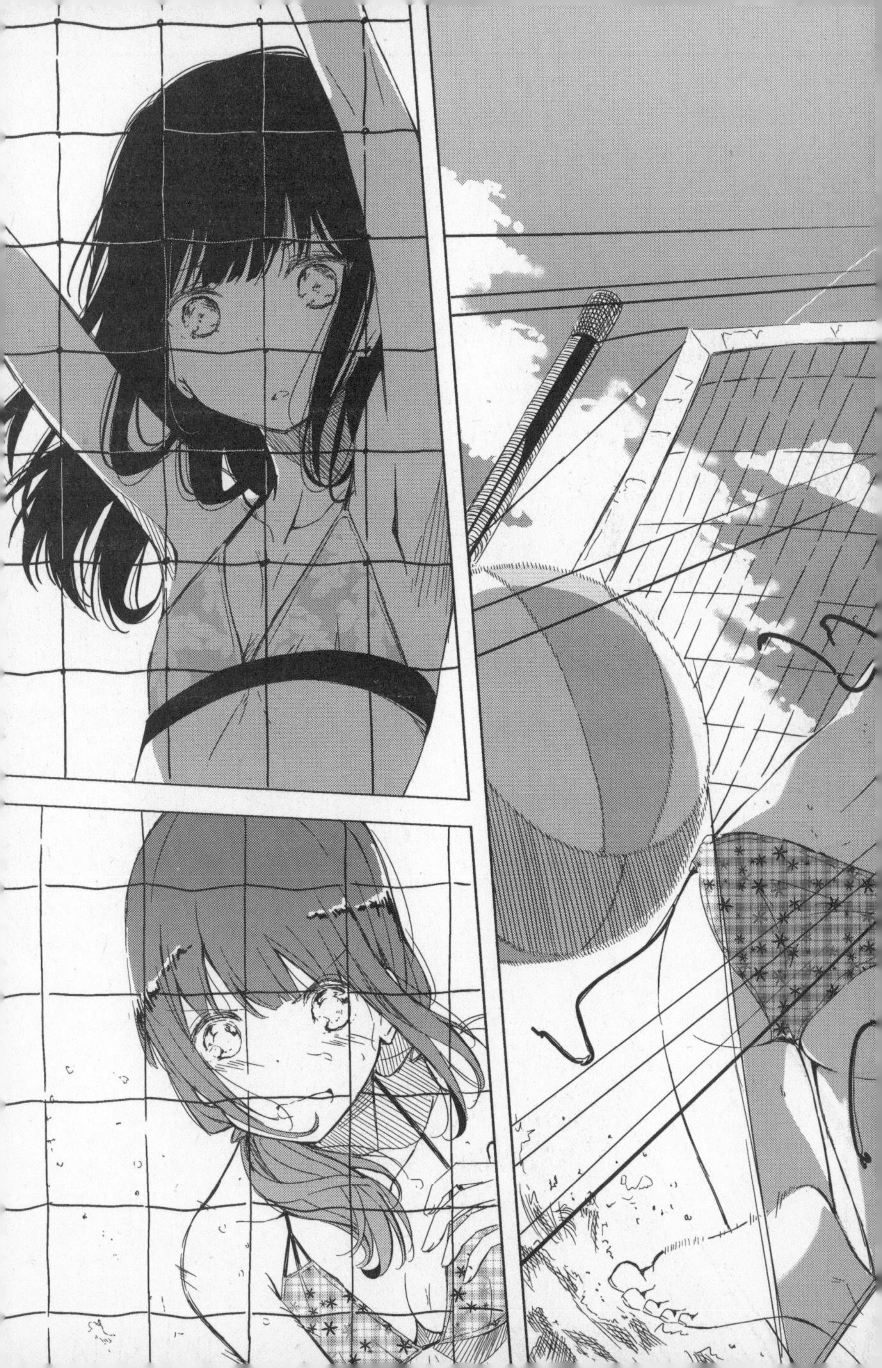

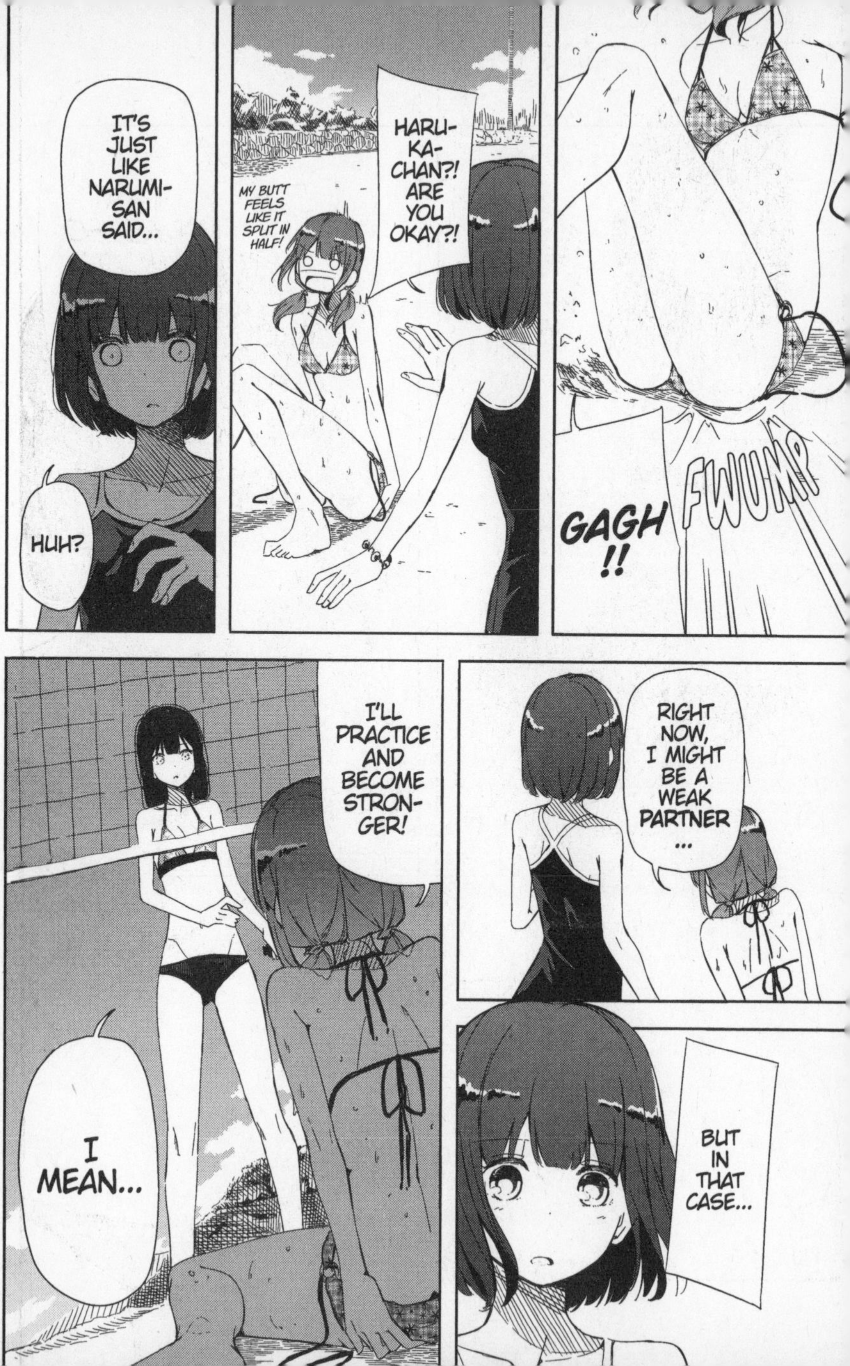
FWUMP
GAGH!!
HARU-KA-CHAN?! ARE YOU OKAY?!
MY BUTT FEELS LIKE IT SPLIT IN HALF!
IT'S JUST LIKE NARUMI-SAN SAID...
HUH?
RIGHT NOW, I MIGHT BE A WEAK PARTNER...
BUT IN THAT CASE...
I'LL PRACTICE AND BECOME STRONGER!
I MEAN...

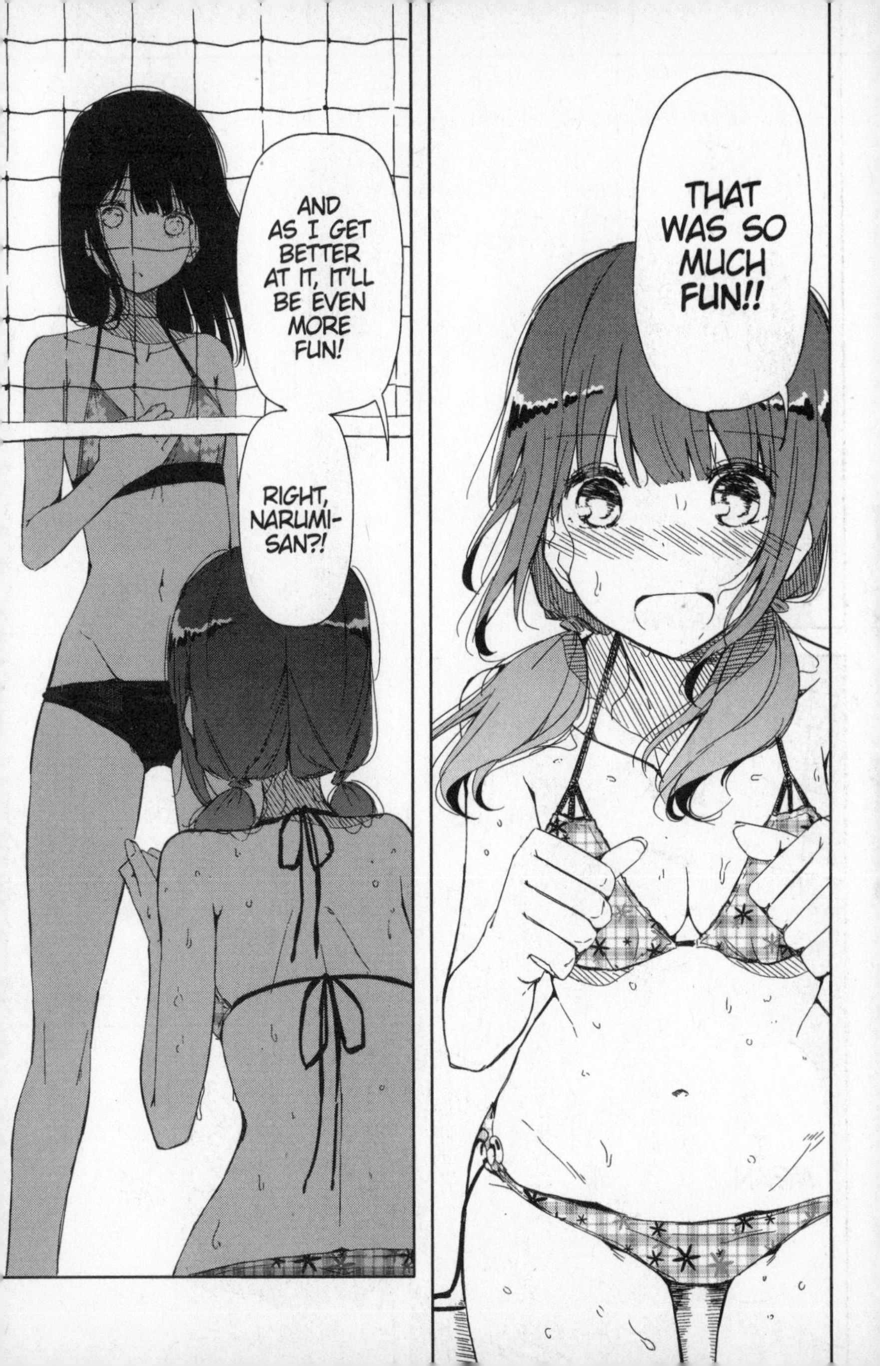
THAT WAS SO MUCH FUN!!
AND AS I GET BETTER AT IT, IT'LL BE EVEN MORE FUN!
RIGHT, NARUMI-SAN?!

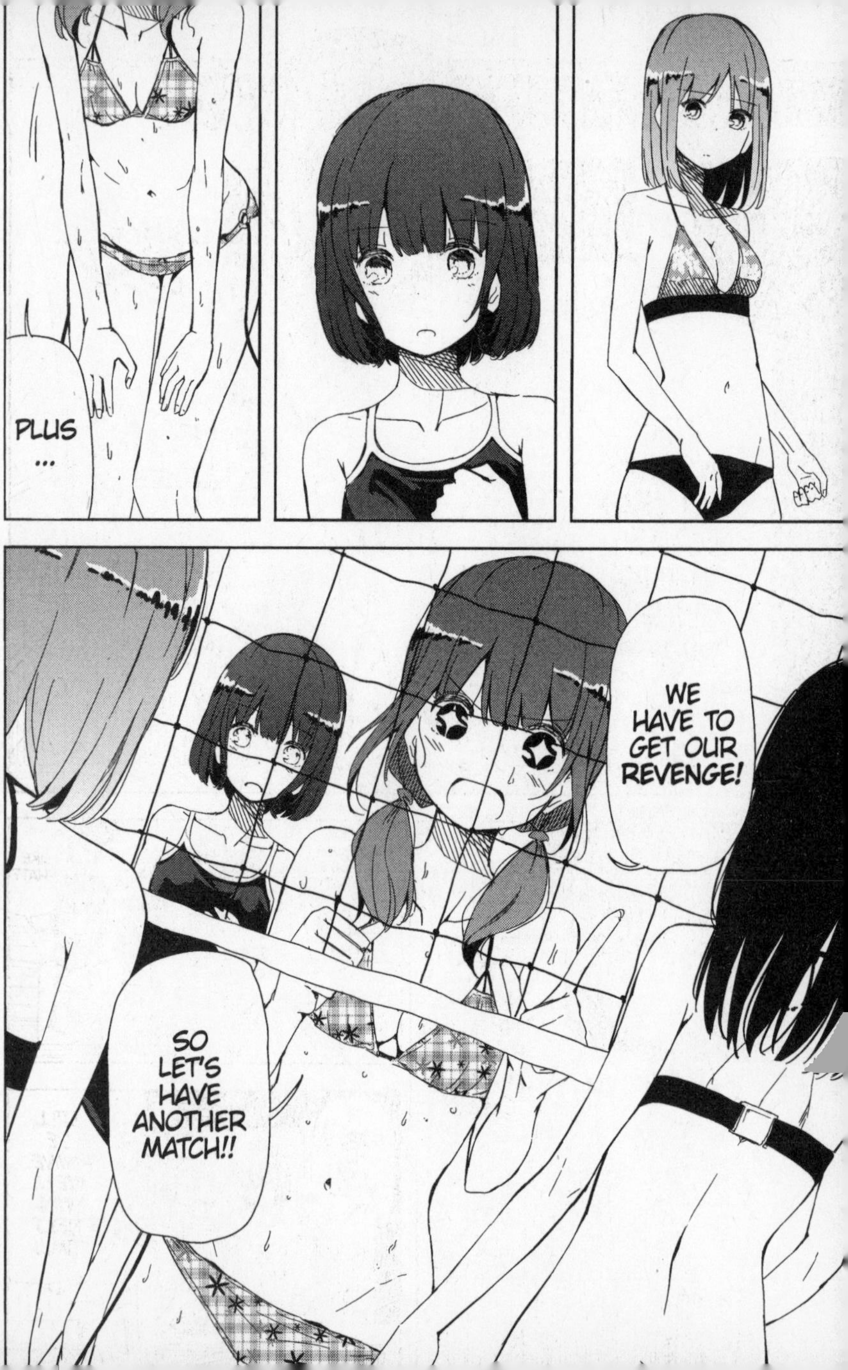
PLUS ...
WE HAVE TO GET OUR REVENGE!
SO LET'S HAVE ANOTHER MATCH!!

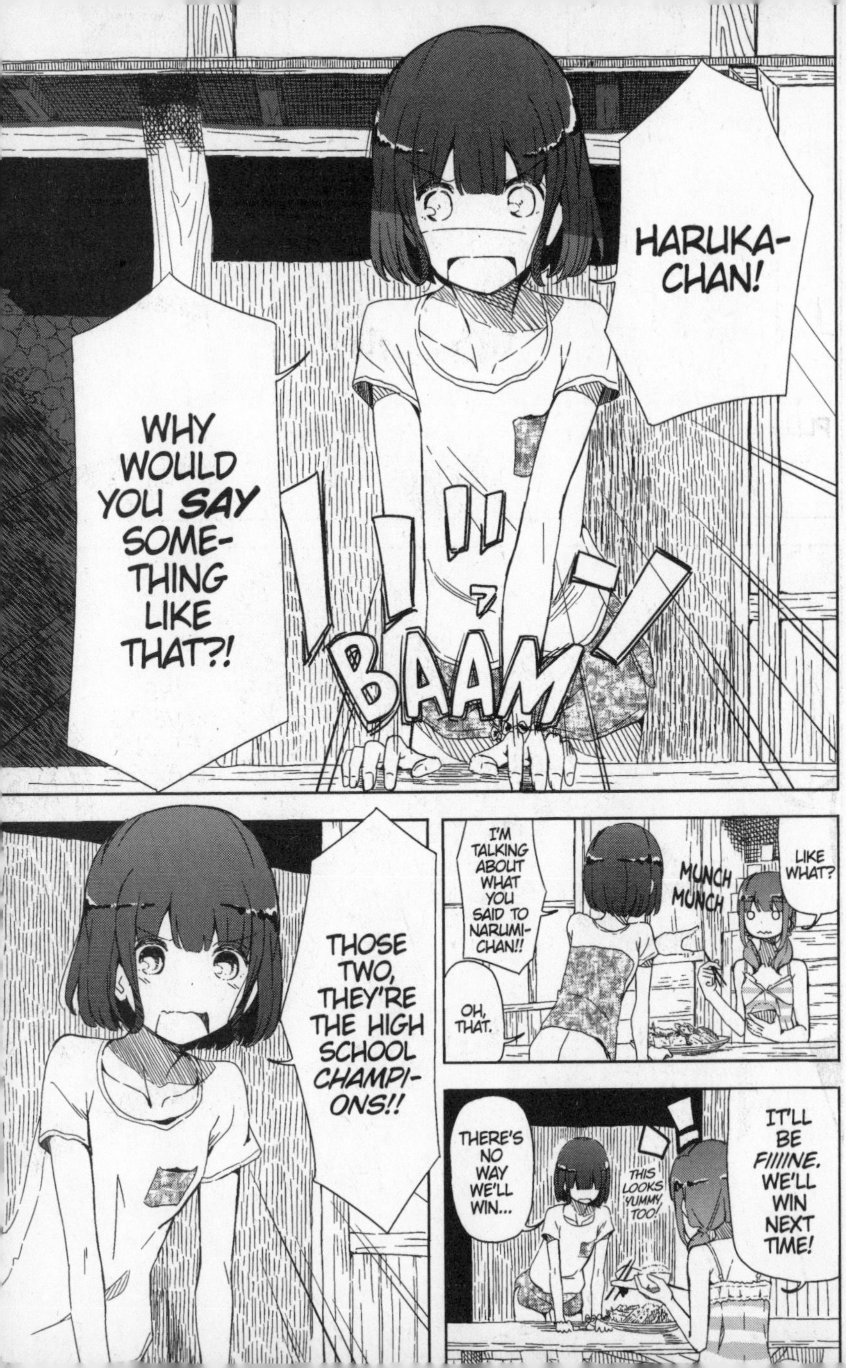
HARUKA-CHAN!
BAAM
WHY WOULD YOU SAY SOMETHING LIKE THAT?!
LIKE WHAT?
MUNCH MUNCH
I'M TALKING ABOUT WHAT YOU SAID TO NARUMI-CHAN!!
OH, THAT.
IT'LL BE FIIIINE. WE'LL WIN NEXT TIME!
!
THIS LOOKS YUMMY, TOO!
THERE'S NO WAY WE'LL WIN...
THOSE TWO, THEY'RE THE HIGH SCHOOL CHAMPIONS!!

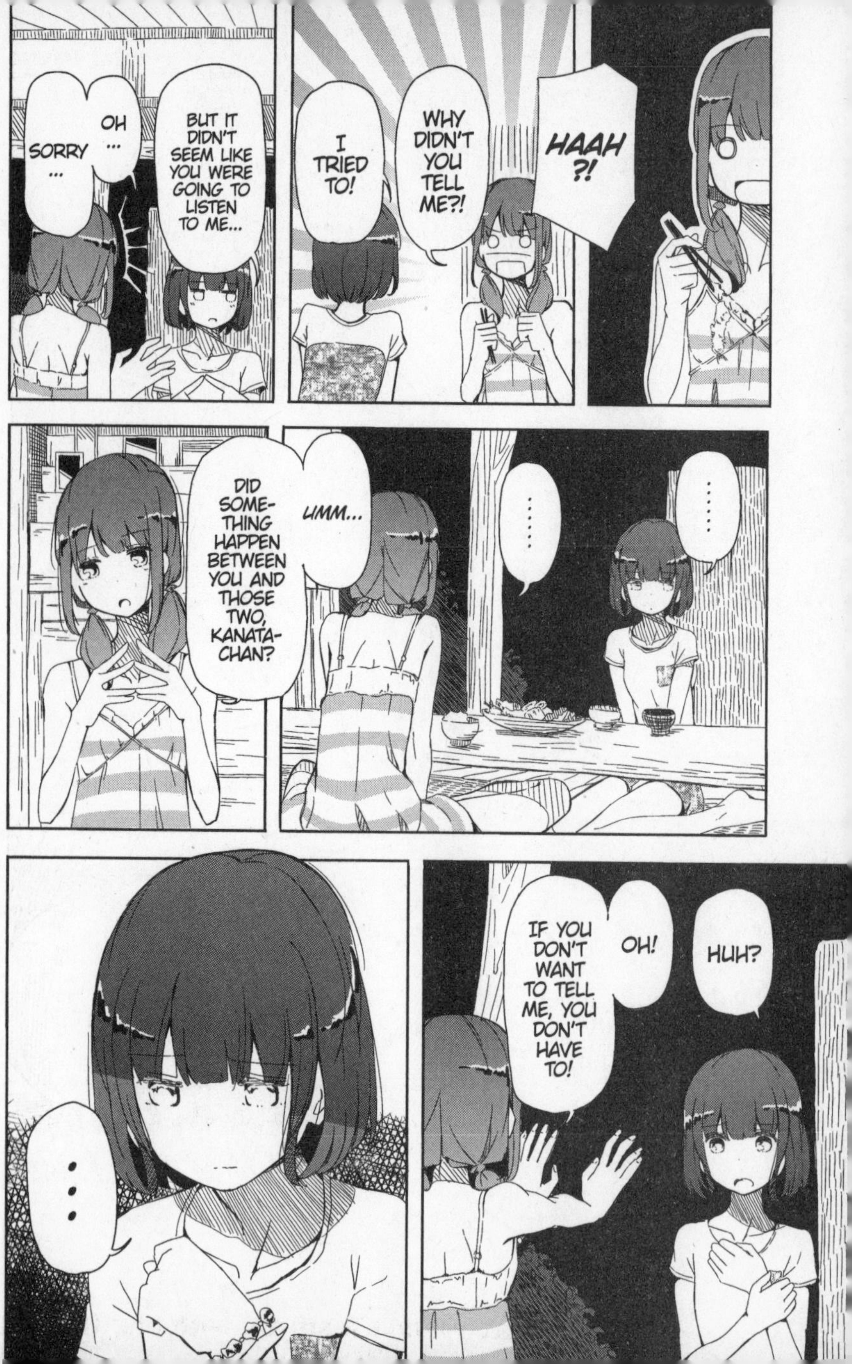
HAAH?!
WHY DIDN'T YOU TELL ME?!
I TRIED TO!
BUT IT DIDN'T SEEM LIKE YOU WERE GOING TO LISTEN TO ME...
OH ...
SORRY ...
......
......
UMM...
DID SOMETHING HAPPEN BETWEEN YOU AND THOSE TWO, KANATA-CHAN?
HUH?
OH!
IF YOU DON'T WANT TO TELL ME, YOU DON'T HAVE TO!
...

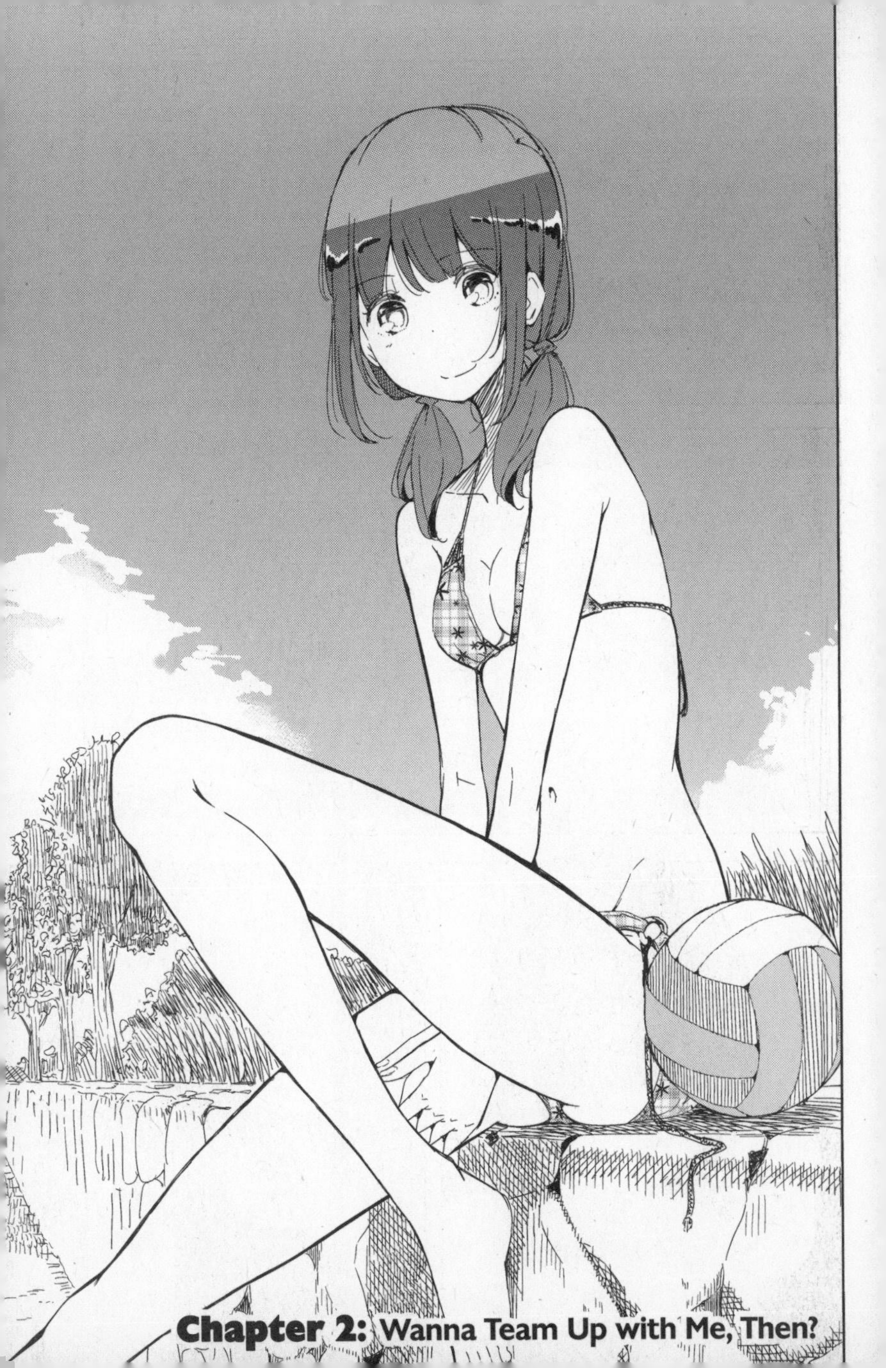
Chapter 2: Wanna Team Up with Me, Then?

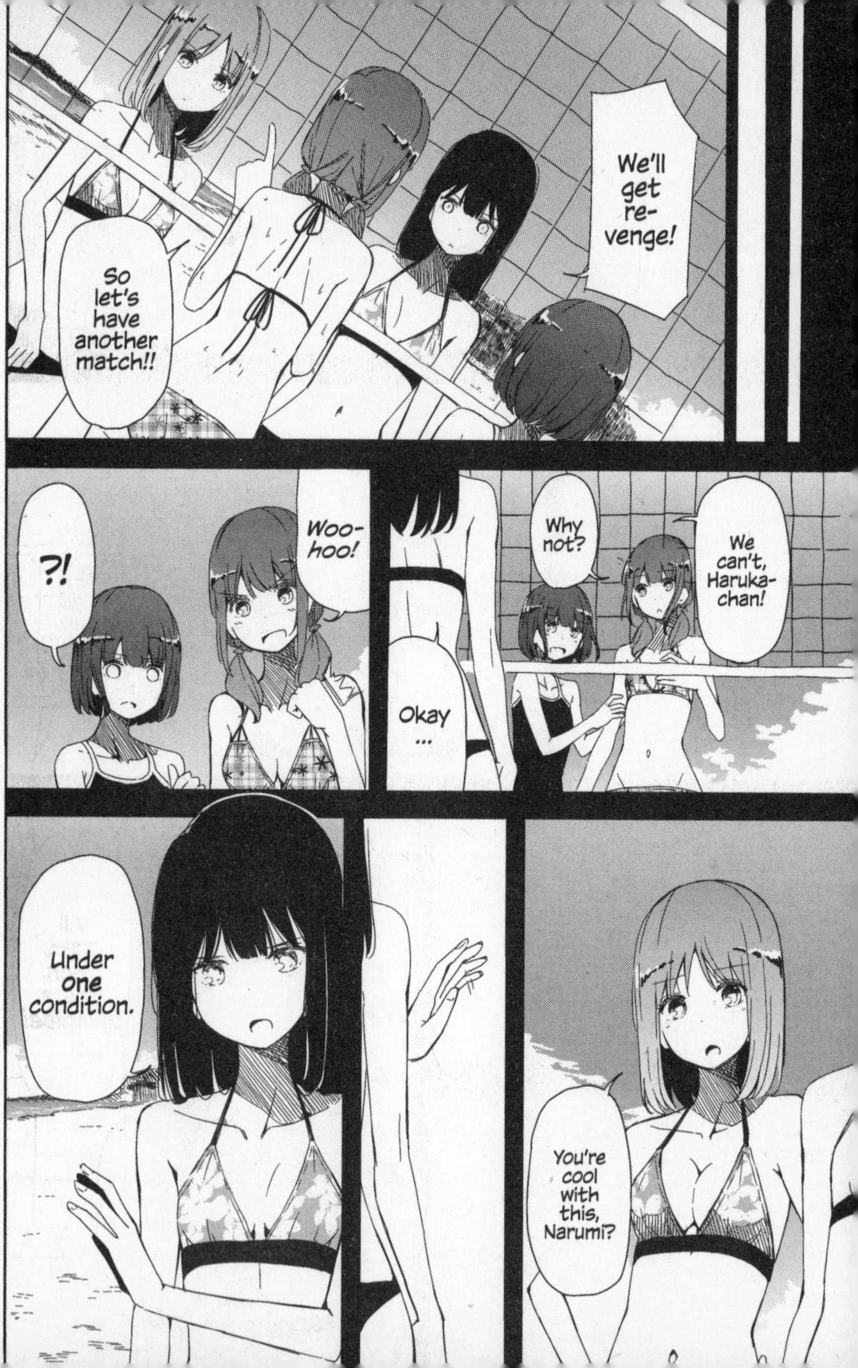
We'll get re-venge!
So let's have another match!!
We can't, Haruka-chan!
Why not?
Okay ...
Woo-hoo!
?!
You're cool with this, Narumi?
Under one condition.

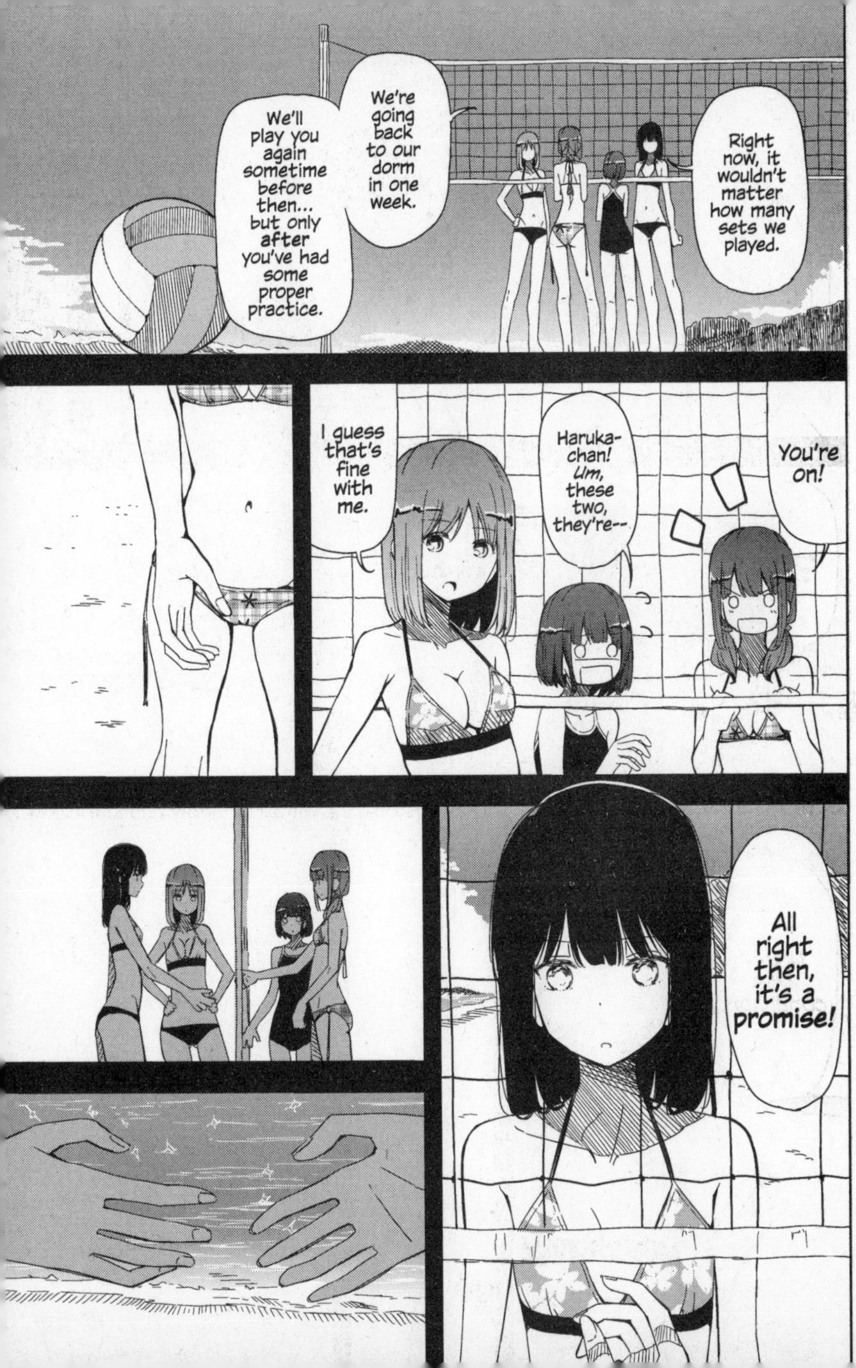
Right now, it wouldn't matter how many sets we played.
We're going back to our dorm in one week.
We'll play you again sometime before then... but only **after** you've had some proper practice.
You're on!
Haruka-chan! *Um,* these two, they're--
I guess that's fine with me.
All right then, it's a **promise!**

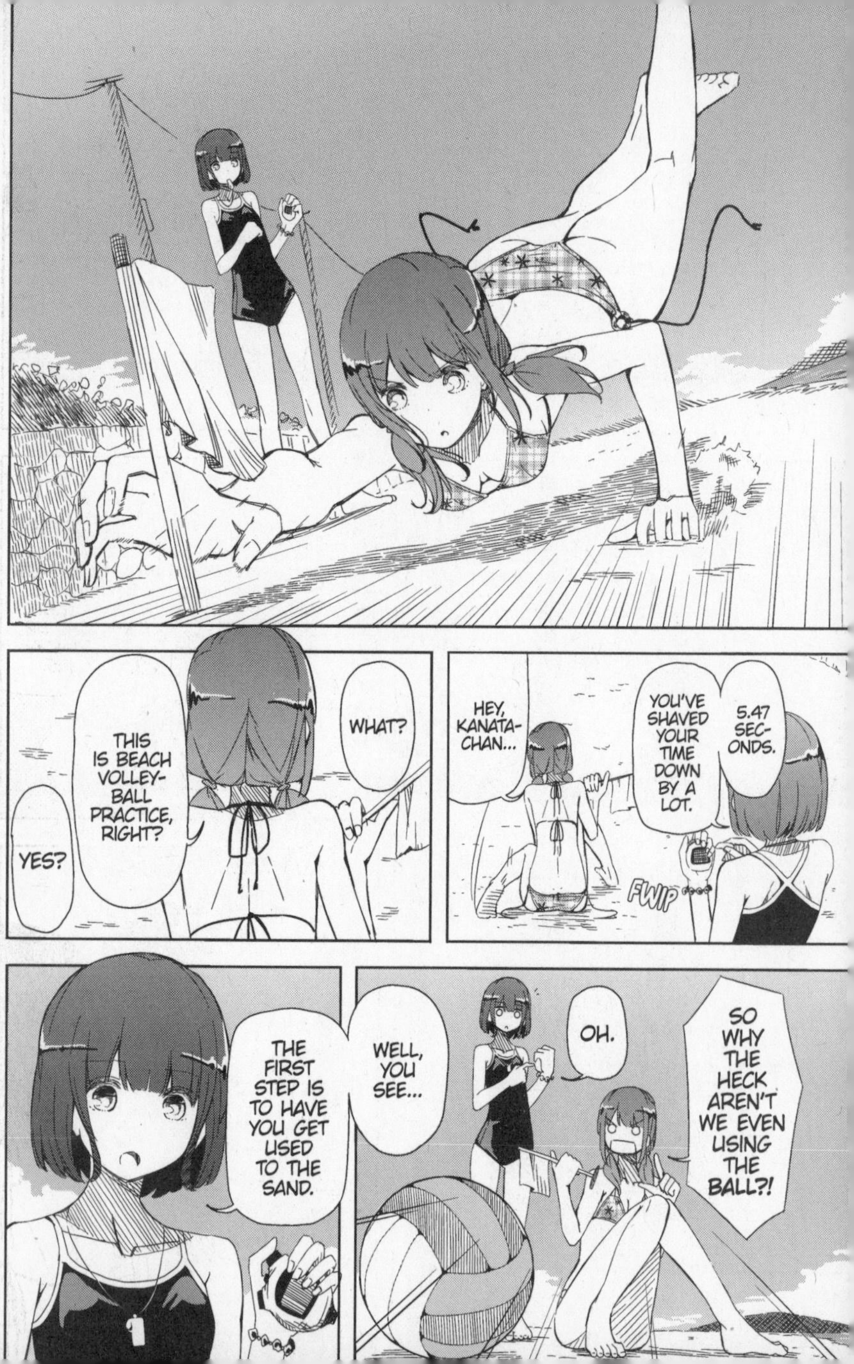
5.47 SECONDS.
YOU'VE SHAVED YOUR TIME DOWN BY A LOT.
HEY, KANATA-CHAN...
FWIP
WHAT?
THIS IS BEACH VOLLEYBALL PRACTICE, RIGHT?
YES?
SO WHY THE HECK AREN'T WE EVEN USING THE BALL?!
OH.
WELL, YOU SEE...
THE FIRST STEP IS TO HAVE YOU GET USED TO THE SAND.

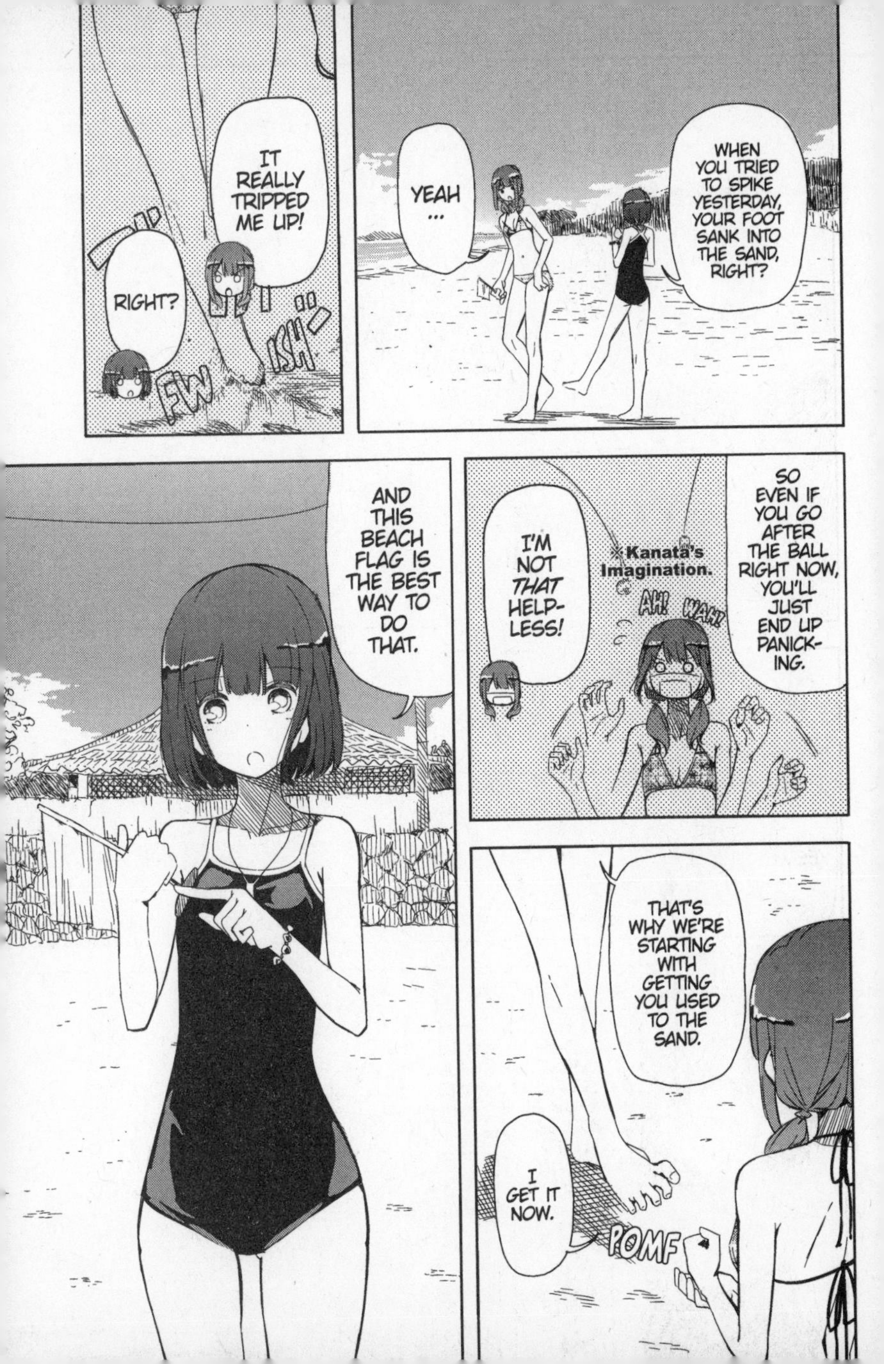
WHEN YOU TRIED TO SPIKE YESTERDAY, YOUR FOOT SANK INTO THE SAND, RIGHT?
YEAH ...
IT REALLY TRIPPED ME UP!
RIGHT?
FWISH
SO EVEN IF YOU GO AFTER THE BALL RIGHT NOW, YOU'LL JUST END UP PANICKING.
※Kanata's Imagination.
AH! WAH!
I'M NOT *THAT* HELPLESS!
THAT'S WHY WE'RE STARTING WITH GETTING YOU USED TO THE SAND.
I GET IT NOW.
POMF
AND THIS BEACH FLAG IS THE BEST WAY TO DO THAT.

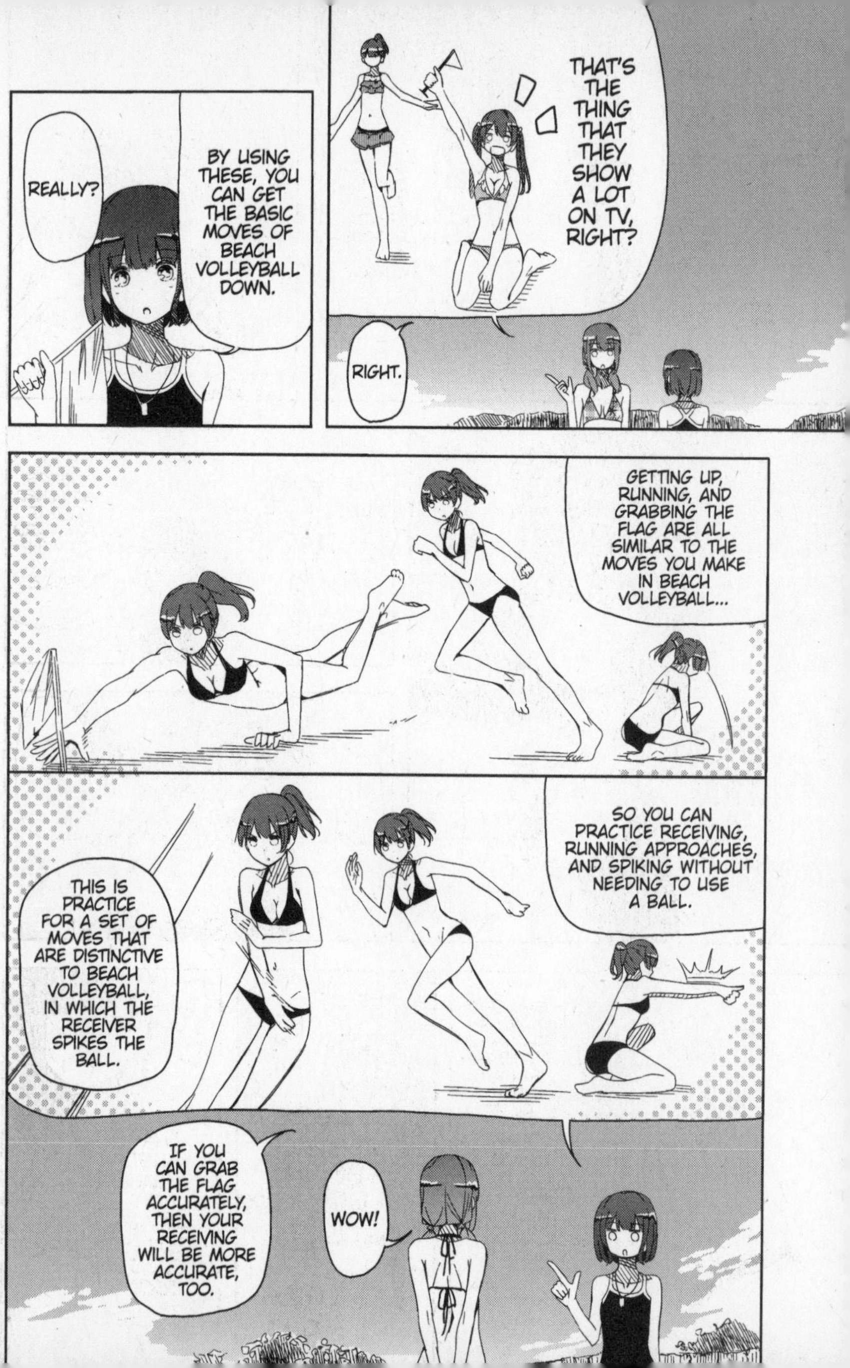
THAT'S THE THING THAT THEY SHOW A LOT ON TV, RIGHT?
RIGHT.
BY USING THESE, YOU CAN GET THE BASIC MOVES OF BEACH VOLLEYBALL DOWN.
REALLY?
GETTING UP, RUNNING, AND GRABBING THE FLAG ARE ALL SIMILAR TO THE MOVES YOU MAKE IN BEACH VOLLEYBALL...
SO YOU CAN PRACTICE RECEIVING, RUNNING APPROACHES, AND SPIKING WITHOUT NEEDING TO USE A BALL.
THIS IS PRACTICE FOR A SET OF MOVES THAT ARE DISTINCTIVE TO BEACH VOLLEYBALL, IN WHICH THE RECEIVER SPIKES THE BALL.
IF YOU CAN GRAB THE FLAG ACCURATELY, THEN YOUR RECEIVING WILL BE MORE ACCURATE, TOO.
WOW!

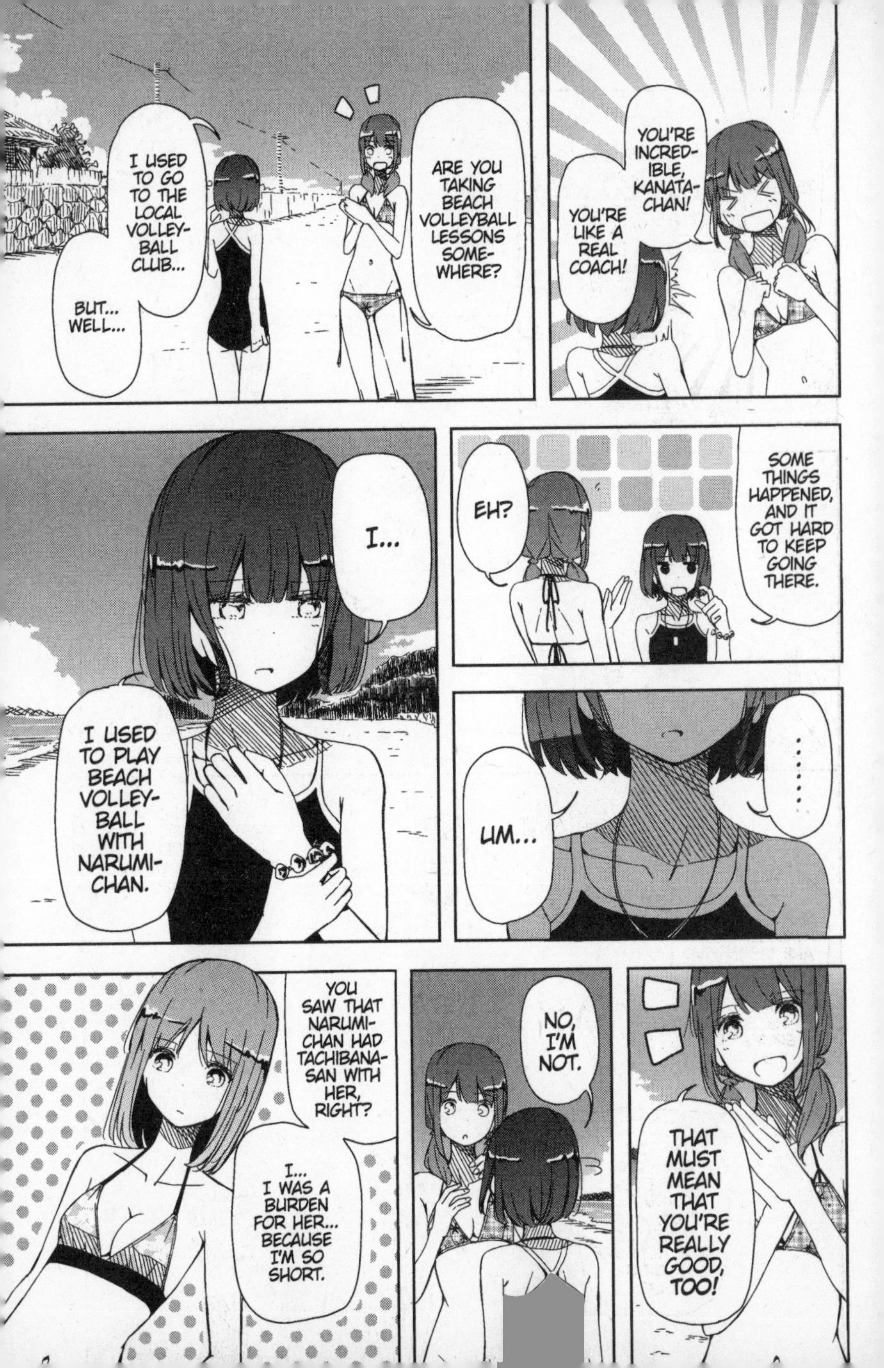
YOU'RE INCREDIBLE, KANATA-CHAN!
YOU'RE LIKE A REAL COACH!
ARE YOU TAKING BEACH VOLLEYBALL LESSONS SOMEWHERE?
I USED TO GO TO THE LOCAL VOLLEYBALL CLUB...
BUT... WELL...
SOME THINGS HAPPENED, AND IT GOT HARD TO KEEP GOING THERE.
EH?
......
UM...
I...
I USED TO PLAY BEACH VOLLEYBALL WITH NARUMI-CHAN.
THAT MUST MEAN THAT YOU'RE REALLY GOOD, TOO!
NO, I'M NOT.
YOU SAW THAT NARUMI-CHAN HAD TACHIBANA-SAN WITH HER, RIGHT?
I... I WAS A BURDEN FOR HER... BECAUSE I'M SO SHORT.

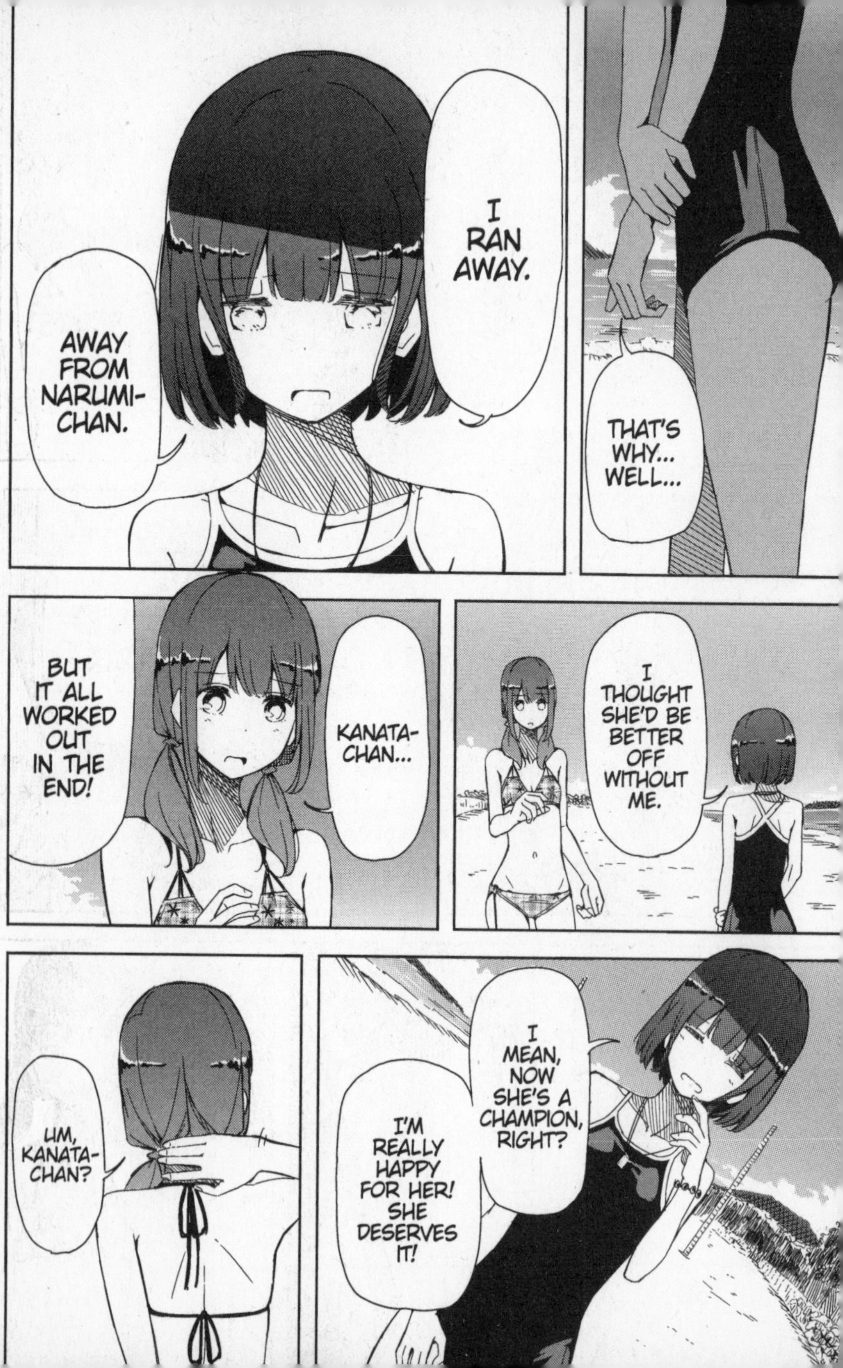
THAT'S WHY... WELL...
I RAN AWAY.
AWAY FROM NARUMI-CHAN.
I THOUGHT SHE'D BE BETTER OFF WITHOUT ME.
KANATA-CHAN...
BUT IT ALL WORKED OUT IN THE END!
I MEAN, NOW SHE'S A CHAMPION, RIGHT?
I'M REALLY HAPPY FOR HER! SHE DESERVES IT!
UM, KANATA-CHAN?

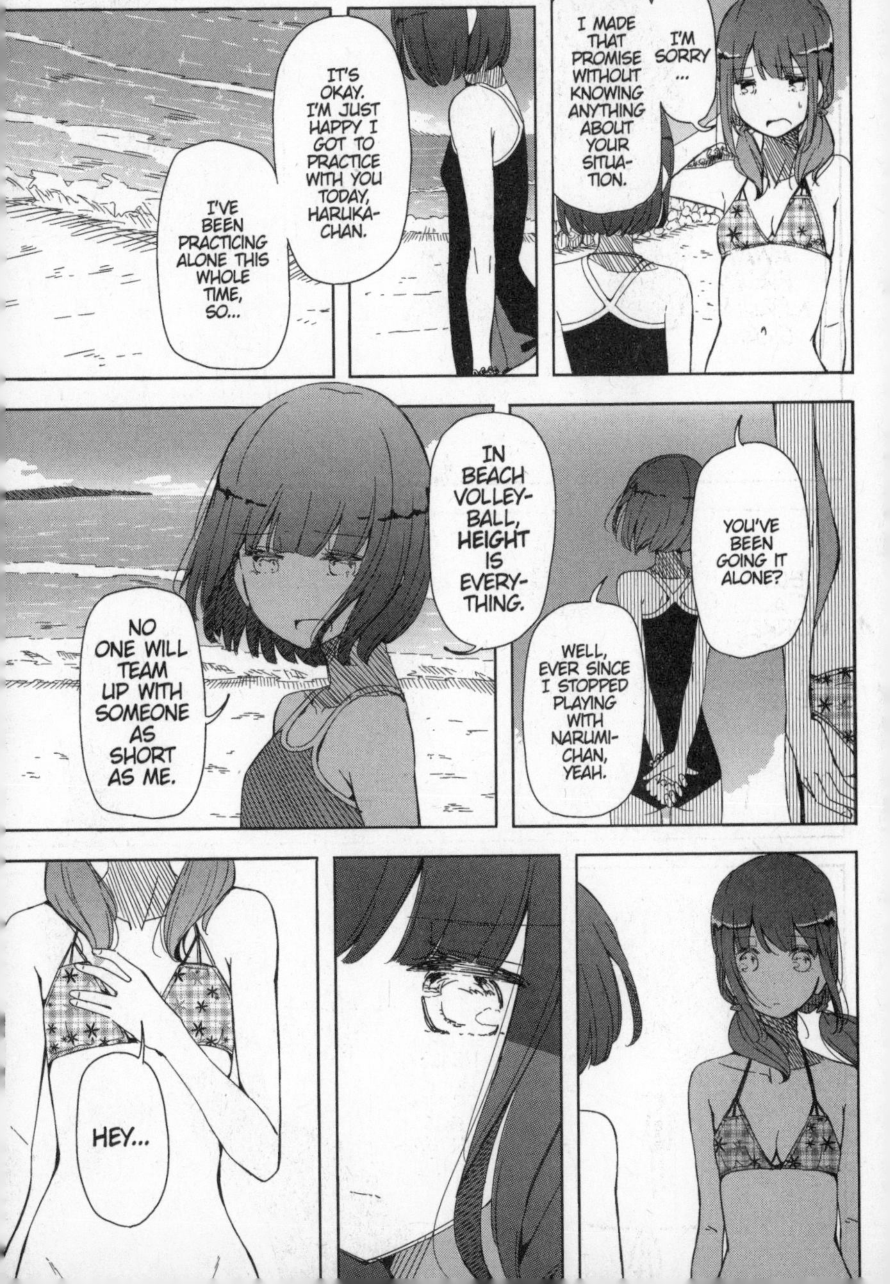
I'M SORRY...
I MADE THAT PROMISE WITHOUT KNOWING ANYTHING ABOUT YOUR SITUATION.
IT'S OKAY. I'M JUST HAPPY I GOT TO PRACTICE WITH YOU TODAY, HARUKA-CHAN.
I'VE BEEN PRACTICING ALONE THIS WHOLE TIME, SO...
YOU'VE BEEN GOING IT ALONE?
WELL, EVER SINCE I STOPPED PLAYING WITH NARUMI-CHAN, YEAH.
IN BEACH VOLLEYBALL, HEIGHT IS EVERYTHING.
NO ONE WILL TEAM UP WITH SOMEONE AS SHORT AS ME.
HEY...

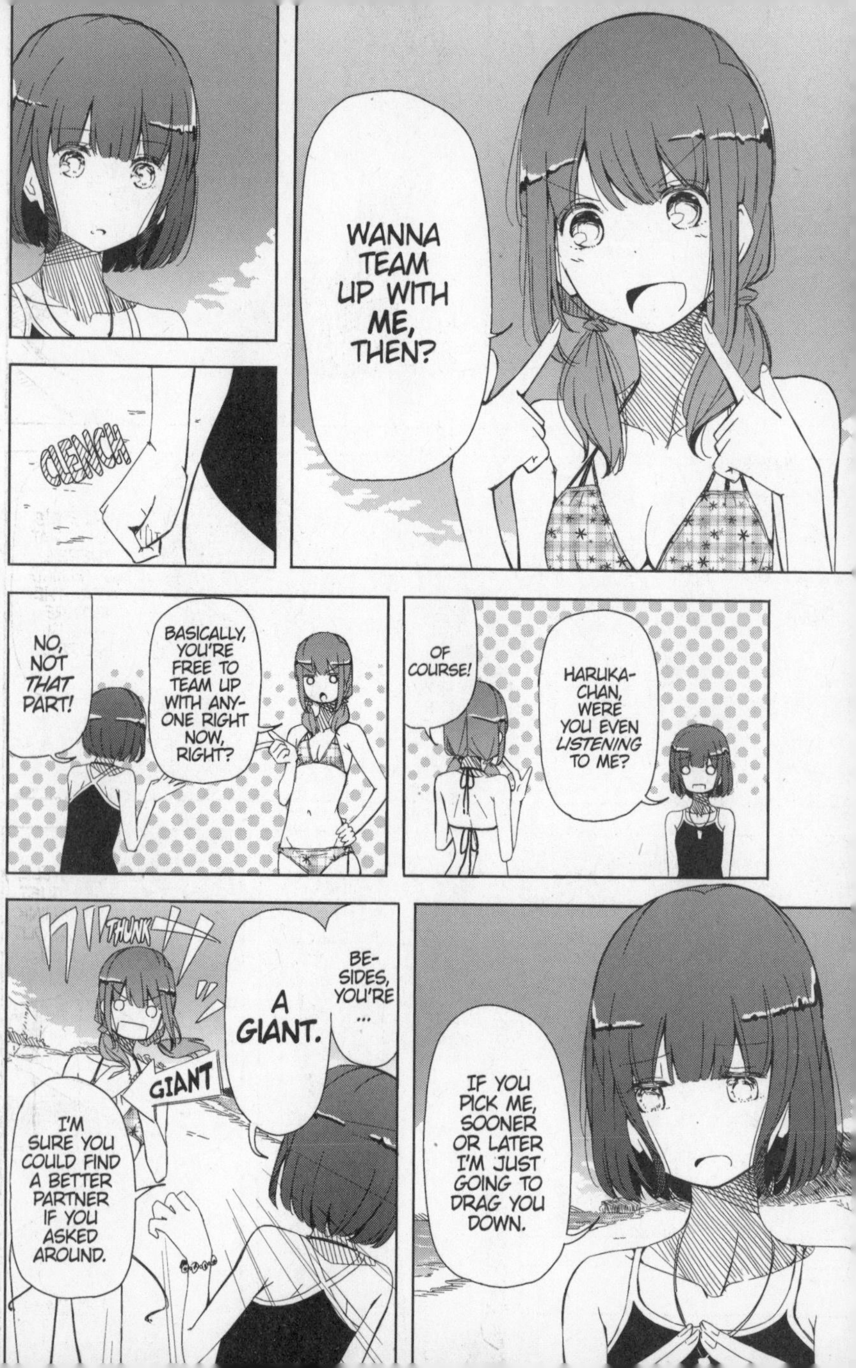
WANNA TEAM UP WITH ME, THEN?
CLENCH
HARUKA-CHAN, WERE YOU EVEN *LISTENING* TO ME?
OF COURSE!
BASICALLY, YOU'RE FREE TO TEAM UP WITH ANYONE RIGHT NOW, RIGHT?
NO, NOT *THAT* PART!
IF YOU PICK ME, SOONER OR LATER I'M JUST GOING TO DRAG YOU DOWN.
BESIDES, YOU'RE ...
A GIANT.
THUNK
GIANT
I'M SURE YOU COULD FIND A BETTER PARTNER IF YOU ASKED AROUND.

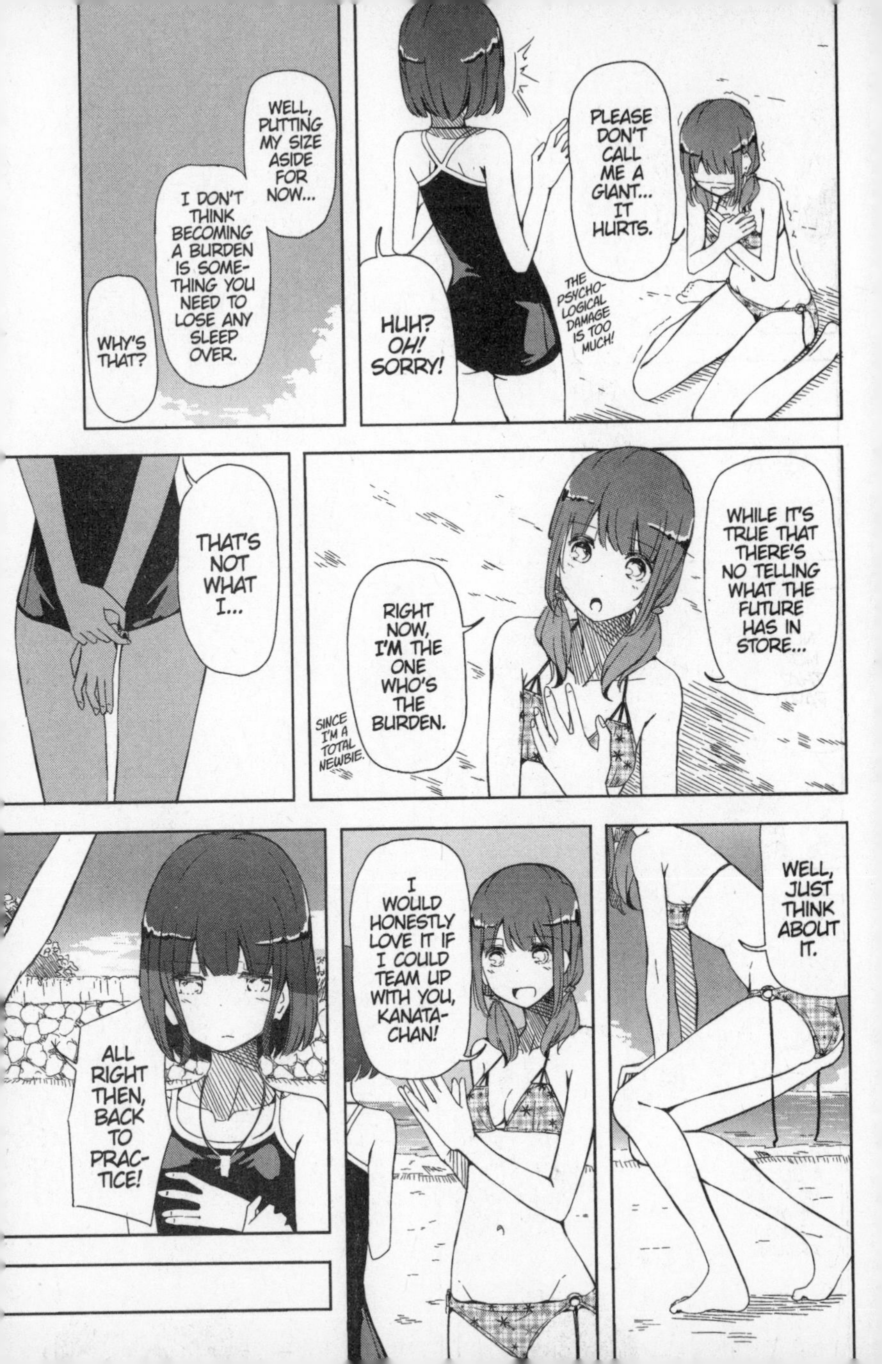
PLEASE DON'T CALL ME A GIANT... IT HURTS.
THE PSYCHOLOGICAL DAMAGE IS TOO MUCH!
HUH? OH! SORRY!
WELL, PUTTING MY SIZE ASIDE FOR NOW...
I DON'T THINK BECOMING A BURDEN IS SOMETHING YOU NEED TO LOSE ANY SLEEP OVER.
WHY'S THAT?
WHILE IT'S TRUE THAT THERE'S NO TELLING WHAT THE FUTURE HAS IN STORE...
RIGHT NOW, I'M THE ONE WHO'S THE BURDEN.
SINCE I'M A TOTAL NEWBIE.
THAT'S NOT WHAT I...
WELL, JUST THINK ABOUT IT.
I WOULD HONESTLY LOVE IT IF I COULD TEAM UP WITH YOU, KANATA-CHAN!
ALL RIGHT THEN, BACK TO PRACTICE!

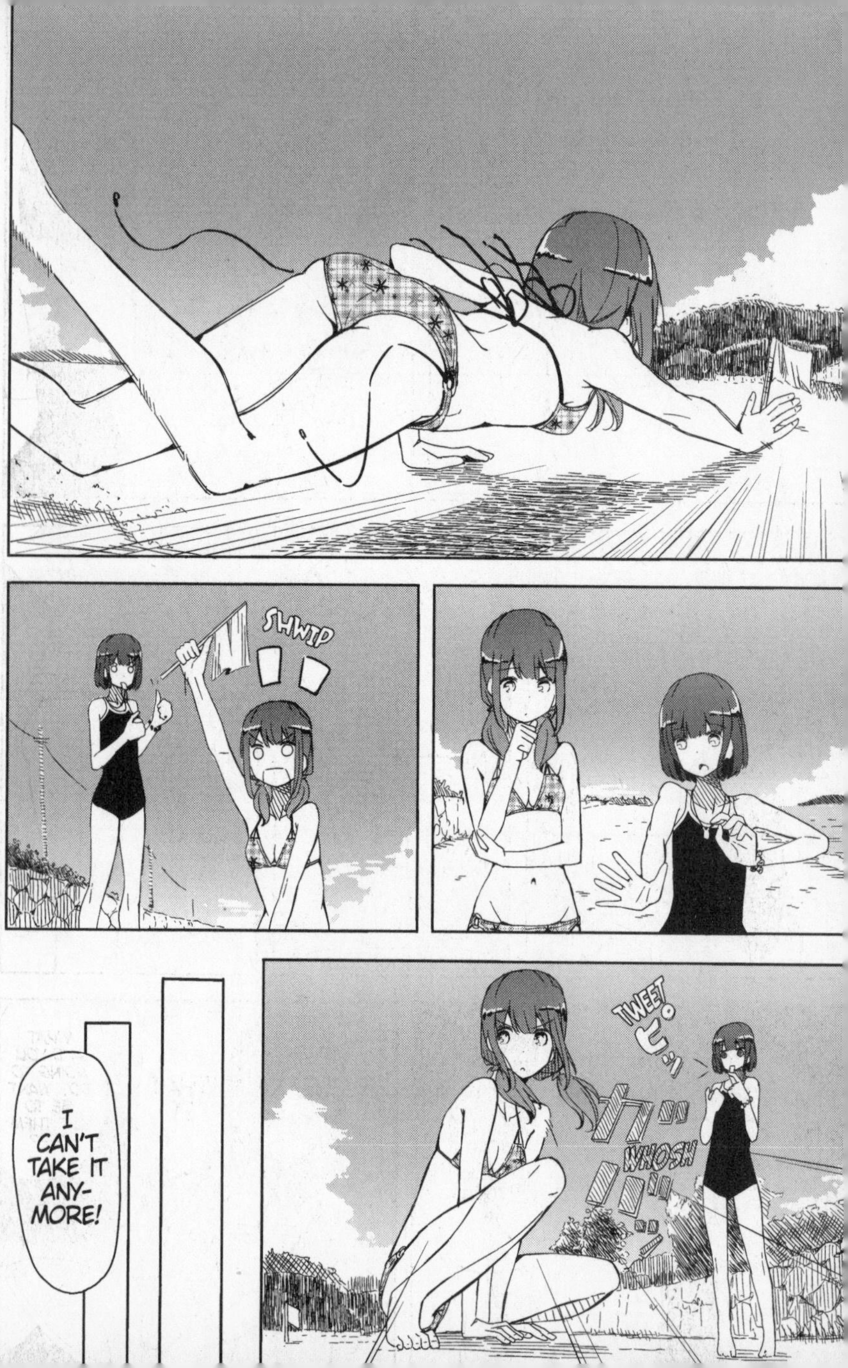
SHWIP
TWEET
ピッ
WHOOSH
I CAN'T TAKE IT ANY-MORE!

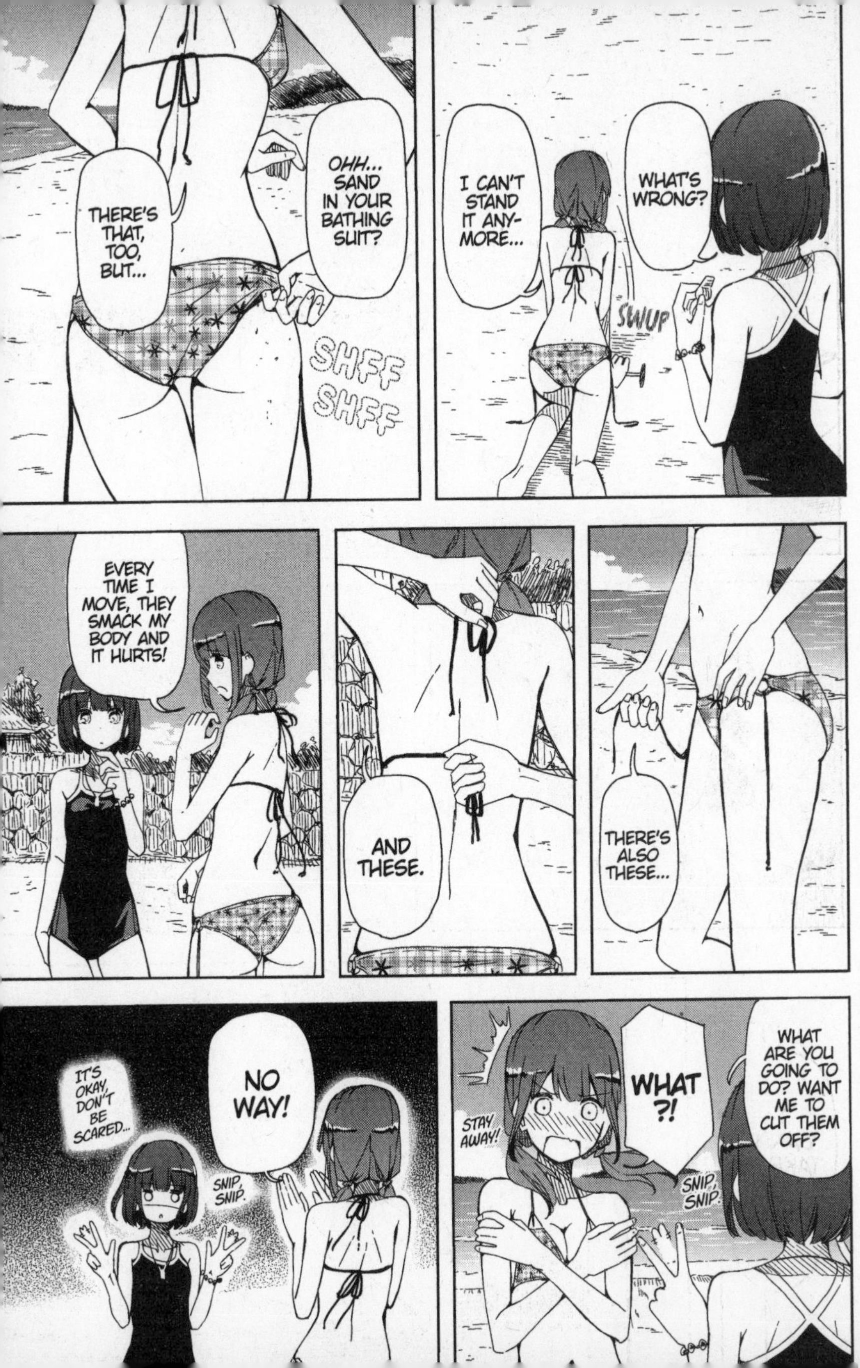
WHAT'S WRONG?
I CAN'T STAND IT ANYMORE...
SWUP
OHH... SAND IN YOUR BATHING SUIT?
THERE'S THAT, TOO, BUT...
SHFF SHFF
THERE'S ALSO THESE...
AND THESE.
EVERY TIME I MOVE, THEY SMACK MY BODY AND IT HURTS!
WHAT ARE YOU GOING TO DO? WANT ME TO CUT THEM OFF?
SNIP, SNIP.
WHAT ?!
STAY AWAY!
NO WAY!
SNIP, SNIP.
IT'S OKAY, DON'T BE SCARED...

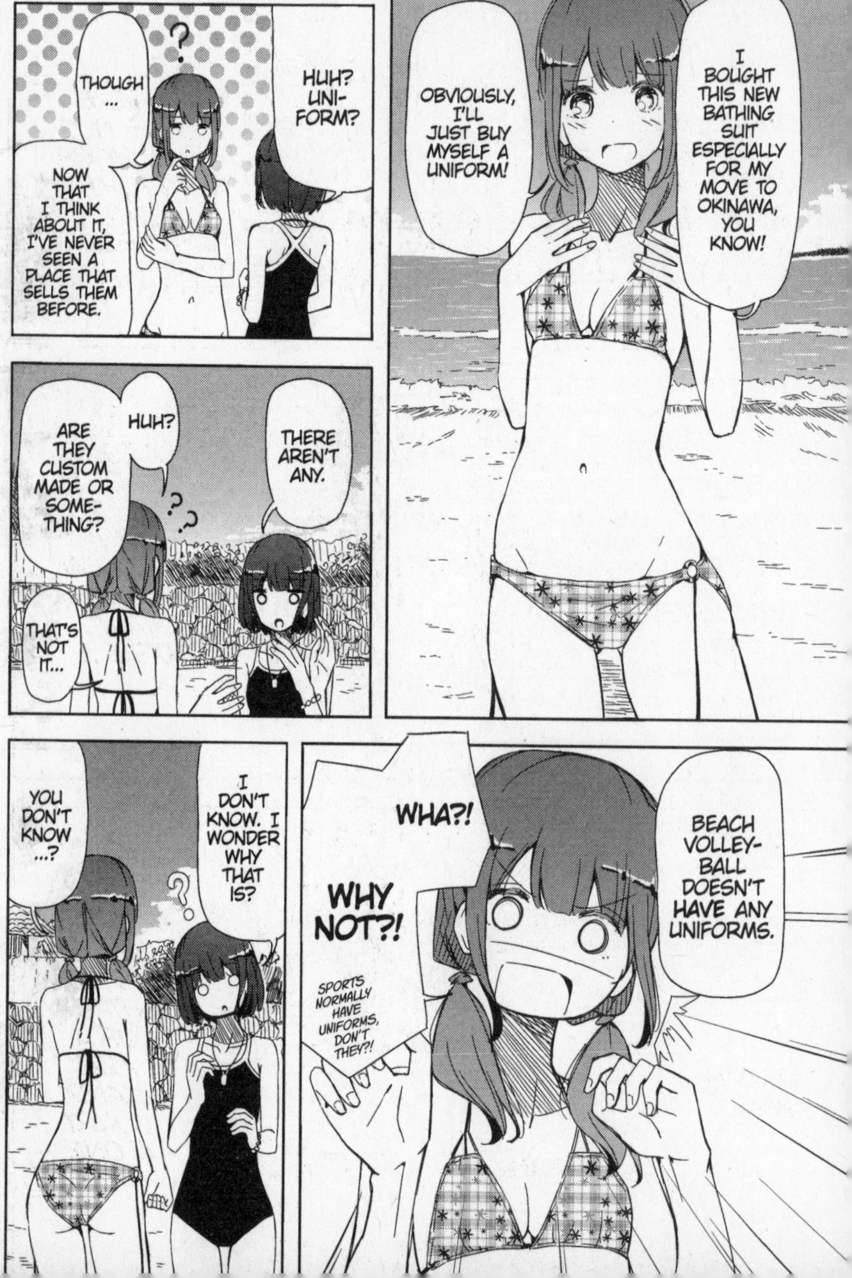
I BOUGHT THIS NEW BATHING SUIT ESPECIALLY FOR MY MOVE TO OKINAWA, YOU KNOW!
OBVIOUSLY, I'LL JUST BUY MYSELF A UNIFORM!
HUH? UNI-FORM?
THOUGH ...
NOW THAT I THINK ABOUT IT, I'VE NEVER SEEN A PLACE THAT SELLS THEM BEFORE.
THERE AREN'T ANY.
HUH?
ARE THEY CUSTOM MADE OR SOME-THING?
THAT'S NOT IT...
BEACH VOLLEY-BALL DOESN'T HAVE ANY UNIFORMS.
WHA?!
WHY NOT?!
SPORTS NORMALLY HAVE UNIFORMS, DON'T THEY?!
I DON'T KNOW. I WONDER WHY THAT IS?
YOU DON'T KNOW ...?

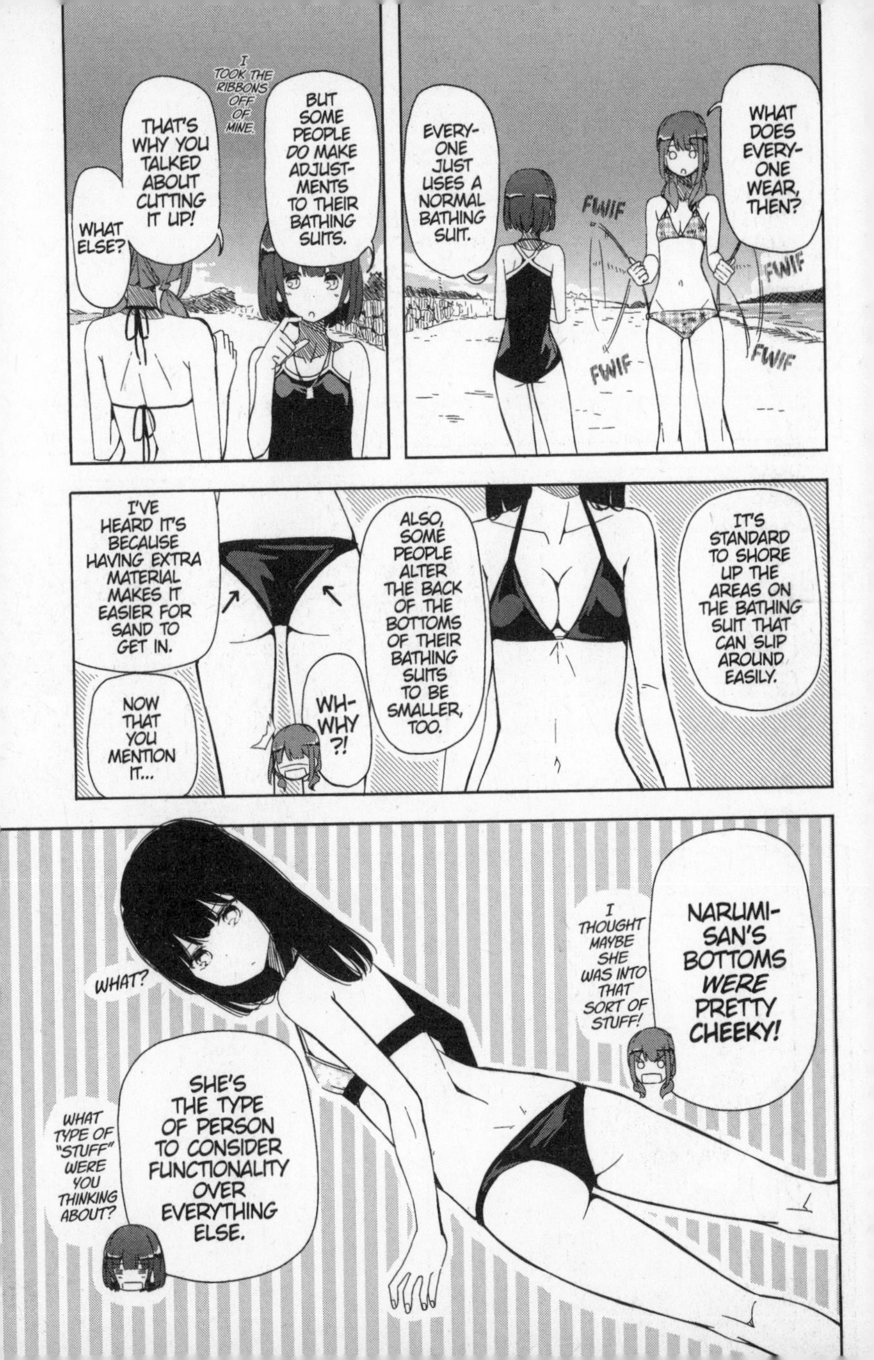
WHAT DOES EVERY-ONE WEAR, THEN?
EVERY-ONE JUST USES A NORMAL BATHING SUIT.
FWIF
FWIF
FWIF
FWIF
BUT SOME PEOPLE DO MAKE ADJUST-MENTS TO THEIR BATHING SUITS.
I TOOK THE RIBBONS OFF OF MINE.
THAT'S WHY YOU TALKED ABOUT CUTTING IT UP!
WHAT ELSE?
IT'S STANDARD TO SHORE UP THE AREAS ON THE BATHING SUIT THAT CAN SLIP AROUND EASILY.
ALSO, SOME PEOPLE ALTER THE BACK OF THE BOTTOMS OF THEIR BATHING SUITS TO BE SMALLER, TOO.
WH-WHY?!
I'VE HEARD IT'S BECAUSE HAVING EXTRA MATERIAL MAKES IT EASIER FOR SAND TO GET IN.
NOW THAT YOU MENTION IT...
NARUMI-SAN'S BOTTOMS WERE PRETTY CHEEKY!
I THOUGHT MAYBE SHE WAS INTO THAT SORT OF STUFF!
WHAT?
SHE'S THE TYPE OF PERSON TO CONSIDER FUNCTIONALITY OVER EVERYTHING ELSE.
WHAT TYPE OF "STUFF" WERE YOU THINKING ABOUT?

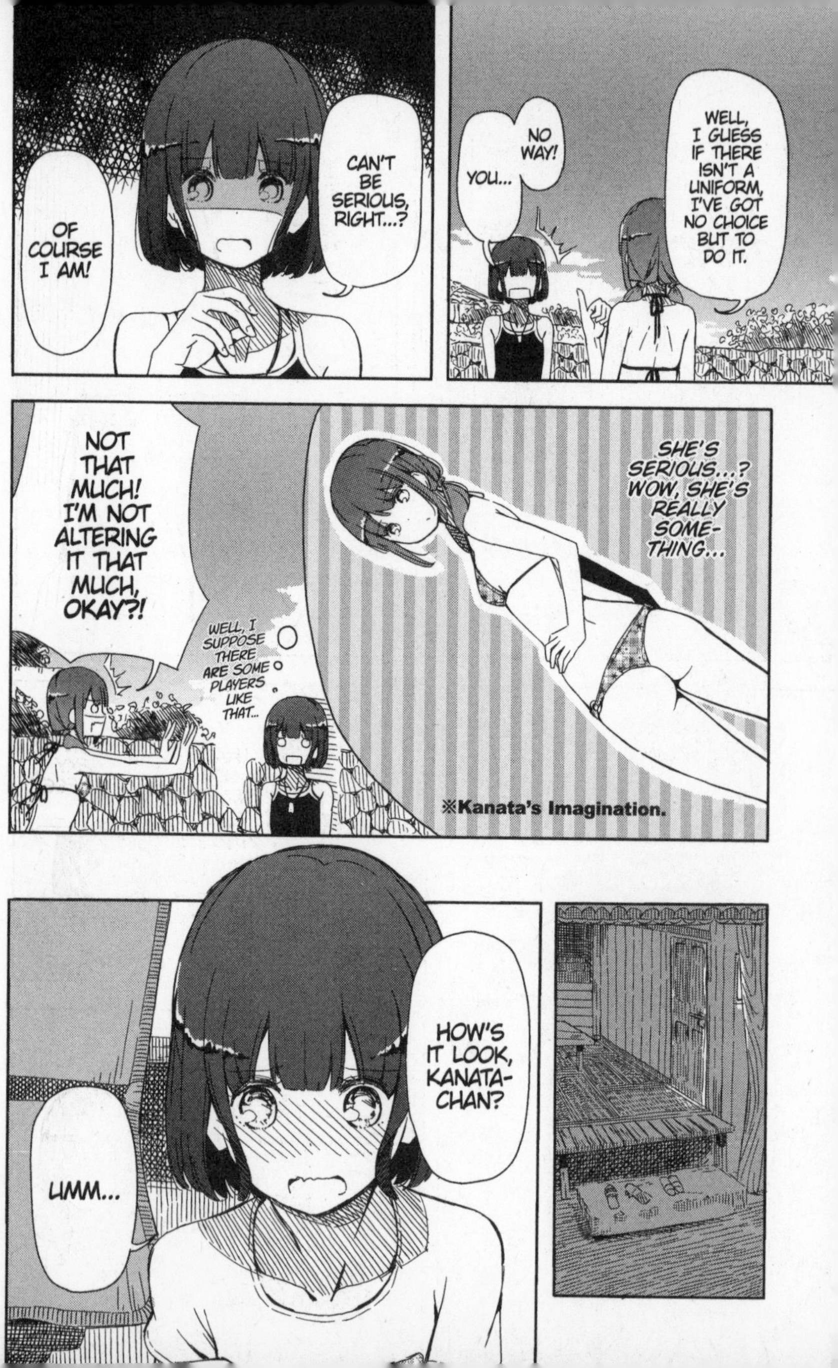
WELL, I GUESS IF THERE ISN'T A UNIFORM, I'VE GOT NO CHOICE BUT TO DO IT.
NO WAY!
YOU...
CAN'T BE SERIOUS, RIGHT...?
OF COURSE I AM!
SHE'S SERIOUS...? WOW, SHE'S REALLY SOME-THING...
WELL, I SUPPOSE THERE ARE SOME PLAYERS LIKE THAT...
NOT THAT MUCH! I'M NOT ALTERING IT THAT MUCH, OKAY?!
※Kanata's Imagination.
HOW'S IT LOOK, KANATA-CHAN?
UMM...

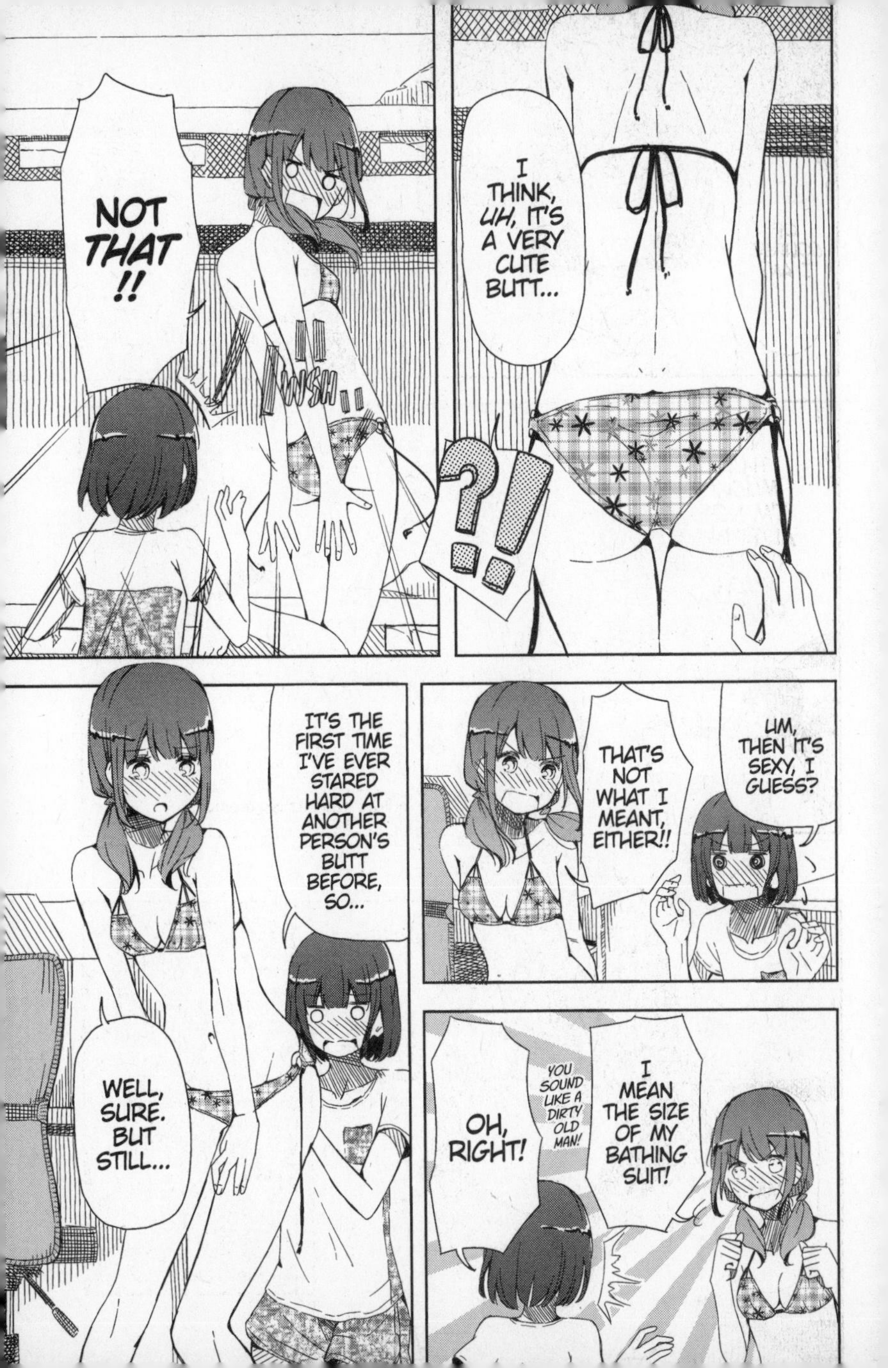
I THINK, UH, IT'S A VERY CUTE BUTT...
?!!
NOT THAT!!
SWISH
UM, THEN IT'S SEXY, I GUESS?
THAT'S NOT WHAT I MEANT, EITHER!!
I MEAN THE SIZE OF MY BATHING SUIT!
YOU SOUND LIKE A DIRTY OLD MAN!
OH, RIGHT!
IT'S THE FIRST TIME I'VE EVER STARED HARD AT ANOTHER PERSON'S BUTT BEFORE, SO...
WELL, SURE. BUT STILL...

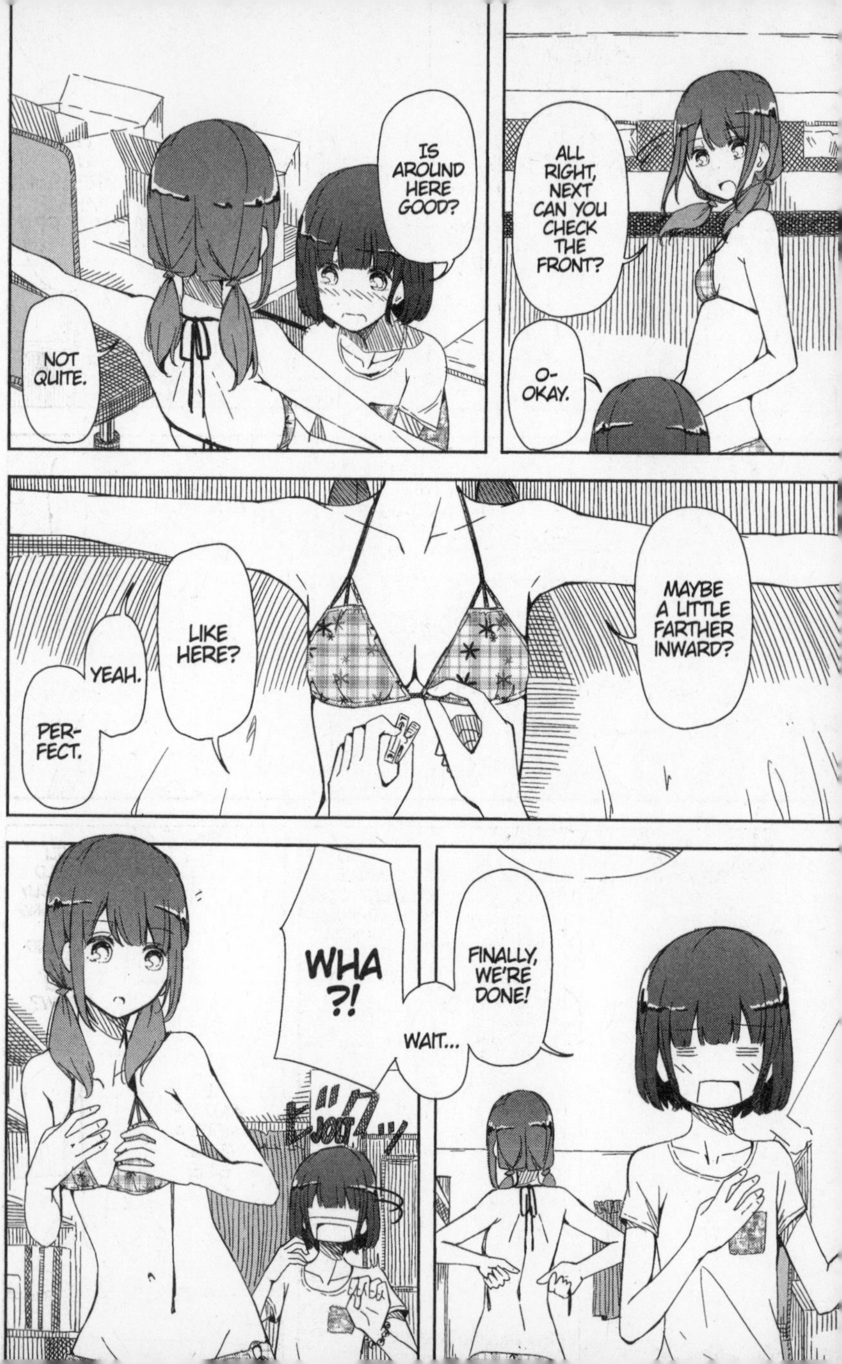
ALL RIGHT, NEXT CAN YOU CHECK THE FRONT?
O-OKAY.
IS AROUND HERE GOOD?
NOT QUITE.
MAYBE A LITTLE FARTHER INWARD?
LIKE HERE?
YEAH.
PER-FECT.
FINALLY, WE'RE DONE!
WAIT...
WHA ?!

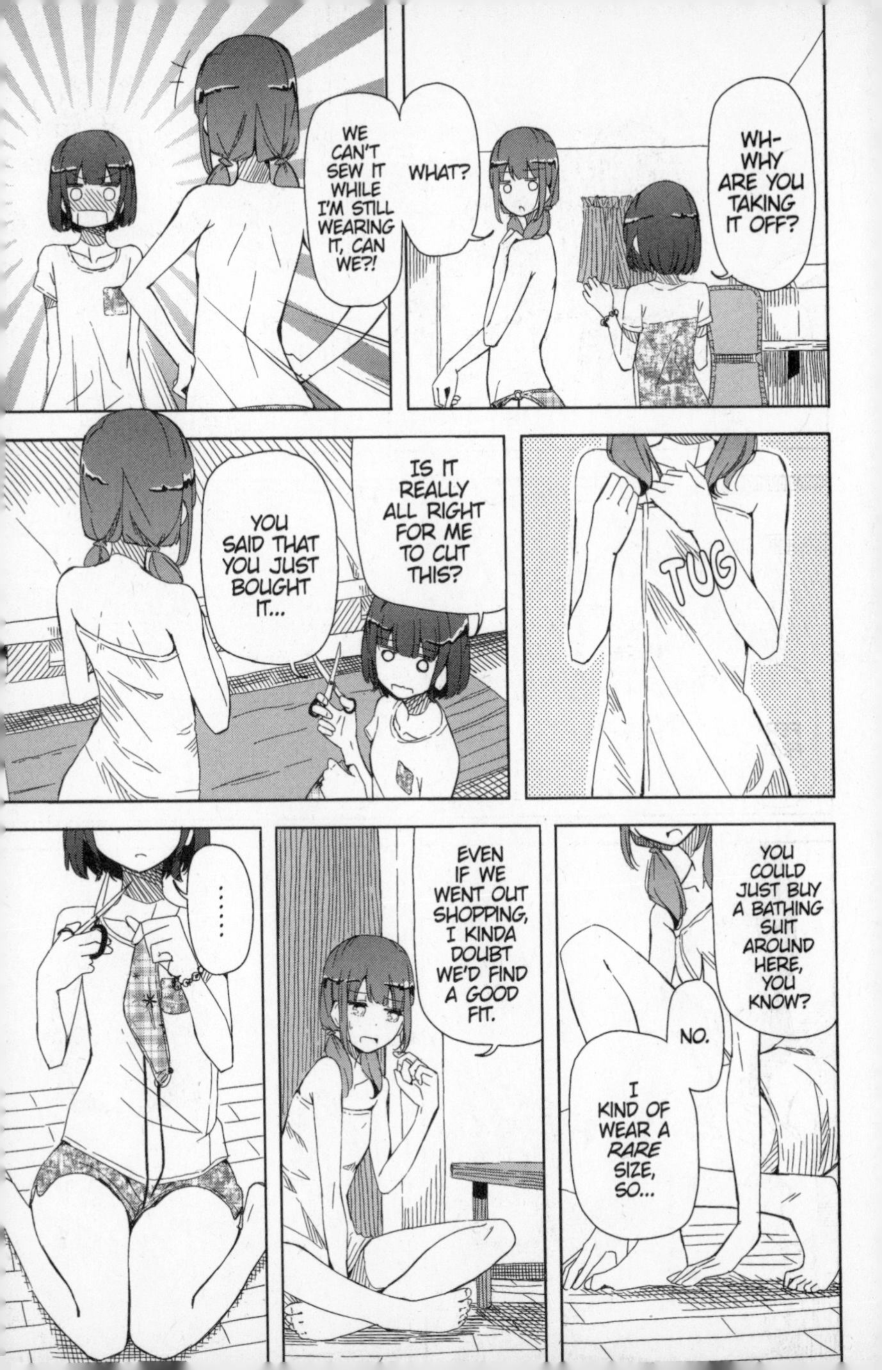
WH- WHY ARE YOU TAKING IT OFF?
WHAT?
WE CAN'T SEW IT WHILE I'M STILL WEARING IT, CAN WE?!
TUG
IS IT REALLY ALL RIGHT FOR ME TO CUT THIS?
YOU SAID THAT YOU JUST BOUGHT IT...
YOU COULD JUST BUY A BATHING SUIT AROUND HERE, YOU KNOW?
NO.
I KIND OF WEAR A *RARE* SIZE, SO...
EVEN IF WE WENT OUT SHOPPING, I KINDA DOUBT WE'D FIND A GOOD FIT.
......

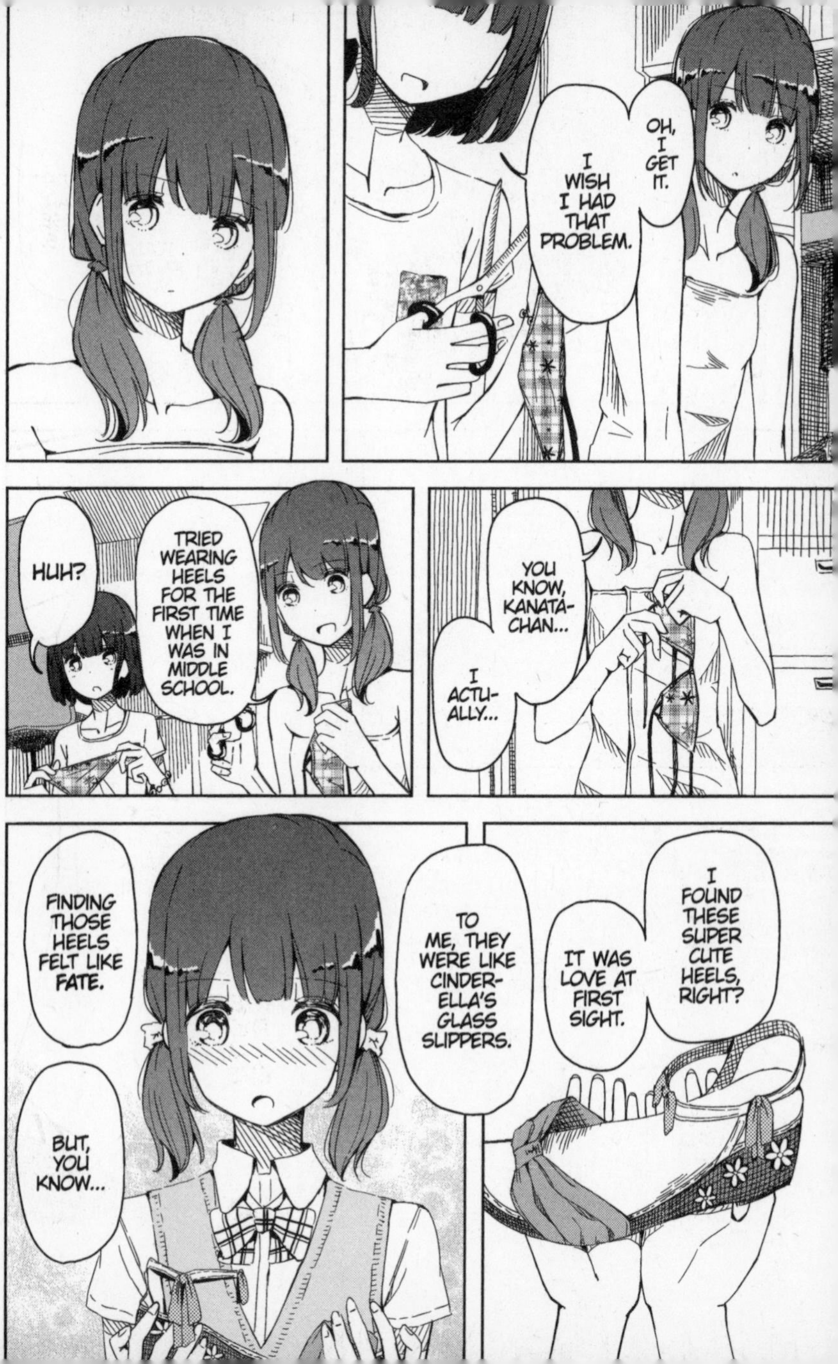
OH, I GET IT.
I WISH I HAD THAT PROBLEM.
YOU KNOW, KANATA-CHAN...
I ACTUALLY...
TRIED WEARING HEELS FOR THE FIRST TIME WHEN I WAS IN MIDDLE SCHOOL.
HUH?
I FOUND THESE SUPER CUTE HEELS, RIGHT?
IT WAS LOVE AT FIRST SIGHT.
TO ME, THEY WERE LIKE CINDERELLA'S GLASS SLIPPERS.
FINDING THOSE HEELS FELT LIKE FATE.
BUT, YOU KNOW...

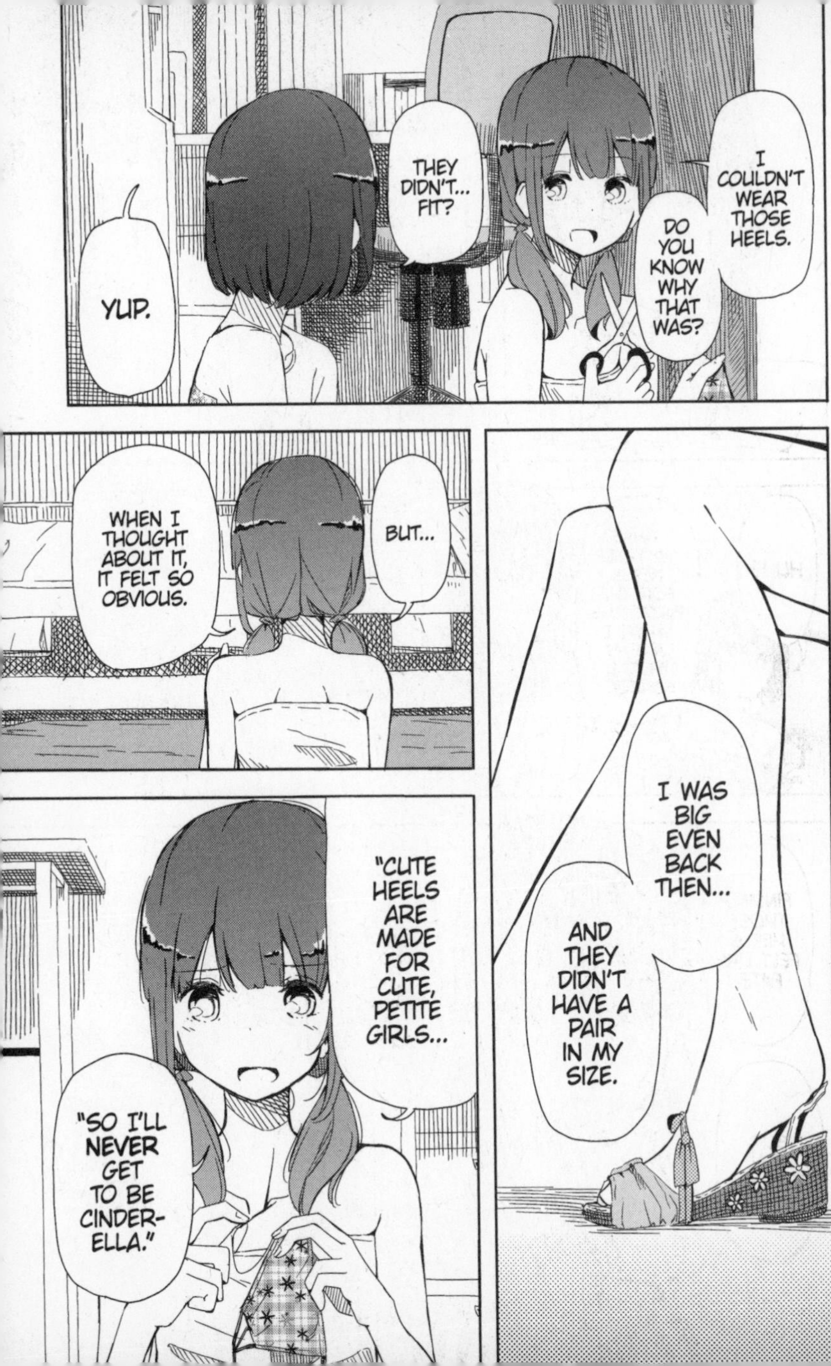
I COULDN'T WEAR THOSE HEELS.
DO YOU KNOW WHY THAT WAS?
THEY DIDN'T... FIT?
YUP.
I WAS BIG EVEN BACK THEN...
AND THEY DIDN'T HAVE A PAIR IN MY SIZE.
BUT...
WHEN I THOUGHT ABOUT IT, IT FELT SO OBVIOUS.
"CUTE HEELS ARE MADE FOR CUTE, PETITE GIRLS...
"SO I'LL NEVER GET TO BE CINDERELLA."

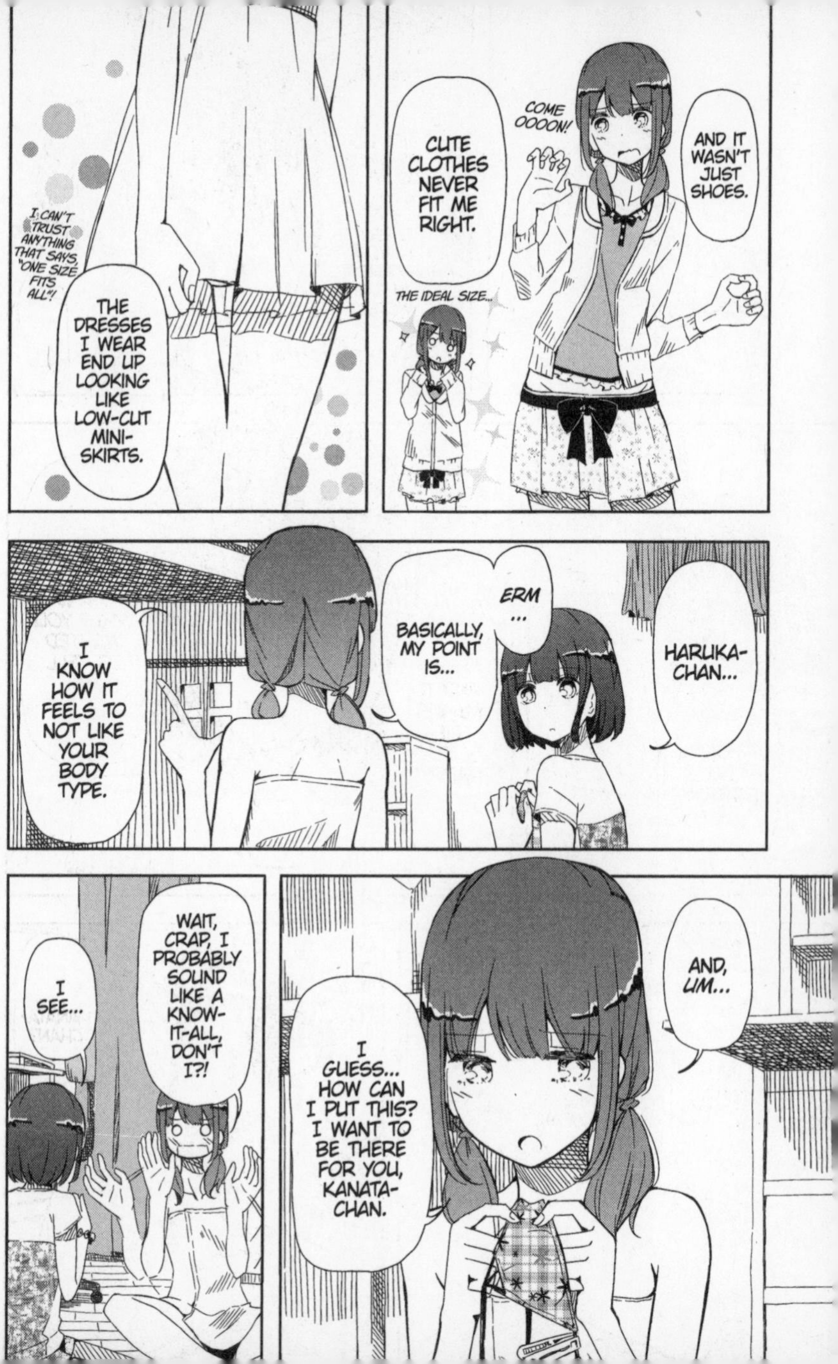
AND IT WASN'T JUST SHOES.
COME OOOON!
CUTE CLOTHES NEVER FIT ME RIGHT.
THE IDEAL SIZE...
THE DRESSES I WEAR END UP LOOKING LIKE LOW-CUT MINI-SKIRTS.
I CAN'T TRUST ANYTHING THAT SAYS, "ONE SIZE FITS ALL"!
HARUKA-CHAN...
ERM ...
BASICALLY, MY POINT IS...
I KNOW HOW IT FEELS TO NOT LIKE YOUR BODY TYPE.
AND, UM...
I GUESS... HOW CAN I PUT THIS? I WANT TO BE THERE FOR YOU, KANATA-CHAN.
WAIT, CRAP, I PROBABLY SOUND LIKE A KNOW-IT-ALL, DON'T I?!
I SEE...

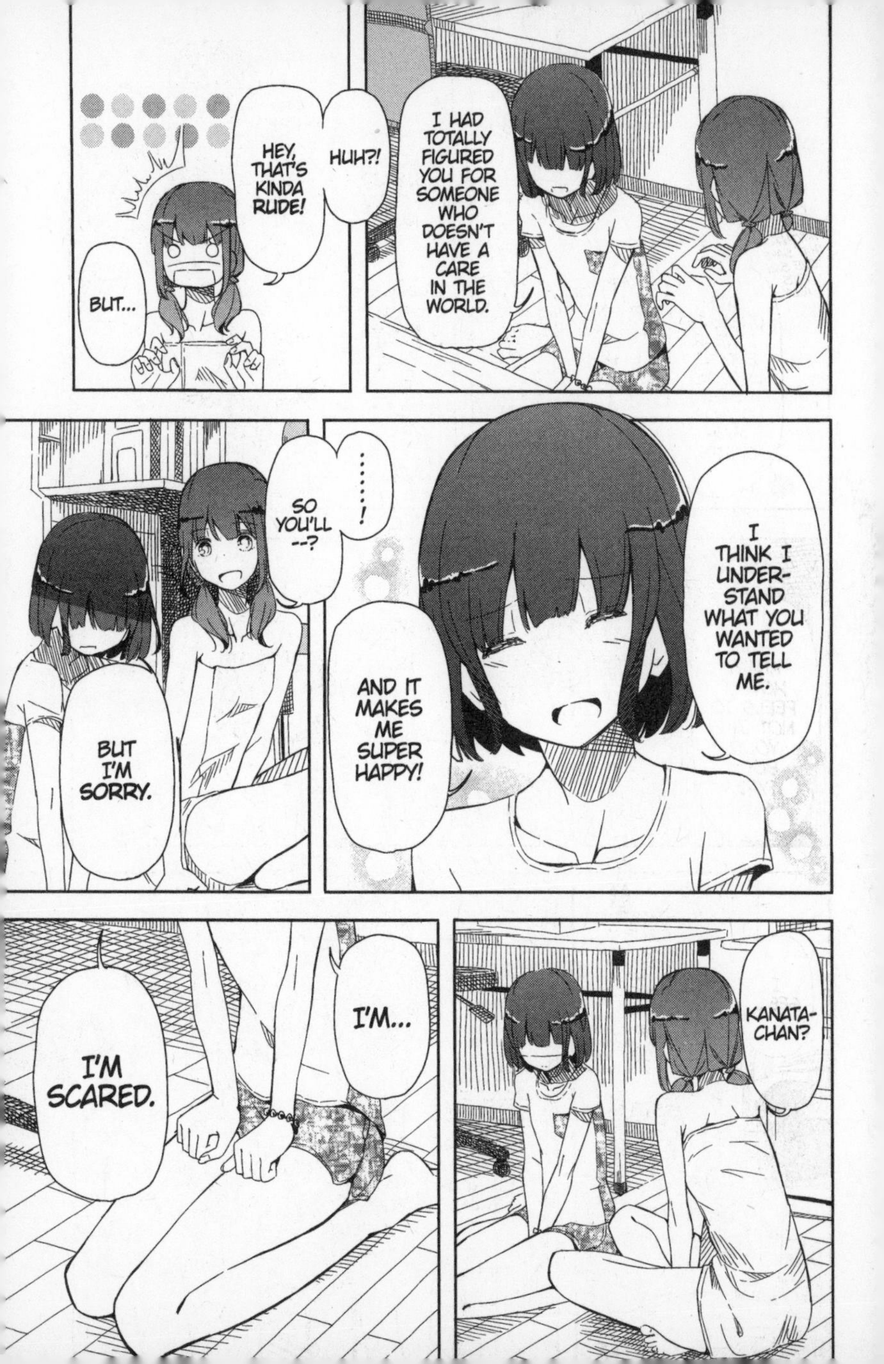
I HAD TOTALLY FIGURED YOU FOR SOMEONE WHO DOESN'T HAVE A CARE IN THE WORLD.
HUH?!
HEY, THAT'S KINDA RUDE!
BUT...
I THINK I UNDERSTAND WHAT YOU WANTED TO TELL ME.
AND IT MAKES ME SUPER HAPPY!
......!
SO YOU'LL --?
BUT I'M SORRY.
KANATA-CHAN?
I'M...
I'M SCARED.

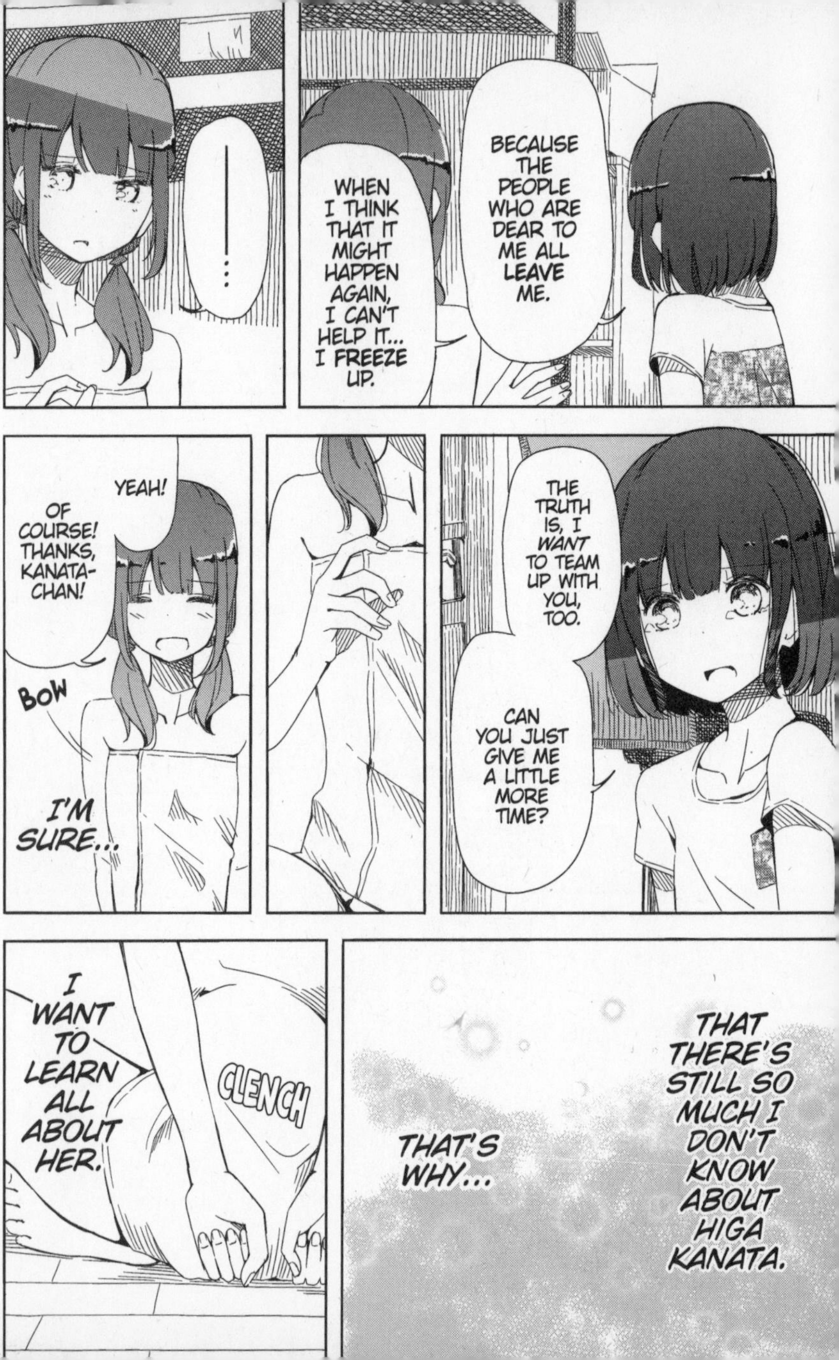
BECAUSE THE PEOPLE WHO ARE DEAR TO ME ALL LEAVE ME.
WHEN I THINK THAT IT MIGHT HAPPEN AGAIN, I CAN'T HELP IT... I FREEZE UP.
......
THE TRUTH IS, I *WANT* TO TEAM UP WITH YOU, TOO.
CAN YOU JUST GIVE ME A LITTLE MORE TIME?
YEAH!
OF COURSE! THANKS, KANATA-CHAN!
BOW
I'M SURE...
THAT THERE'S STILL SO MUCH I DON'T KNOW ABOUT HIGA KANATA.
THAT'S WHY...
CLENCH
I WANT TO LEARN ALL ABOUT HER.

Presented by Nyoijizai

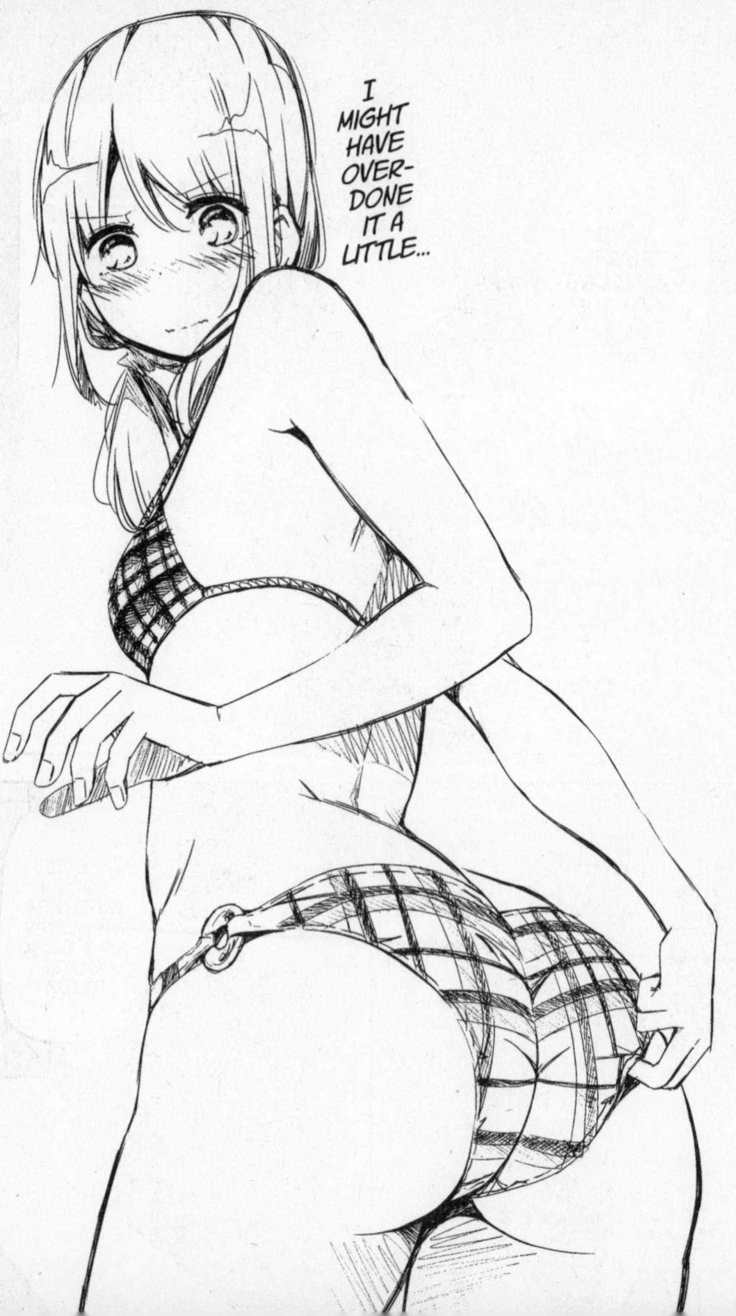
I MIGHT HAVE OVER-DONE IT A LITTLE...

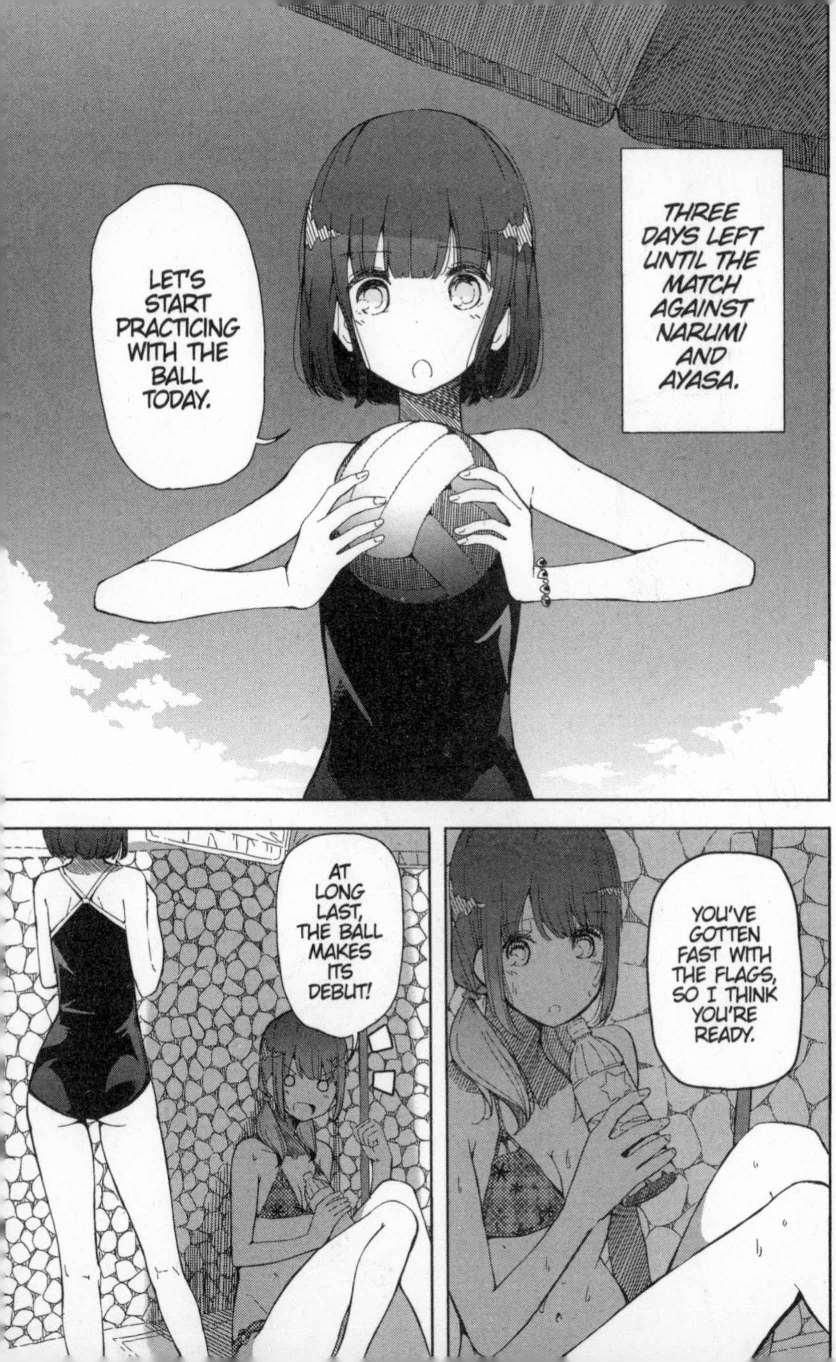
THREE DAYS LEFT UNTIL THE MATCH AGAINST NARUMI AND AYASA.
LET'S START PRACTICING WITH THE BALL TODAY.
YOU'VE GOTTEN FAST WITH THE FLAGS, SO I THINK YOU'RE READY.
AT LONG LAST, THE BALL MAKES ITS DEBUT!

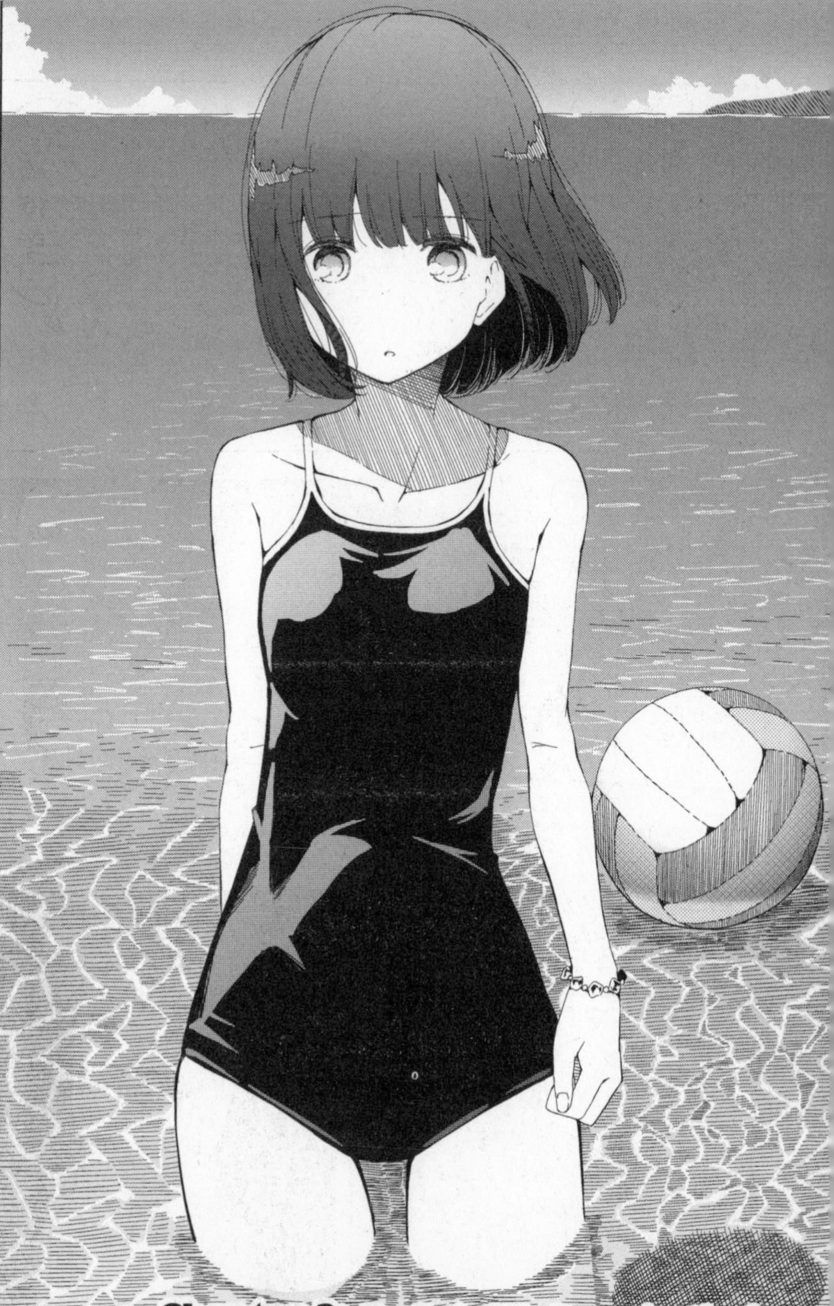

Chapter 3: She Ended Up Becoming the Ace.

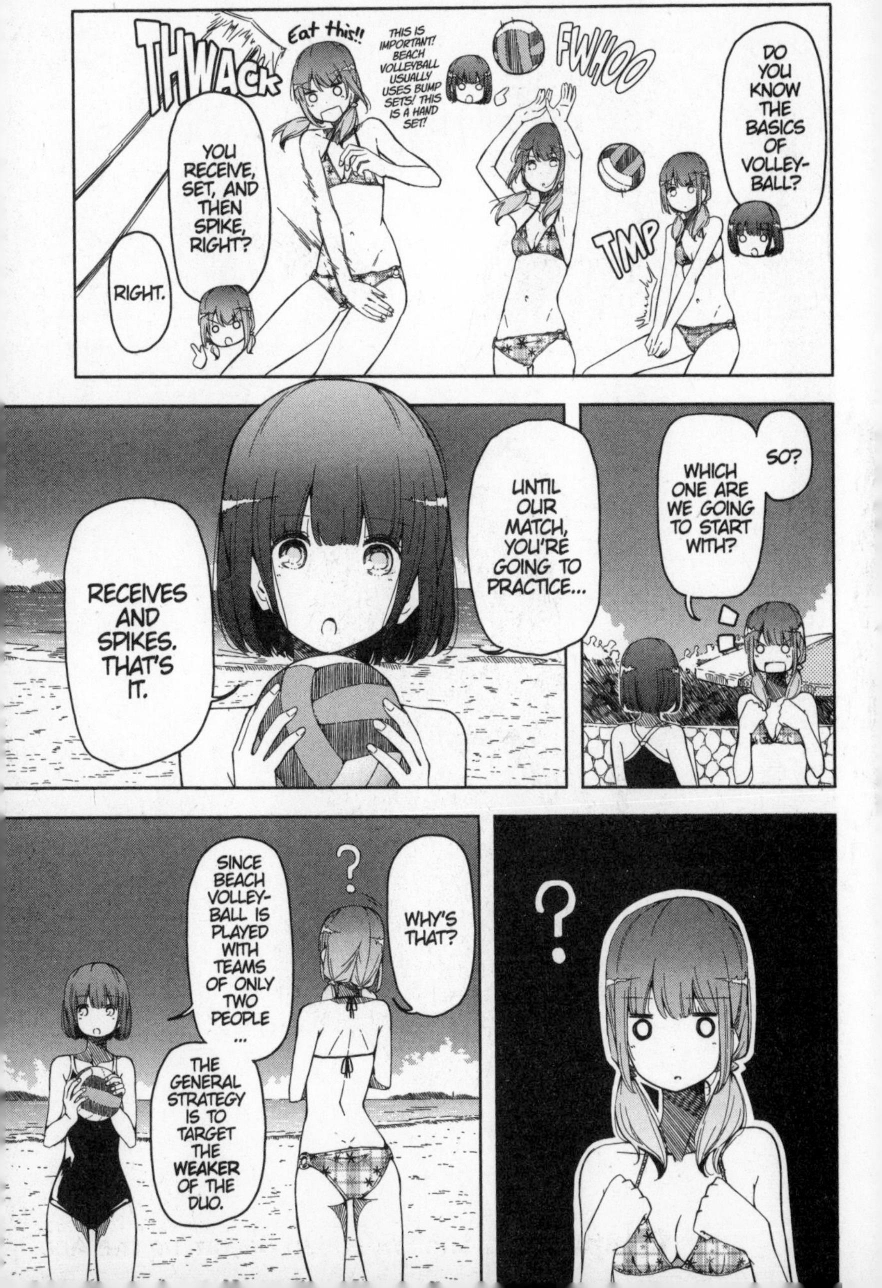
DO YOU KNOW THE BASICS OF VOLLEY-BALL?
TMP
FWHOO
THIS IS IMPORTANT! BEACH VOLLEYBALL USUALLY USES BUMP SETS! THIS IS A HAND SET!
Eat this!!
THWACK
YOU RECEIVE, SET, AND THEN SPIKE, RIGHT?
RIGHT.
SO?
WHICH ONE ARE WE GOING TO START WITH?
UNTIL OUR MATCH, YOU'RE GOING TO PRACTICE...
RECEIVES AND SPIKES. THAT'S IT.
?
WHY'S THAT?
?
SINCE BEACH VOLLEY-BALL IS PLAYED WITH TEAMS OF ONLY TWO PEOPLE ...
THE GENERAL STRATEGY IS TO TARGET THE WEAKER OF THE DUO.

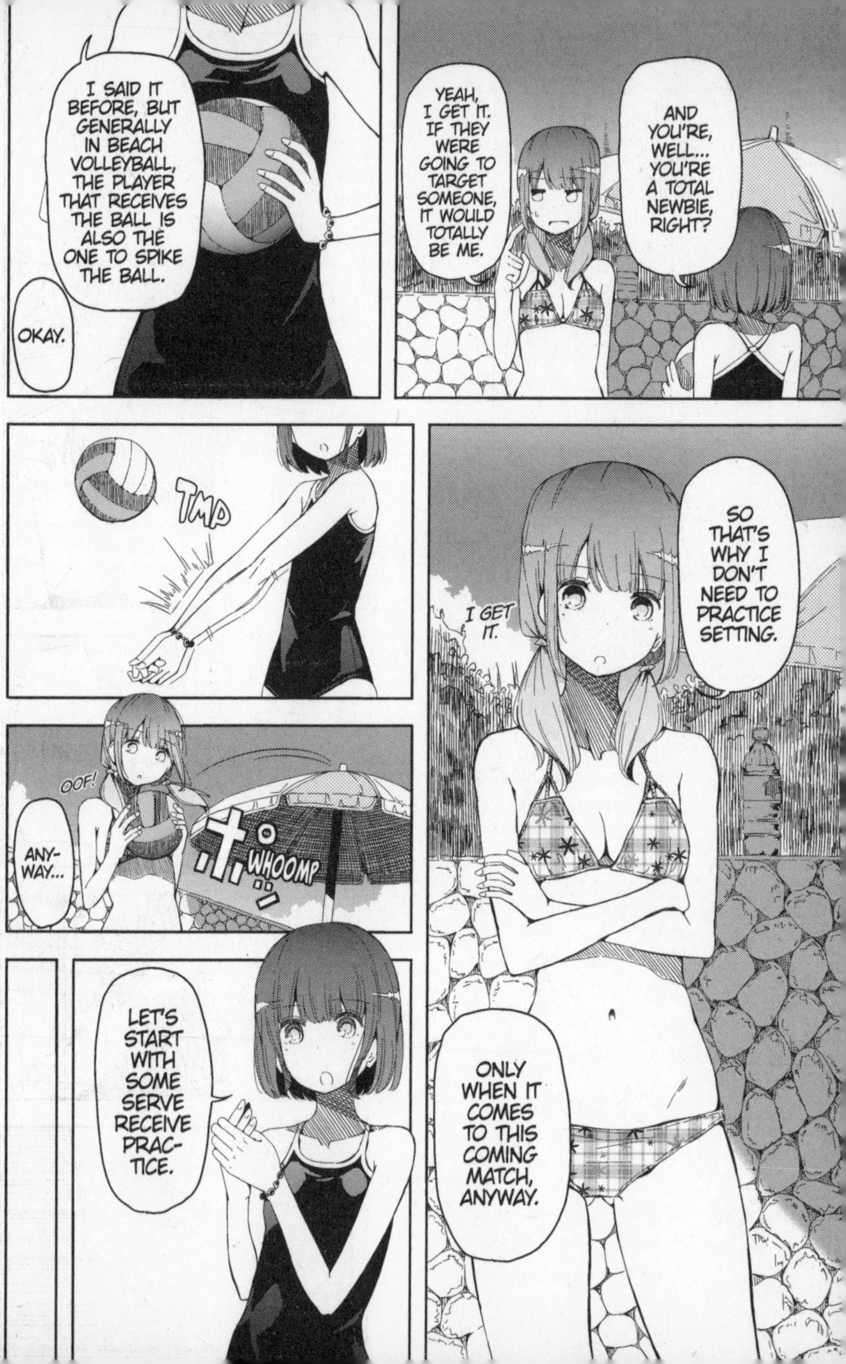
AND YOU'RE, WELL... YOU'RE A TOTAL NEWBIE, RIGHT?
YEAH, I GET IT. IF THEY WERE GOING TO TARGET SOMEONE, IT WOULD TOTALLY BE ME.
I SAID IT BEFORE, BUT GENERALLY IN BEACH VOLLEYBALL, THE PLAYER THAT RECEIVES THE BALL IS ALSO THE ONE TO SPIKE THE BALL.
OKAY.
SO THAT'S WHY I DON'T NEED TO PRACTICE SETTING.
I GET IT.
ONLY WHEN IT COMES TO THIS COMING MATCH, ANYWAY.
TMP
OOF!
WHOOMP
ANY-WAY...
LET'S START WITH SOME SERVE RECEIVE PRAC-TICE.

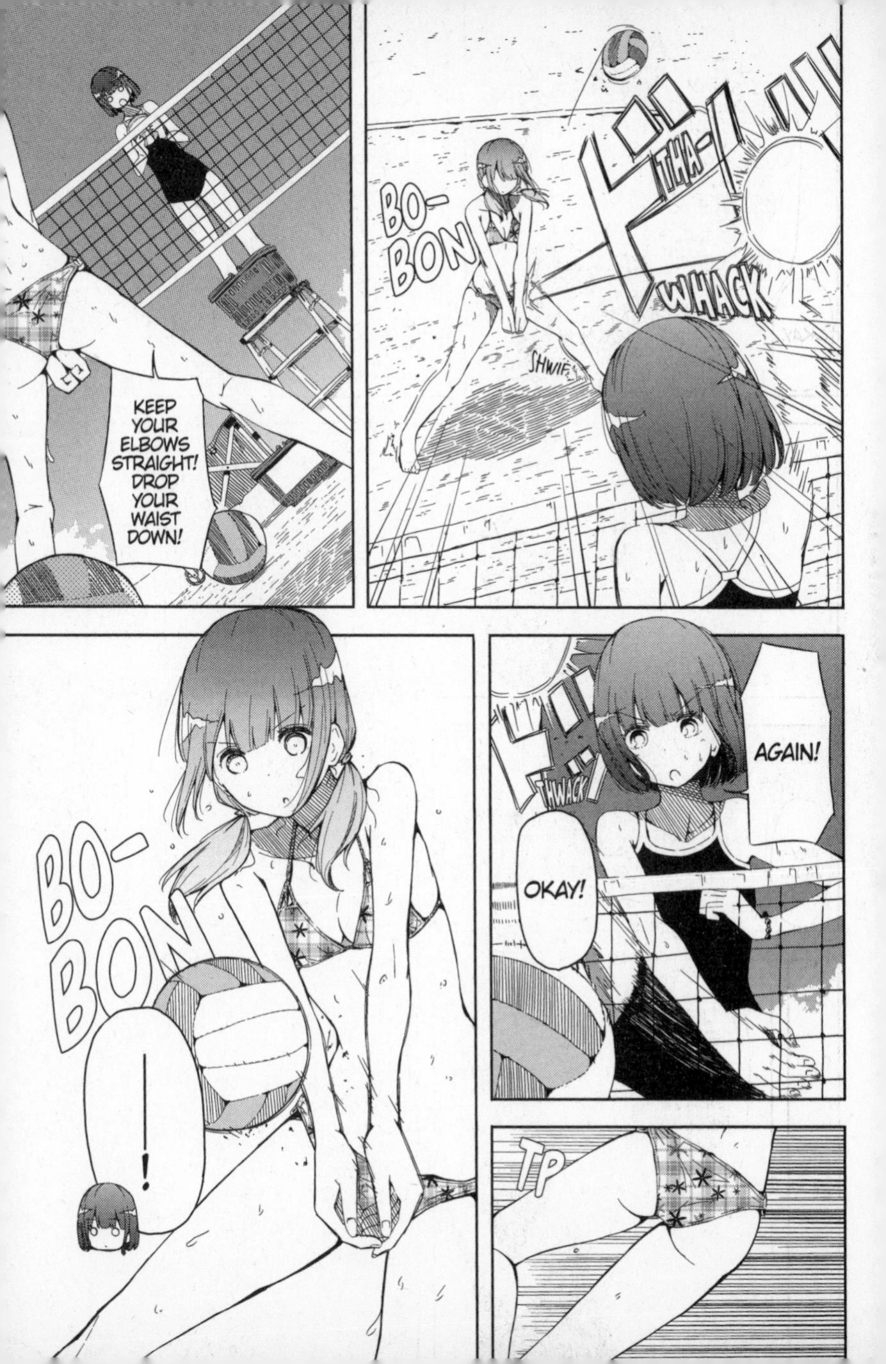
THA-
WHACK
BO-BON
SHWIF
KEEP YOUR ELBOWS STRAIGHT! DROP YOUR WAIST DOWN!
AGAIN!
THWACK
OKAY!
TP
BO-BON
—!

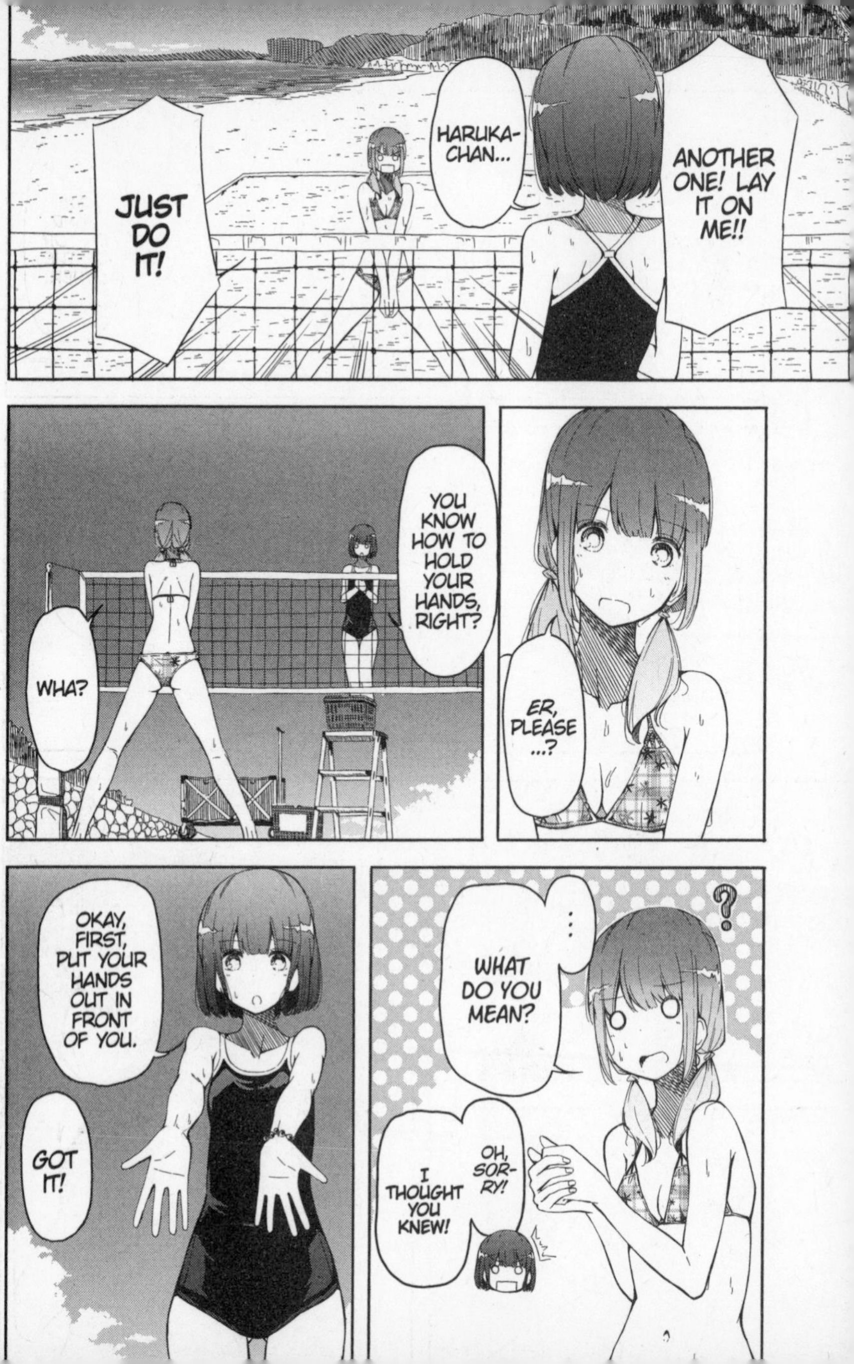
ANOTHER ONE! LAY IT ON ME!!
HARUKA-CHAN...
JUST DO IT!
ER, PLEASE ...?
YOU KNOW HOW TO HOLD YOUR HANDS, RIGHT?
WHA?
...
WHAT DO YOU MEAN?
OH, SORRY!
I THOUGHT YOU KNEW!
OKAY, FIRST, PUT YOUR HANDS OUT IN FRONT OF YOU.
GOT IT!

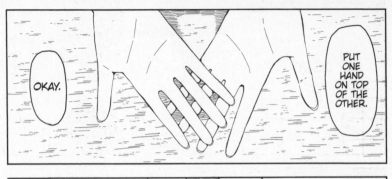

PUT ONE HAND ON TOP OF THE OTHER.
OKAY.
CLOSE YOUR THUMBS OVER YOUR HANDS.
GOT IT.
THIS IS THE CORRECT WAY TO BRING YOUR HANDS TOGE-THER.
THAT SHOULD GIVE YOU BETTER CONTROL OVER YOUR RECEIVES.
HUH, OKAY.
NOW HOLD THAT POSE FOR ANOTHER ONE!
HUH ?!
LEAN

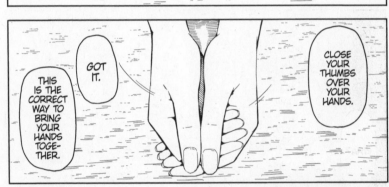

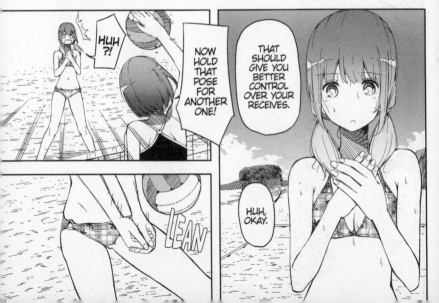

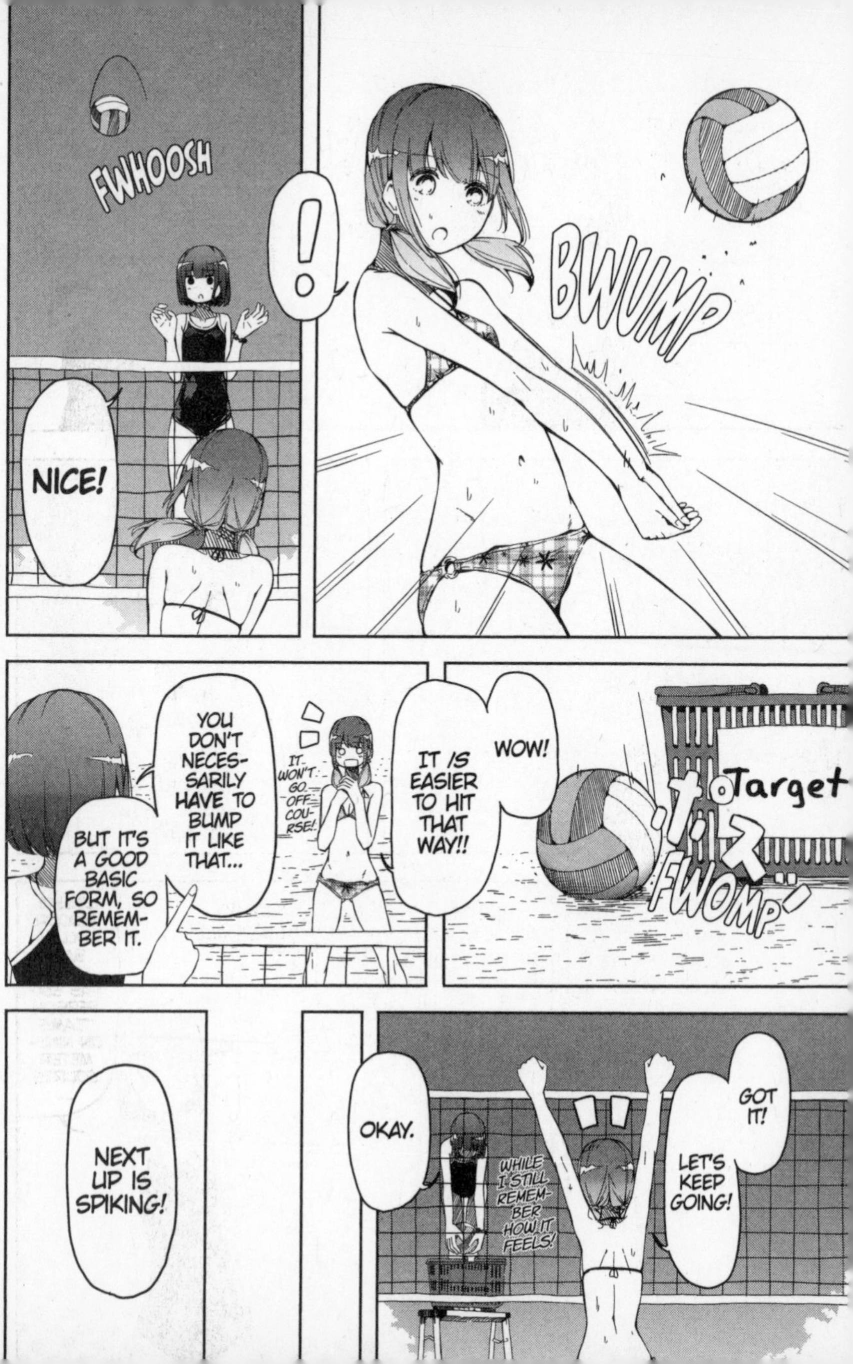
!
BWUMP
FWHOOSH
NICE!
Target
FWOMP
WOW!
IT IS EASIER TO HIT THAT WAY!!
IT WON'T GO OFF COURSE!
YOU DON'T NECES-SARILY HAVE TO BUMP IT LIKE THAT...
BUT IT'S A GOOD BASIC FORM, SO REMEM-BER IT.
GOT IT!
LET'S KEEP GOING!
WHILE I STILL REMEM-BER HOW IT FEELS!
OKAY.
NEXT UP IS SPIKING!

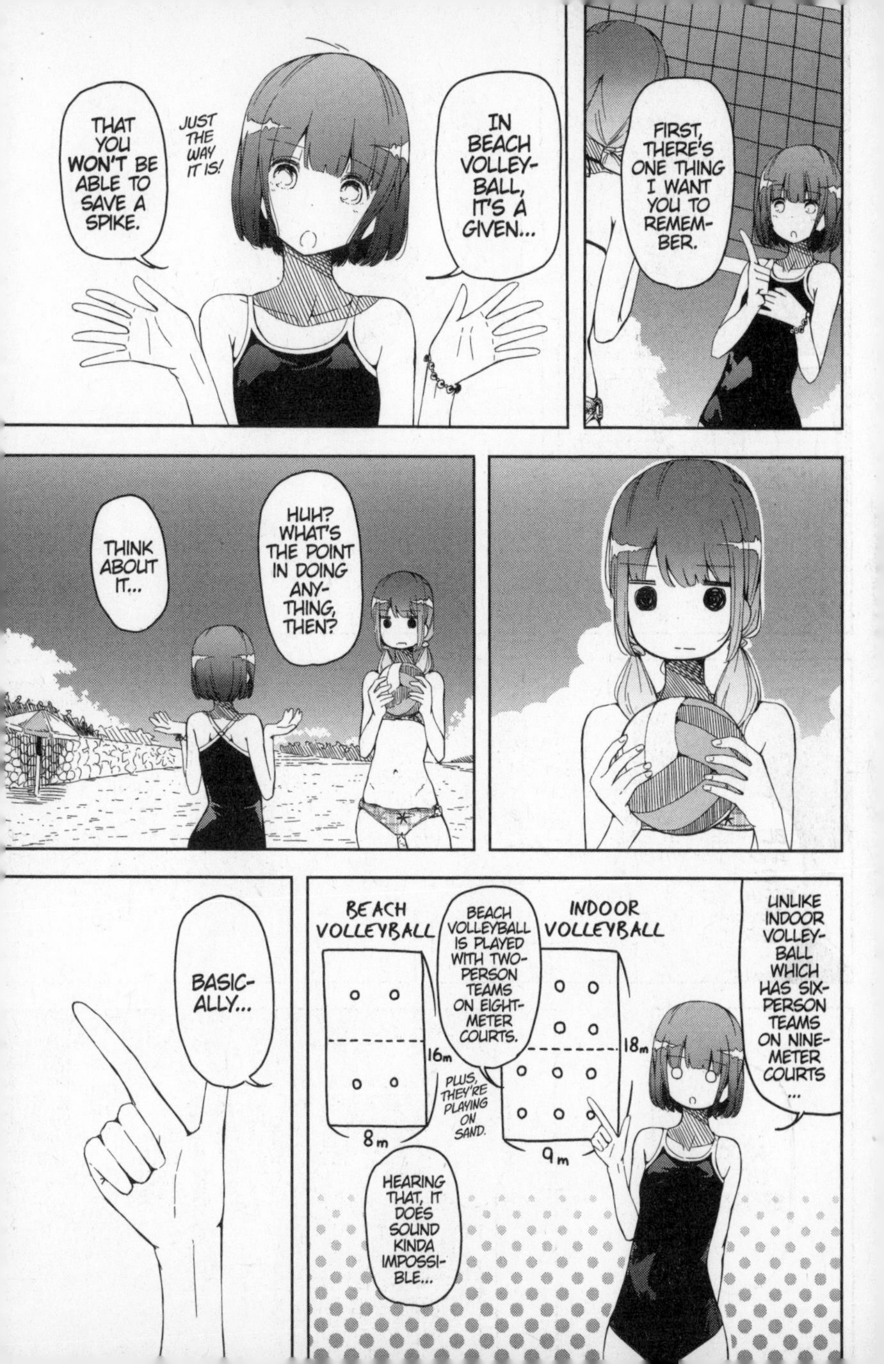
FIRST, THERE'S ONE THING I WANT YOU TO REMEMBER.
IN BEACH VOLLEYBALL, IT'S A GIVEN...
JUST THE WAY IT IS!
THAT YOU WON'T BE ABLE TO SAVE A SPIKE.
HUH? WHAT'S THE POINT IN DOING ANYTHING, THEN?
THINK ABOUT IT...
UNLIKE INDOOR VOLLEYBALL WHICH HAS SIX-PERSON TEAMS ON NINE-METER COURTS...
INDOOR VOLLEYBALL
18m
9m
BEACH VOLLEYBALL IS PLAYED WITH TWO-PERSON TEAMS ON EIGHT-METER COURTS.
PLUS, THEY'RE PLAYING ON SAND.
BEACH VOLLEYBALL
16m
8m
HEARING THAT, IT DOES SOUND KINDA IMPOSSIBLE...
BASICALLY...

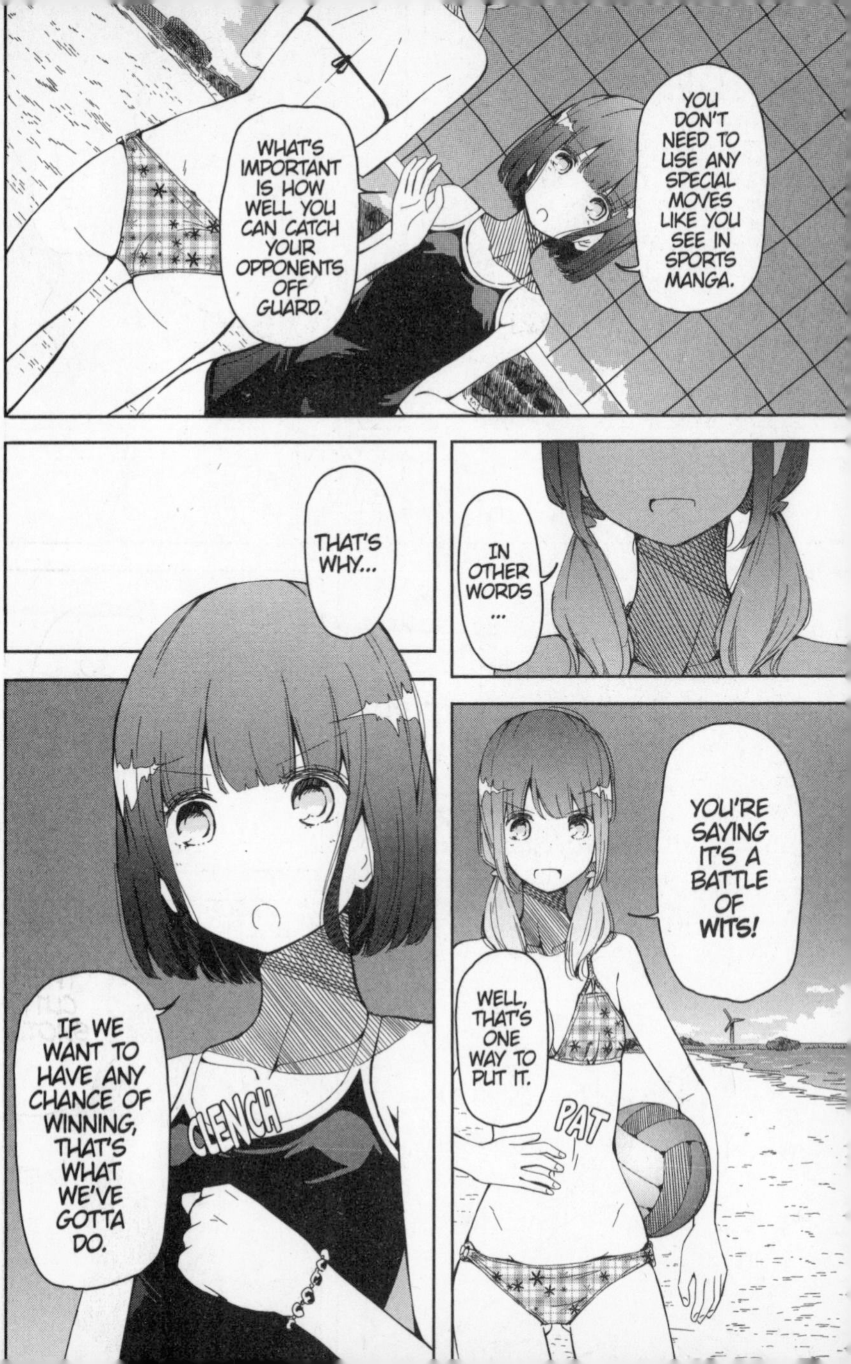
YOU DON'T NEED TO USE ANY SPECIAL MOVES LIKE YOU SEE IN SPORTS MANGA.
WHAT'S IMPORTANT IS HOW WELL YOU CAN CATCH YOUR OPPONENTS OFF GUARD.
IN OTHER WORDS...
THAT'S WHY...
YOU'RE SAYING IT'S A BATTLE OF WITS!
WELL, THAT'S ONE WAY TO PUT IT.
PAT
IF WE WANT TO HAVE ANY CHANCE OF WINNING, THAT'S WHAT WE'VE GOTTA DO.
CLENCH

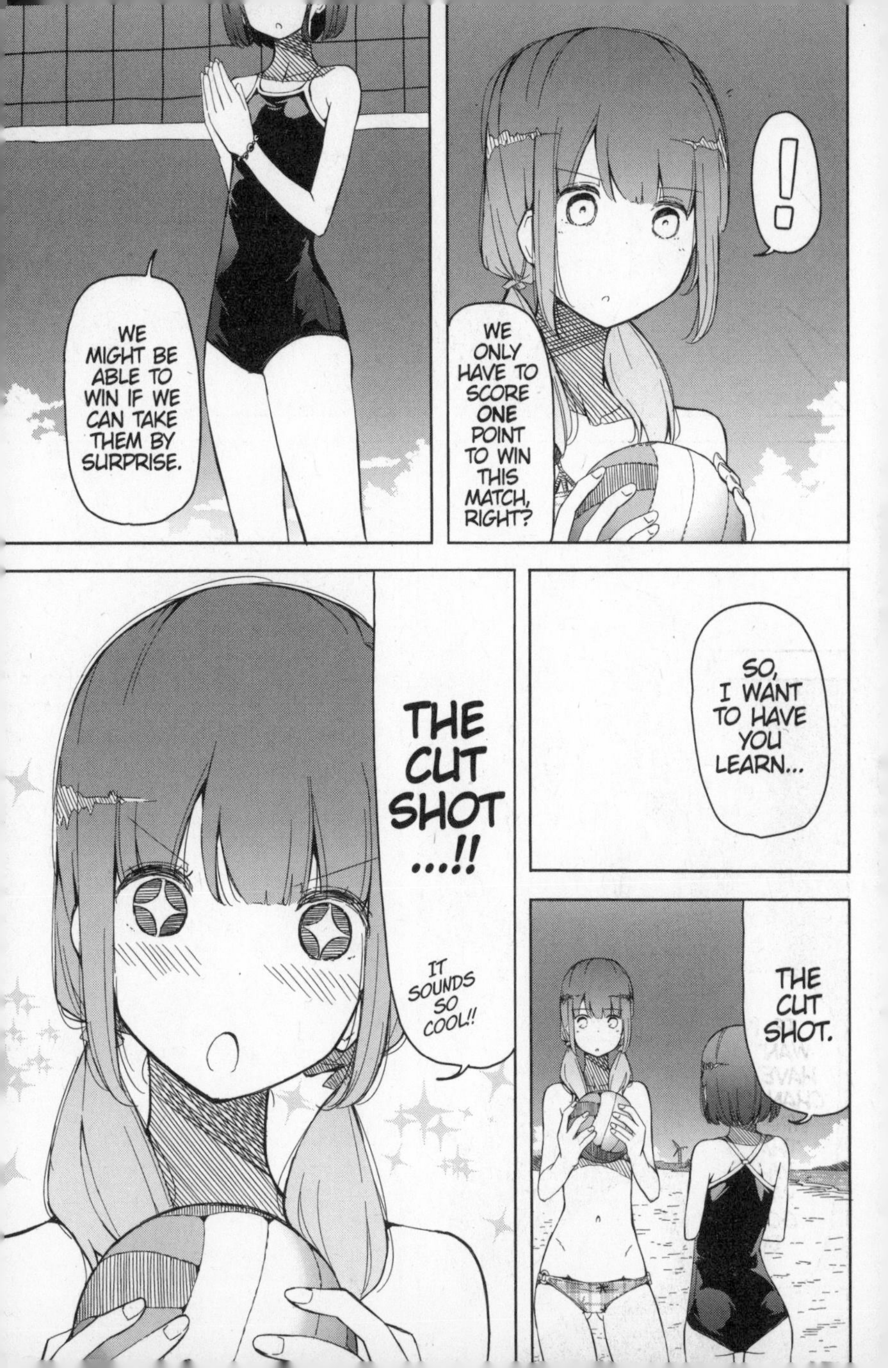
!
WE ONLY HAVE TO SCORE ONE POINT TO WIN THIS MATCH, RIGHT?
WE MIGHT BE ABLE TO WIN IF WE CAN TAKE THEM BY SURPRISE.
SO, I WANT TO HAVE YOU LEARN...
THE CUT SHOT.
THE CUT SHOT ...!!
IT SOUNDS SO COOL!!

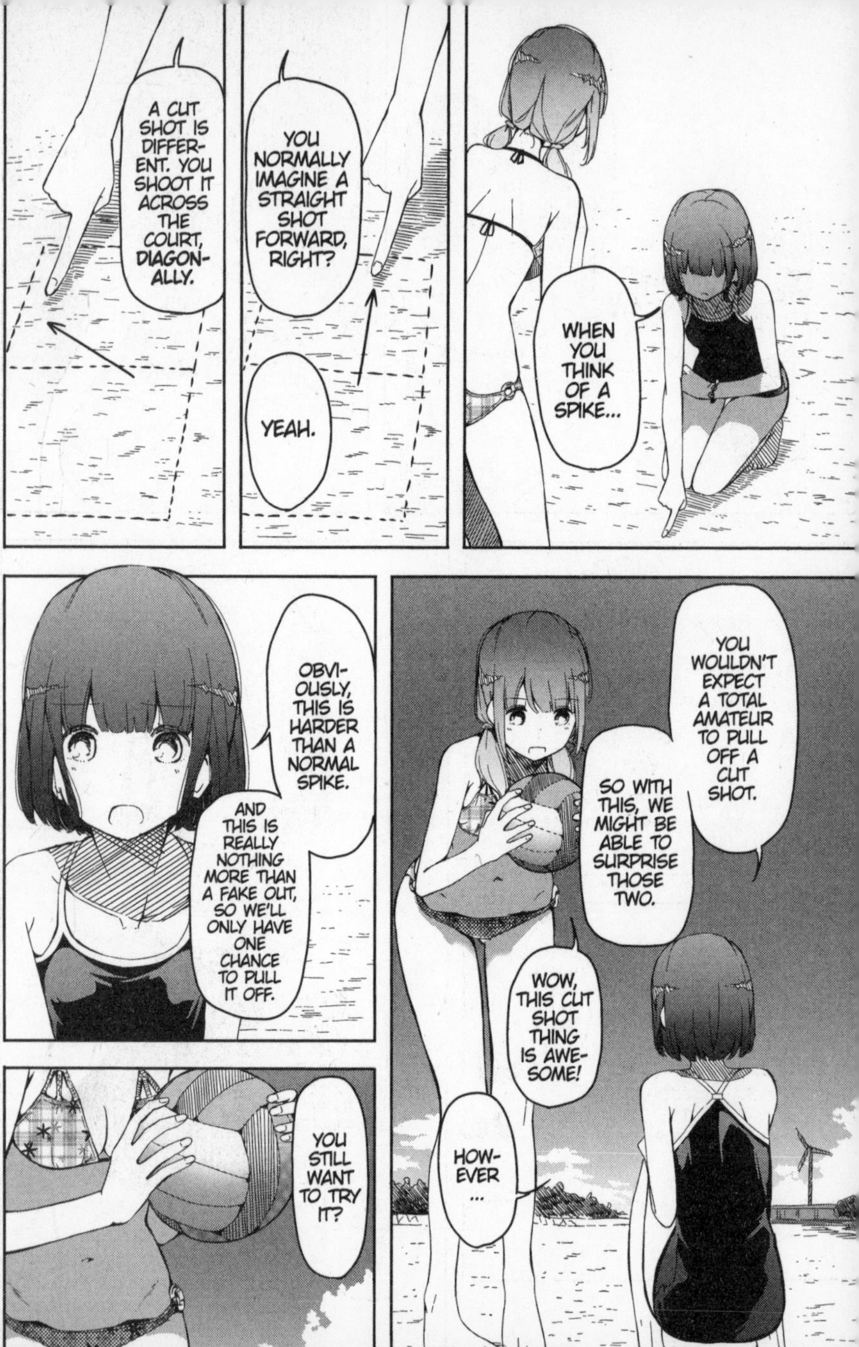
WHEN YOU THINK OF A SPIKE...
YOU NORMALLY IMAGINE A STRAIGHT SHOT FORWARD, RIGHT?
YEAH.
A CUT SHOT IS DIFFERENT. YOU SHOOT IT ACROSS THE COURT, DIAGONALLY.
YOU WOULDN'T EXPECT A TOTAL AMATEUR TO PULL OFF A CUT SHOT.
SO WITH THIS, WE MIGHT BE ABLE TO SURPRISE THOSE TWO.
WOW, THIS CUT SHOT THING IS AWESOME!
HOWEVER ...
OBVIOUSLY, THIS IS HARDER THAN A NORMAL SPIKE.
AND THIS IS REALLY NOTHING MORE THAN A FAKE OUT, SO WE'LL ONLY HAVE ONE CHANCE TO PULL IT OFF.
YOU STILL WANT TO TRY IT?

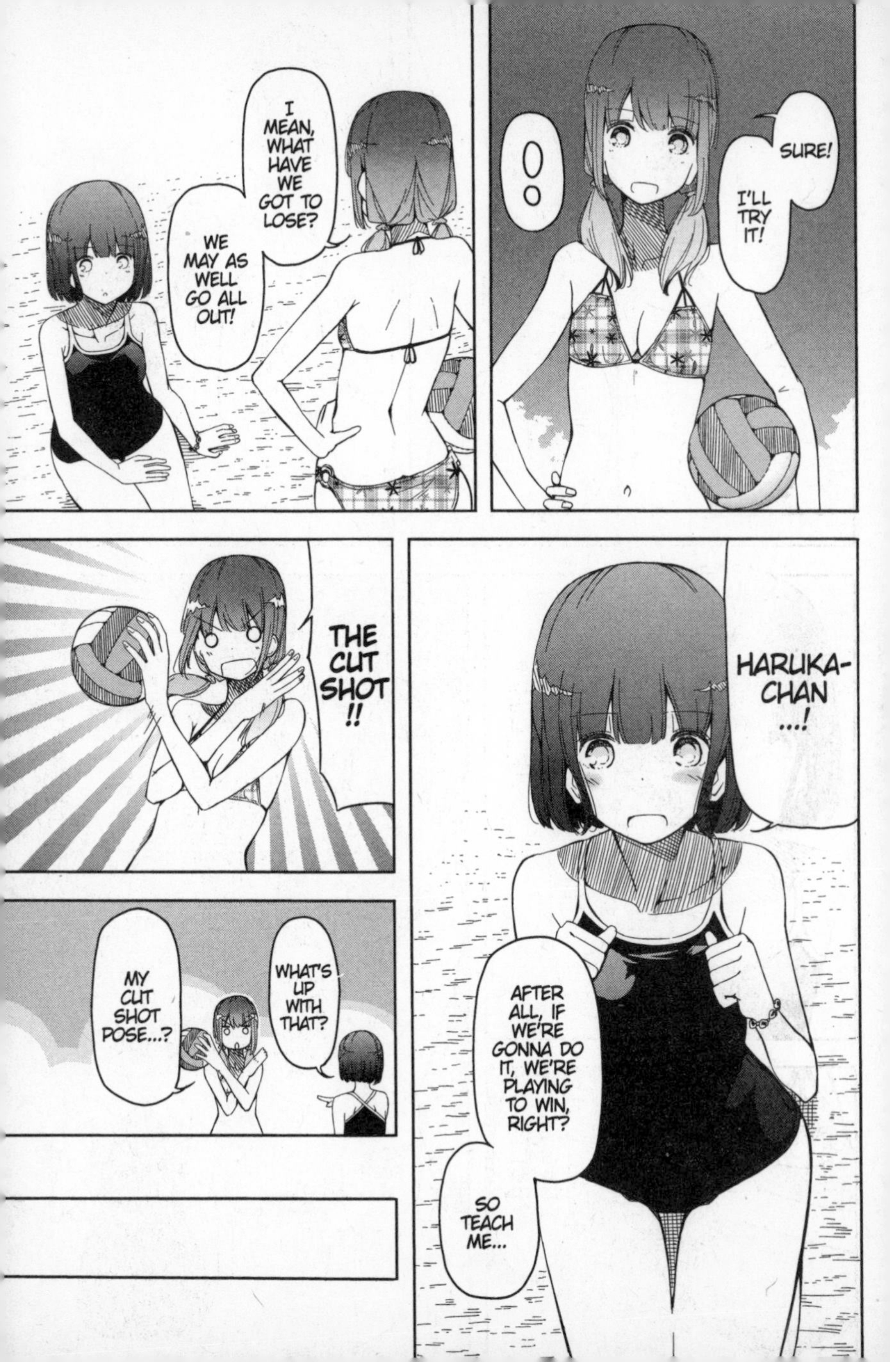
SURE!
I'LL TRY IT!
I MEAN, WHAT HAVE WE GOT TO LOSE?
WE MAY AS WELL GO ALL OUT!
HARUKA-CHAN...!
AFTER ALL, IF WE'RE GONNA DO IT, WE'RE PLAYING TO WIN, RIGHT?
SO TEACH ME...
THE CUT SHOT!!
WHAT'S UP WITH THAT?
MY CUT SHOT POSE...?

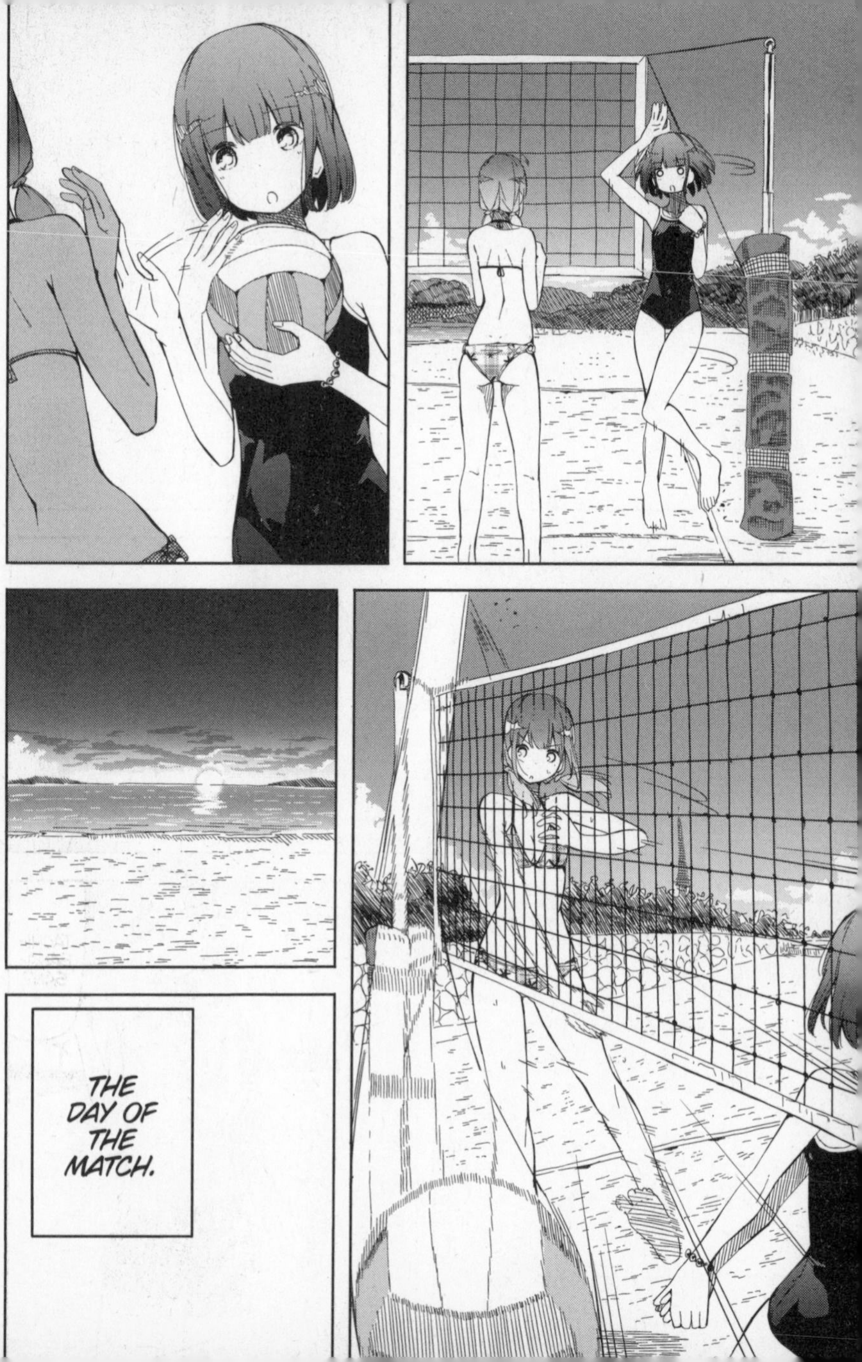
THE DAY OF THE MATCH.

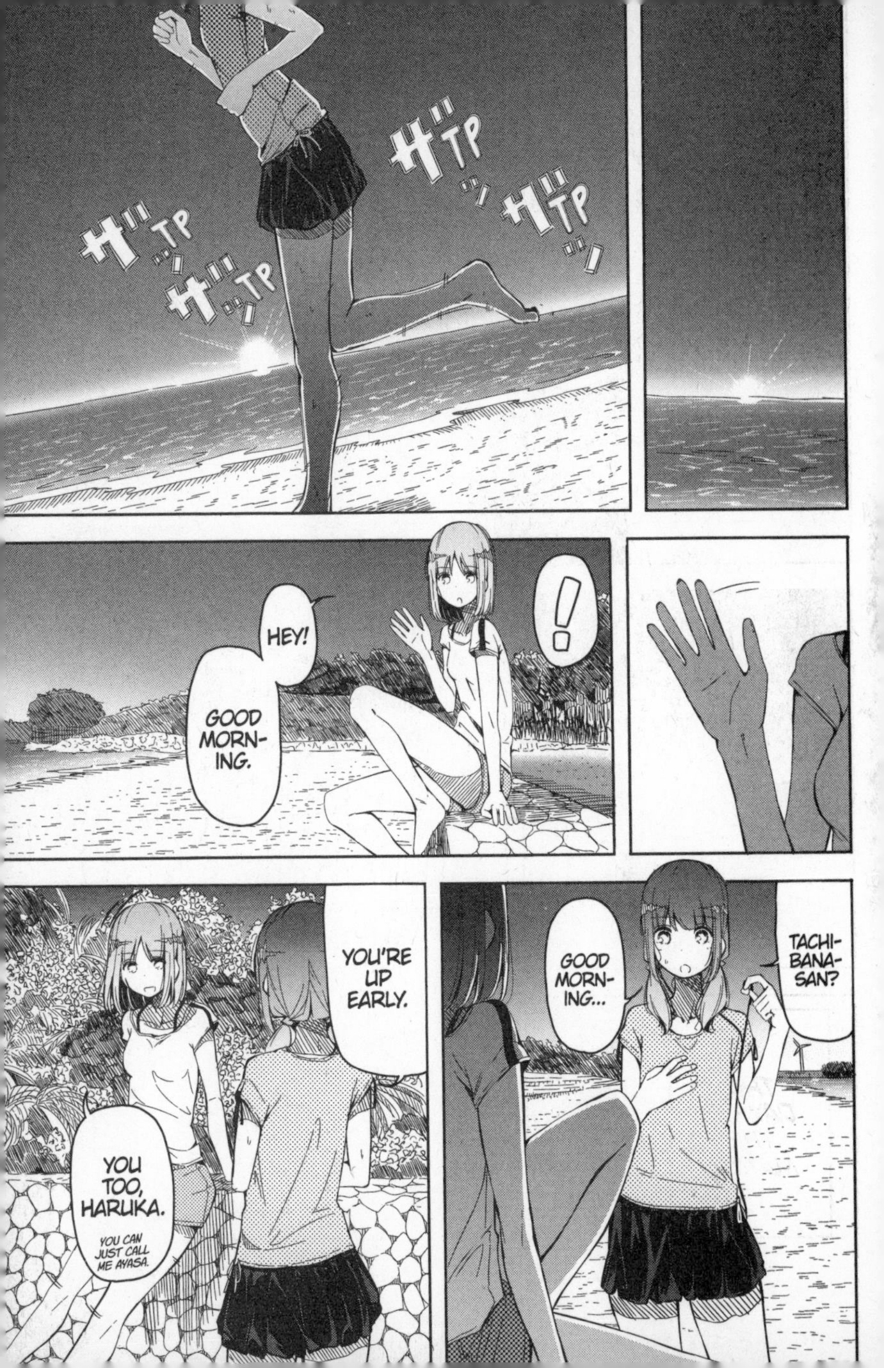
ザッ TP
ザッ TP
ザッ TP
ザッ TP
!
HEY!
GOOD MORN-ING.
TACHI-BANA-SAN?
GOOD MORN-ING...
YOU'RE UP EARLY.
YOU TOO, HARUKA.
YOU CAN JUST CALL ME AYASA.

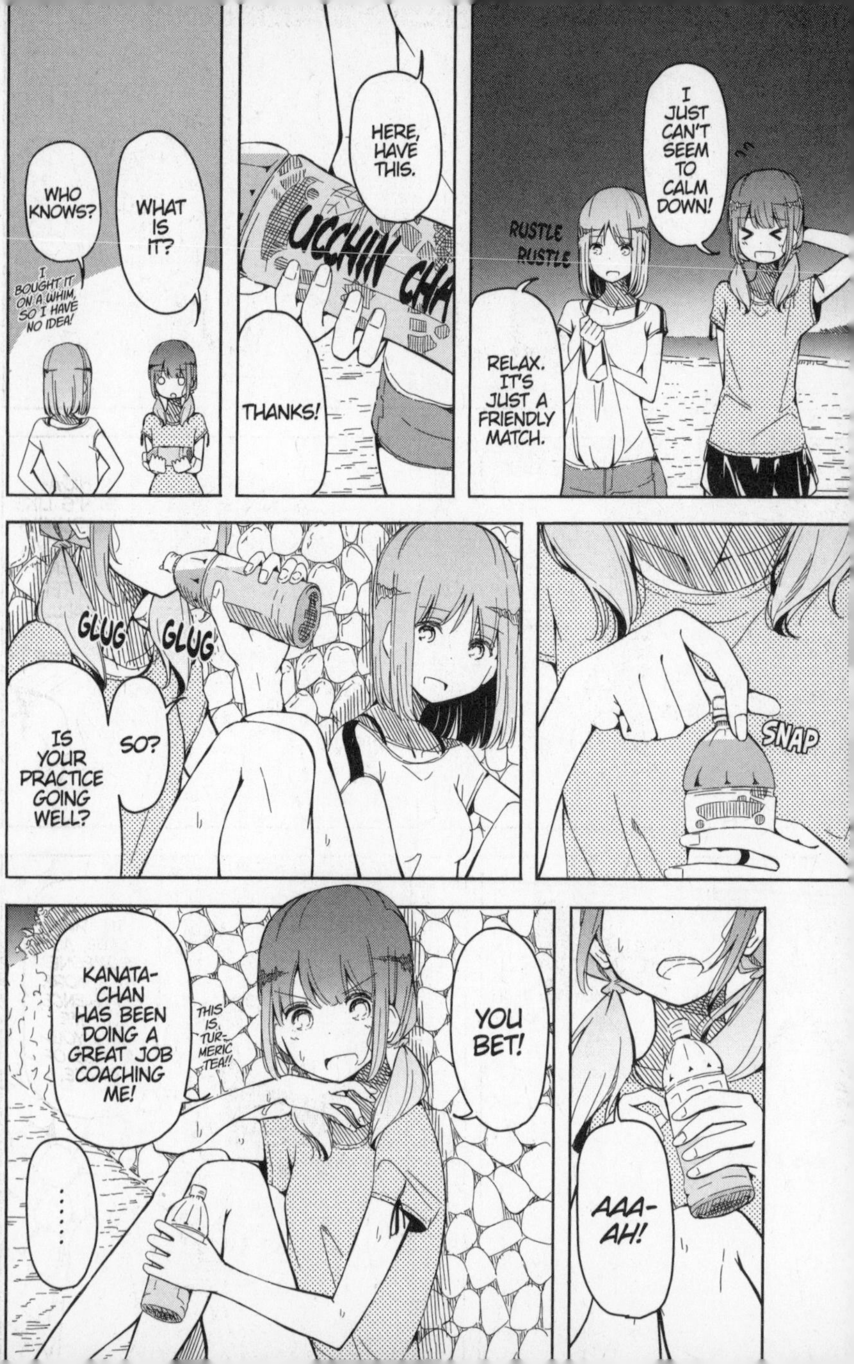
I JUST CAN'T SEEM TO CALM DOWN!
RUSTLE RUSTLE
RELAX. IT'S JUST A FRIENDLY MATCH.
HERE, HAVE THIS.
UCCHIN CHA
THANKS!
WHAT IS IT?
WHO KNOWS?
I BOUGHT IT ON A WHIM, SO I HAVE NO IDEA!
SNAP
GLUG GLUG
SO?
IS YOUR PRACTICE GOING WELL?
AAA-AH!
YOU BET!
THIS IS, TURMERIC TEA!!
KANATA-CHAN HAS BEEN DOING A GREAT JOB COACHING ME!
......

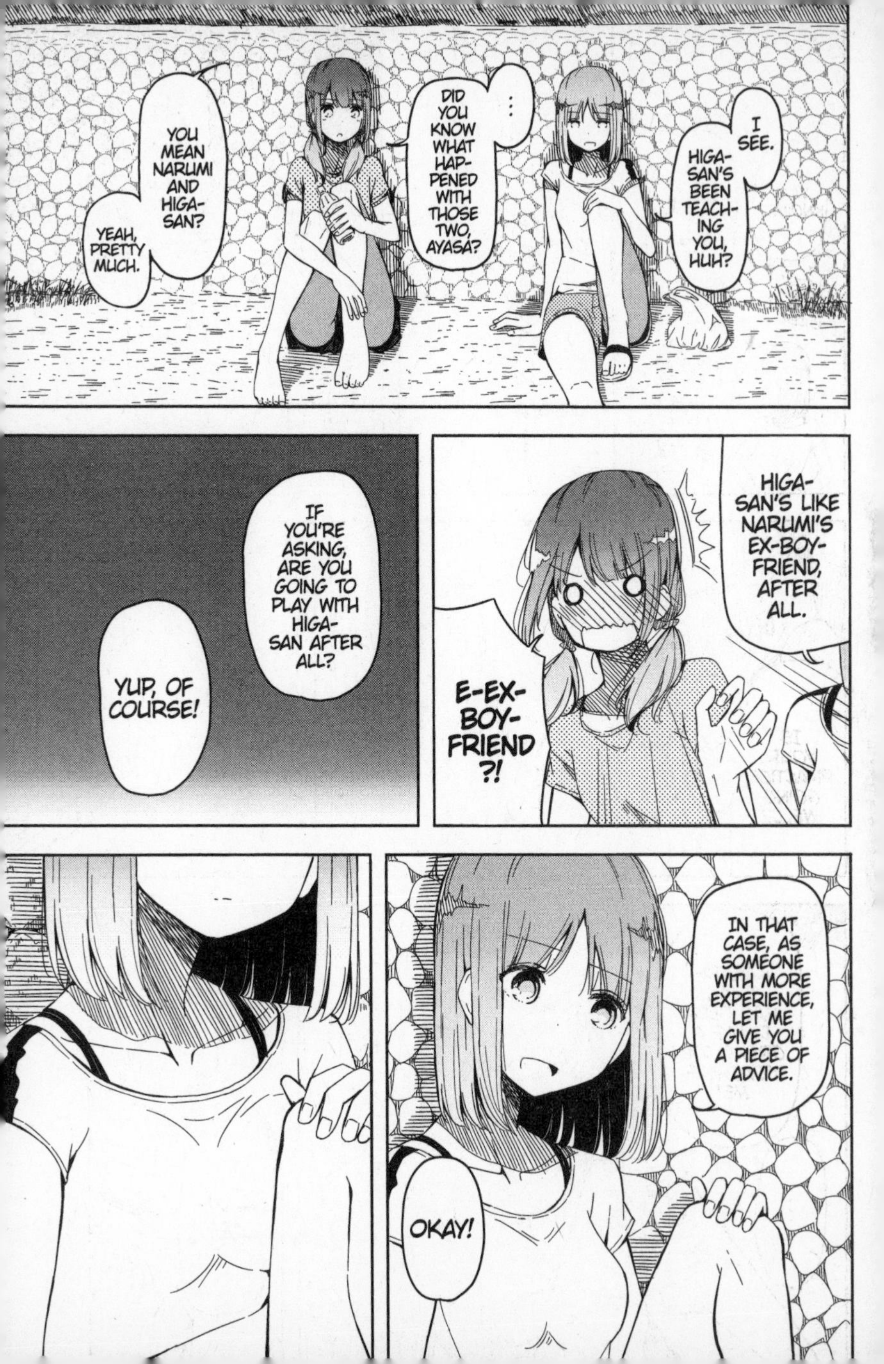
I SEE.
HIGA-SAN'S BEEN TEACHING YOU, HUH?
...
DID YOU KNOW WHAT HAPPENED WITH THOSE TWO, AYASA?
YOU MEAN NARUMI AND HIGA-SAN?
YEAH, PRETTY MUCH.
HIGA-SAN'S LIKE NARUMI'S EX-BOYFRIEND, AFTER ALL.
E-EX-BOYFRIEND?!
IF YOU'RE ASKING, ARE YOU GOING TO PLAY WITH HIGA-SAN AFTER ALL?
YUP, OF COURSE!
IN THAT CASE, AS SOMEONE WITH MORE EXPERIENCE, LET ME GIVE YOU A PIECE OF ADVICE.
OKAY!

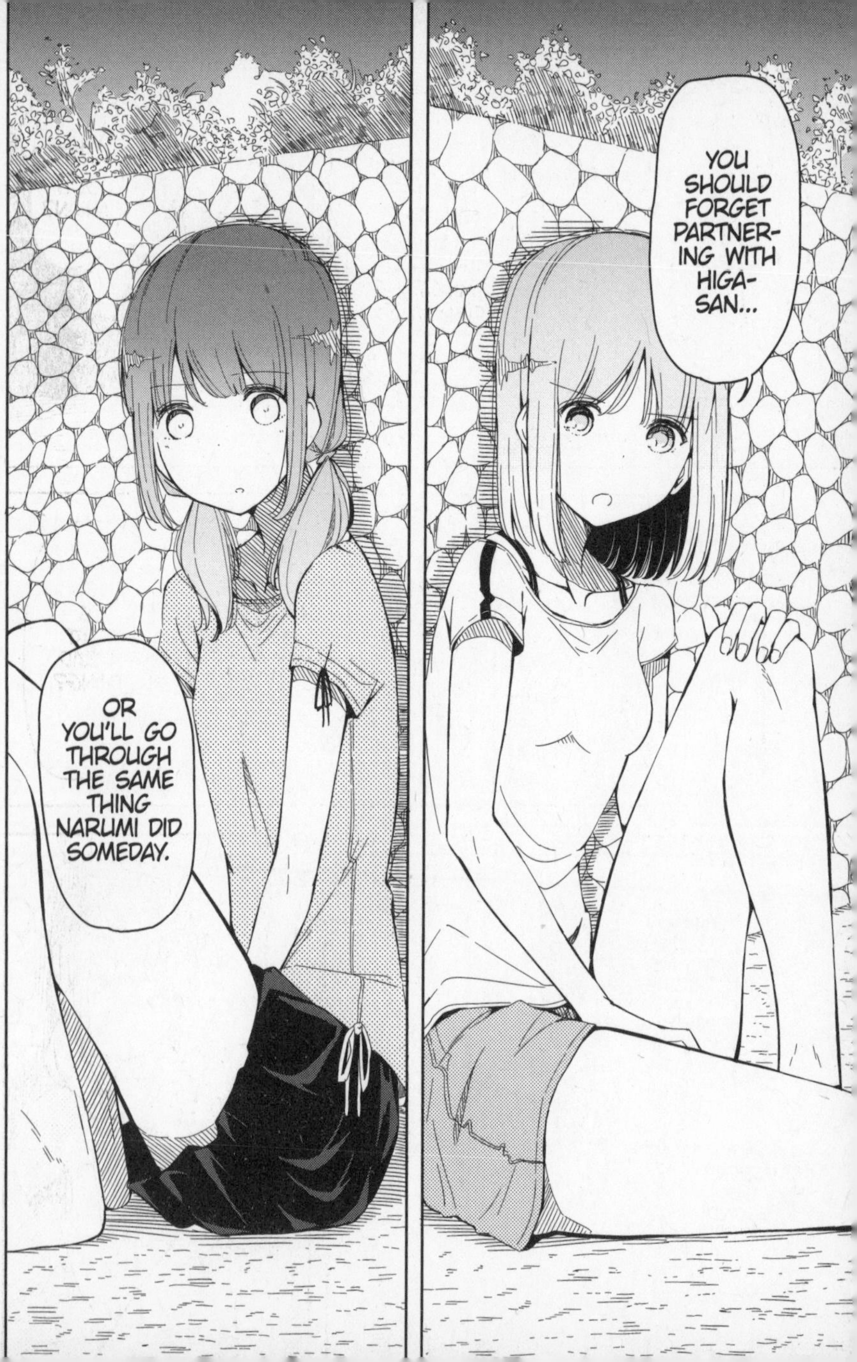
YOU SHOULD FORGET PARTNER-ING WITH HIGA-SAN...
OR YOU'LL GO THROUGH THE SAME THING NARUMI DID SOMEDAY.

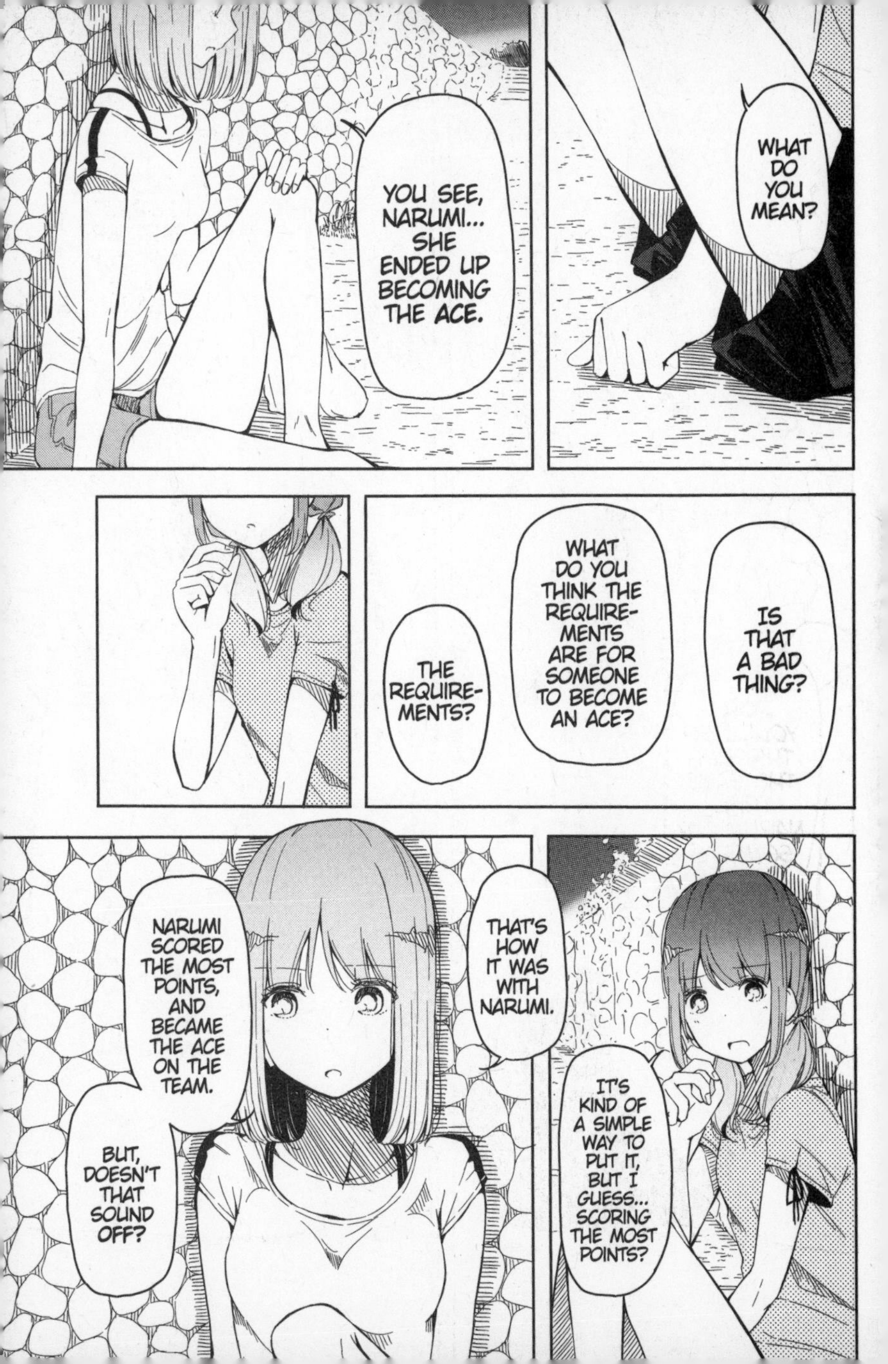
WHAT DO YOU MEAN?
YOU SEE, NARUMI... SHE ENDED UP BECOMING THE ACE.
IS THAT A BAD THING?
WHAT DO YOU THINK THE REQUIRE-MENTS ARE FOR SOMEONE TO BECOME AN ACE?
THE REQUIRE-MENTS?
IT'S KIND OF A SIMPLE WAY TO PUT IT, BUT I GUESS... SCORING THE MOST POINTS?
THAT'S HOW IT WAS WITH NARUMI.
NARUMI SCORED THE MOST POINTS, AND BECAME THE ACE ON THE TEAM.
BUT, DOESN'T THAT SOUND OFF?

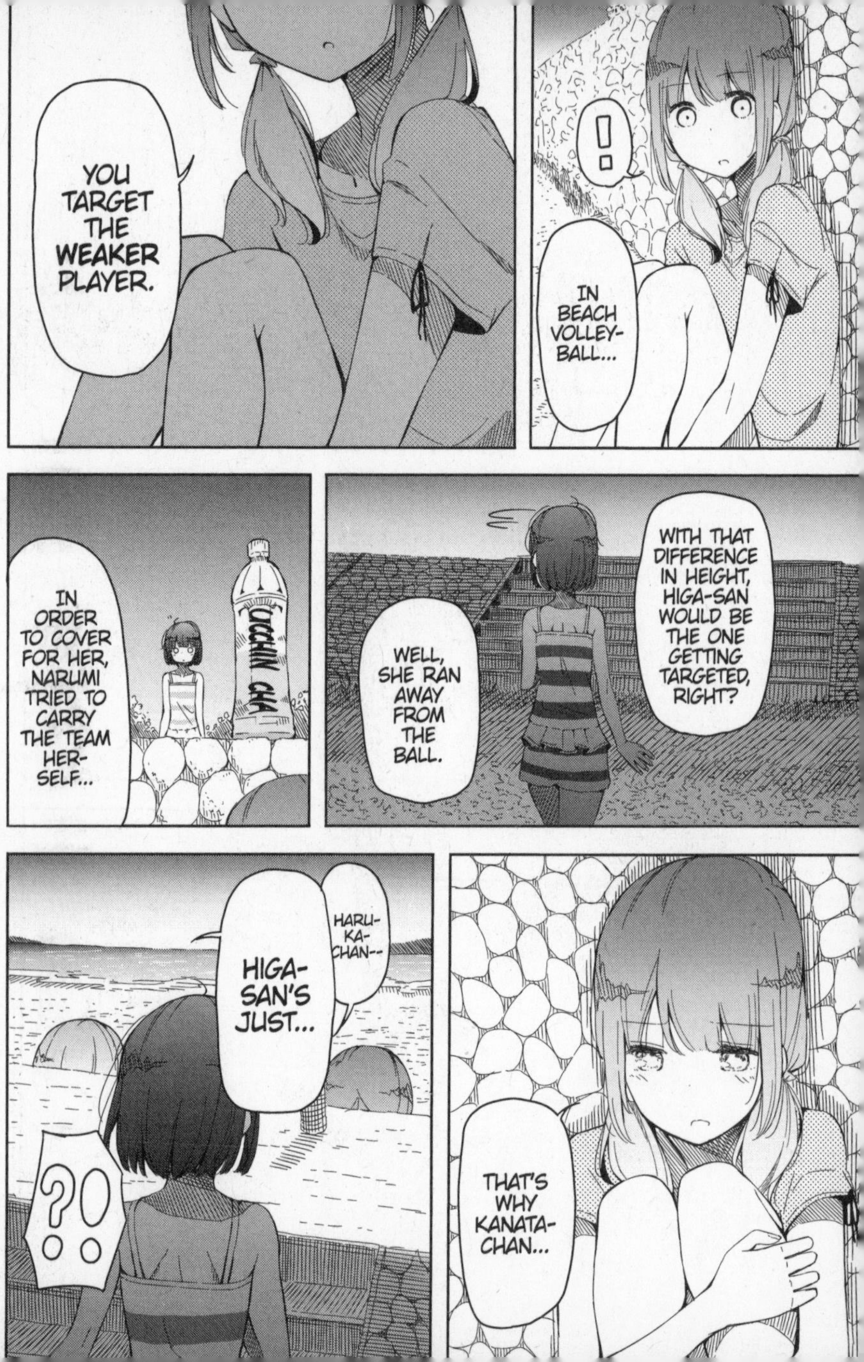
!
IN BEACH VOLLEY-BALL...
YOU TARGET THE WEAKER PLAYER.
WITH THAT DIFFERENCE IN HEIGHT, HIGA-SAN WOULD BE THE ONE GETTING TARGETED, RIGHT?
WELL, SHE RAN AWAY FROM THE BALL.
IN ORDER TO COVER FOR HER, NARUMI TRIED TO CARRY THE TEAM HER-SELF...
THAT'S WHY KANATA-CHAN...
HARU-KA-CHAN--
HIGA-SAN'S JUST...
?!

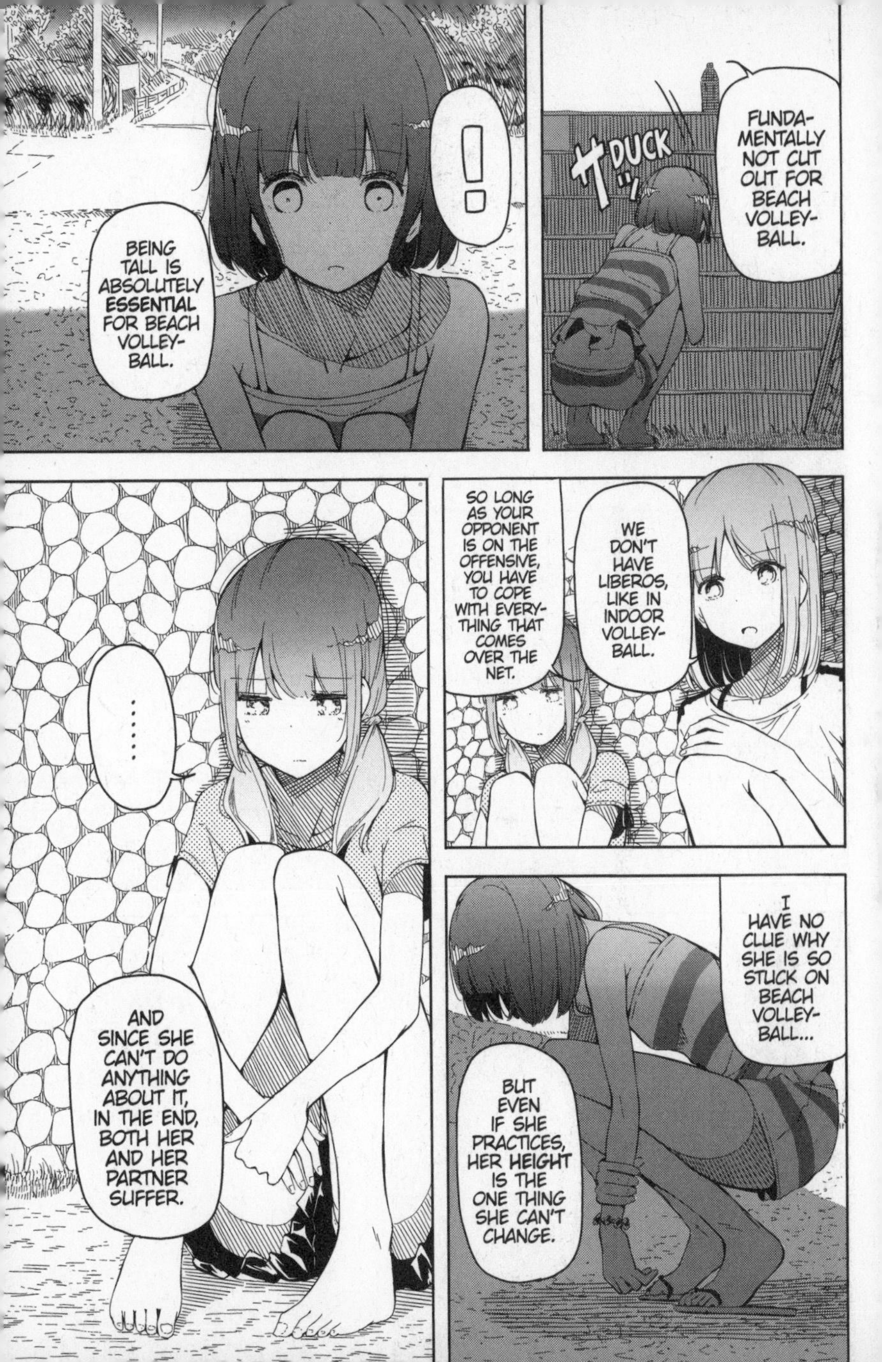
FUNDA-MENTALLY NOT CUT OUT FOR BEACH VOLLEY-BALL.
DUCK
!
BEING TALL IS ABSOLUTELY ESSENTIAL FOR BEACH VOLLEY-BALL.
WE DON'T HAVE LIBEROS, LIKE IN INDOOR VOLLEY-BALL.
SO LONG AS YOUR OPPONENT IS ON THE OFFENSIVE, YOU HAVE TO COPE WITH EVERY-THING THAT COMES OVER THE NET.
I HAVE NO CLUE WHY SHE IS SO STUCK ON BEACH VOLLEY-BALL...
BUT EVEN IF SHE PRACTICES, HER HEIGHT IS THE ONE THING SHE CAN'T CHANGE.
......
AND SINCE SHE CAN'T DO ANYTHING ABOUT IT, IN THE END, BOTH HER AND HER PARTNER SUFFER.

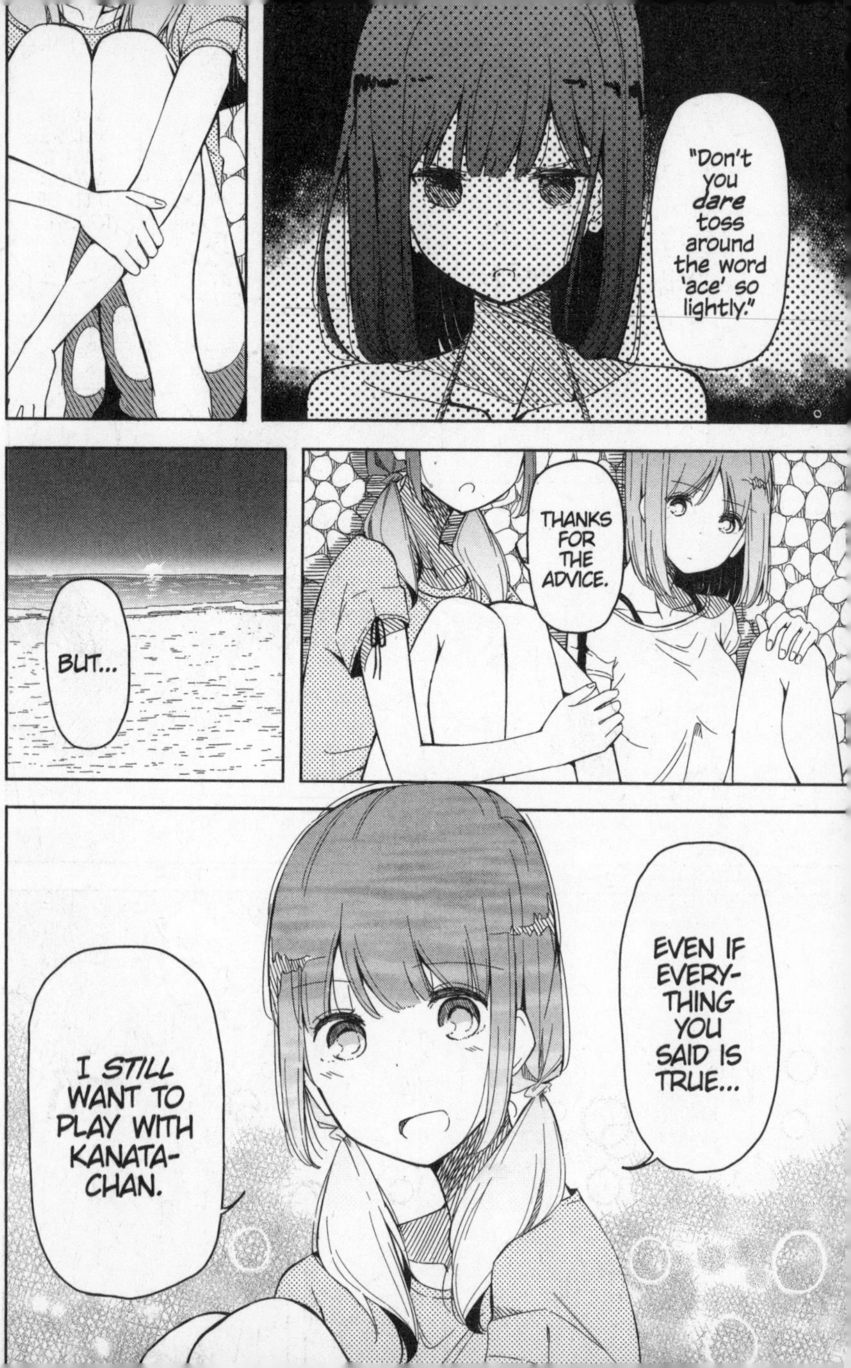
"Don't you dare toss around the word 'ace' so lightly."
THANKS FOR THE ADVICE.
BUT...
EVEN IF EVERY-THING YOU SAID IS TRUE...
I STILL WANT TO PLAY WITH KANATA-CHAN.

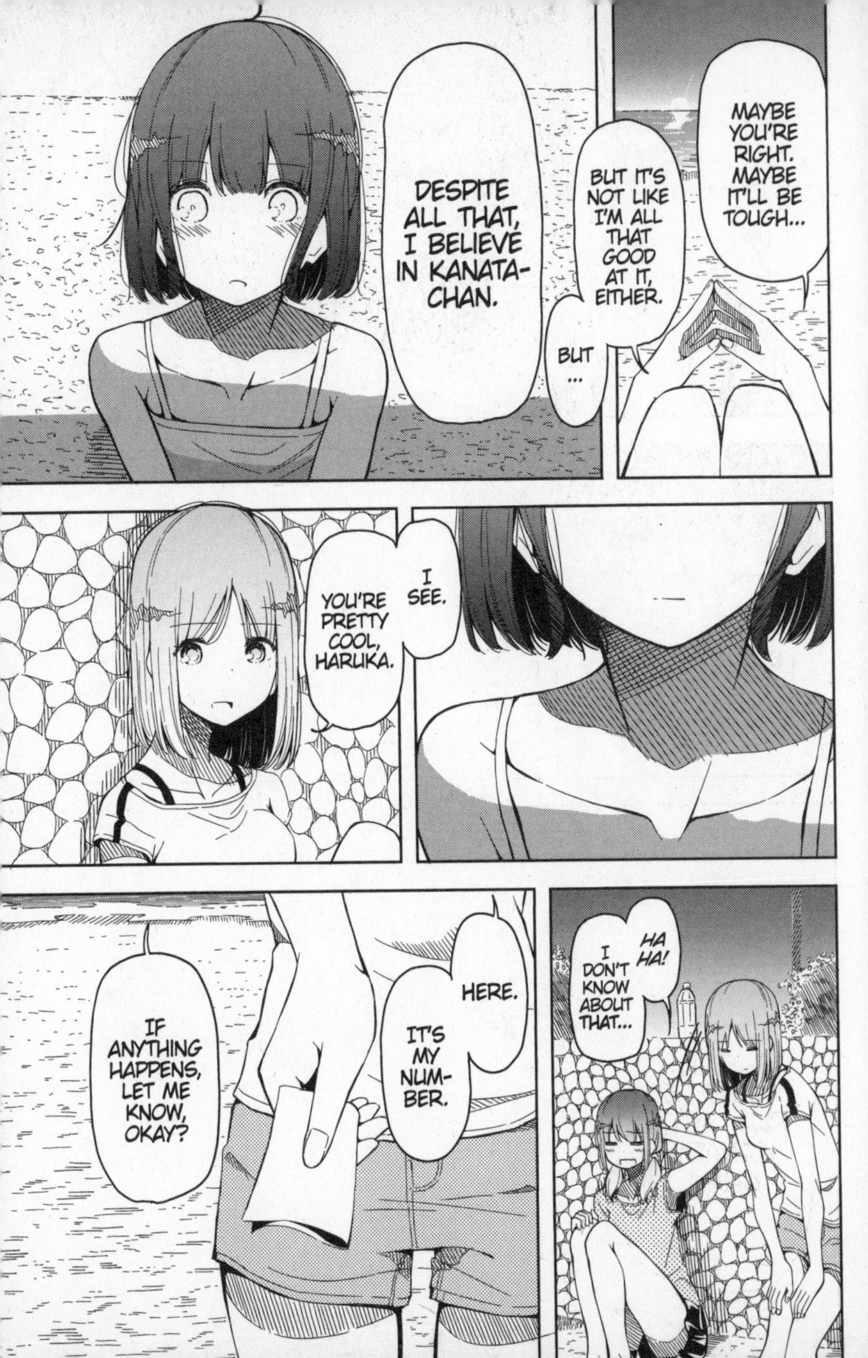
MAYBE YOU'RE RIGHT. MAYBE IT'LL BE TOUGH...
BUT IT'S NOT LIKE I'M ALL THAT GOOD AT IT, EITHER.
BUT ...
DESPITE ALL THAT, I BELIEVE IN KANATA-CHAN.
I SEE.
YOU'RE PRETTY COOL, HARUKA.
HA HA!
I DON'T KNOW ABOUT THAT...
HERE.
IT'S MY NUMBER.
IF ANYTHING HAPPENS, LET ME KNOW, OKAY?

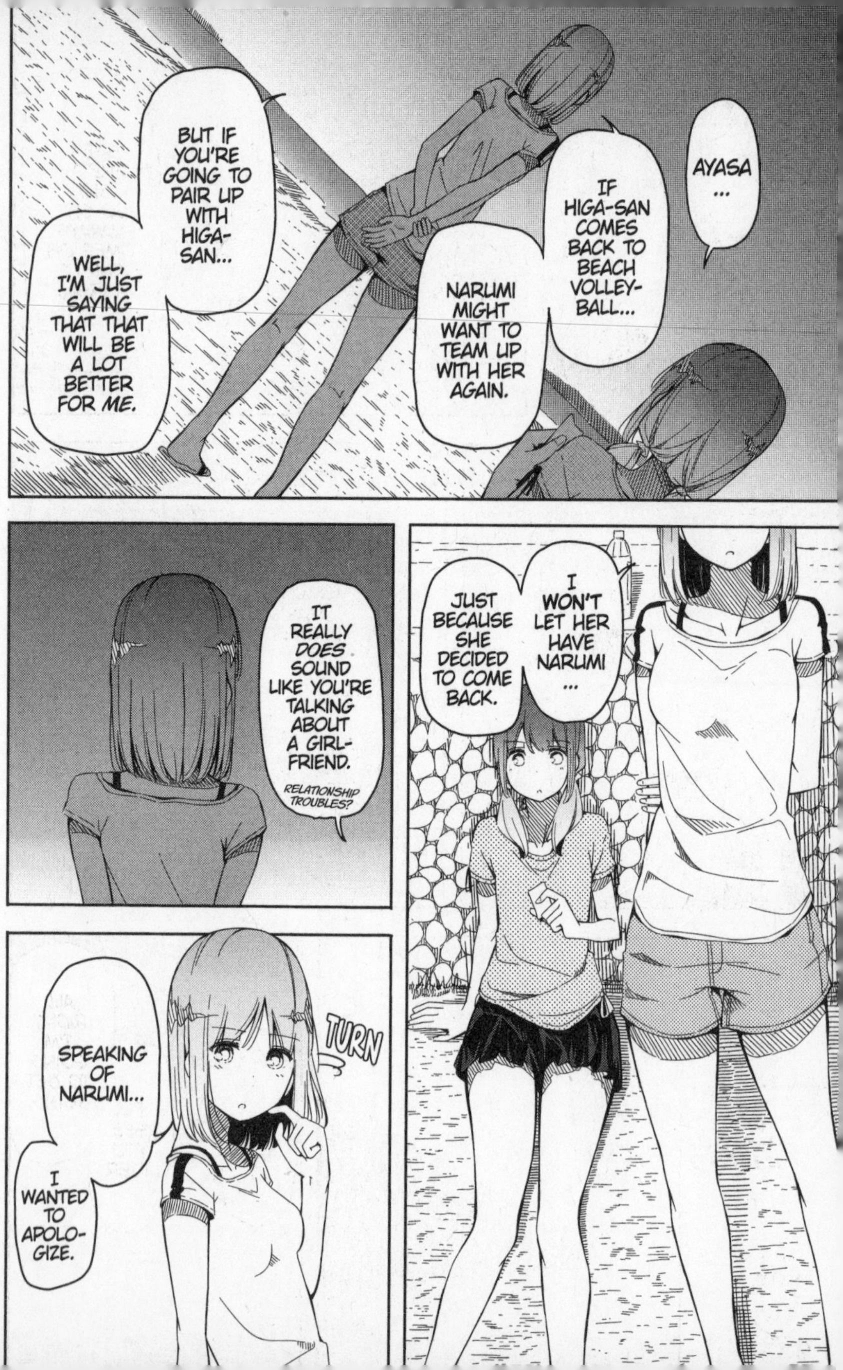
AYASA...
IF HIGA-SAN COMES BACK TO BEACH VOLLEY-BALL...
NARUMI MIGHT WANT TO TEAM UP WITH HER AGAIN.
BUT IF YOU'RE GOING TO PAIR UP WITH HIGA-SAN...
WELL, I'M JUST SAYING THAT THAT WILL BE A LOT BETTER FOR *ME*.
I WON'T LET HER HAVE NARUMI...
JUST BECAUSE SHE DECIDED TO COME BACK.
IT REALLY *DOES* SOUND LIKE YOU'RE TALKING ABOUT A GIRL-FRIEND.
RELATIONSHIP TROUBLES?
TURN
SPEAKING OF NARUMI...
I WANTED TO APOLO-GIZE.

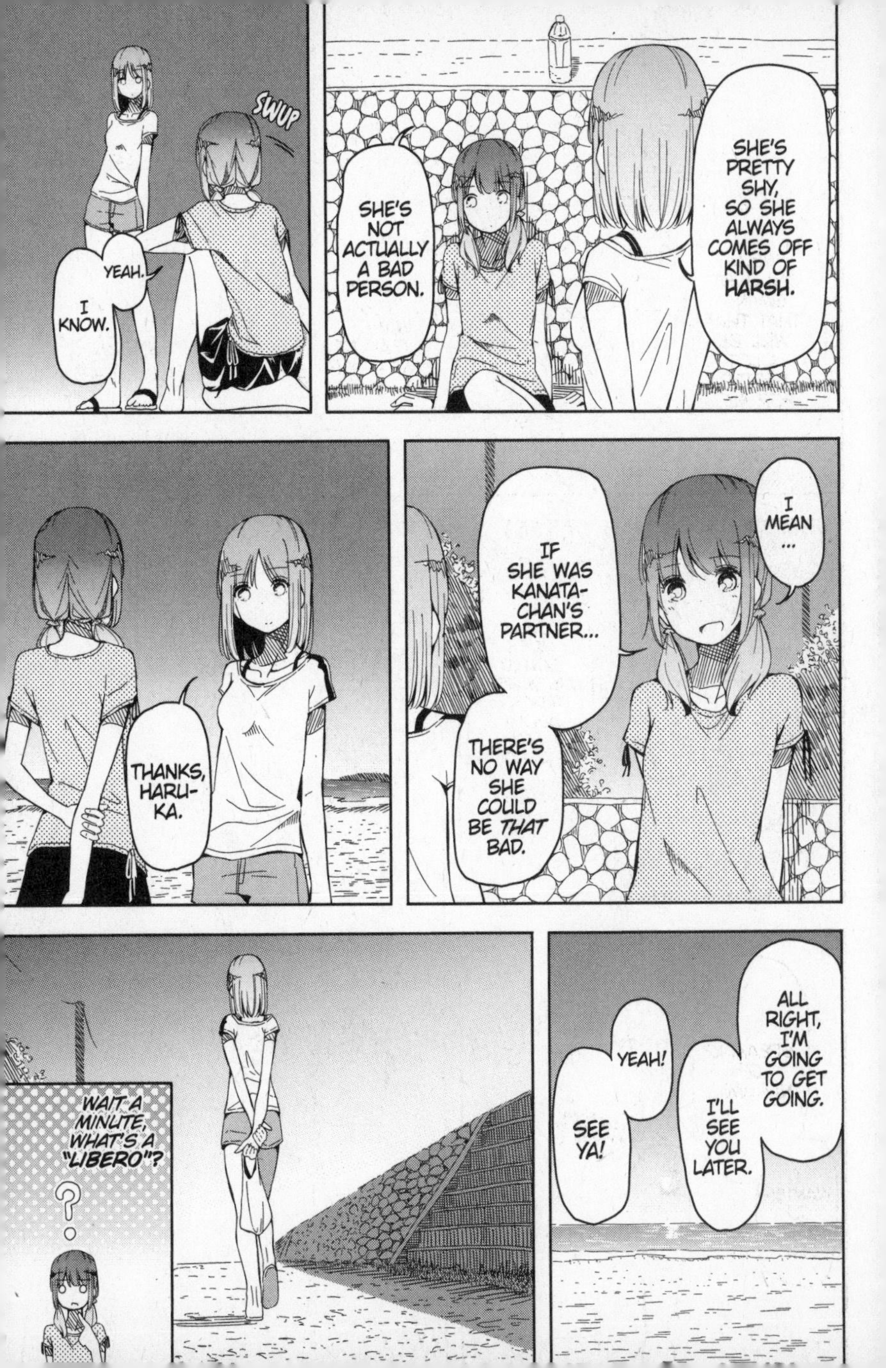
SHE'S PRETTY SHY, SO SHE ALWAYS COMES OFF KIND OF HARSH.
SHE'S NOT ACTUALLY A BAD PERSON.
SWUP
YEAH.
I KNOW.
I MEAN ...
IF SHE WAS KANATA-CHAN'S PARTNER...
THERE'S NO WAY SHE COULD BE *THAT* BAD.
THANKS, HARU-KA.
ALL RIGHT, I'M GOING TO GET GOING.
I'LL SEE YOU LATER.
YEAH!
SEE YA!
WAIT A MINUTE, WHAT'S A "LIBERO"?
?

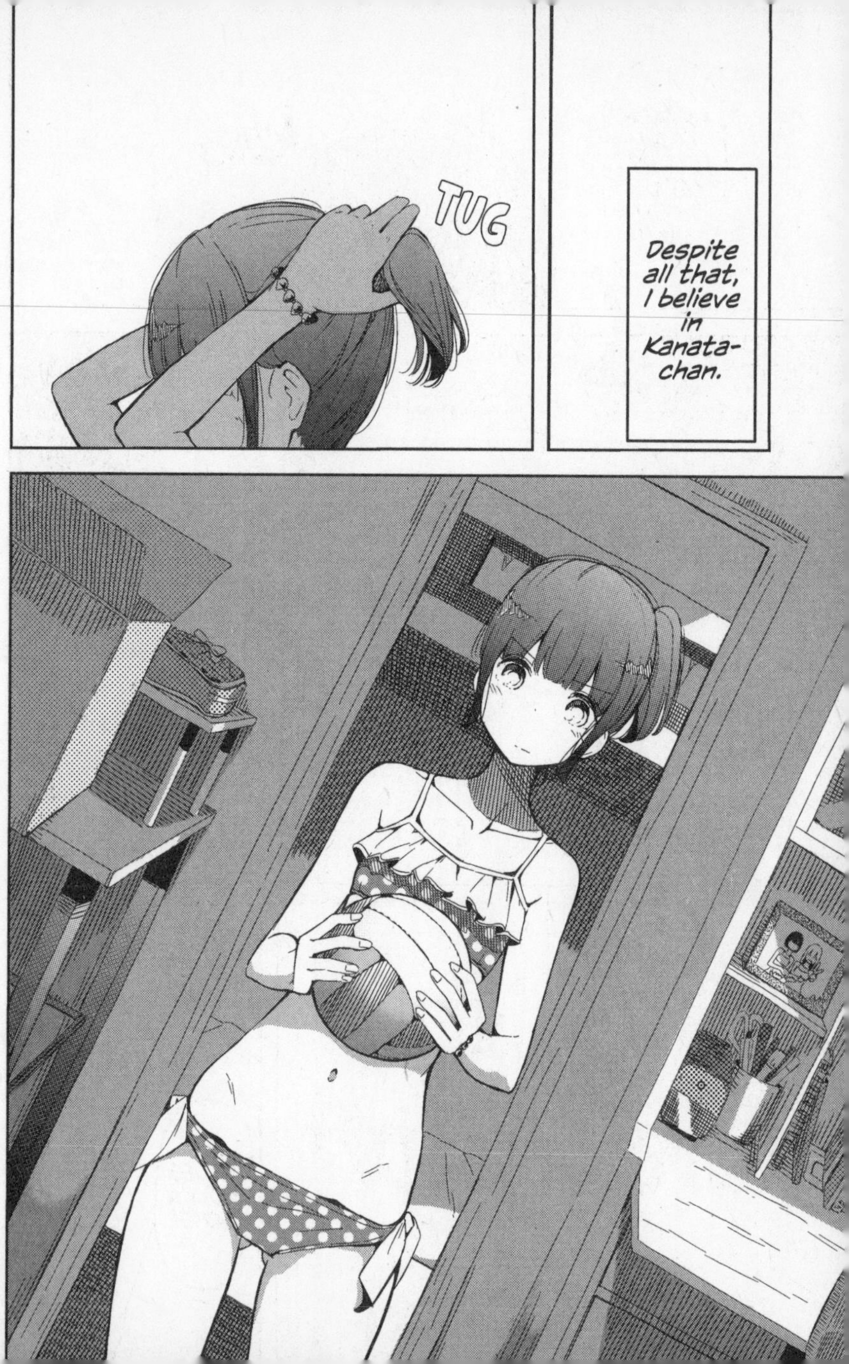
Despite all that, I believe in Kanata-chan.
TUG

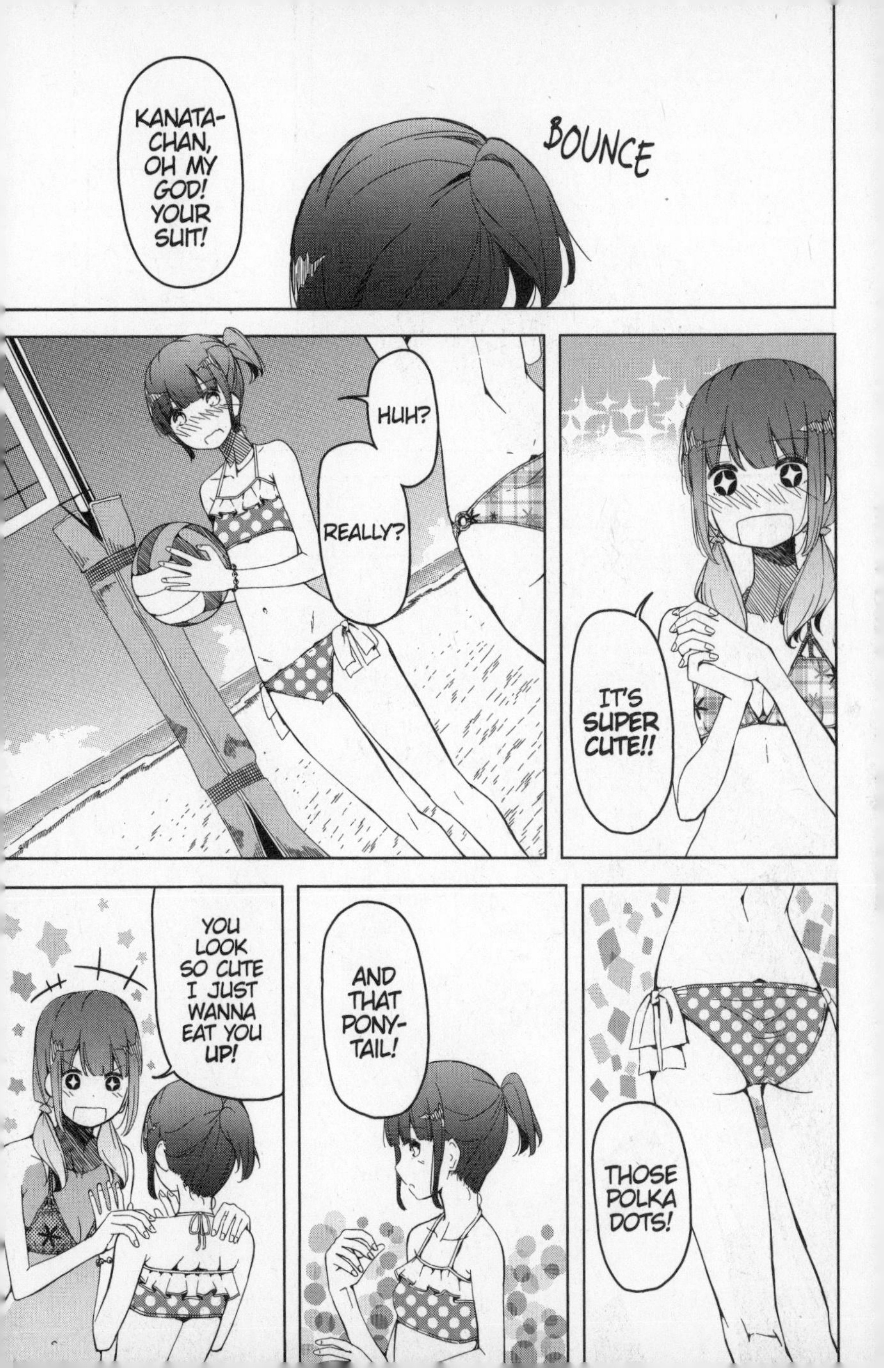
BOUNCE
KANATA-CHAN, OH MY GOD! YOUR SUIT!
IT'S SUPER CUTE!!
HUH?
REALLY?
THOSE POLKA DOTS!
AND THAT PONY-TAIL!
YOU LOOK SO CUTE I JUST WANNA EAT YOU UP!

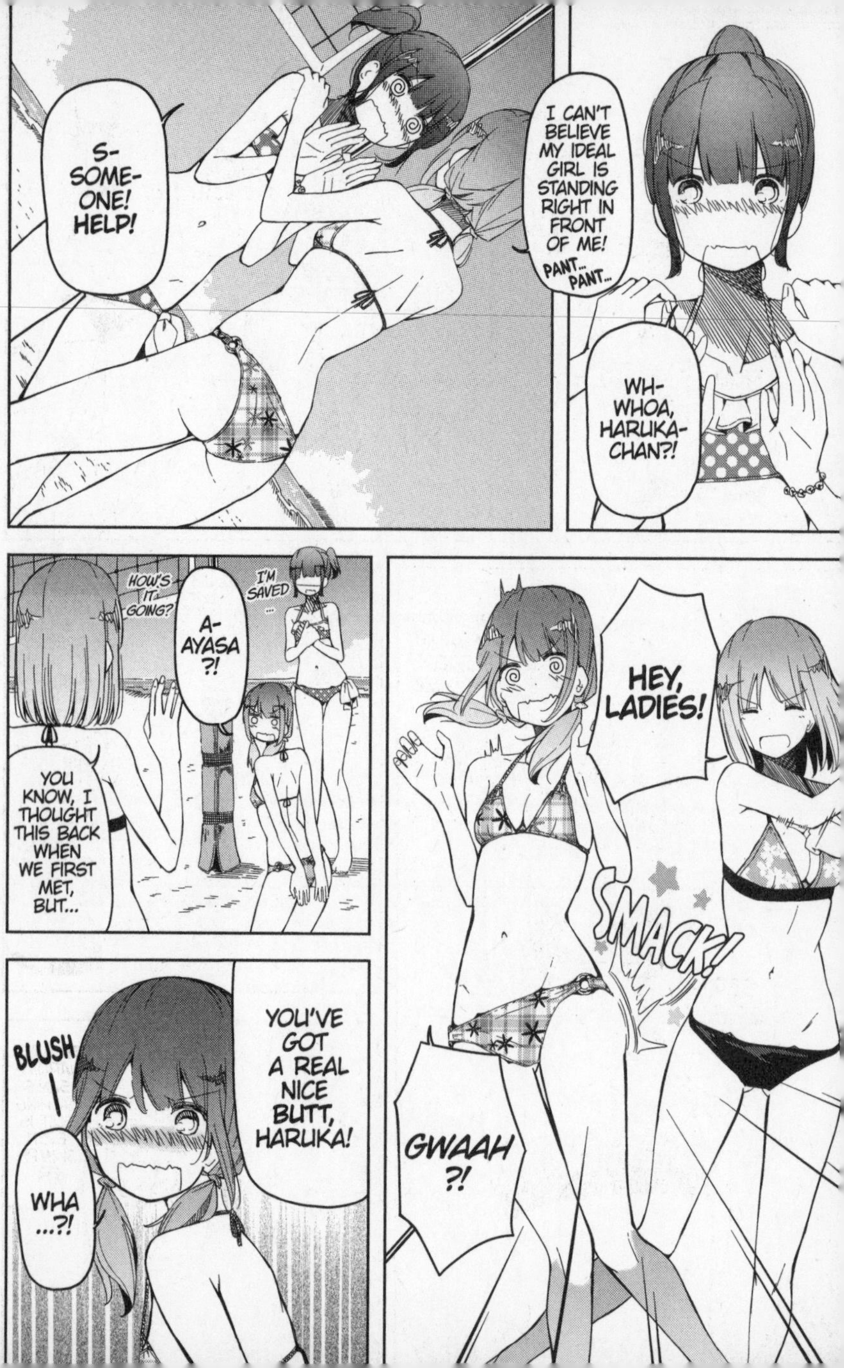
I CAN'T BELIEVE MY IDEAL GIRL IS STANDING RIGHT IN FRONT OF ME!
PANT... PANT...
WH-WHOA, HARUKA-CHAN?!
S-SOME-ONE! HELP!
HEY, LADIES!
SMACK!
GWAAH ?!
I'M SAVED ...
A-AYASA ?!
HOW'S IT GOING?
YOU KNOW, I THOUGHT THIS BACK WHEN WE FIRST MET, BUT...
YOU'VE GOT A REAL NICE BUTT, HARUKA!
BLUSH
WHA ...?!

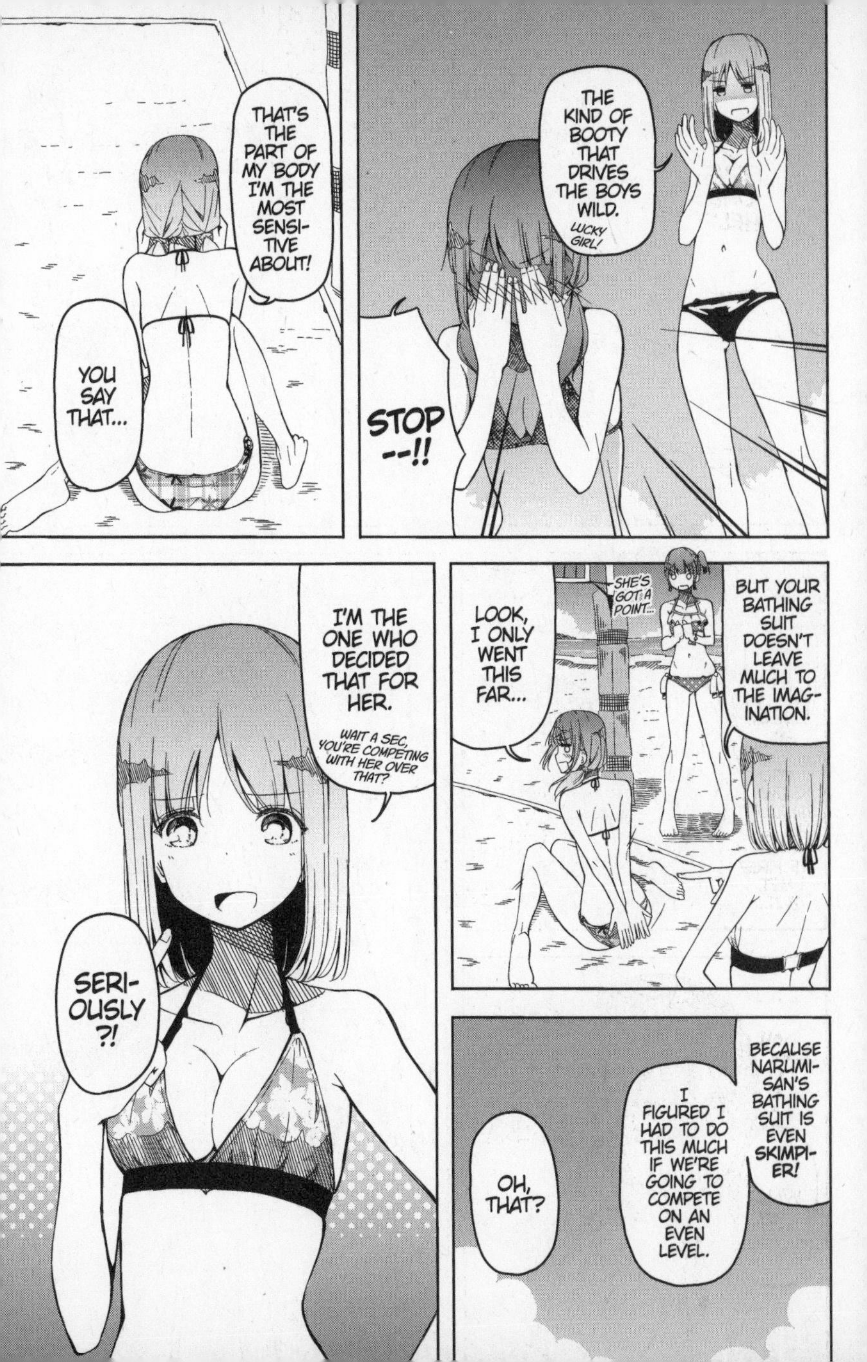
THE KIND OF BOOTY THAT DRIVES THE BOYS WILD.
LUCKY GIRL!
STOP--!!
THAT'S THE PART OF MY BODY I'M THE MOST SENSITIVE ABOUT!
YOU SAY THAT...
BUT YOUR BATHING SUIT DOESN'T LEAVE MUCH TO THE IMAGINATION.
SHE'S GOT A POINT...
LOOK, I ONLY WENT THIS FAR...
BECAUSE NARUMI-SAN'S BATHING SUIT IS EVEN SKIMPIER!
I FIGURED I HAD TO DO THIS MUCH IF WE'RE GOING TO COMPETE ON AN EVEN LEVEL.
OH, THAT?
I'M THE ONE WHO DECIDED THAT FOR HER.
WAIT A SEC, YOU'RE COMPETING WITH HER OVER THAT?
SERIOUSLY?!

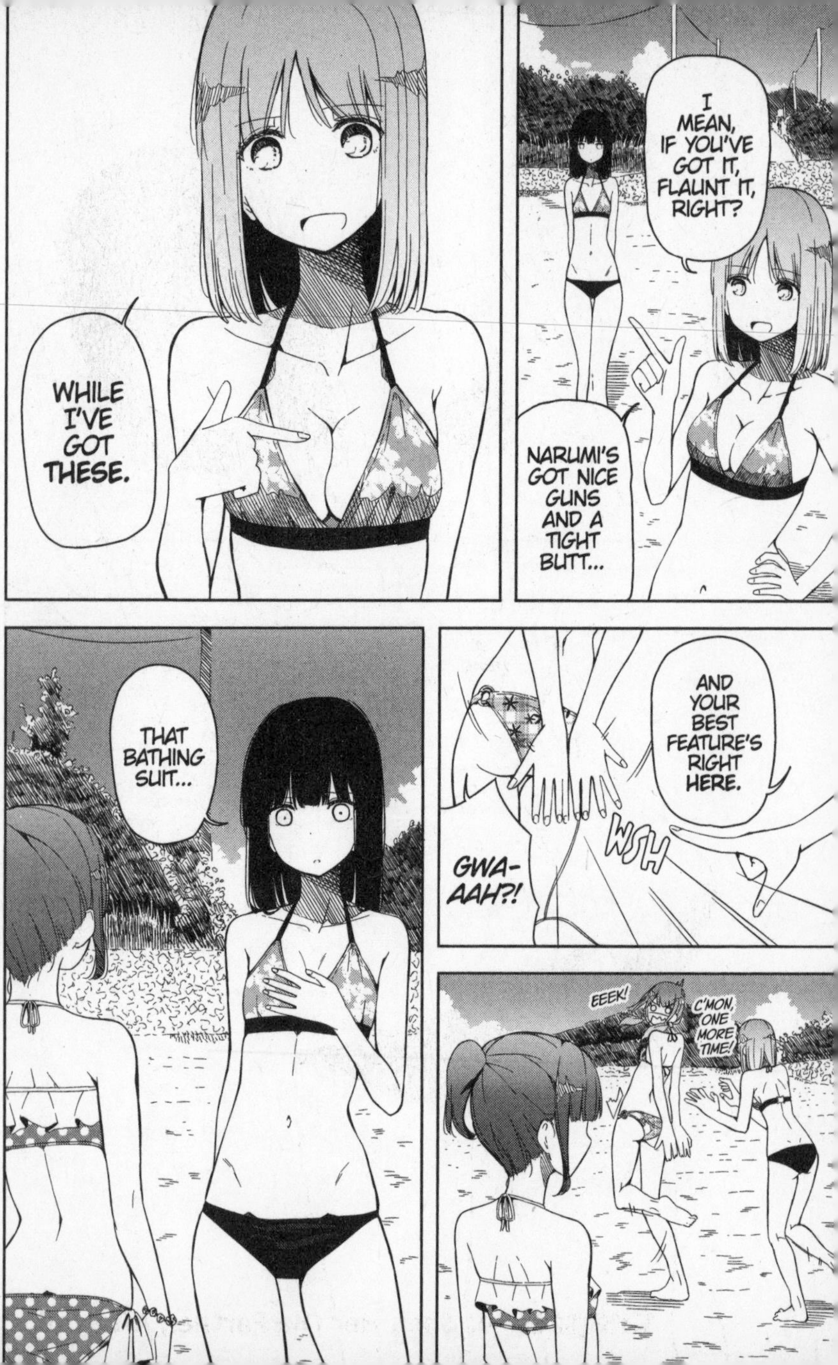
I MEAN, IF YOU'VE GOT IT, FLAUNT IT, RIGHT?
NARUMI'S GOT NICE GUNS AND A TIGHT BUTT...
WHILE I'VE GOT THESE.
AND YOUR BEST FEATURE'S RIGHT HERE.
WSH
GWA-AAH?!
C'MON, ONE MORE TIME!
EEEK!
THAT BATHING SUIT...

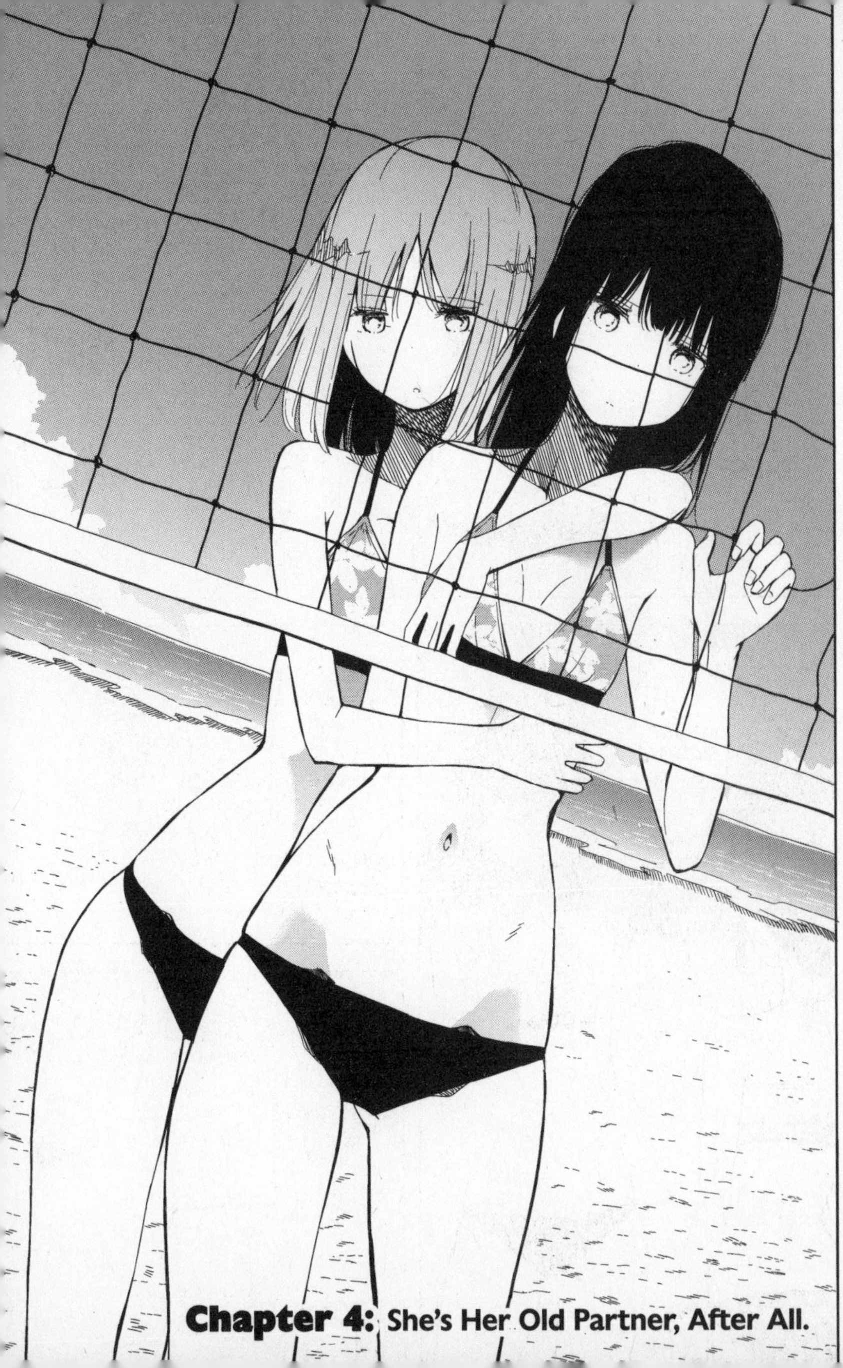

Chapter 4: She's Her Old Partner, After All.

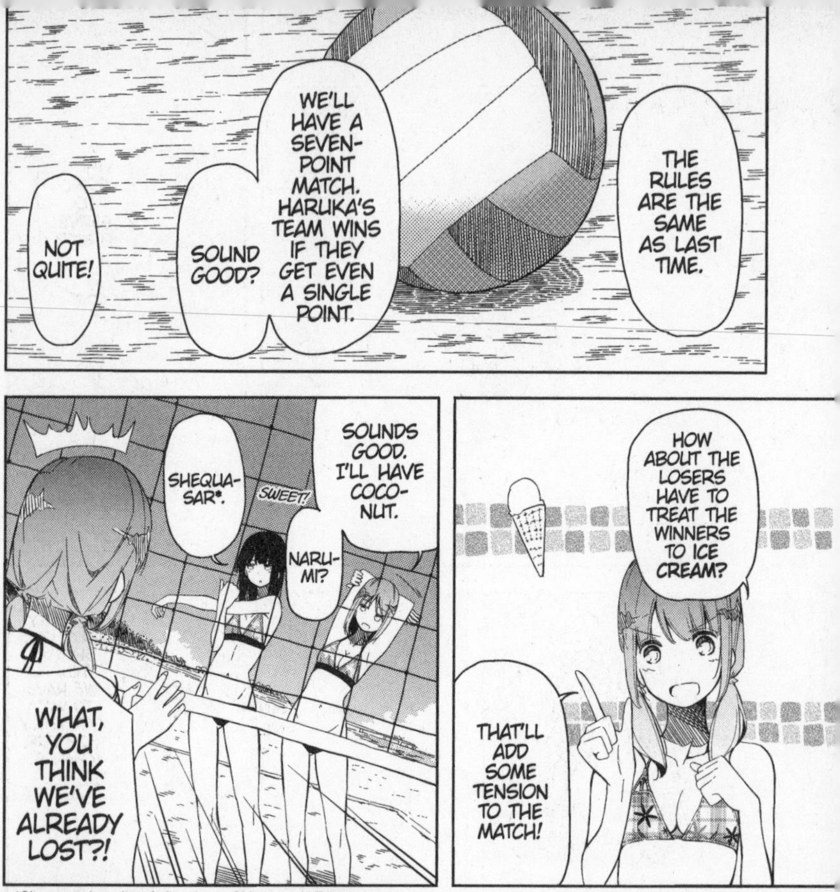
THE RULES ARE THE SAME AS LAST TIME.
WE'LL HAVE A SEVEN-POINT MATCH. HARUKA'S TEAM WINS IF THEY GET EVEN A SINGLE POINT.
SOUND GOOD?
NOT QUITE!
HOW ABOUT THE LOSERS HAVE TO TREAT THE WINNERS TO ICE CREAM?
THAT'LL ADD SOME TENSION TO THE MATCH!
SOUNDS GOOD. I'LL HAVE COCONUT.
SWEET!
SHEQUASAR*.
NARUMI?
WHAT, YOU THINK WE'VE ALREADY LOST?!

*Shequasar is a citrus fruit native to Okinawa and Taiwan.

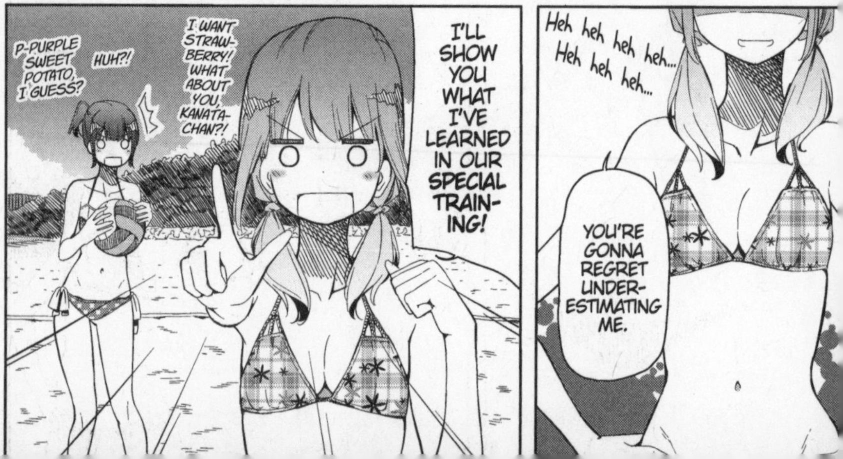
Heh heh heh heh... Heh heh heh...
YOU'RE GONNA REGRET UNDER-ESTIMATING ME.
I'LL SHOW YOU WHAT I'VE LEARNED IN OUR SPECIAL TRAIN-ING!
I WANT STRAW-BERRY! WHAT ABOUT YOU, KANATA-CHAN?!
HUH?!
P-PURPLE SWEET POTATO, I GUESS?

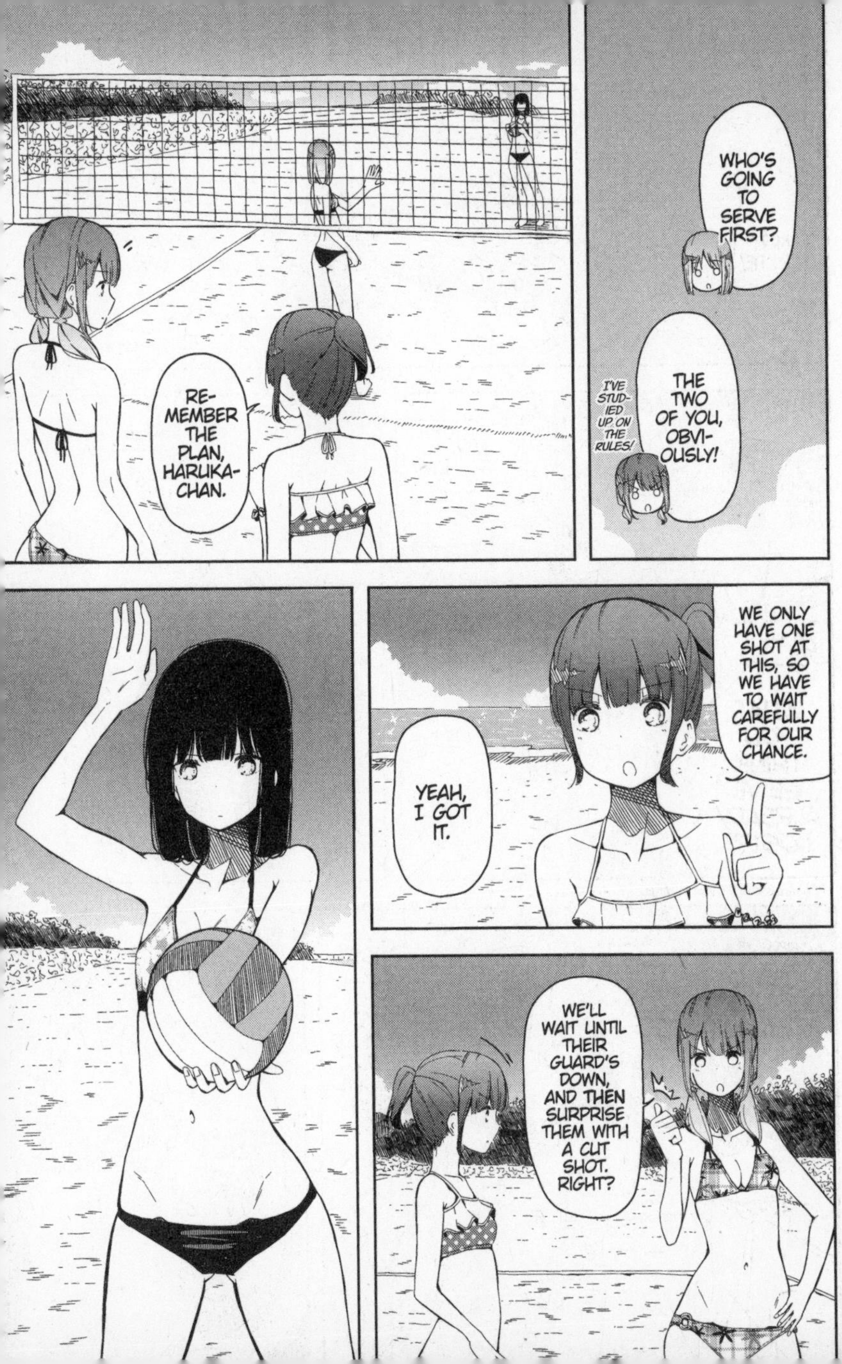
WHO'S GOING TO SERVE FIRST?
THE TWO OF YOU, OBVI-OUSLY!
I'VE STUD-IED UP ON THE RULES!
RE-MEMBER THE PLAN, HARUKA-CHAN.
WE ONLY HAVE ONE SHOT AT THIS, SO WE HAVE TO WAIT CAREFULLY FOR OUR CHANCE.
YEAH, I GOT IT.
WE'LL WAIT UNTIL THEIR GUARD'S DOWN, AND THEN SURPRISE THEM WITH A CUT SHOT. RIGHT?

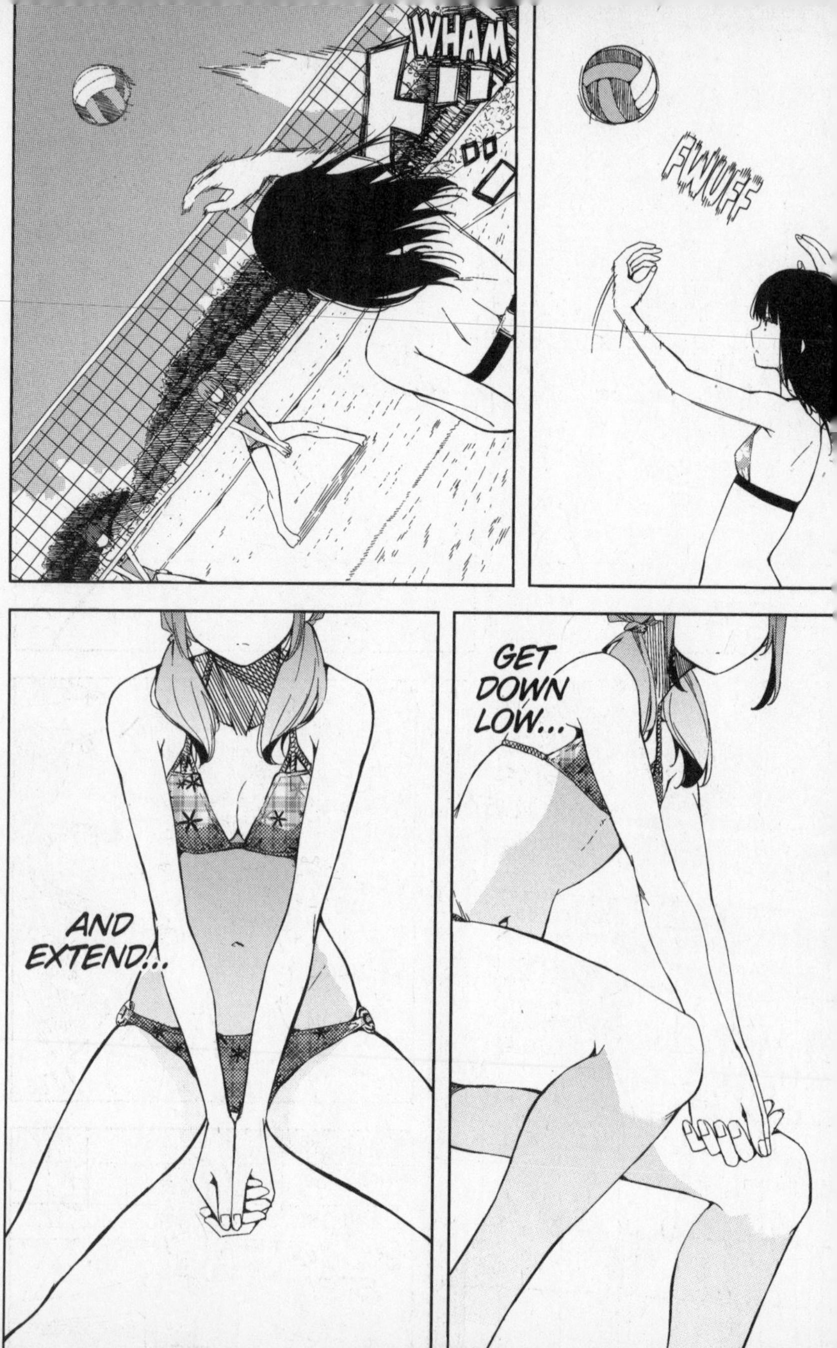
FWUFF
WHAM
GET DOWN LOW...
AND EXTEND...

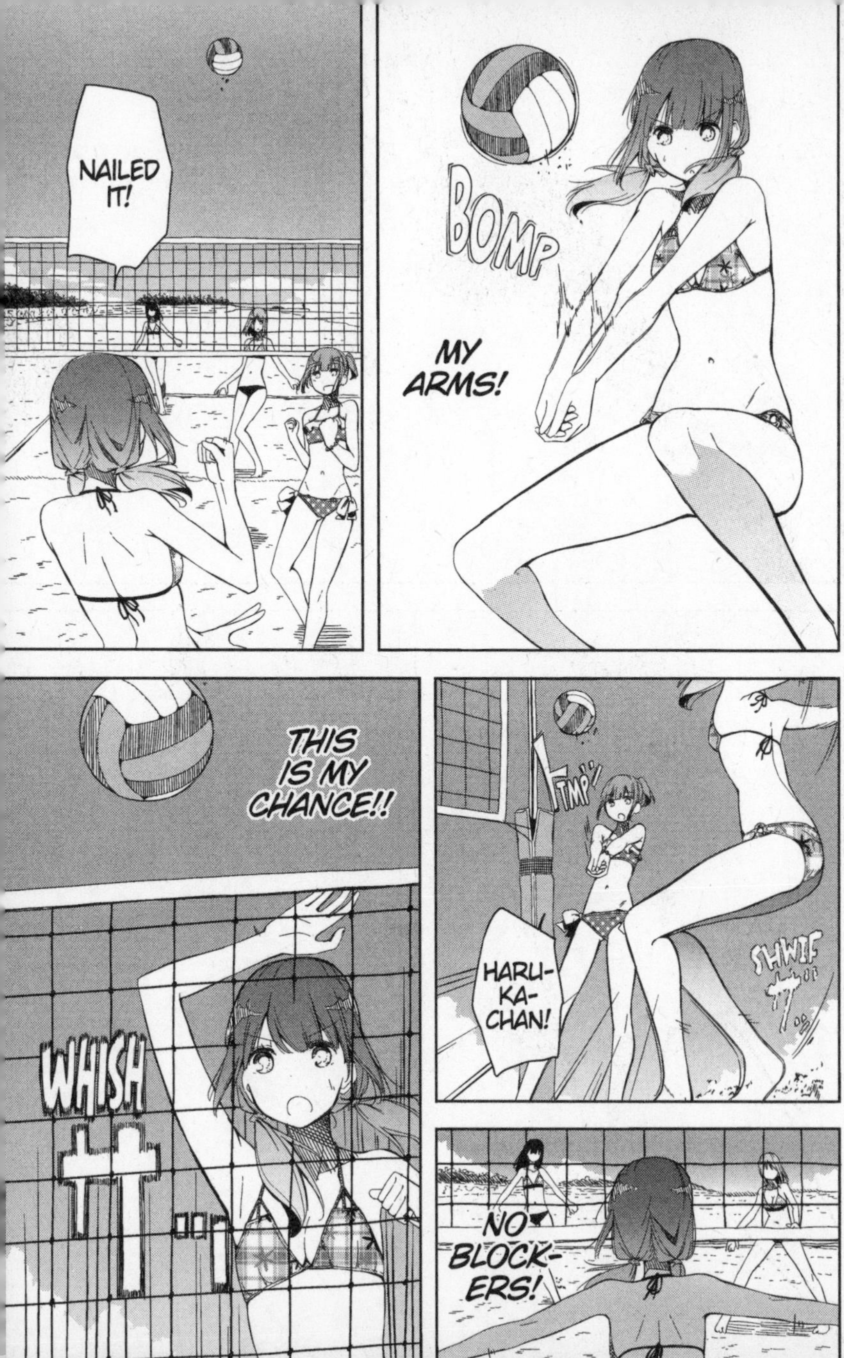
BOMP
MY ARMS!
NAILED IT!
TMP
HARU-KA-CHAN!
SHWIF
NO BLOCK-ERS!
THIS IS MY CHANCE!!
WHISH

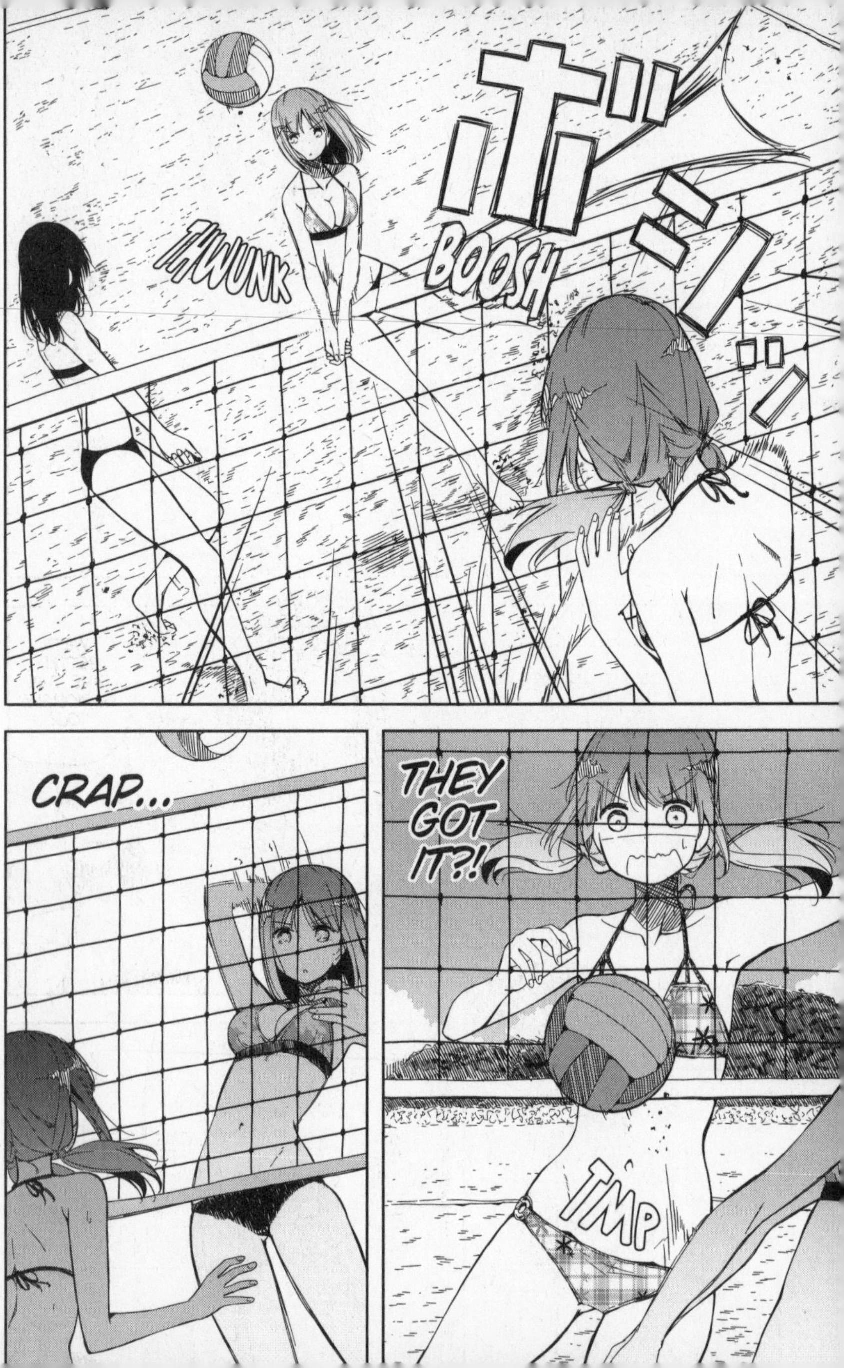
BOOSH
THWUNK
THEY GOT IT?!
TMP
CRAP...

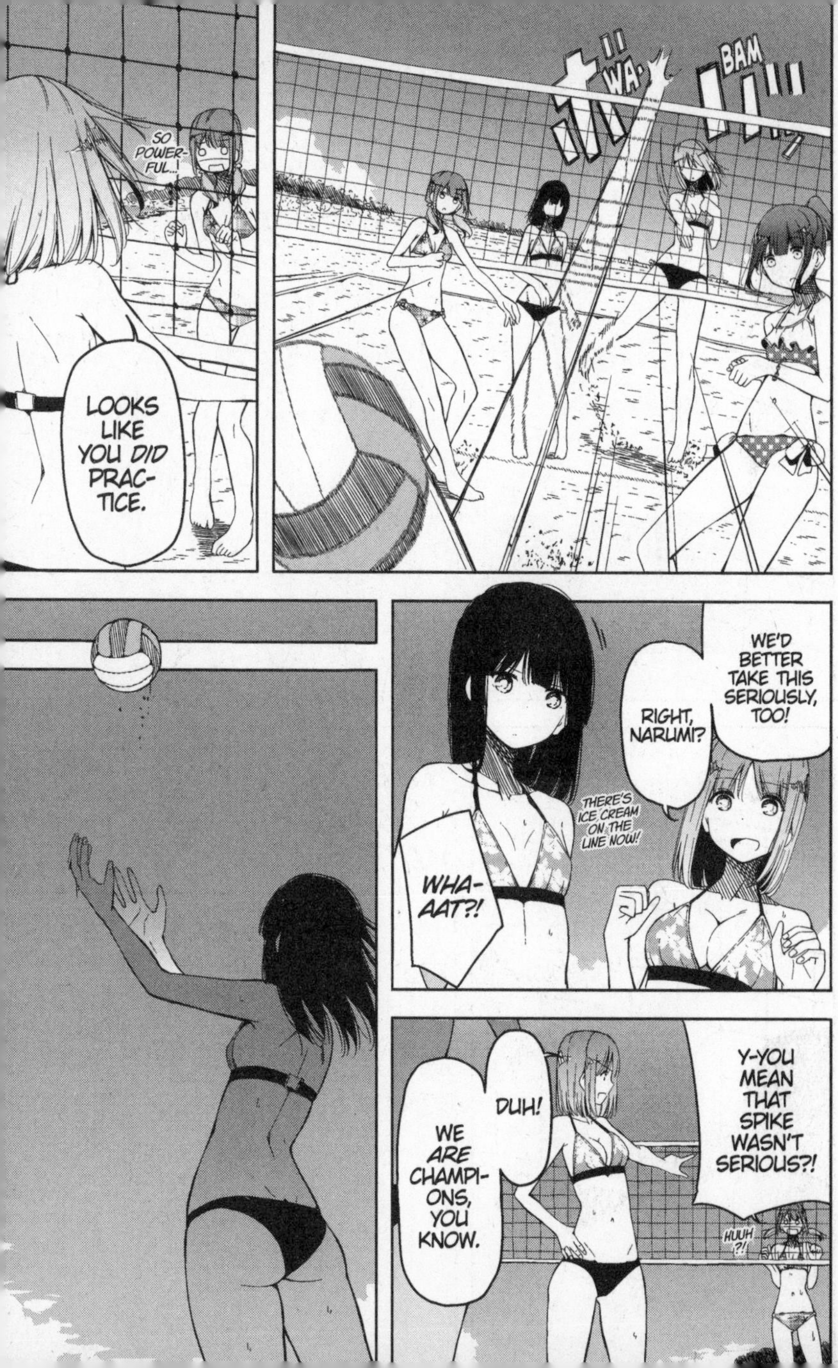
WA
BAM
SO POWER-FUL...!
LOOKS LIKE YOU DID PRAC-TICE.
WE'D BETTER TAKE THIS SERIOUSLY, TOO!
RIGHT, NARUMI?
THERE'S ICE CREAM ON THE LINE NOW!
WHA-AAT?!
Y-YOU MEAN THAT SPIKE WASN'T SERIOUS?!
DUH!
WE ARE CHAMPI-ONS, YOU KNOW.
HUUH?!

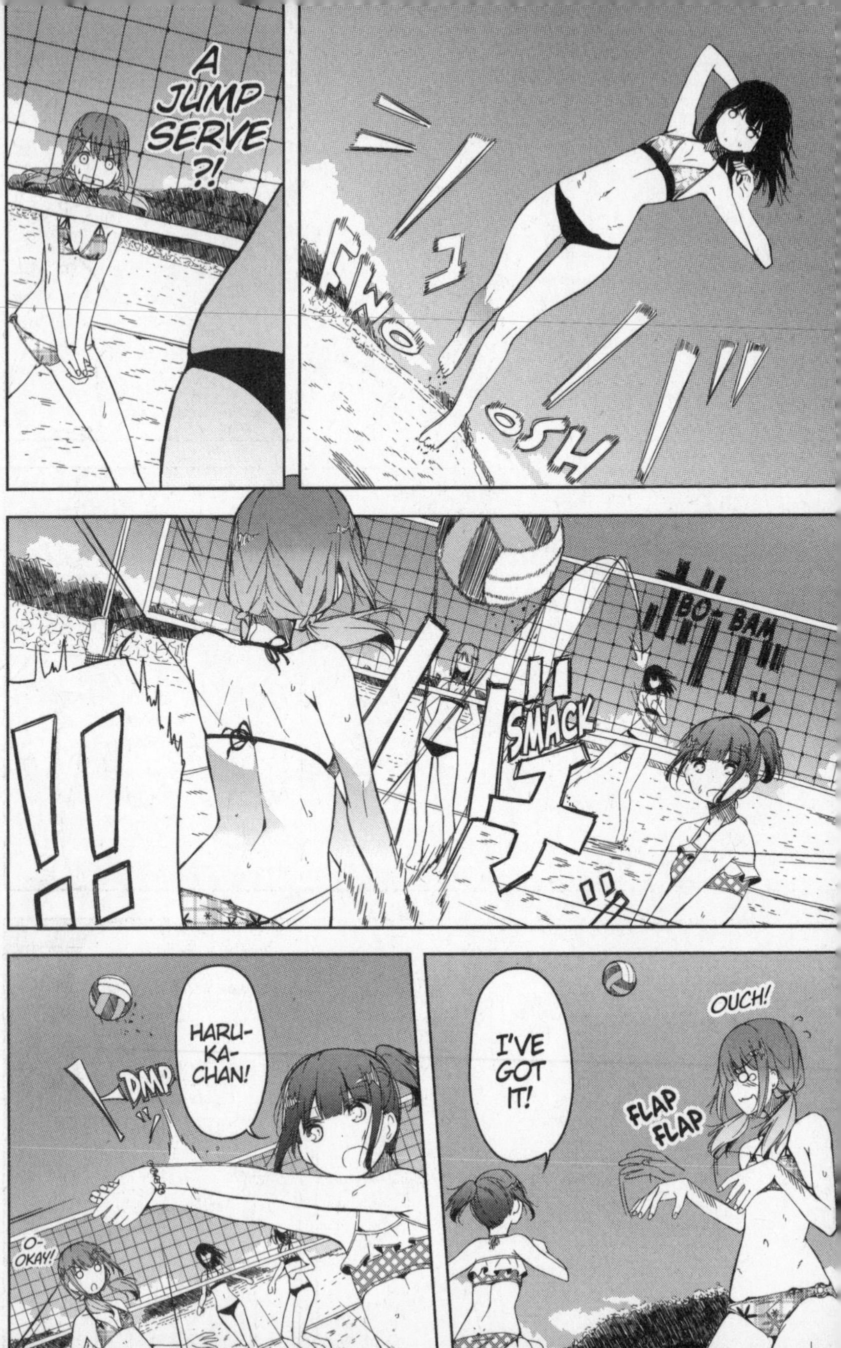
FWOOSH
A JUMP SERVE ?!
BO-BAM
SMACK
!!
OUCH!
I'VE GOT IT!
FLAP FLAP
HARU-KA-CHAN!
DMP
O-OKAY!

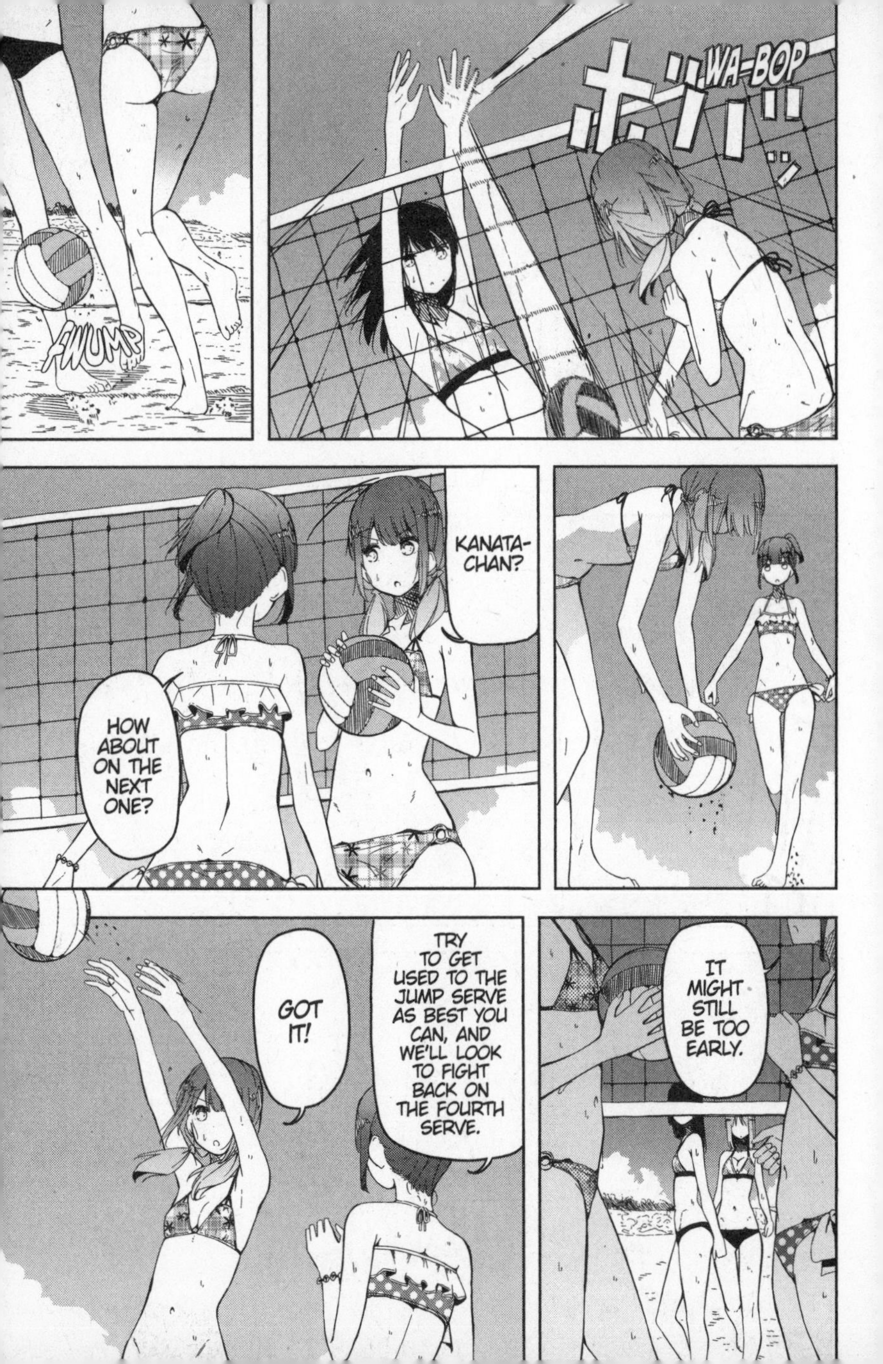
WA-BOP
FWUMP
KANATA-CHAN?
HOW ABOUT ON THE NEXT ONE?
IT MIGHT STILL BE TOO EARLY.
TRY TO GET USED TO THE JUMP SERVE AS BEST YOU CAN, AND WE'LL LOOK TO FIGHT BACK ON THE FOURTH SERVE.
GOT IT!

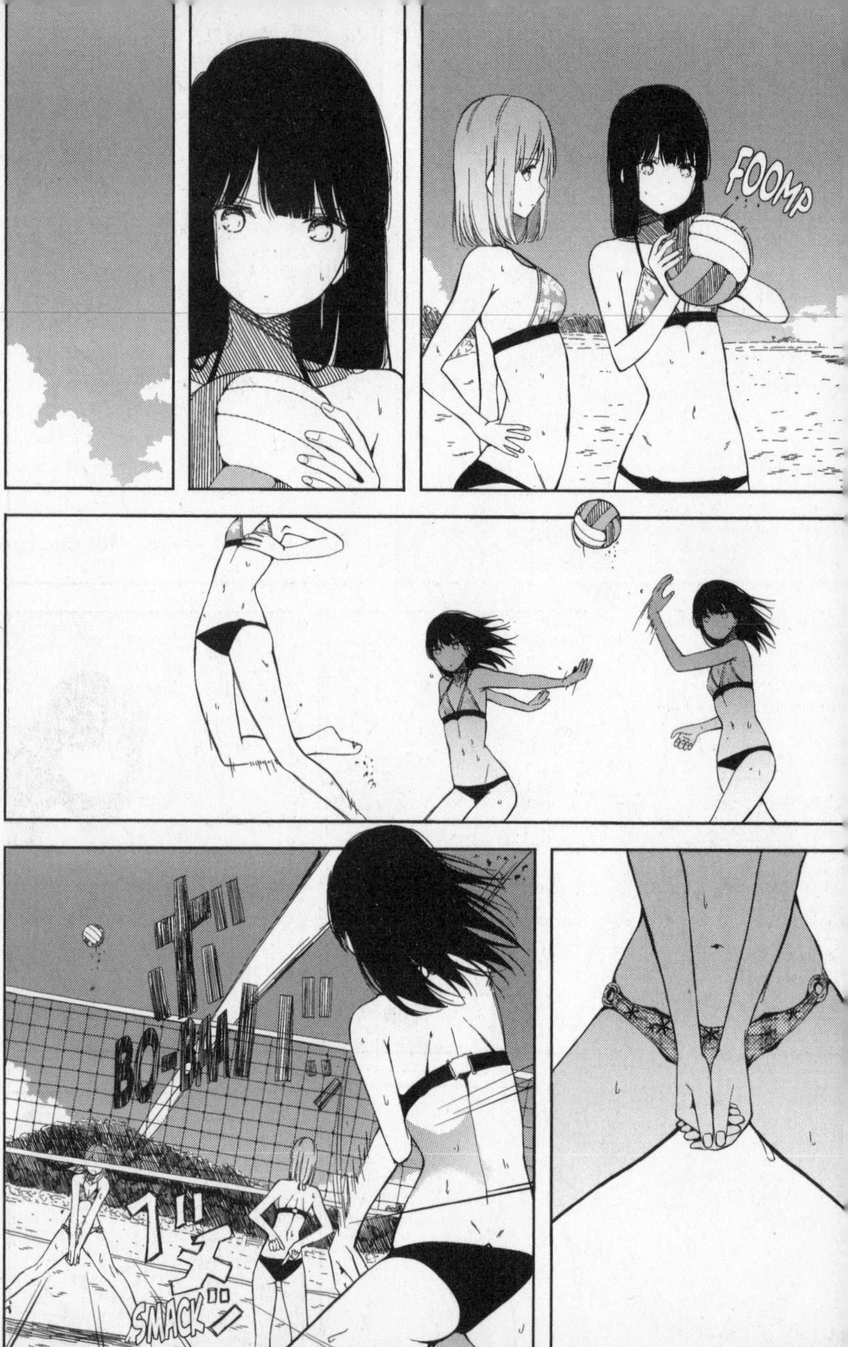
FOOMP
BO-BAM!!
SMACK!!

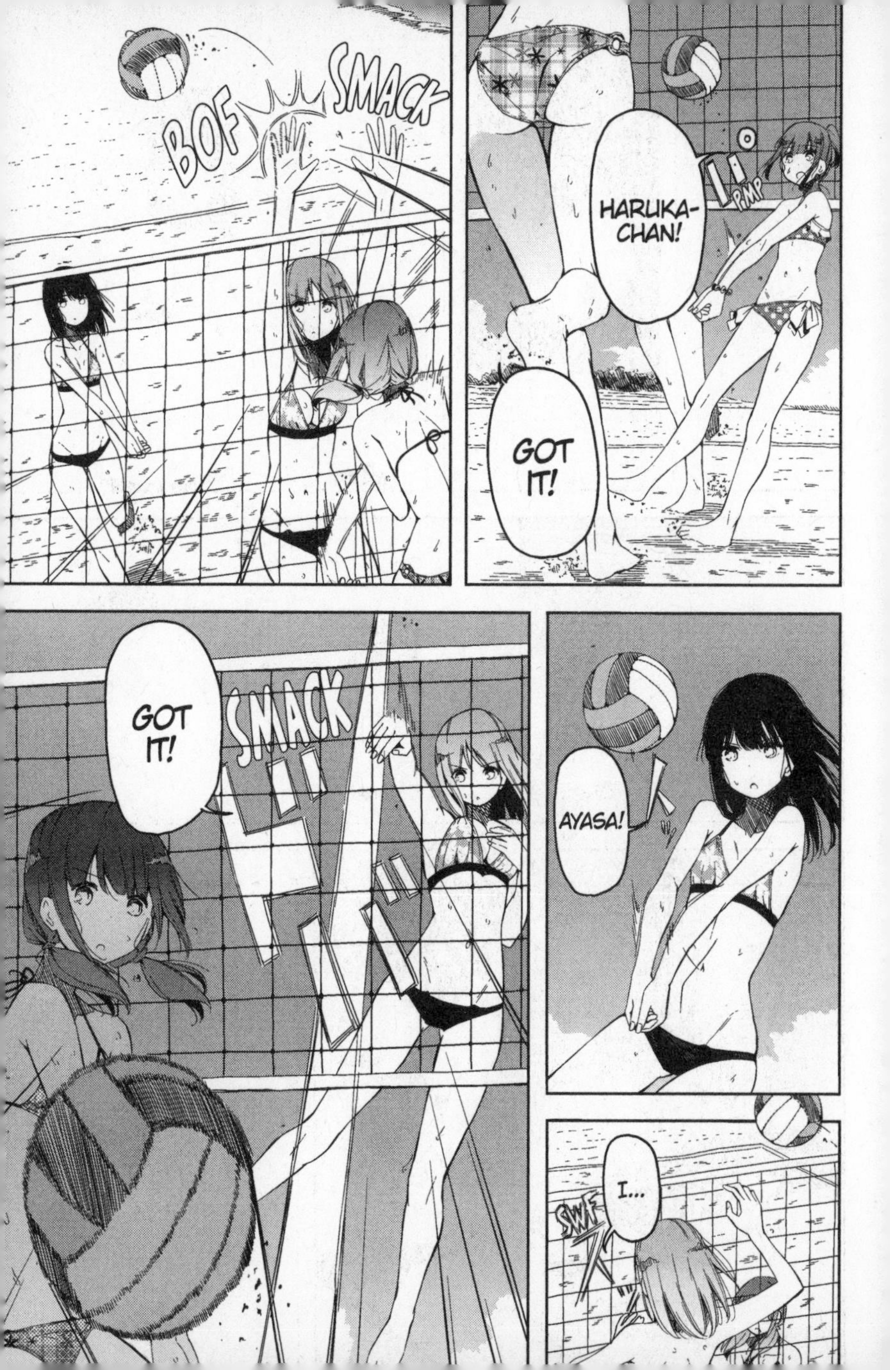
HARUKA-CHAN!
PMP
GOT IT!
BOF
SMACK
AYASA!
I...
GOT IT!
SMACK

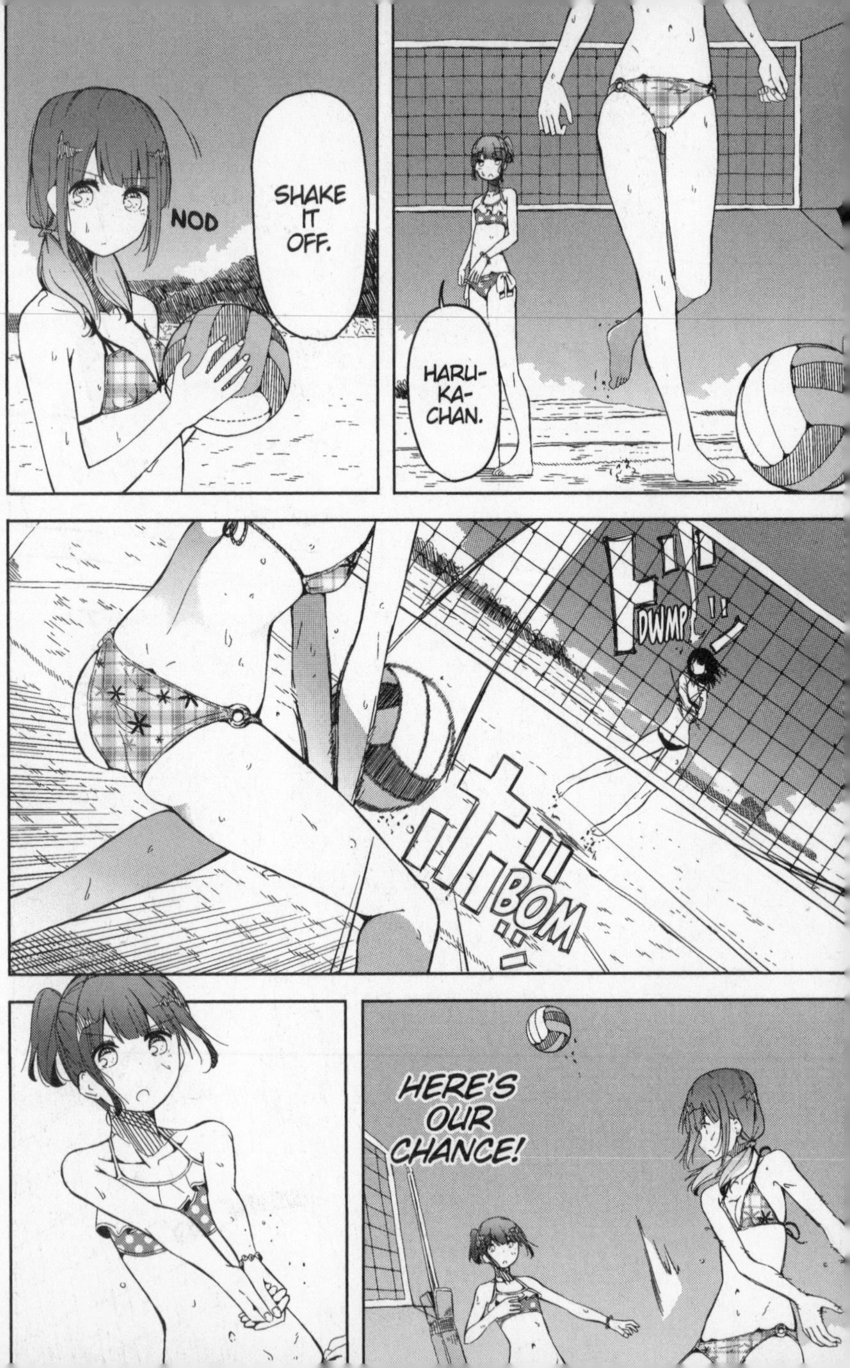
HARU-KA-CHAN.
SHAKE IT OFF.
NOD
DWMP
BOM
HERE'S OUR CHANCE!

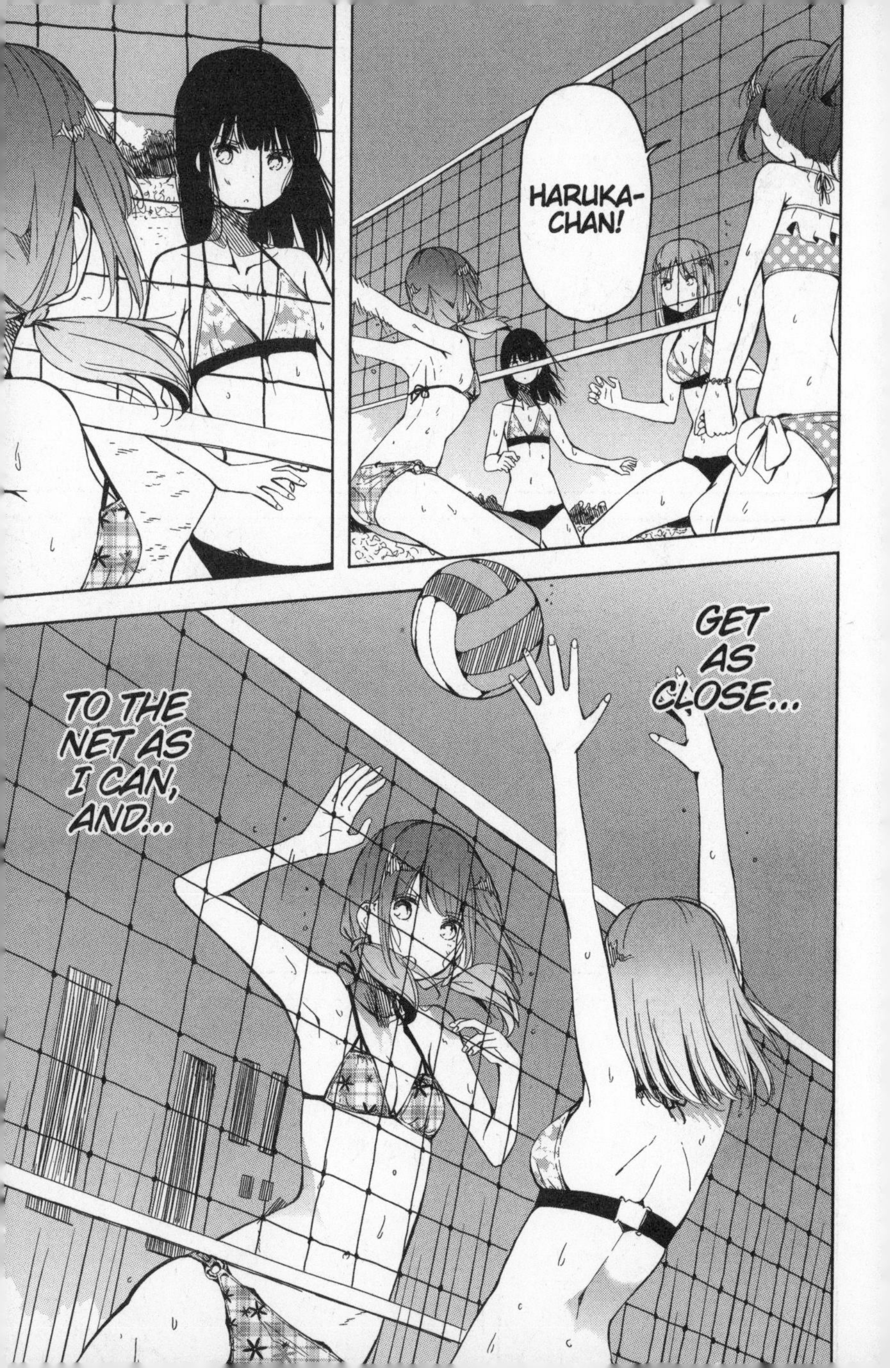
HARUKA-CHAN!
GET AS CLOSE...
TO THE NET AS I CAN, AND...

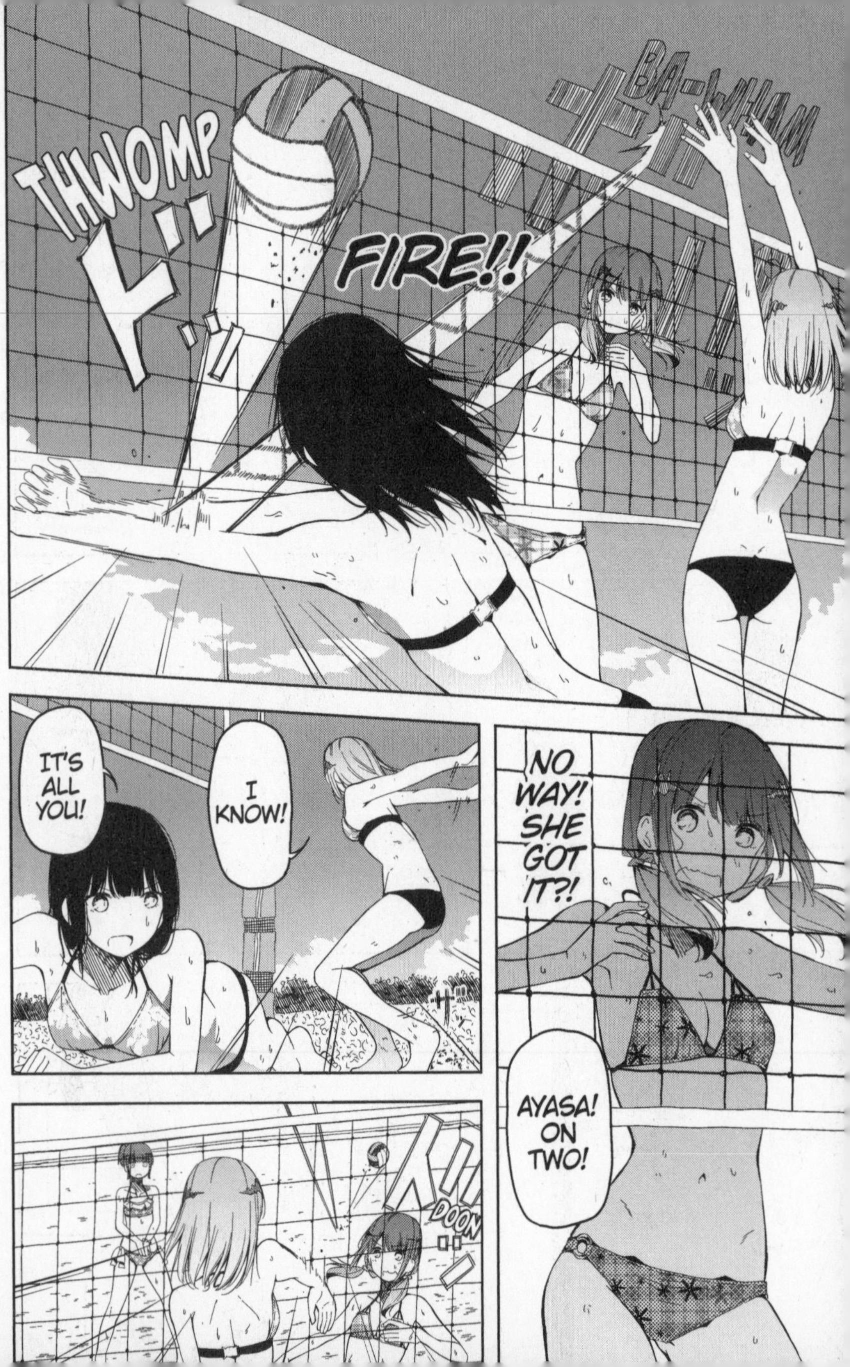
BA-WHAM
FIRE!!
THWOMP
NO WAY! SHE GOT IT?!
AYASA! ON TWO!
IT'S ALL YOU!
I KNOW!
DOON

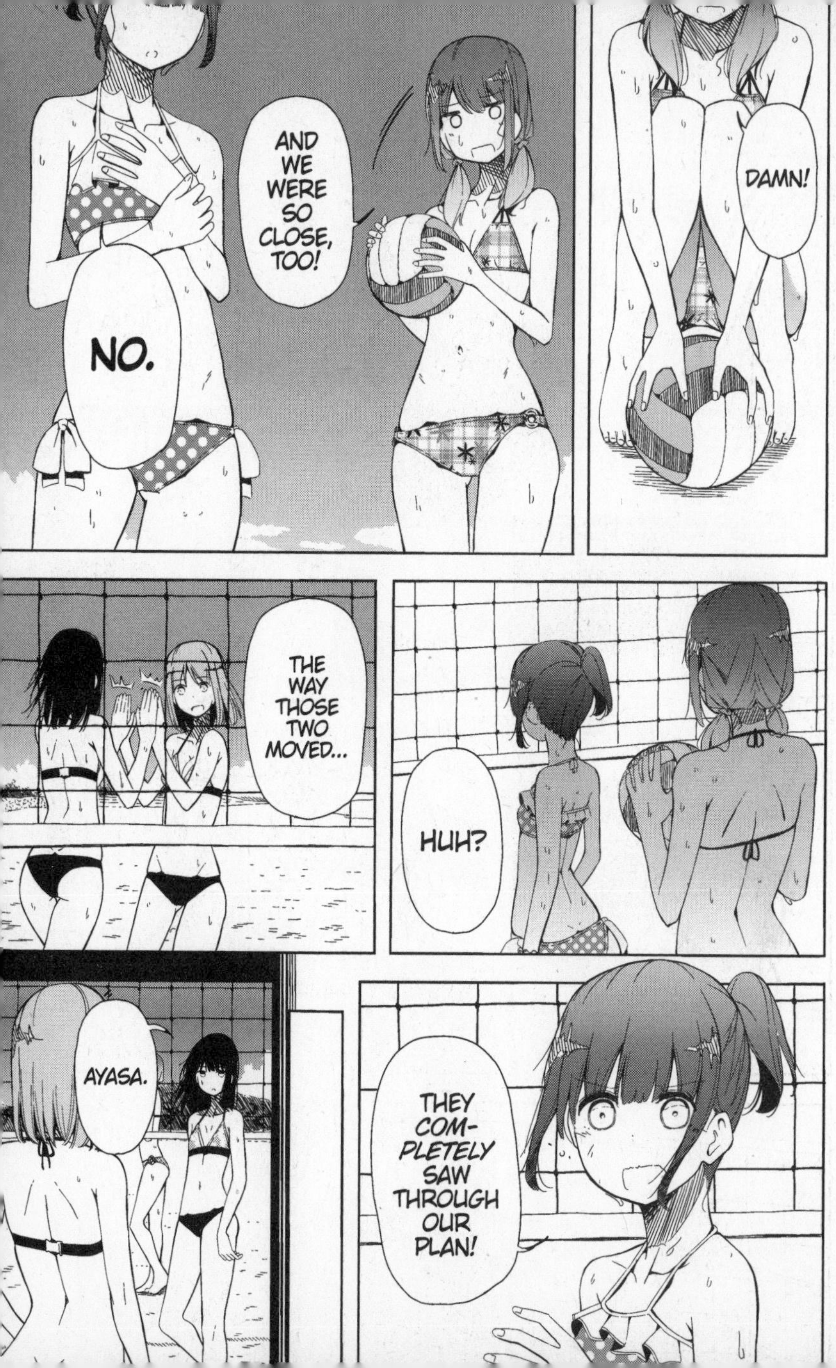
DAMN!
AND WE WERE SO CLOSE, TOO!
NO.
HUH?
THE WAY THOSE TWO MOVED...
THEY COMPLETELY SAW THROUGH OUR PLAN!
AYASA.

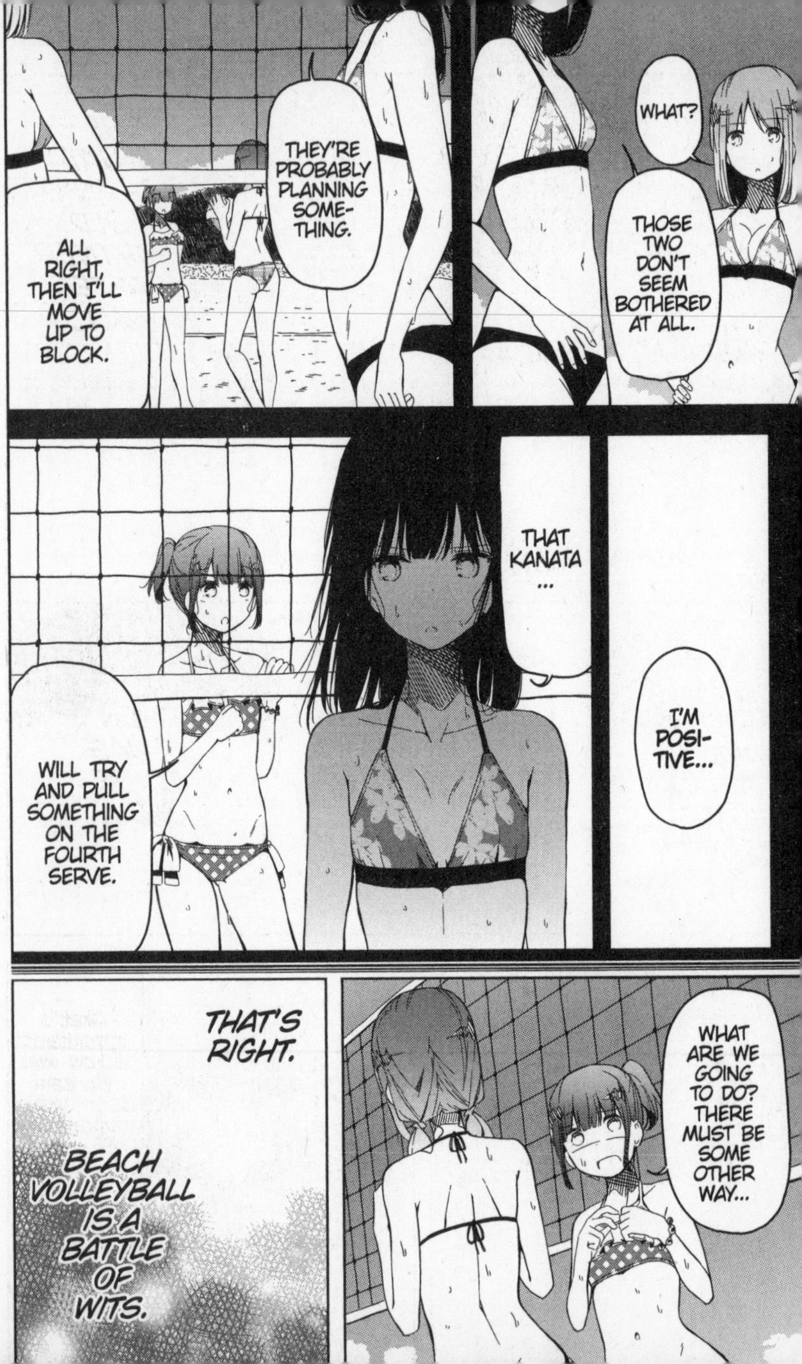
WHAT?
THOSE TWO DON'T SEEM BOTHERED AT ALL.
THEY'RE PROBABLY PLANNING SOME-THING.
ALL RIGHT, THEN I'LL MOVE UP TO BLOCK.
I'M POSI-TIVE...
THAT KANATA ...
WILL TRY AND PULL SOMETHING ON THE FOURTH SERVE.
WHAT ARE WE GOING TO DO? THERE MUST BE SOME OTHER WAY...
THAT'S RIGHT.
BEACH VOLLEYBALL IS A BATTLE OF WITS.

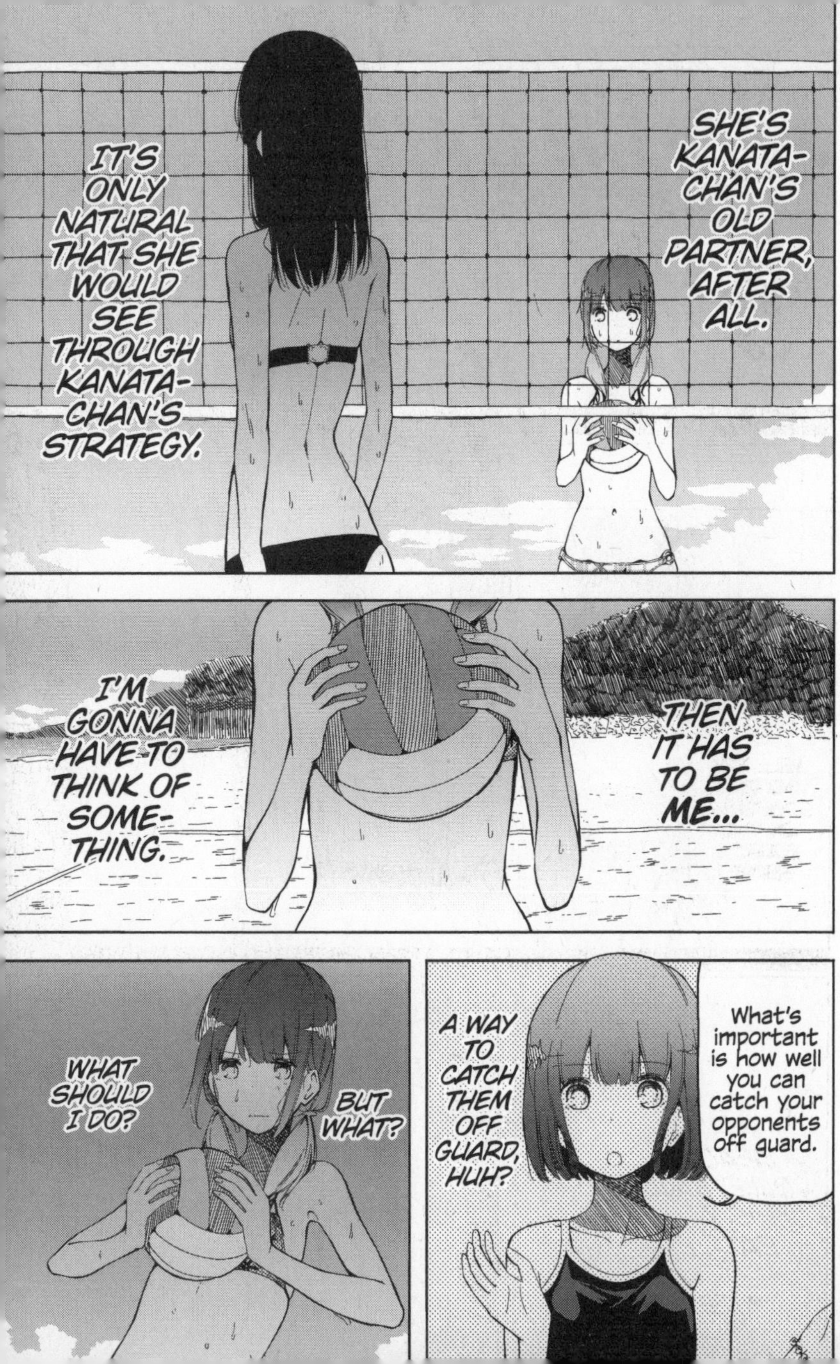
SHE'S KANATA-CHAN'S OLD PARTNER, AFTER ALL.
IT'S ONLY NATURAL THAT SHE WOULD SEE THROUGH KANATA-CHAN'S STRATEGY.
THEN IT HAS TO BE ME...
I'M GONNA HAVE TO THINK OF SOME-THING.
What's important is how well you can catch your opponents off guard.
A WAY TO CATCH THEM OFF GUARD, HUH?
BUT WHAT?
WHAT SHOULD I DO?

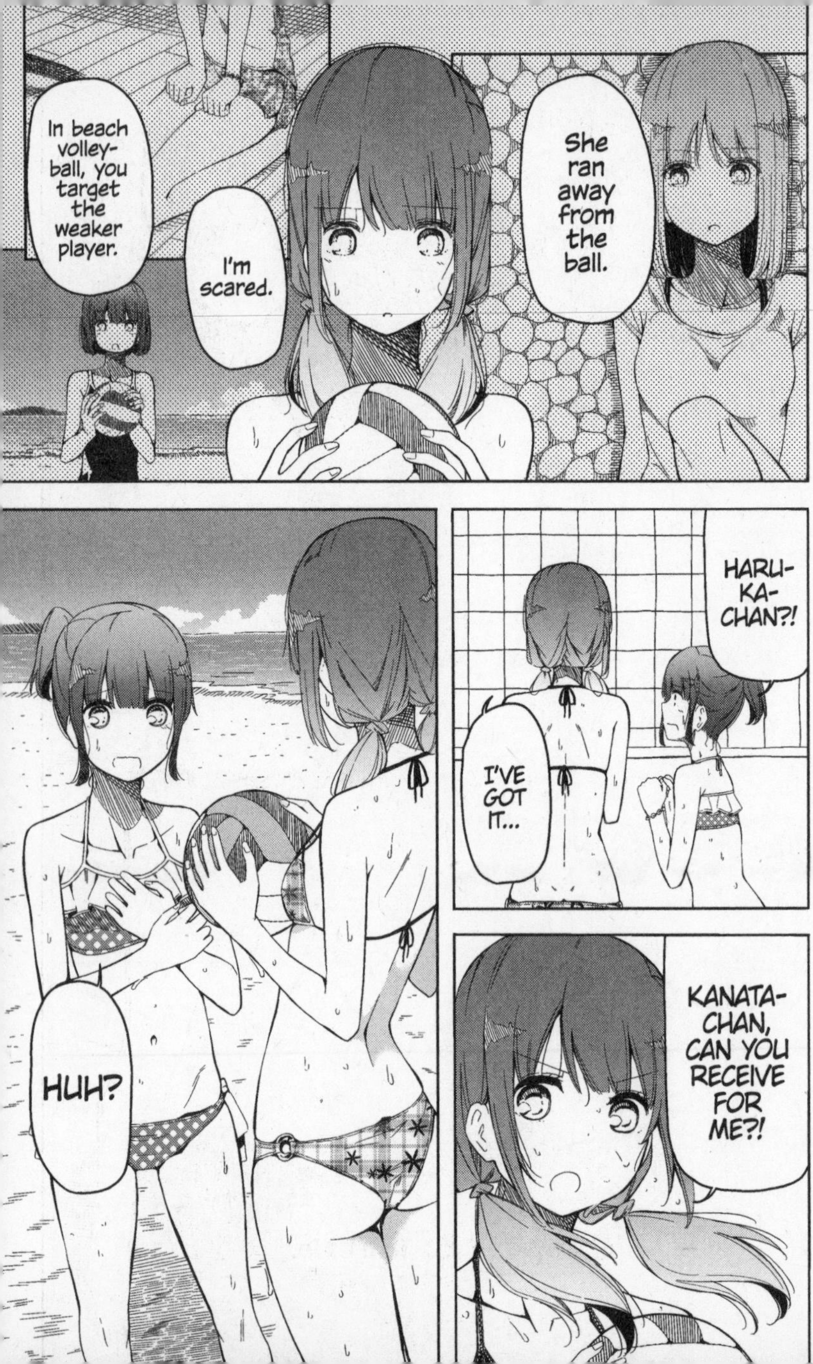
She ran away from the ball.
I'm scared.
In beach volley-ball, you target the weaker player.
HARU-KA-CHAN?!
I'VE GOT IT...
KANATA-CHAN, CAN YOU RECEIVE FOR ME?!
HUH?

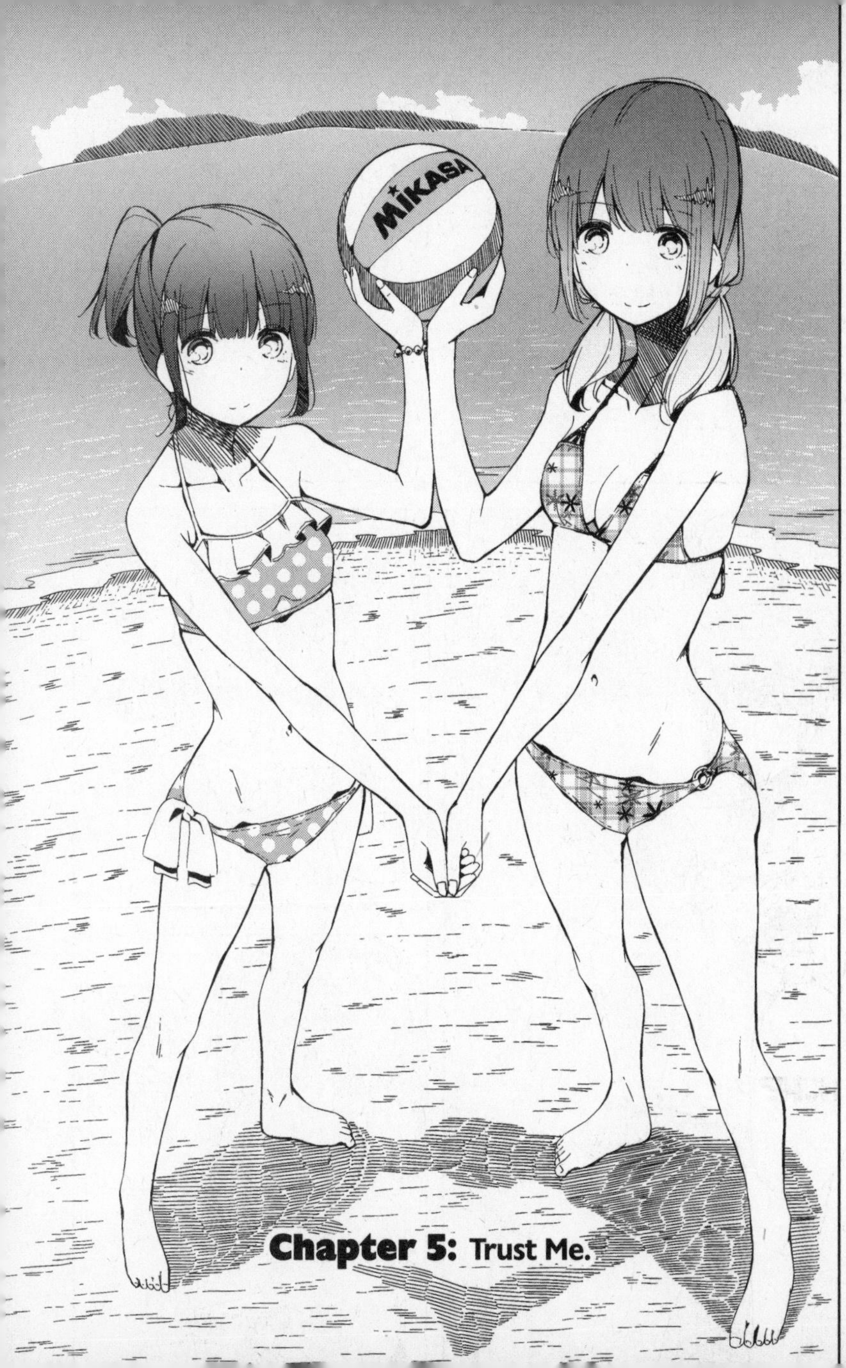
MIKASA

Chapter 5: Trust Me.

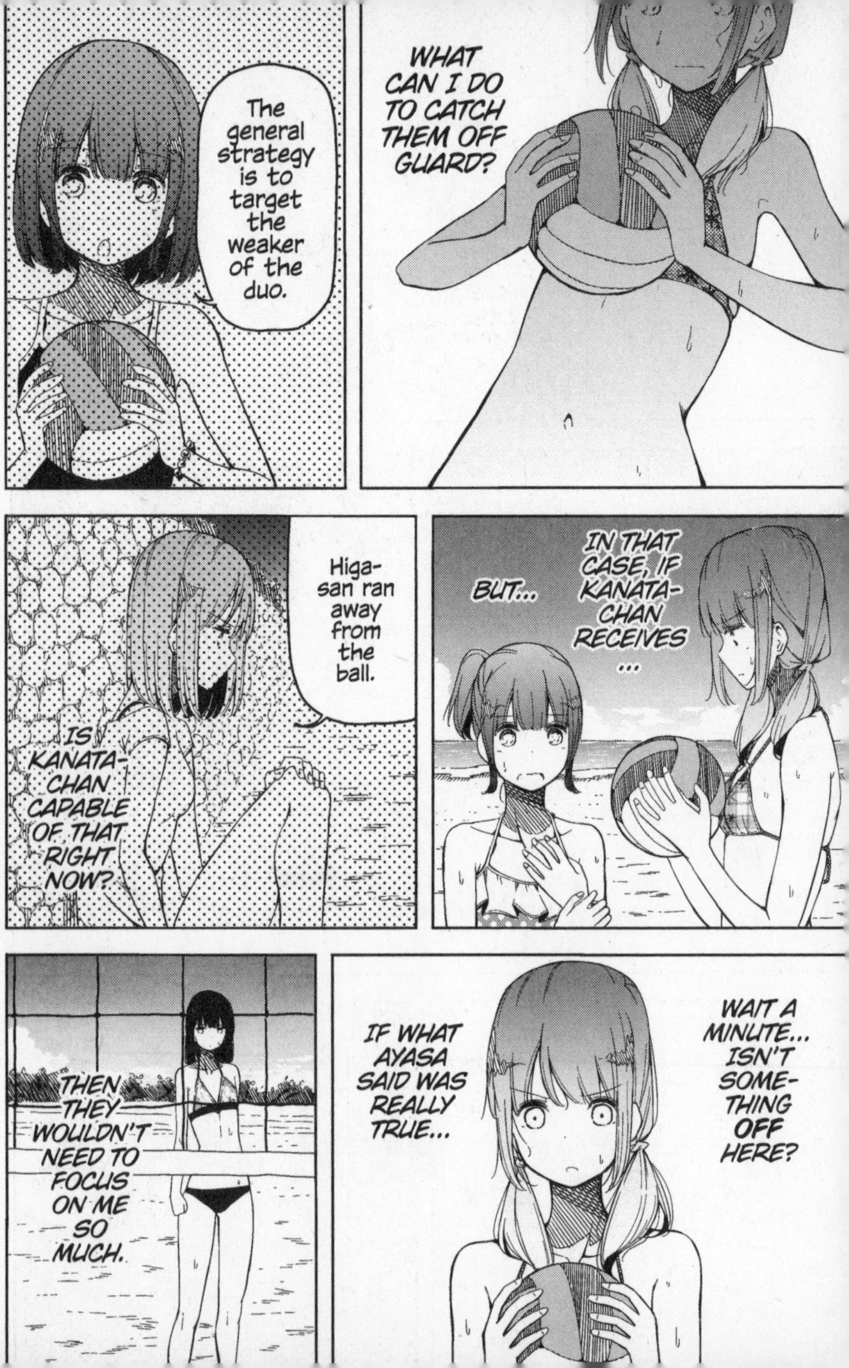
WHAT CAN I DO TO CATCH THEM OFF GUARD?
The general strategy is to target the weaker of the duo.
IN THAT CASE, IF KANATA-CHAN RECEIVES...
BUT...
Higa-san ran away from the ball.
IS KANATA-CHAN CAPABLE OF THAT RIGHT NOW?
WAIT A MINUTE... ISN'T SOMETHING OFF HERE?
IF WHAT AYASA SAID WAS REALLY TRUE...
THEN THEY WOULDN'T NEED TO FOCUS ON ME SO MUCH.

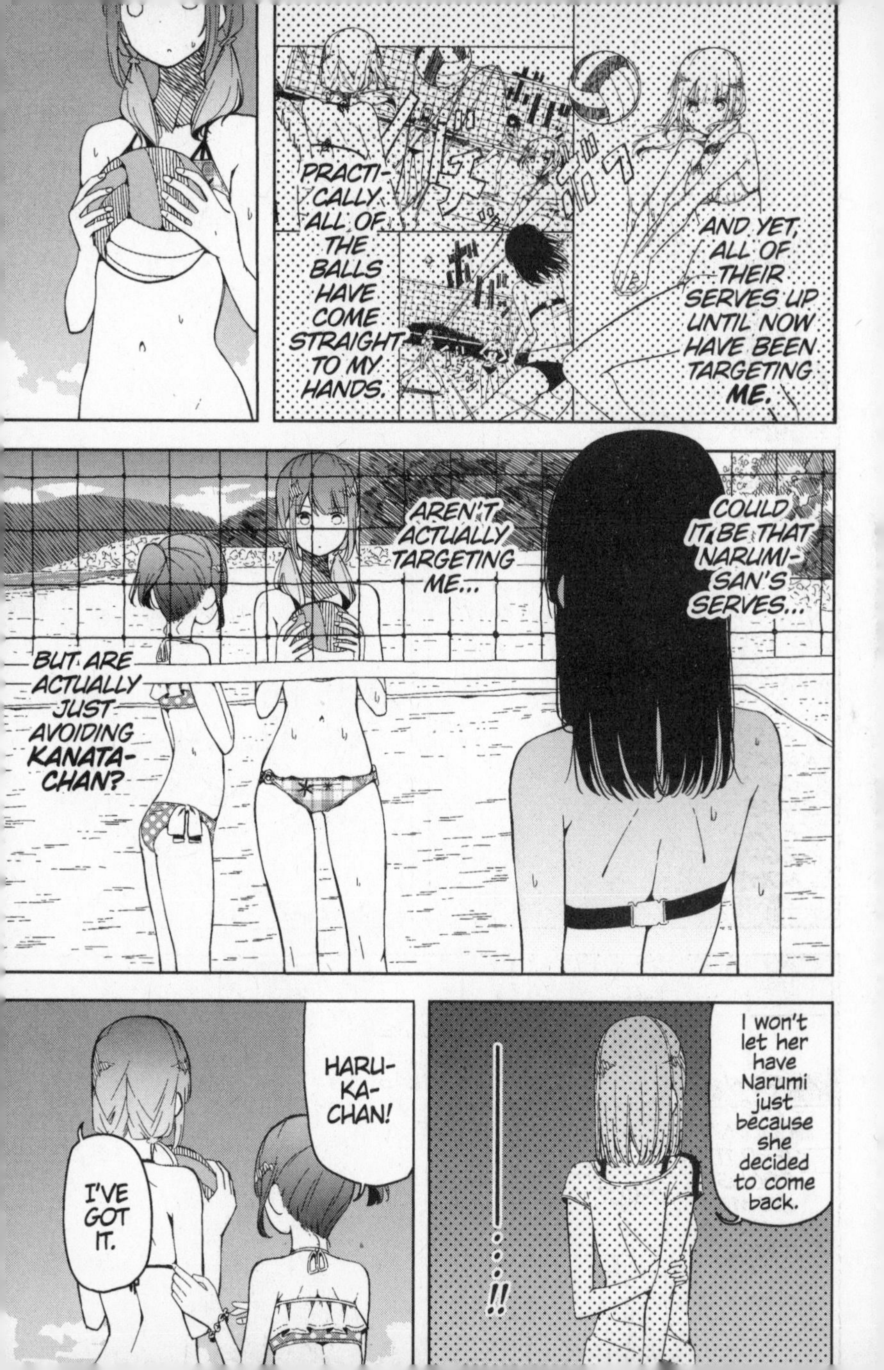
AND YET, ALL OF THEIR SERVES UP UNTIL NOW HAVE BEEN TARGETING ME.
PRACTI-CALLY ALL OF THE BALLS HAVE COME STRAIGHT TO MY HANDS.
COULD IT BE THAT NARUMI-SAN'S SERVES...
AREN'T ACTUALLY TARGETING ME...
BUT ARE ACTUALLY JUST AVOIDING KANATA-CHAN?
I won't let her have Narumi just because she decided to come back.
——......!!
HARU-KA-CHAN!
I'VE GOT IT.

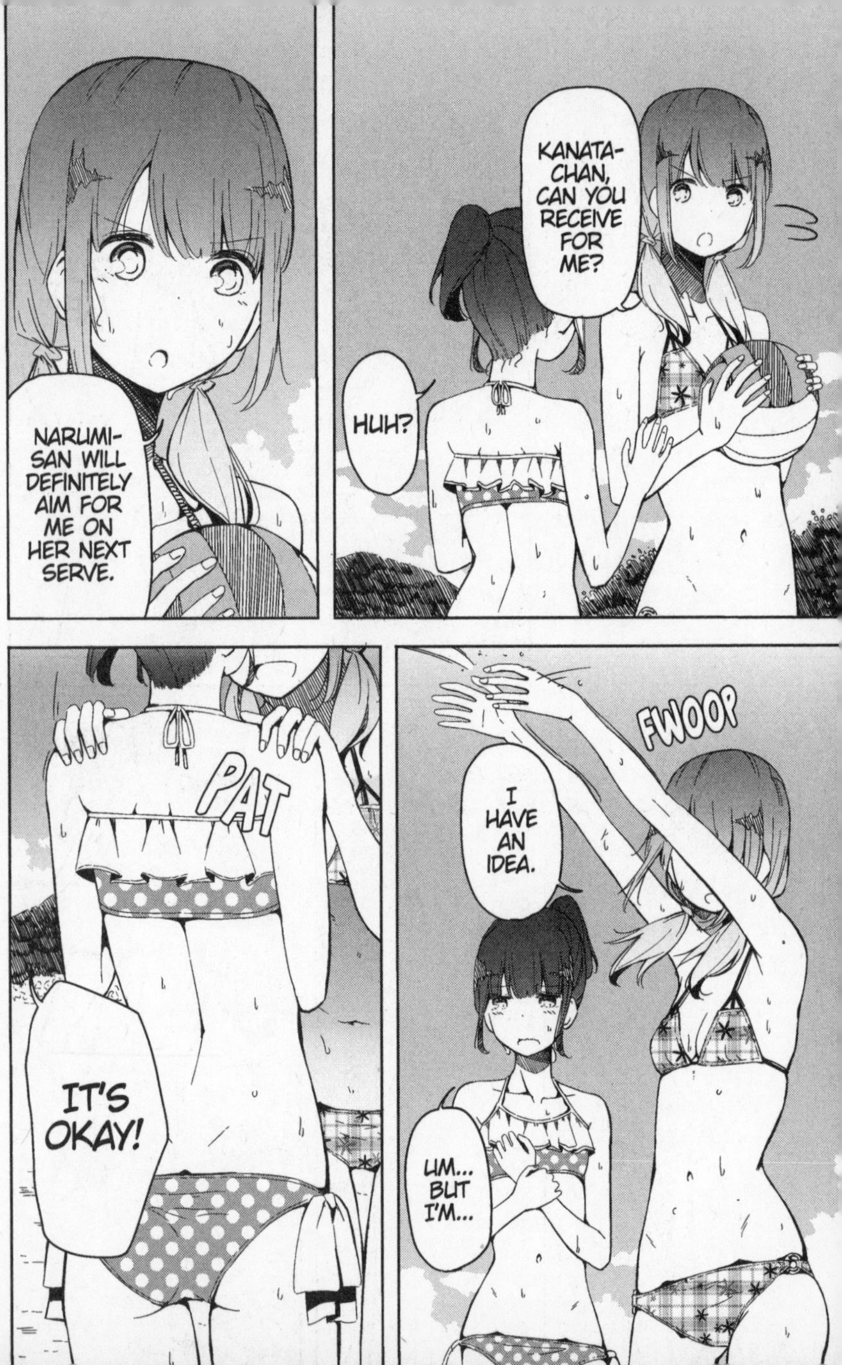
KANATA-CHAN, CAN YOU RECEIVE FOR ME?
HUH?
NARUMI-SAN WILL DEFINITELY AIM FOR ME ON HER NEXT SERVE.
FWOOP
I HAVE AN IDEA.
UM... BUT I'M...
PAT
IT'S OKAY!

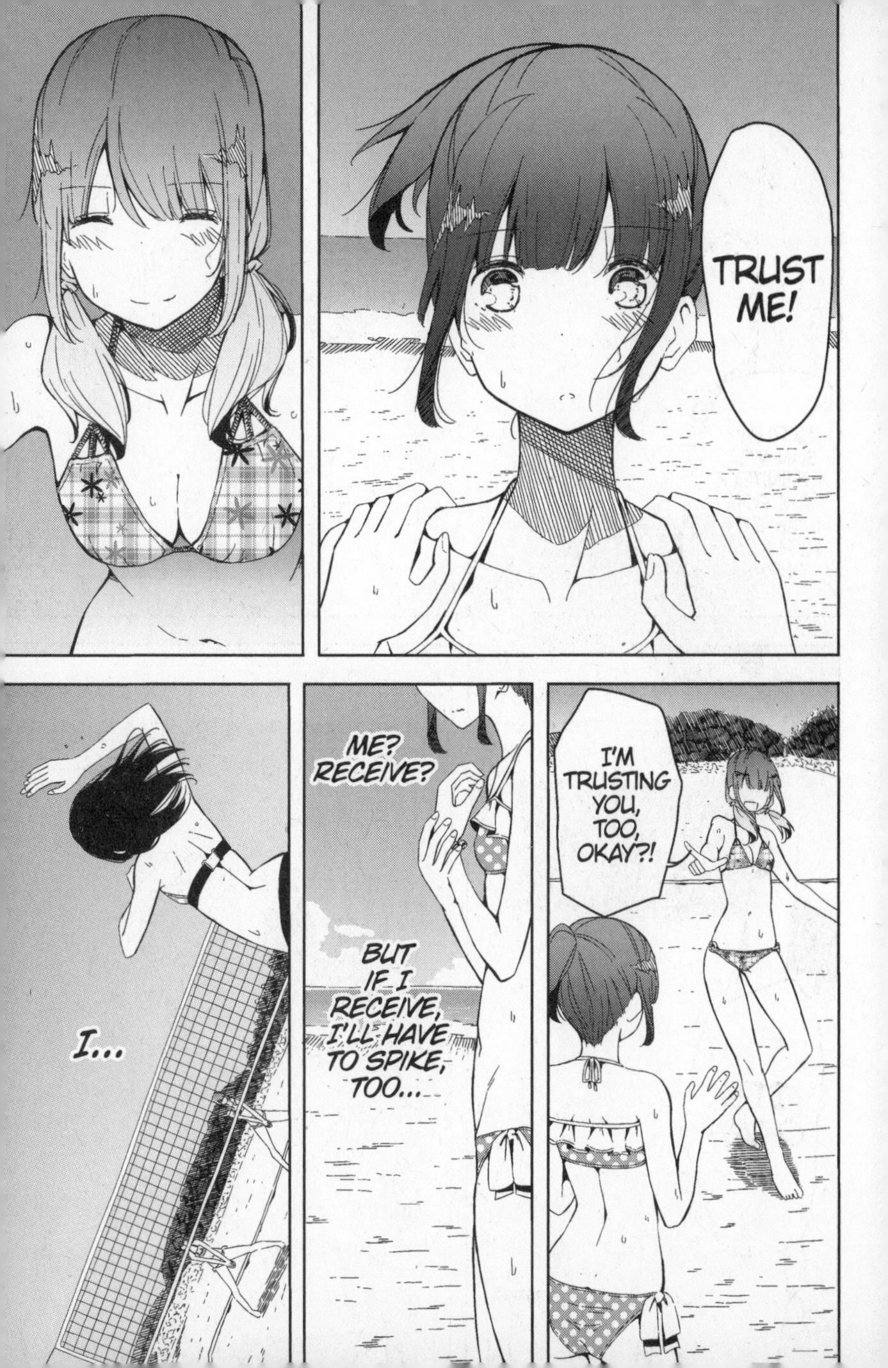
TRUST ME!
I'M TRUSTING YOU, TOO, OKAY?!
ME? RECEIVE?
BUT IF I RECEIVE, I'LL HAVE TO SPIKE, TOO...
I...

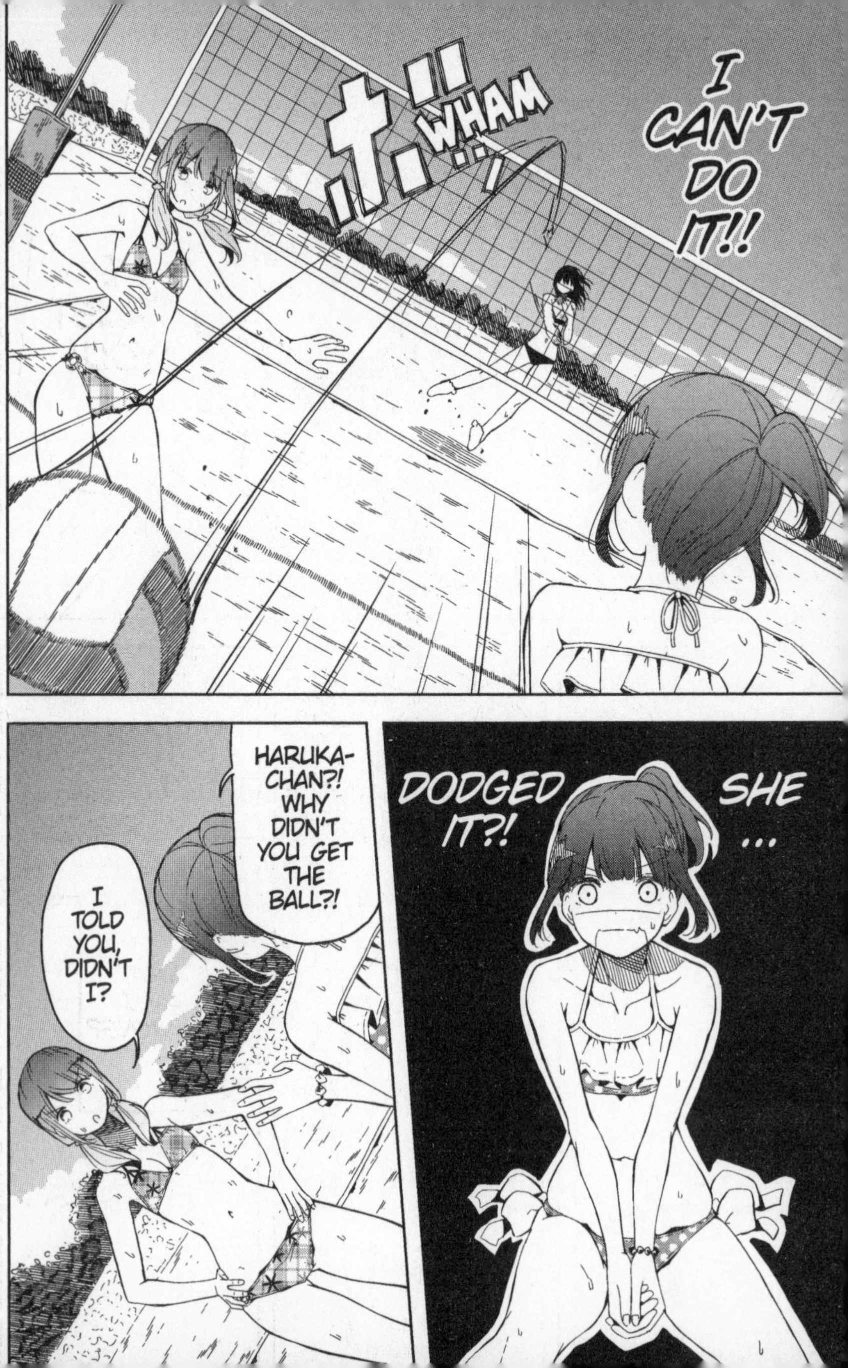
I CAN'T DO IT!!
WHAM
SHE ...
DODGED IT?!
HARUKA-CHAN?! WHY DIDN'T YOU GET THE BALL?!
I TOLD YOU, DIDN'T I?

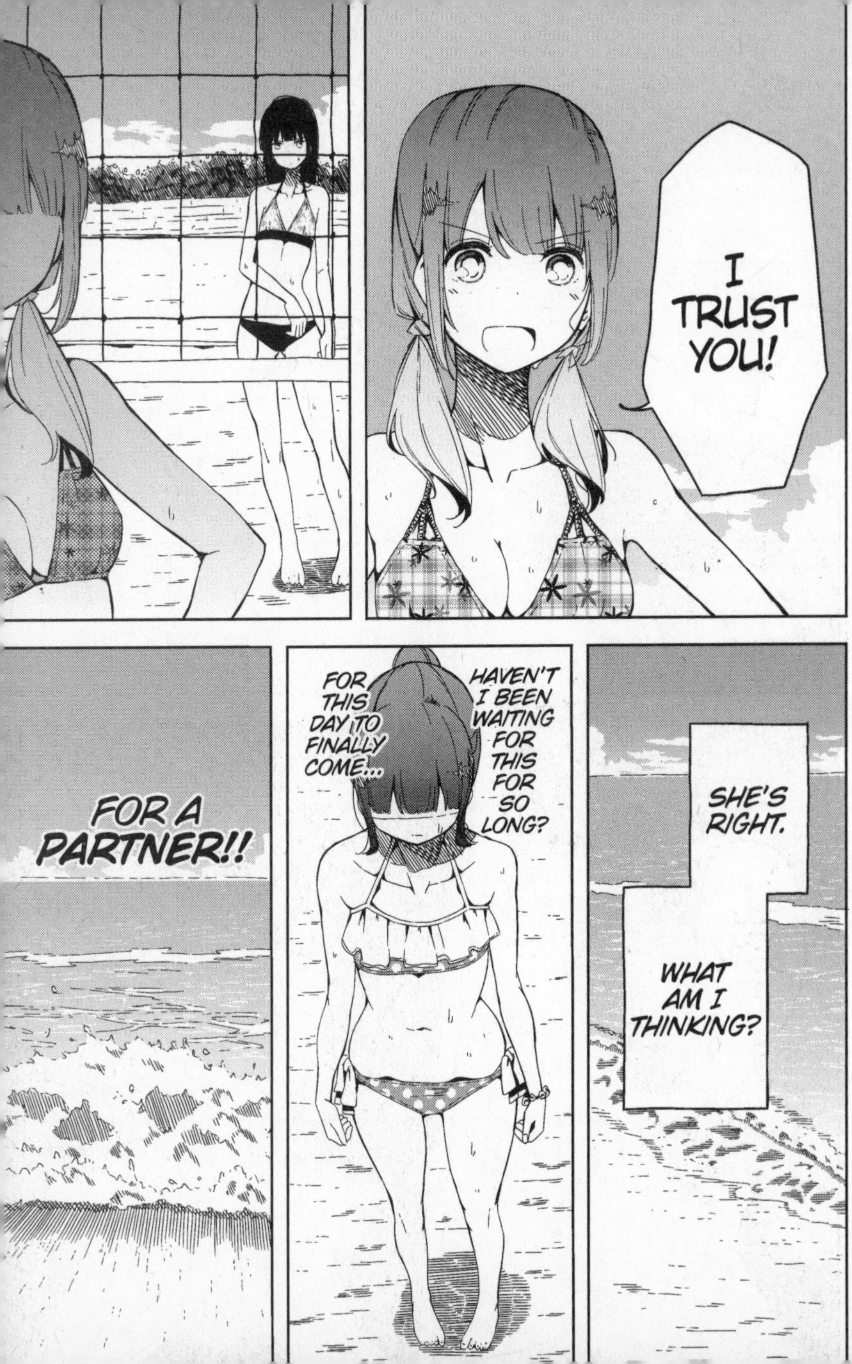
I TRUST YOU!
SHE'S RIGHT.
WHAT AM I THINKING?
HAVEN'T I BEEN WAITING FOR THIS FOR SO LONG?
FOR THIS DAY TO FINALLY COME...
FOR A PARTNER!!

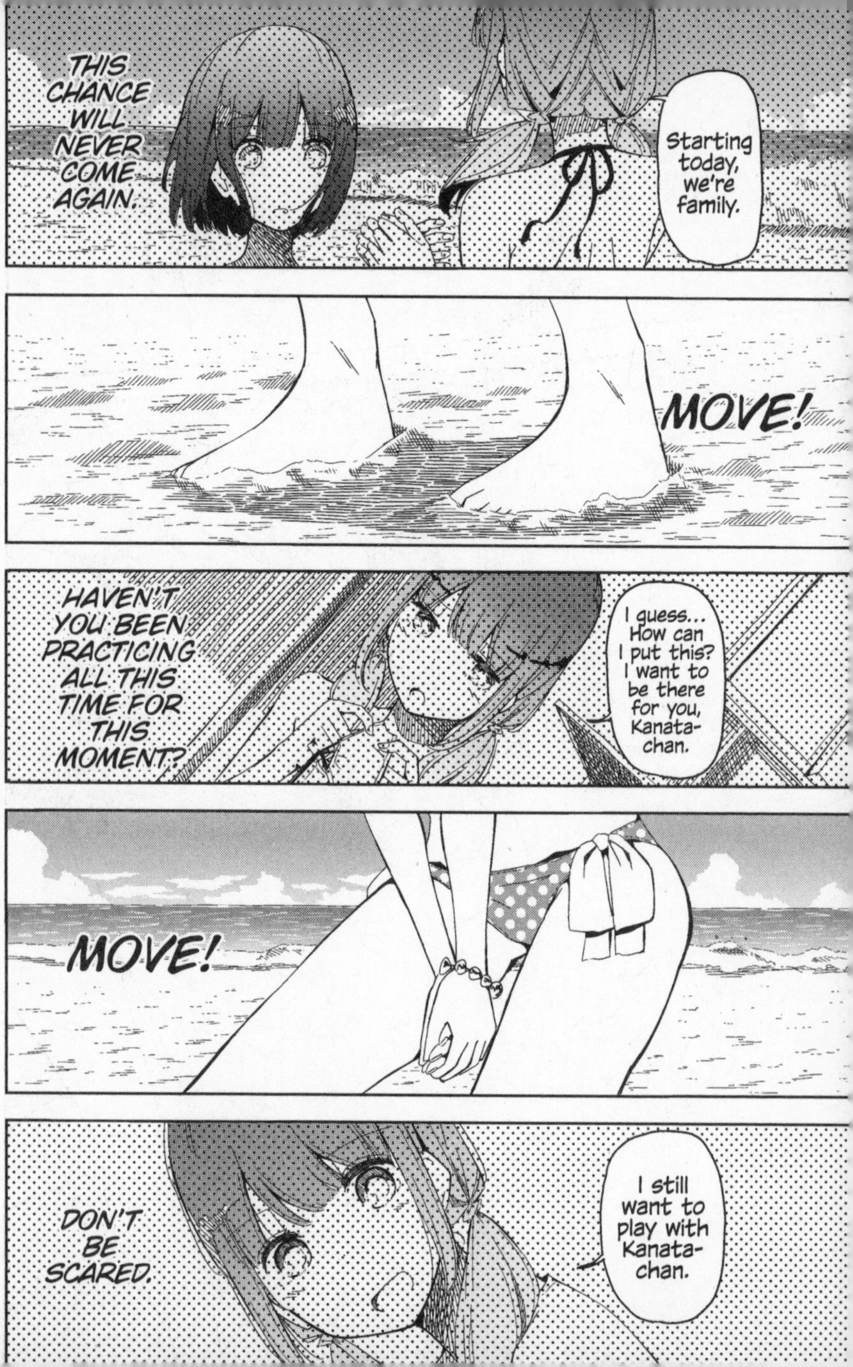
Starting today, we're family.
THIS CHANCE WILL NEVER COME AGAIN.
MOVE!
I guess... How can I put this? I want to be there for you, Kanata-chan.
HAVEN'T YOU BEEN PRACTICING ALL THIS TIME FOR THIS MOMENT?
MOVE!
I still want to play with Kanata-chan.
DON'T BE SCARED.

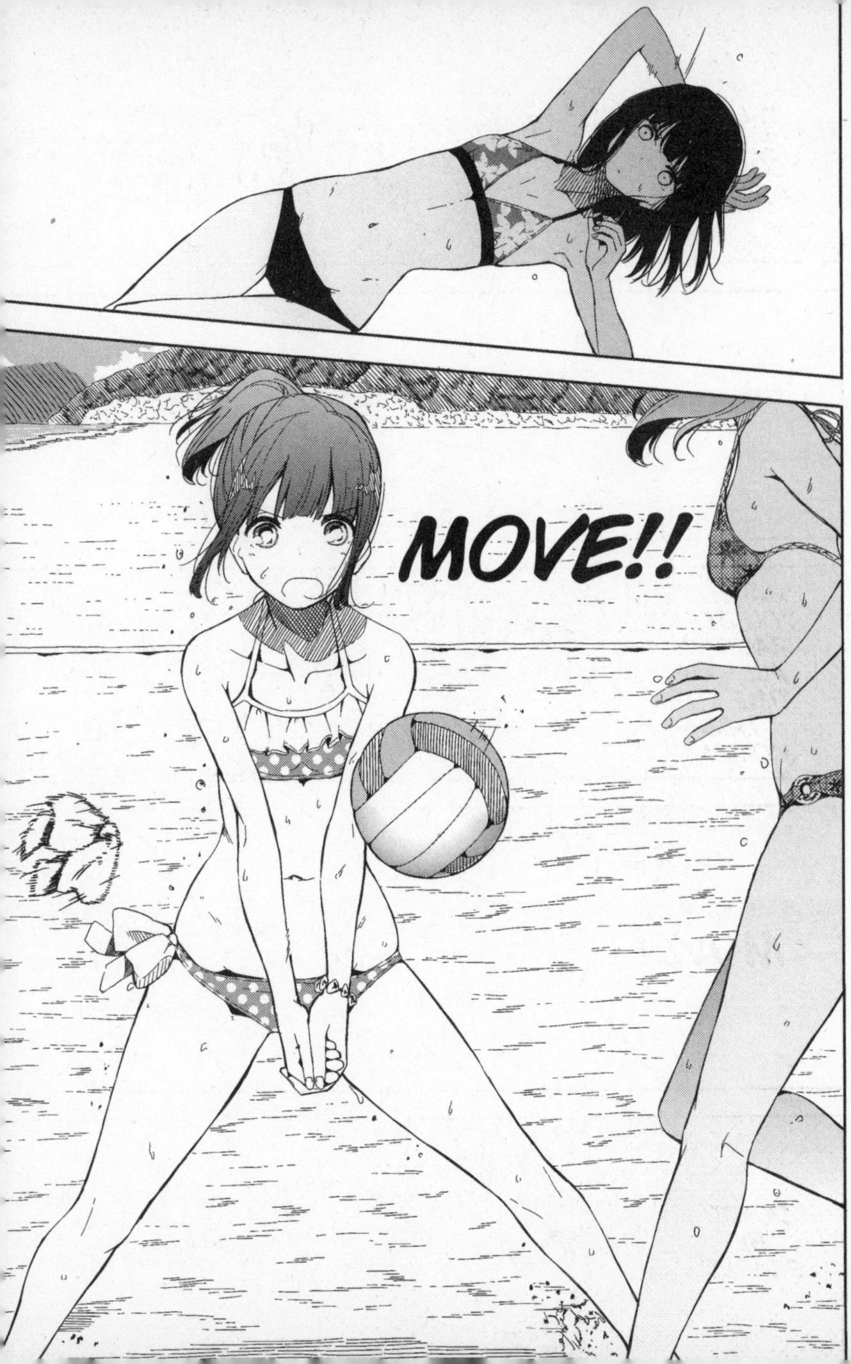
MOVE!!

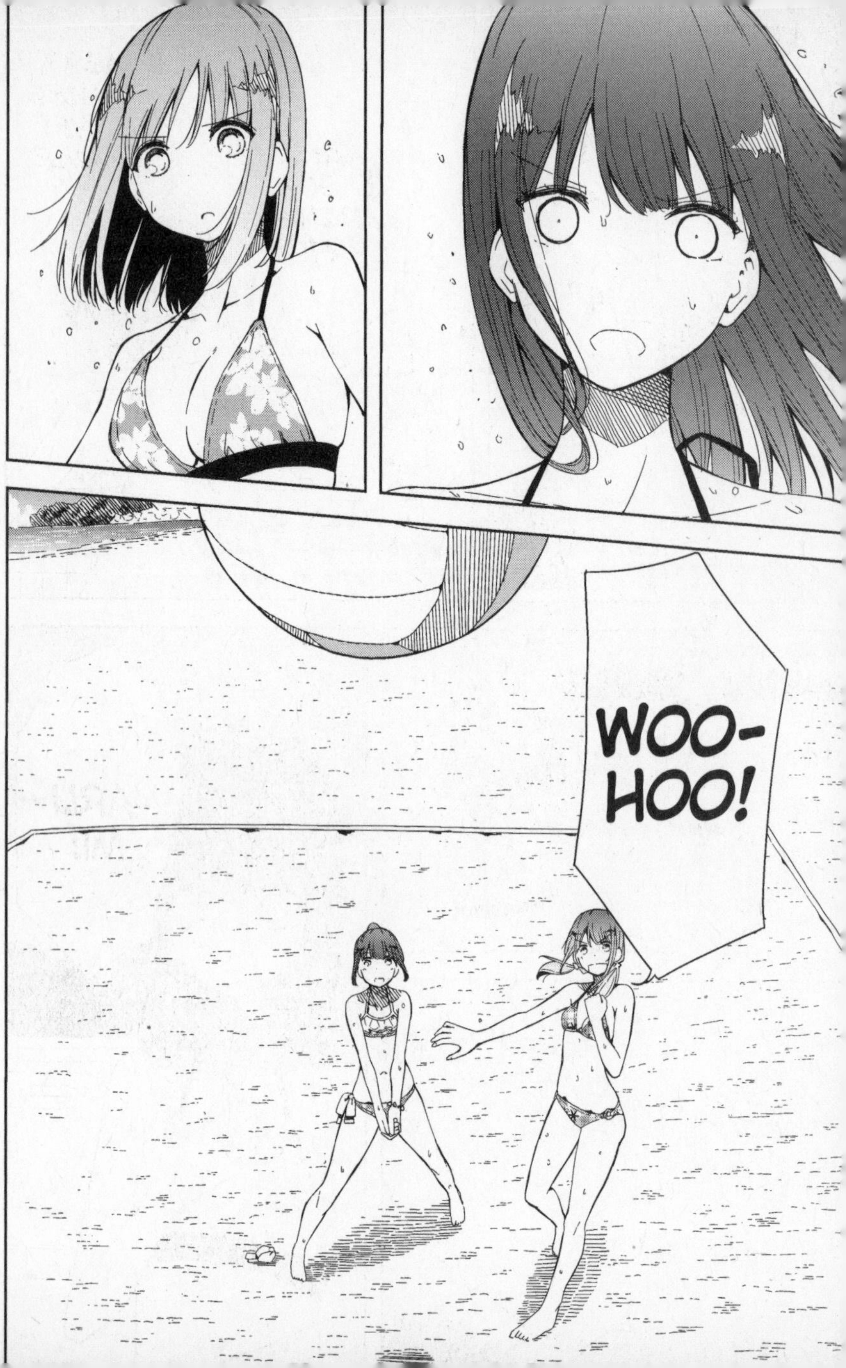
WOO-HOO!

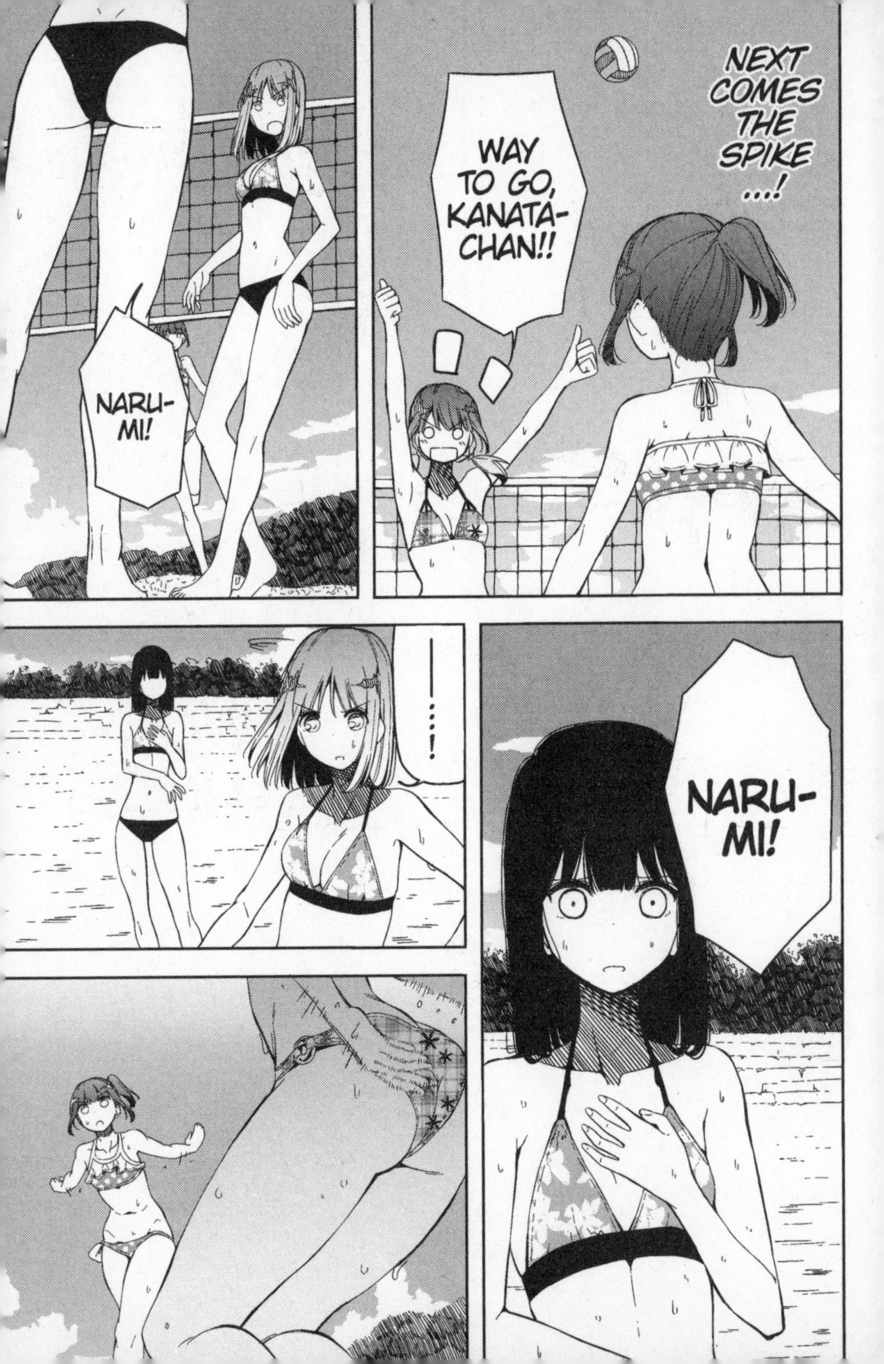
NEXT COMES THE SPIKE...!
WAY TO GO, KANATA-CHAN!!
NARUMI!
NARUMI!
...!

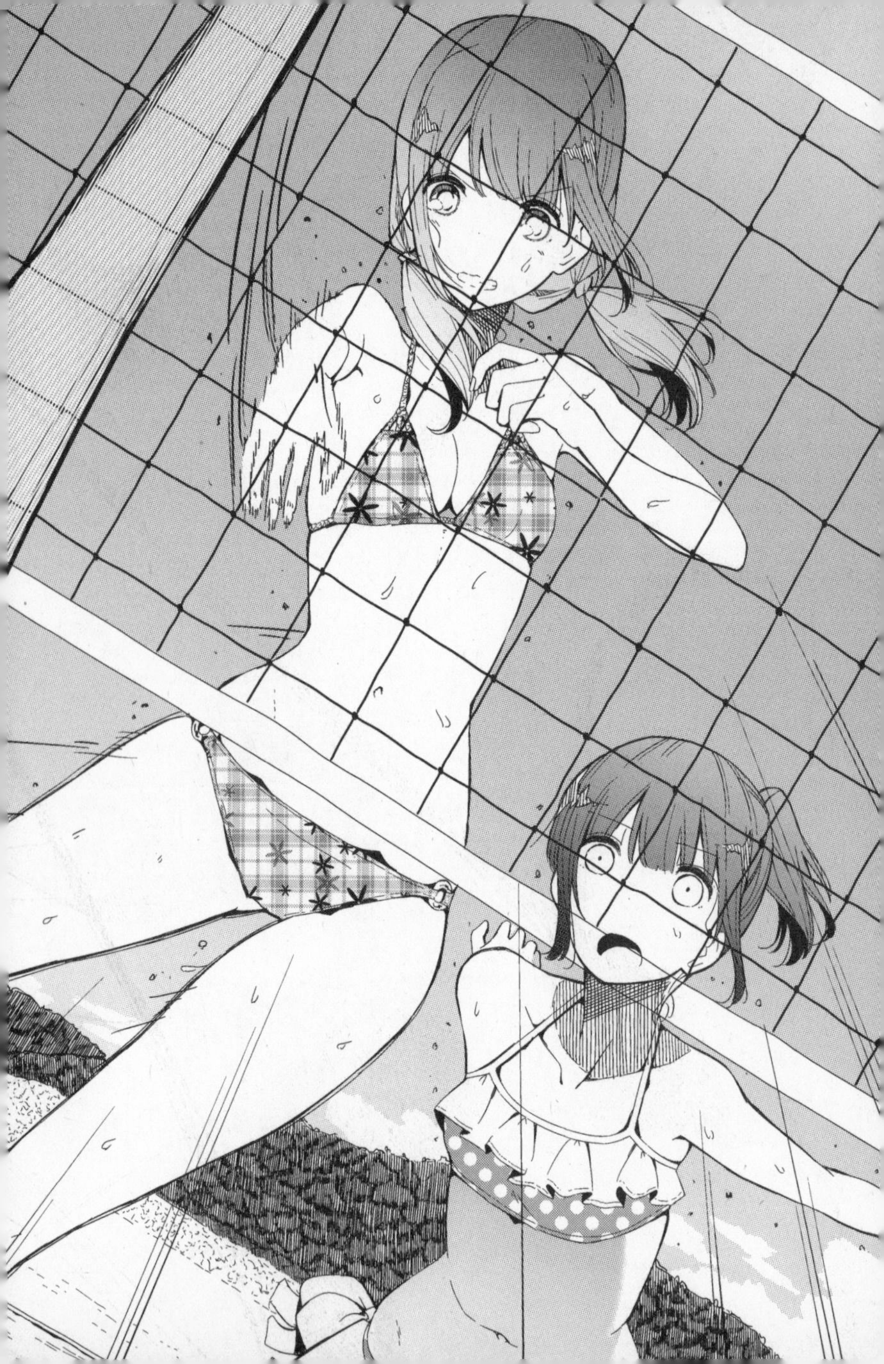

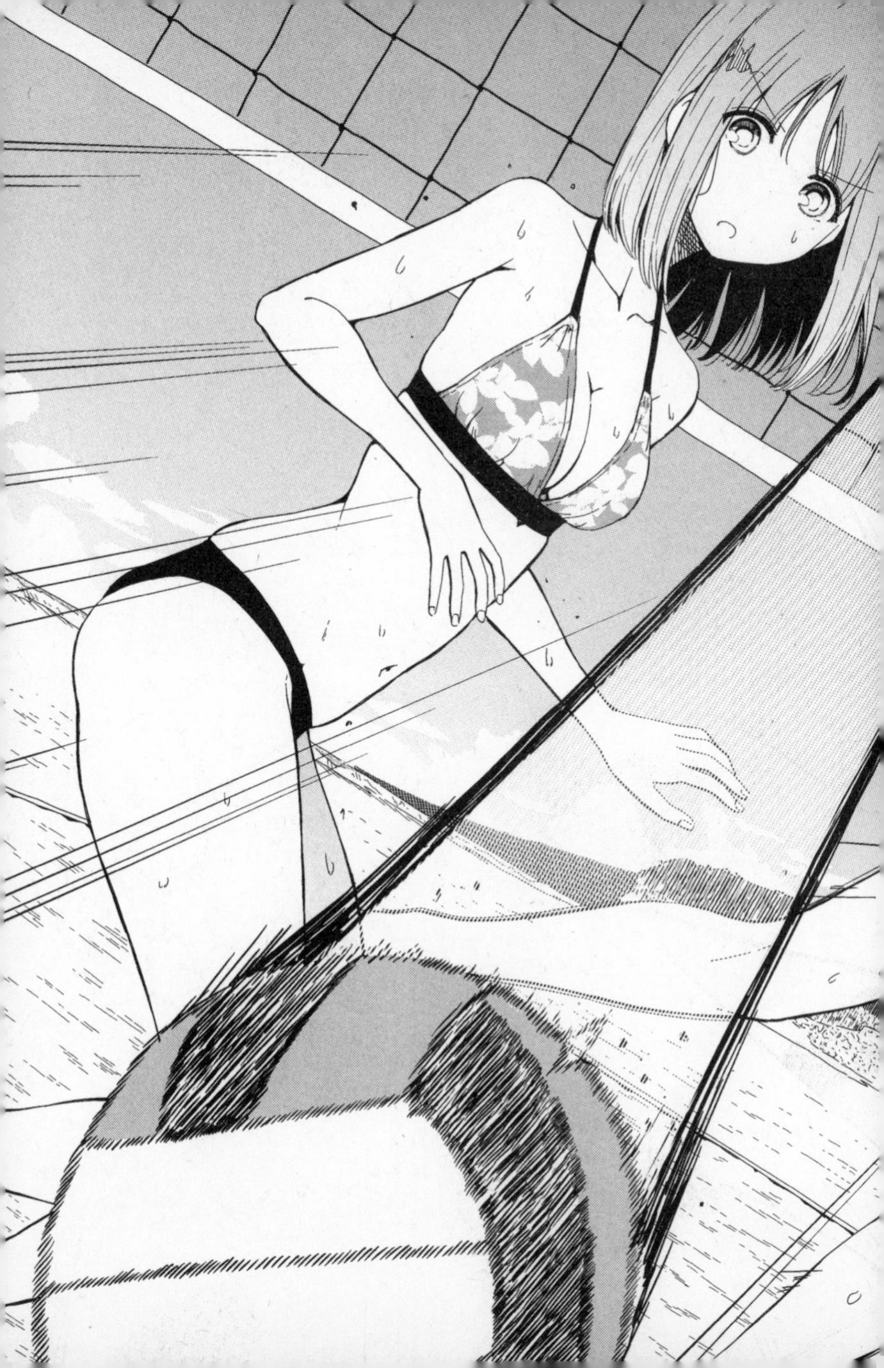

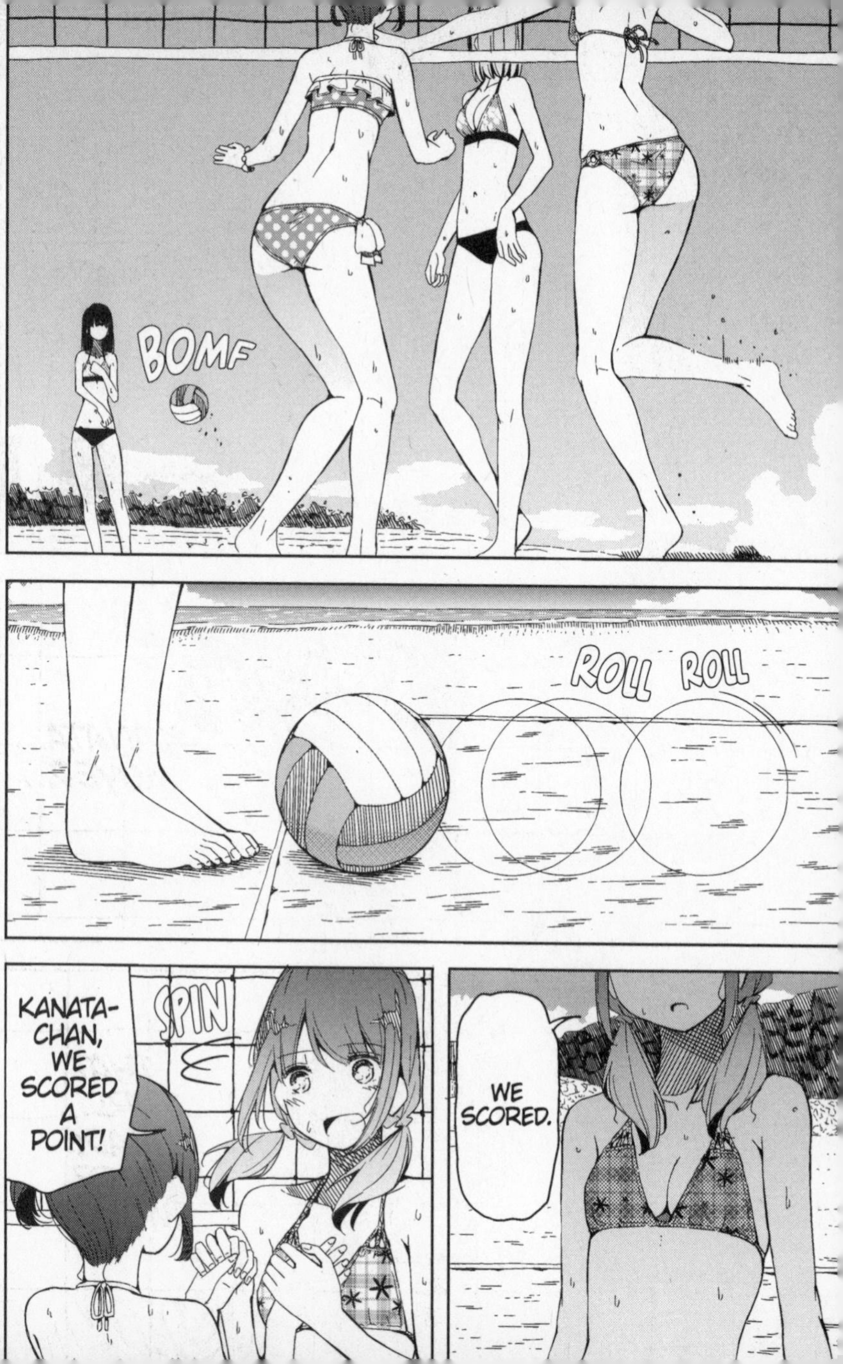
BOMF
ROLL ROLL
WE SCORED.
SPIN
KANATA-CHAN, WE SCORED A POINT!

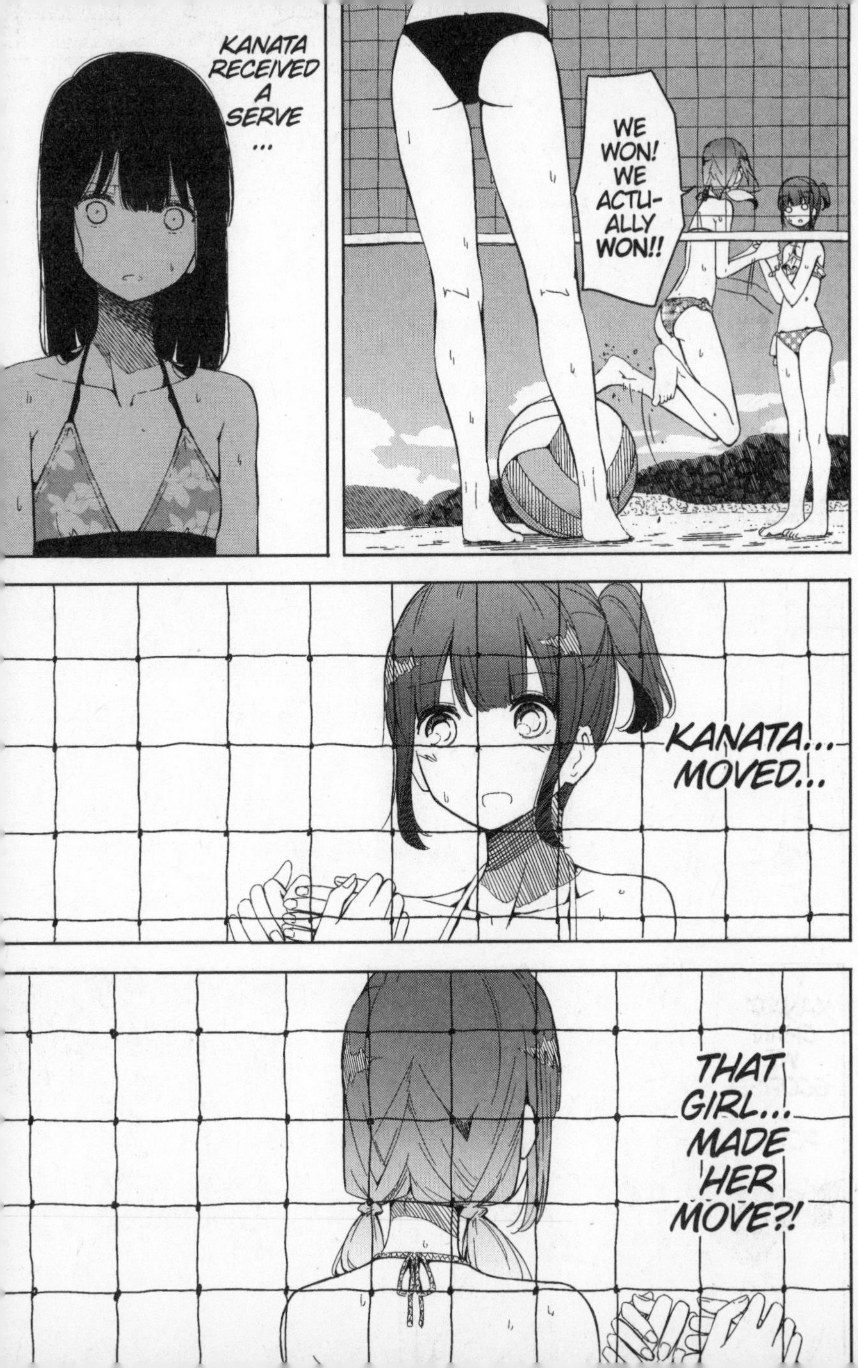
WE WON! WE ACTUALLY WON!!
KANATA RECEIVED A SERVE ...
KANATA... MOVED...
THAT GIRL... MADE HER MOVE?!

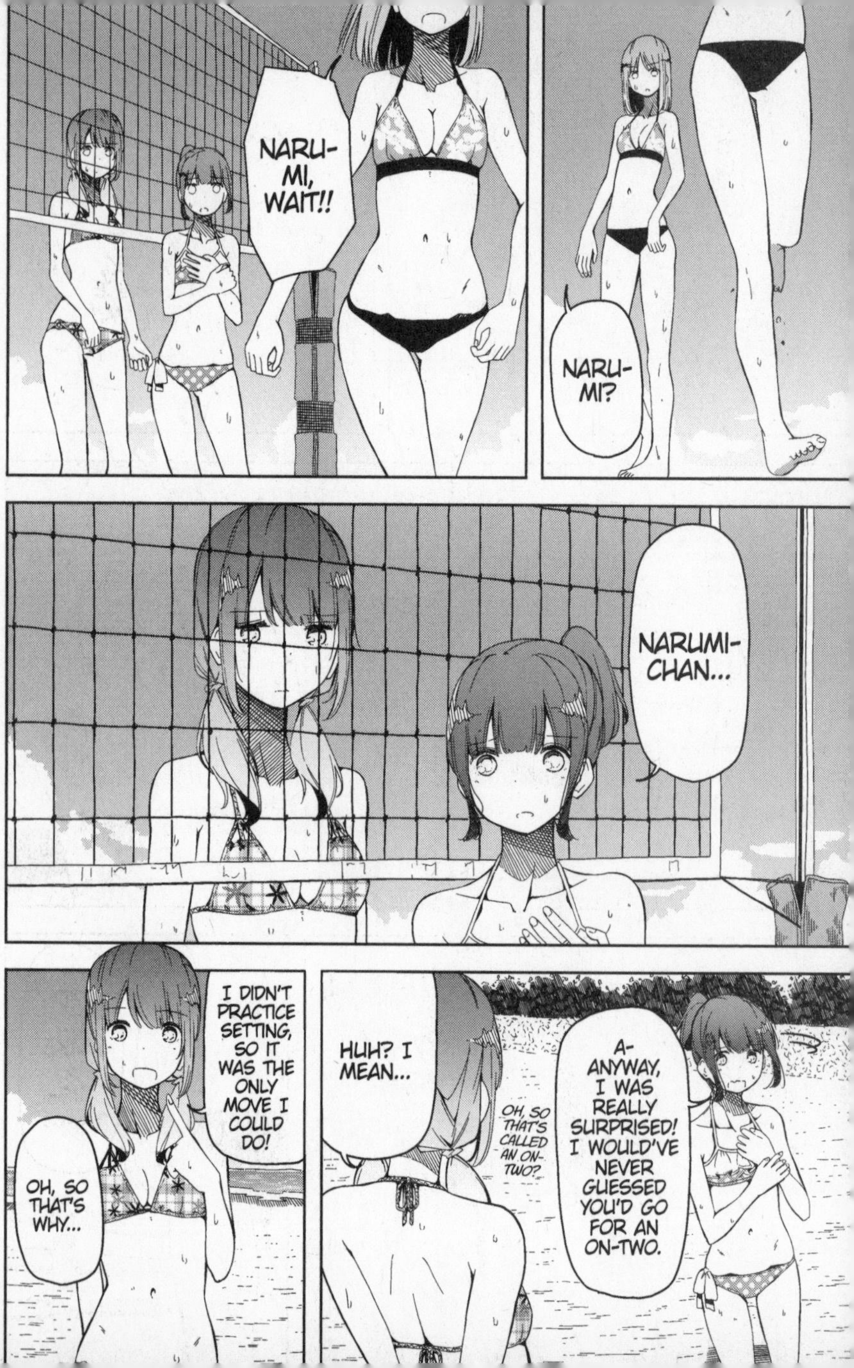
NARU-MI?
NARU-MI, WAIT!!
NARUMI-CHAN...
A-ANYWAY, I WAS REALLY SURPRISED! I WOULD'VE NEVER GUESSED YOU'D GO FOR AN ON-TWO.
OH, SO THAT'S CALLED AN ON-TWO?
HUH? I MEAN...
I DIDN'T PRACTICE SETTING, SO IT WAS THE ONLY MOVE I COULD DO!
OH, SO THAT'S WHY...

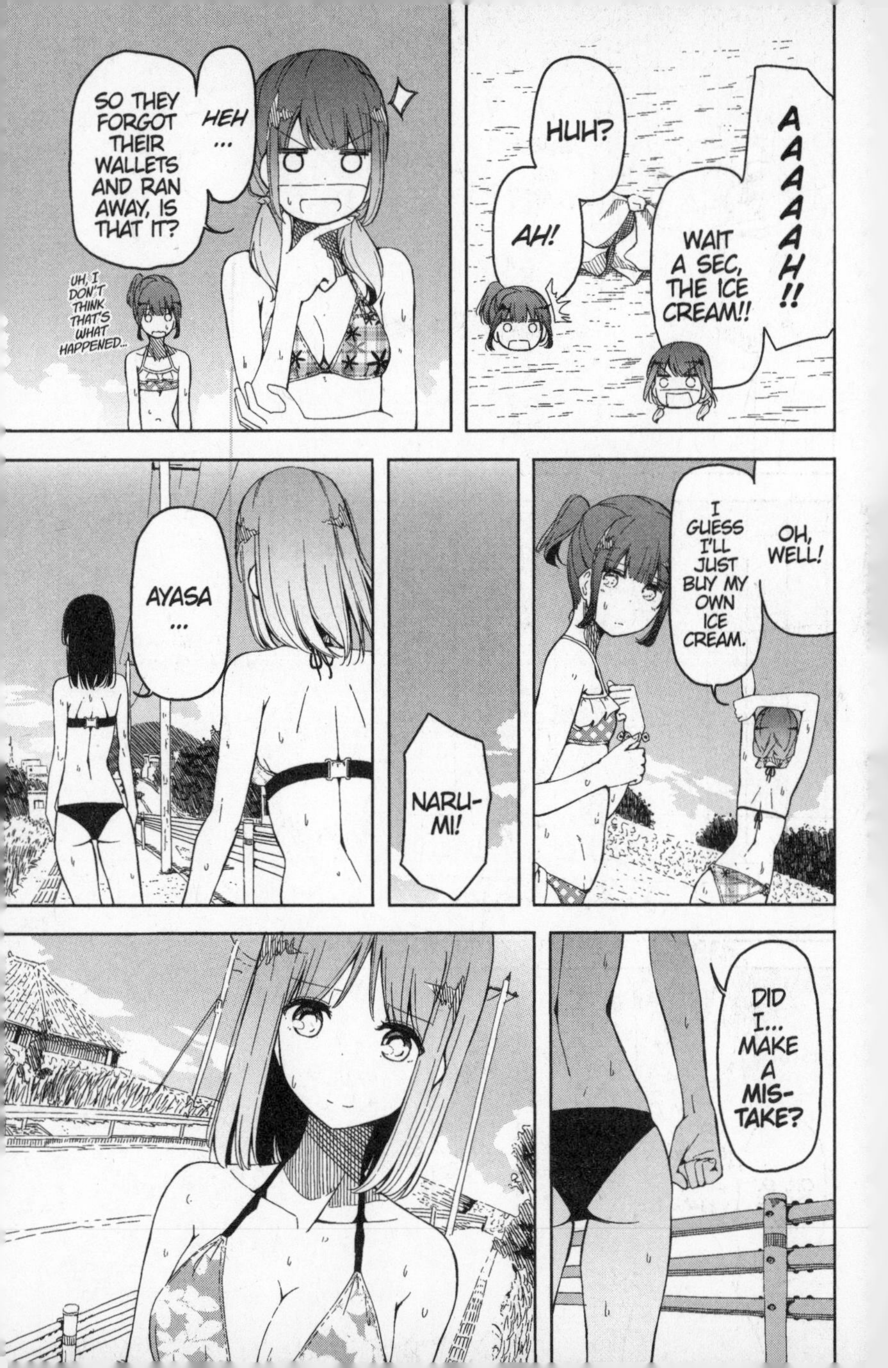
AAAAAAH!!
WAIT A SEC, THE ICE CREAM!!
HUH?
AH!
HEH ...
SO THEY FORGOT THEIR WALLETS AND RAN AWAY, IS THAT IT?
UH, I DON'T THINK THAT'S WHAT HAPPENED...
OH, WELL!
I GUESS I'LL JUST BUY MY OWN ICE CREAM.
NARU-MI!
AYASA ...
DID I... MAKE A MIS-TAKE?

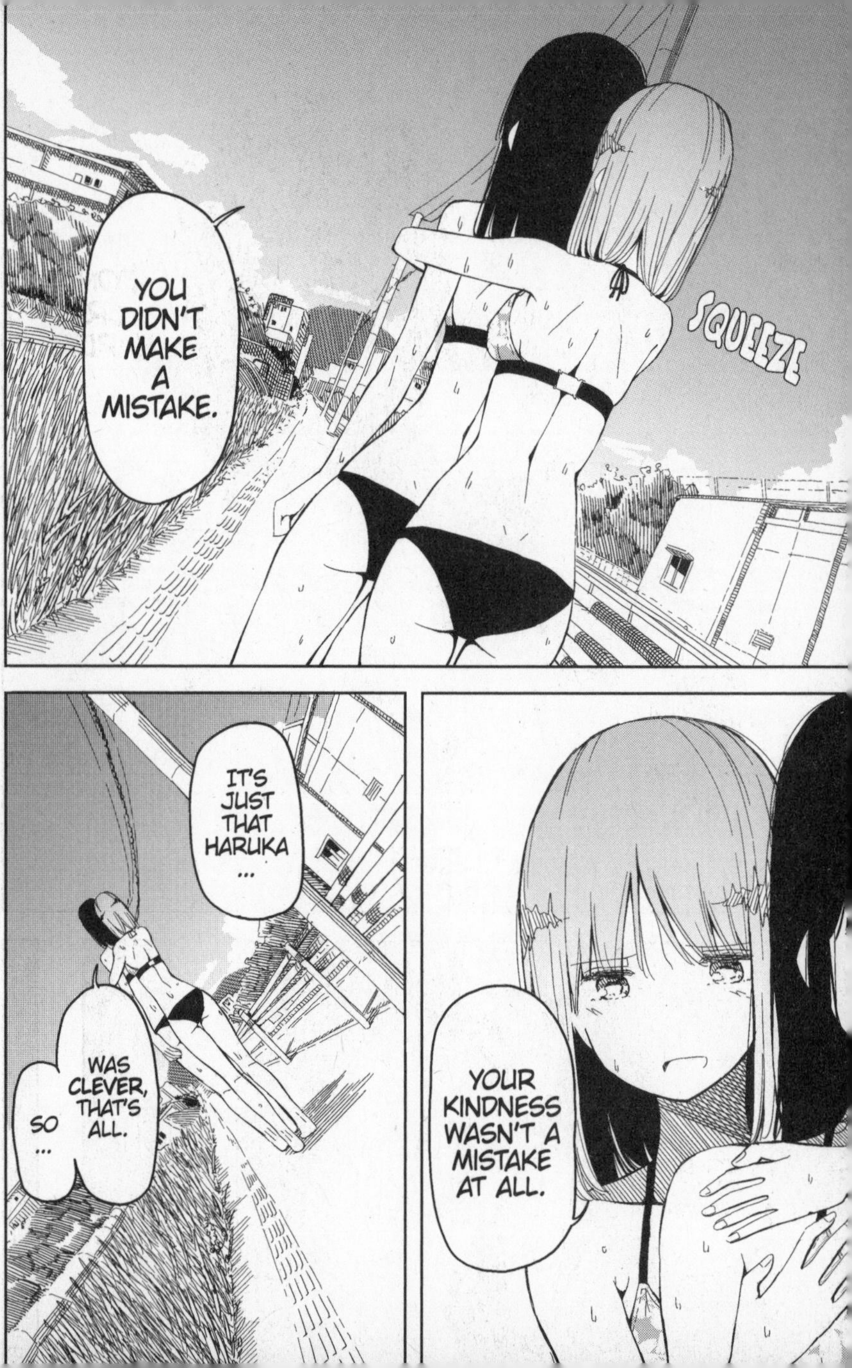
SQUEEZE
YOU DIDN'T MAKE A MISTAKE.
YOUR KINDNESS WASN'T A MISTAKE AT ALL.
IT'S JUST THAT HARUKA ...
WAS CLEVER, THAT'S ALL.
SO ...

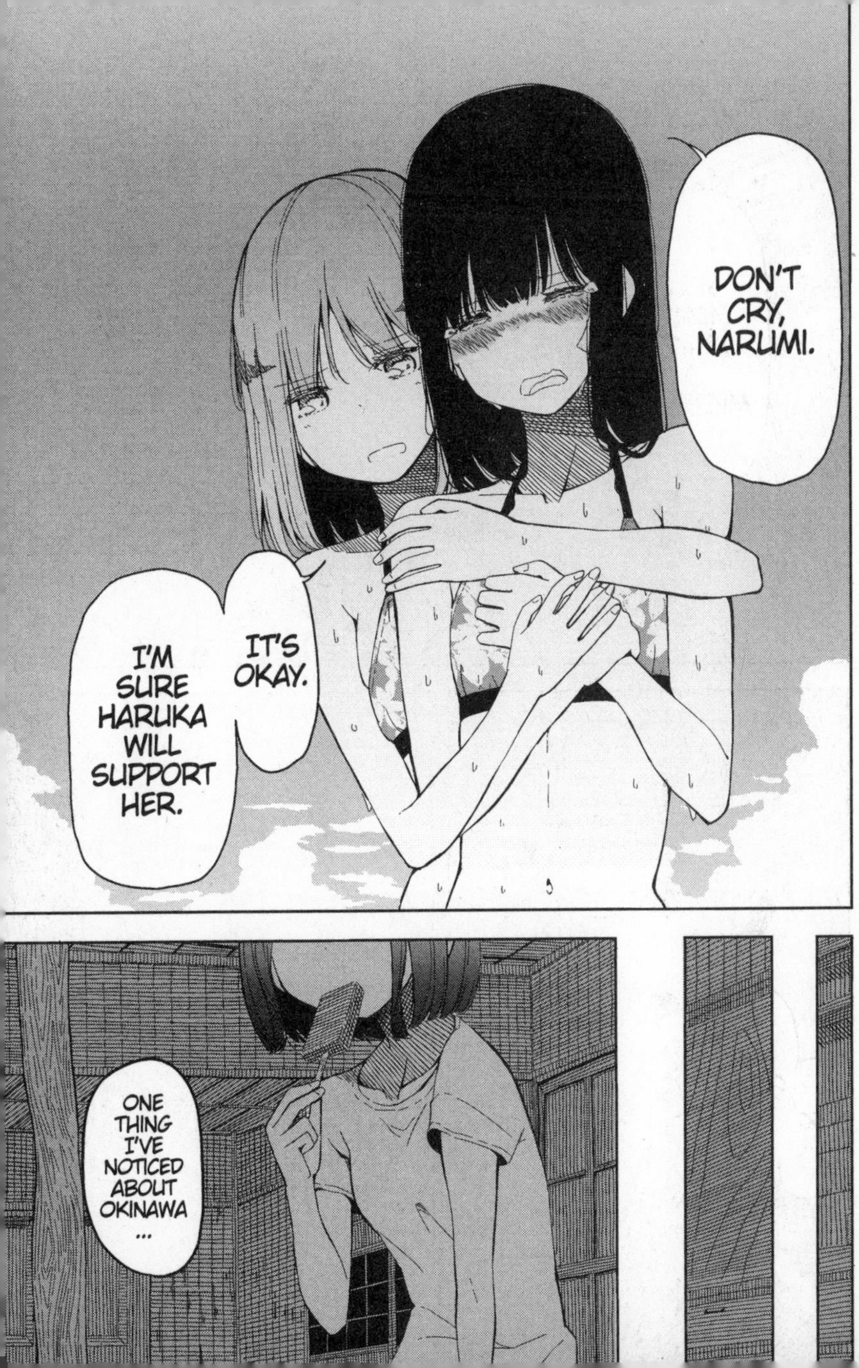
DON'T CRY, NARUMI.
IT'S OKAY.
I'M SURE HARUKA WILL SUPPORT HER.
ONE THING I'VE NOTICED ABOUT OKINAWA ...

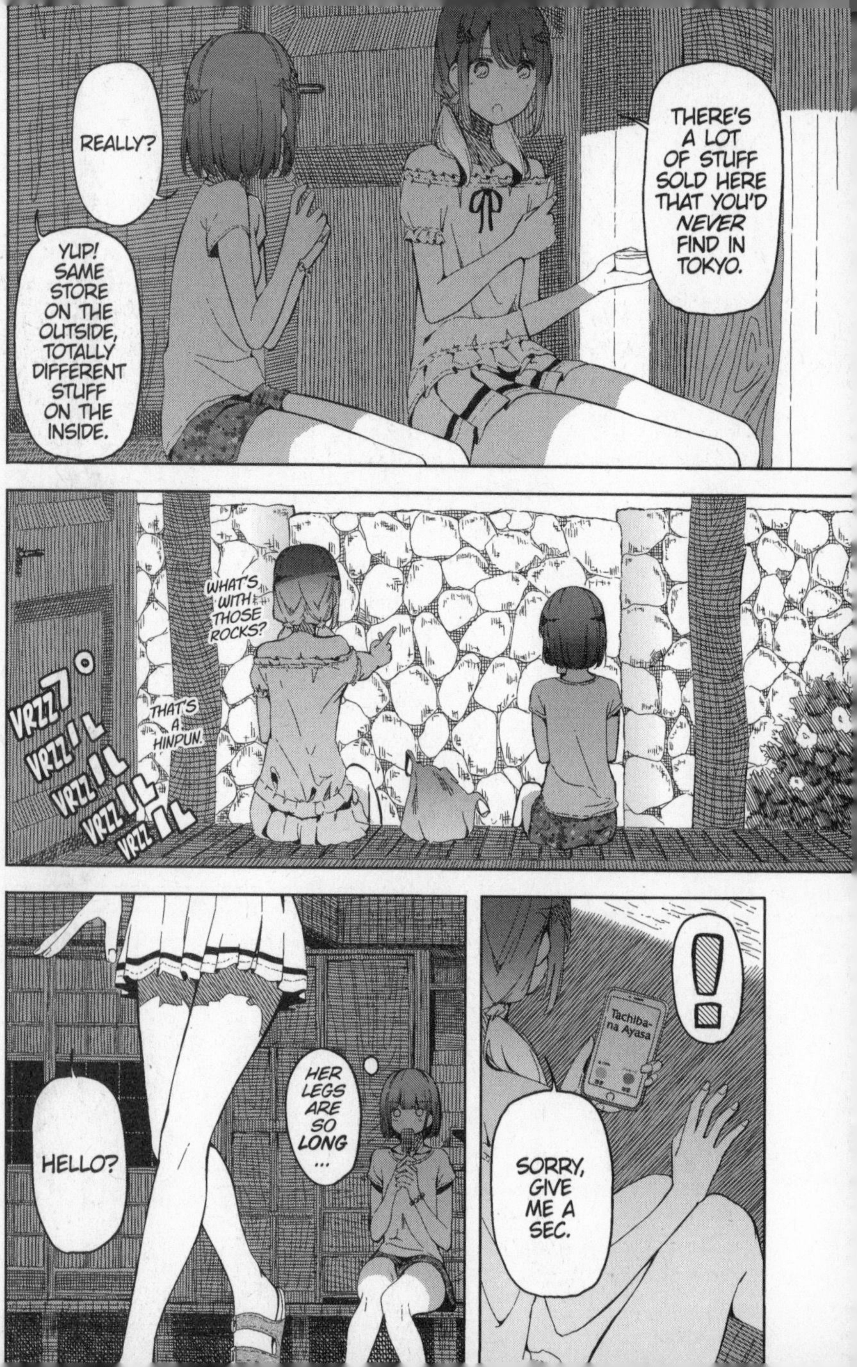
THERE'S A LOT OF STUFF SOLD HERE THAT YOU'D *NEVER* FIND IN TOKYO.
REALLY?
YUP! SAME STORE ON THE OUTSIDE, TOTALLY DIFFERENT STUFF ON THE INSIDE.
WHAT'S WITH THOSE ROCKS?
THAT'S A HINPUN.
VRZZ
VRZZ
VRZZ
VRZZ
VRZZ
!
Tachibana Ayasa
SORRY, GIVE ME A SEC.
HER LEGS ARE SO LONG...
HELLO?

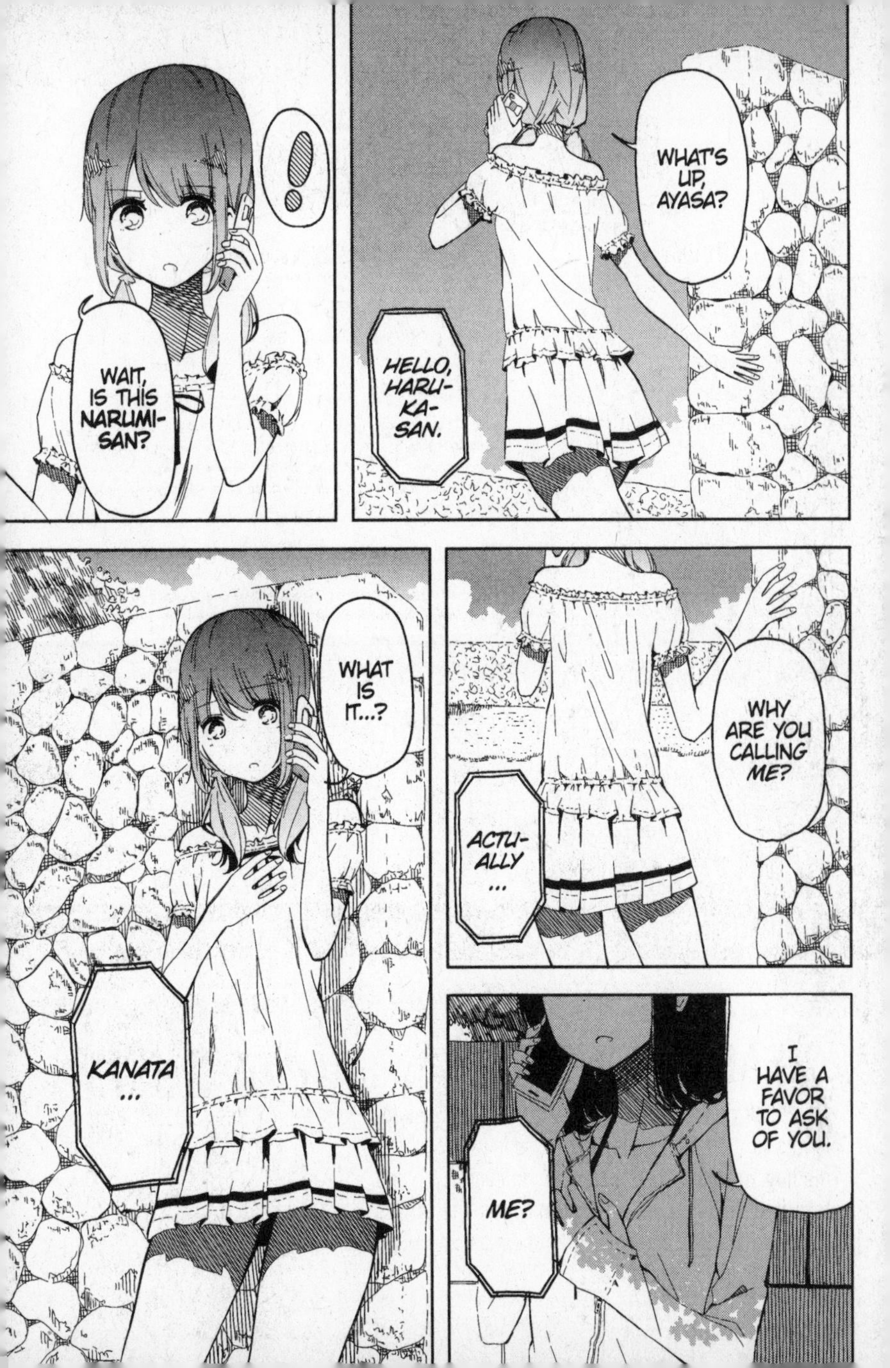
WHAT'S UP, AYASA?
HELLO, HARU-KA-SAN.
!
WAIT, IS THIS NARUMI-SAN?
WHY ARE YOU CALLING ME?
ACTU-ALLY ...
I HAVE A FAVOR TO ASK OF YOU.
ME?
WHAT IS IT...?
KANATA ...

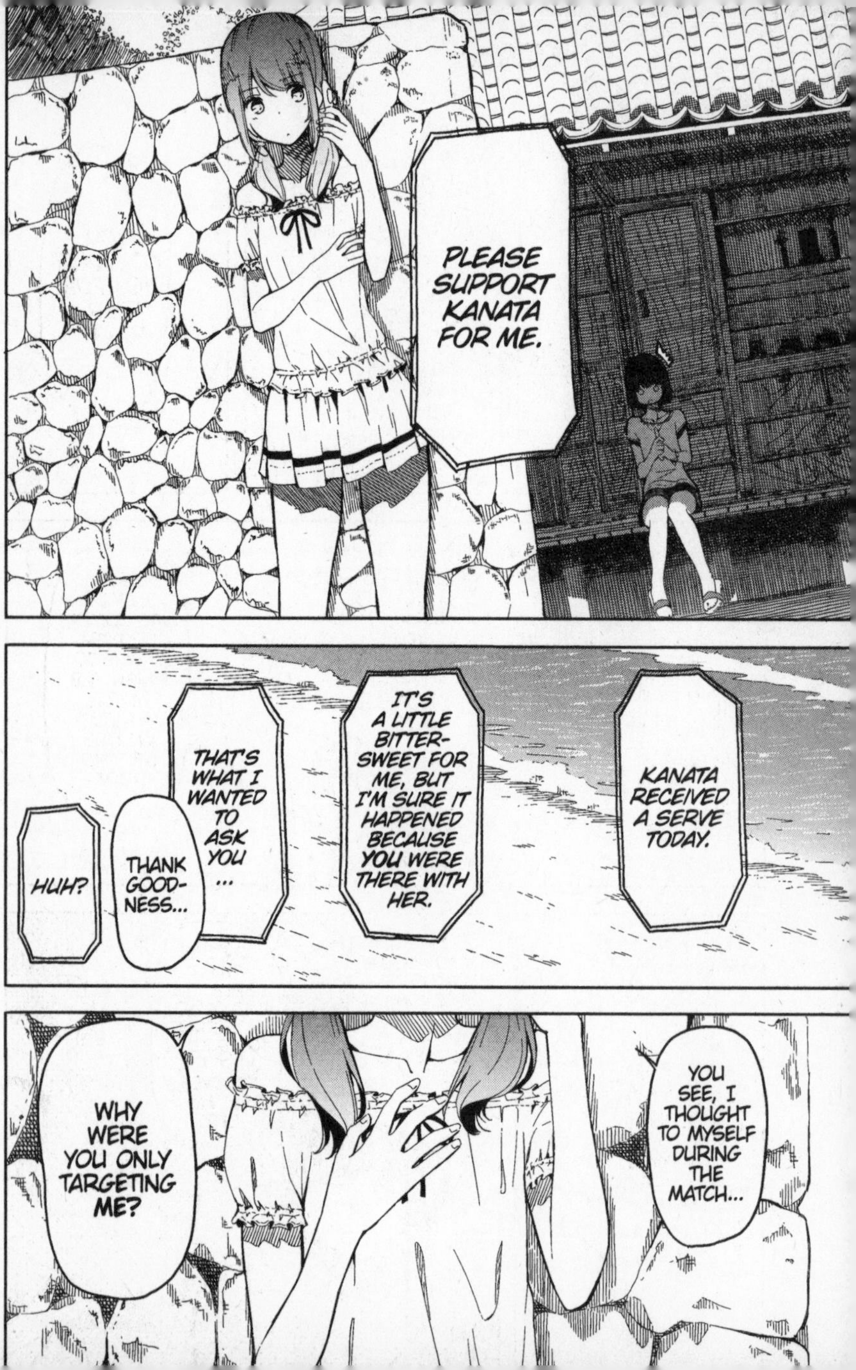
PLEASE SUPPORT KANATA FOR ME.
KANATA RECEIVED A SERVE TODAY.
IT'S A LITTLE BITTER-SWEET FOR ME, BUT I'M SURE IT HAPPENED BECAUSE YOU WERE THERE WITH HER.
THAT'S WHAT I WANTED TO ASK YOU...
THANK GOODNESS...
HUH?
YOU SEE, I THOUGHT TO MYSELF DURING THE MATCH...
WHY WERE YOU ONLY TARGETING ME?

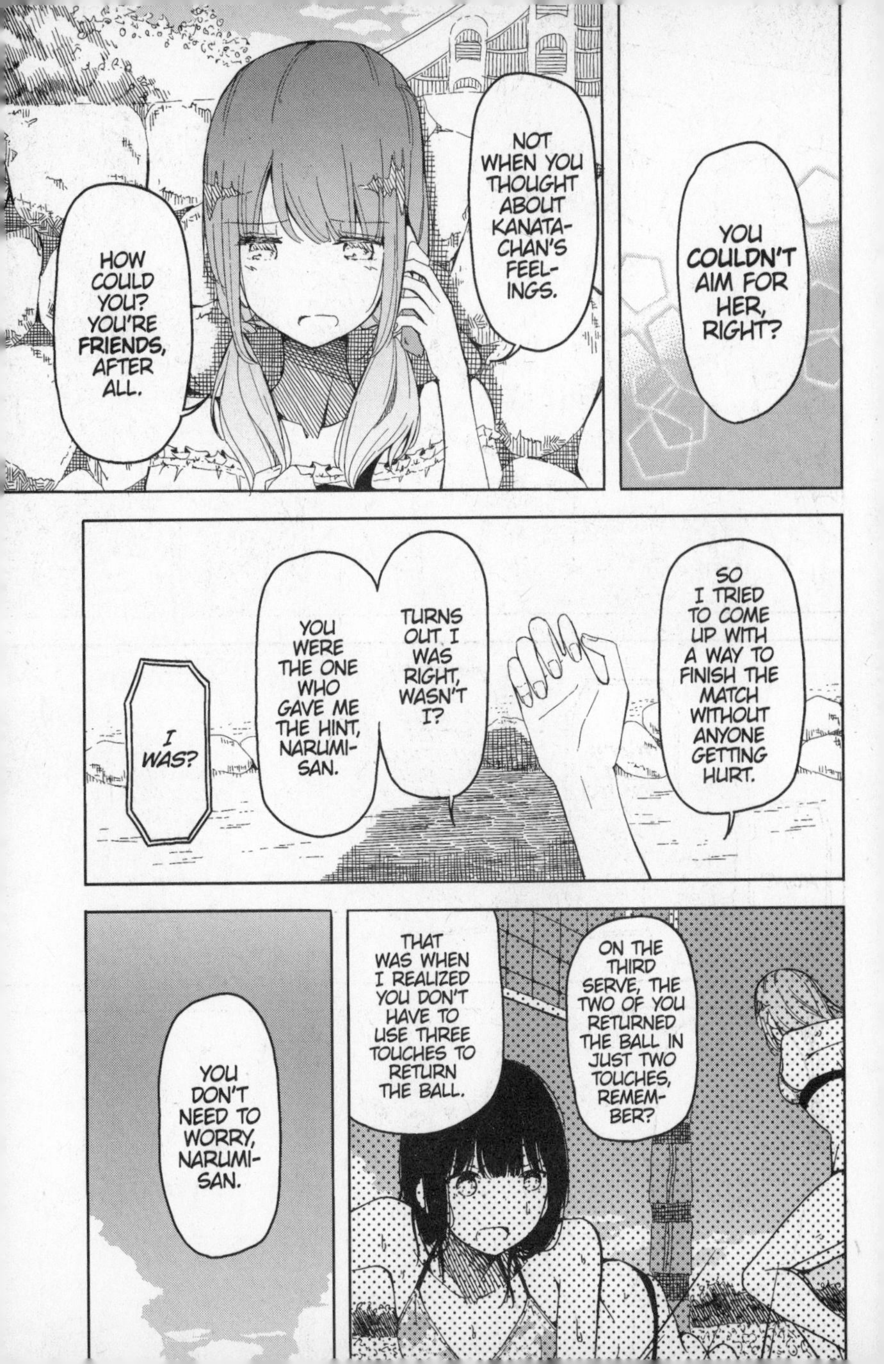
YOU COULDN'T AIM FOR HER, RIGHT?
NOT WHEN YOU THOUGHT ABOUT KANATA-CHAN'S FEELINGS.
HOW COULD YOU? YOU'RE FRIENDS, AFTER ALL.
SO I TRIED TO COME UP WITH A WAY TO FINISH THE MATCH WITHOUT ANYONE GETTING HURT.
TURNS OUT I WAS RIGHT, WASN'T I?
YOU WERE THE ONE WHO GAVE ME THE HINT, NARUMI-SAN.
I WAS?
ON THE THIRD SERVE, THE TWO OF YOU RETURNED THE BALL IN JUST TWO TOUCHES, REMEMBER?
THAT WAS WHEN I REALIZED YOU DON'T HAVE TO USE THREE TOUCHES TO RETURN THE BALL.
YOU DON'T NEED TO WORRY, NARUMI-SAN.

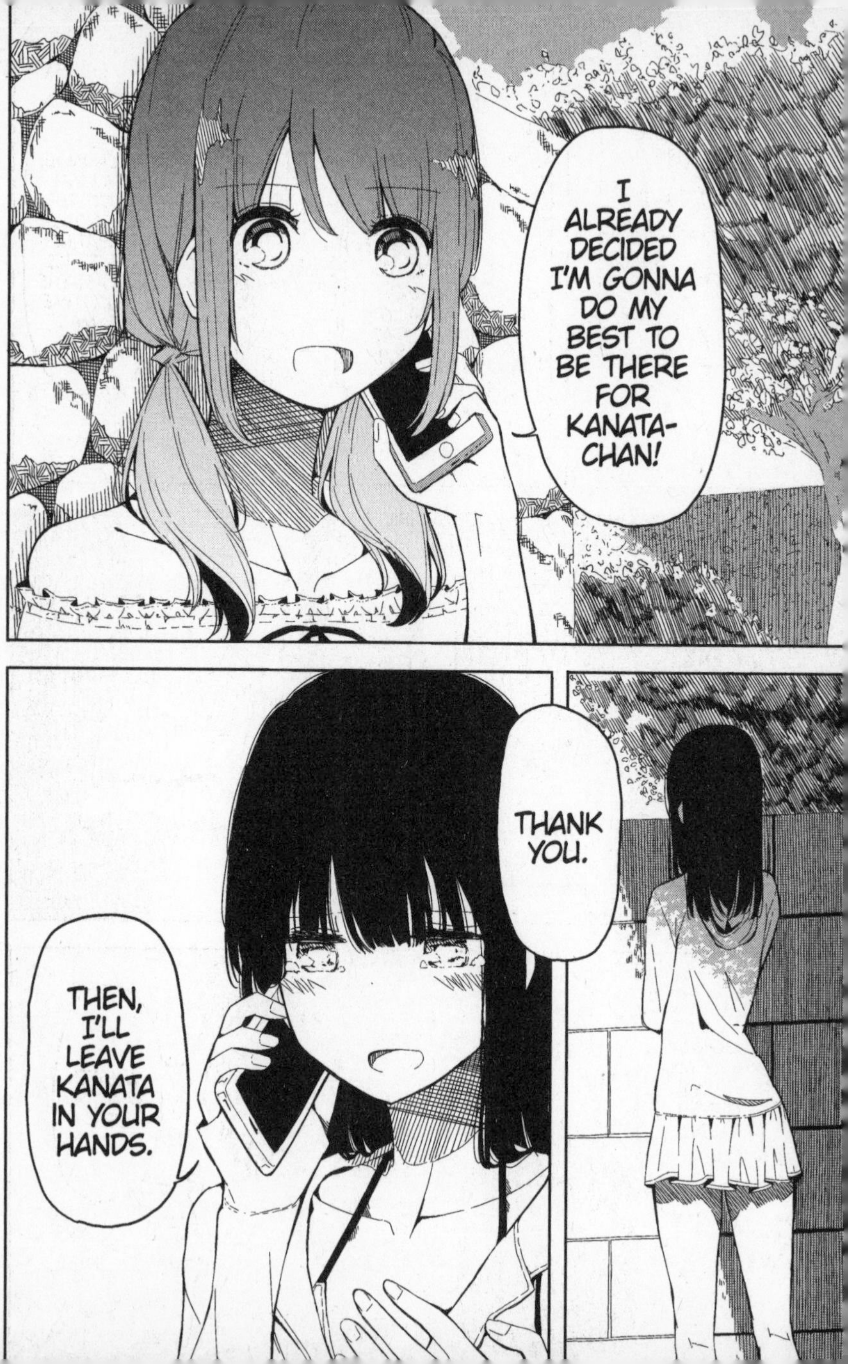
I ALREADY DECIDED I'M GONNA DO MY BEST TO BE THERE FOR KANATA-CHAN!
THANK YOU.
THEN, I'LL LEAVE KANATA IN YOUR HANDS.

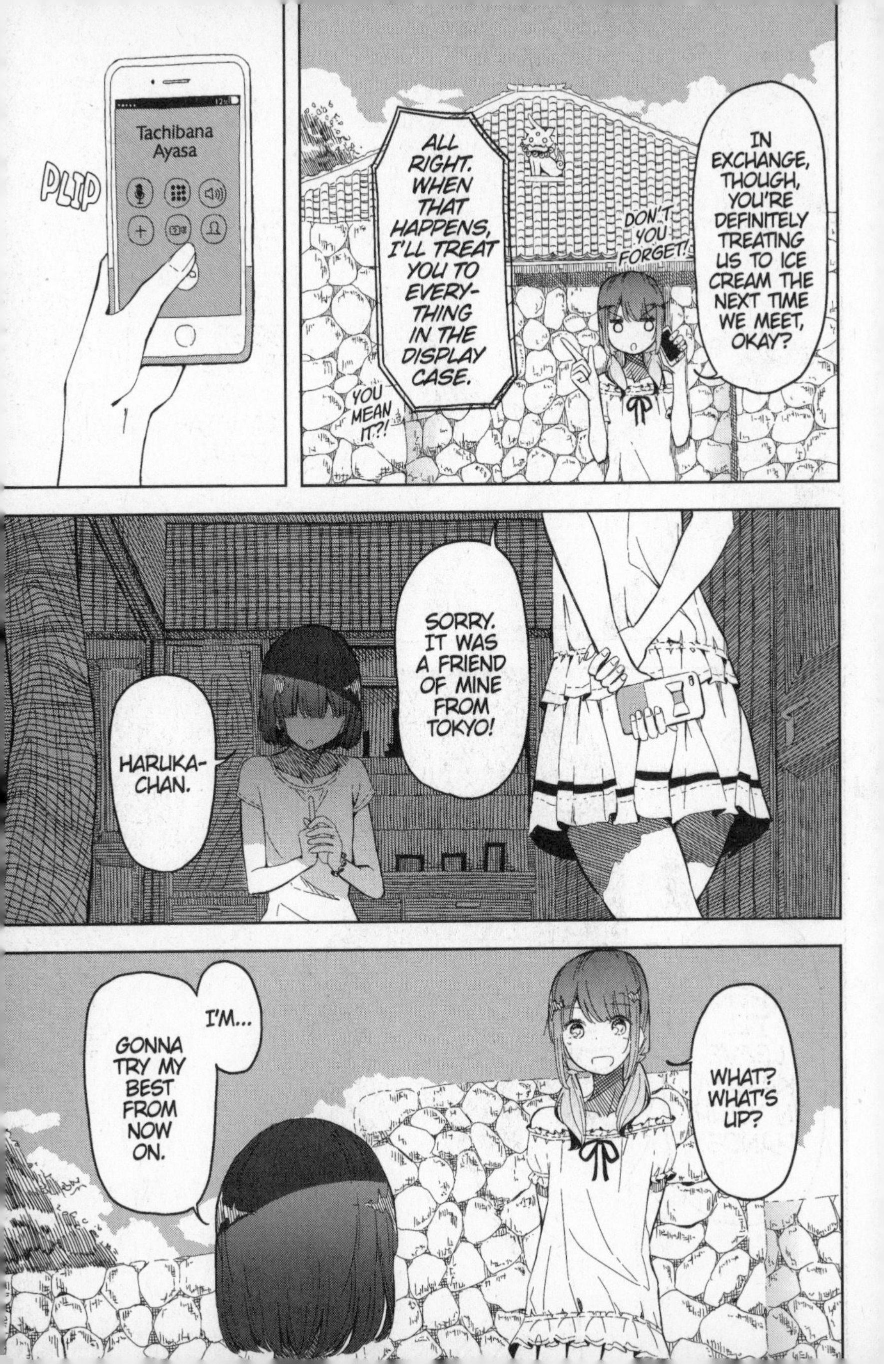
IN EXCHANGE, THOUGH, YOU'RE DEFINITELY TREATING US TO ICE CREAM THE NEXT TIME WE MEET, OKAY?
DON'T YOU FORGET!
ALL RIGHT. WHEN THAT HAPPENS, I'LL TREAT YOU TO EVERY-THING IN THE DISPLAY CASE.
YOU MEAN IT?!
Tachibana Ayasa
PLIP
SORRY. IT WAS A FRIEND OF MINE FROM TOKYO!
HARUKA-CHAN.
WHAT? WHAT'S UP?
I'M...
GONNA TRY MY BEST FROM NOW ON.

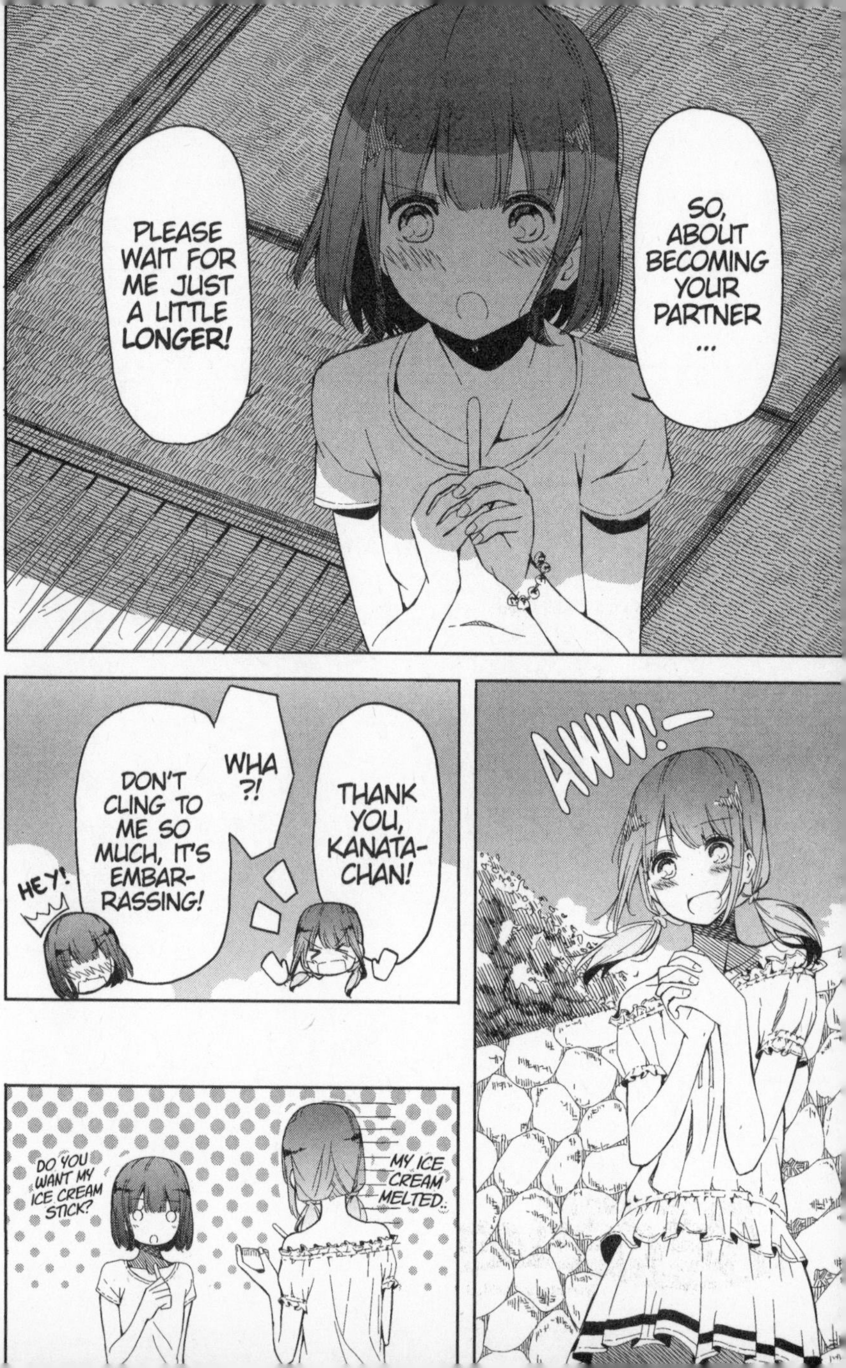
SO, ABOUT BECOMING YOUR PARTNER ...
PLEASE WAIT FOR ME JUST A LITTLE LONGER!
AWW!—
THANK YOU, KANATA-CHAN!
WHA ?!
DON'T CLING TO ME SO MUCH, IT'S EMBARRASSING!
HEY!
MY ICE CREAM MELTED..
DO YOU WANT MY ICE CREAM STICK?

Harukana★Receive

Presented by Nyoijizai

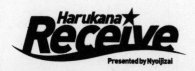

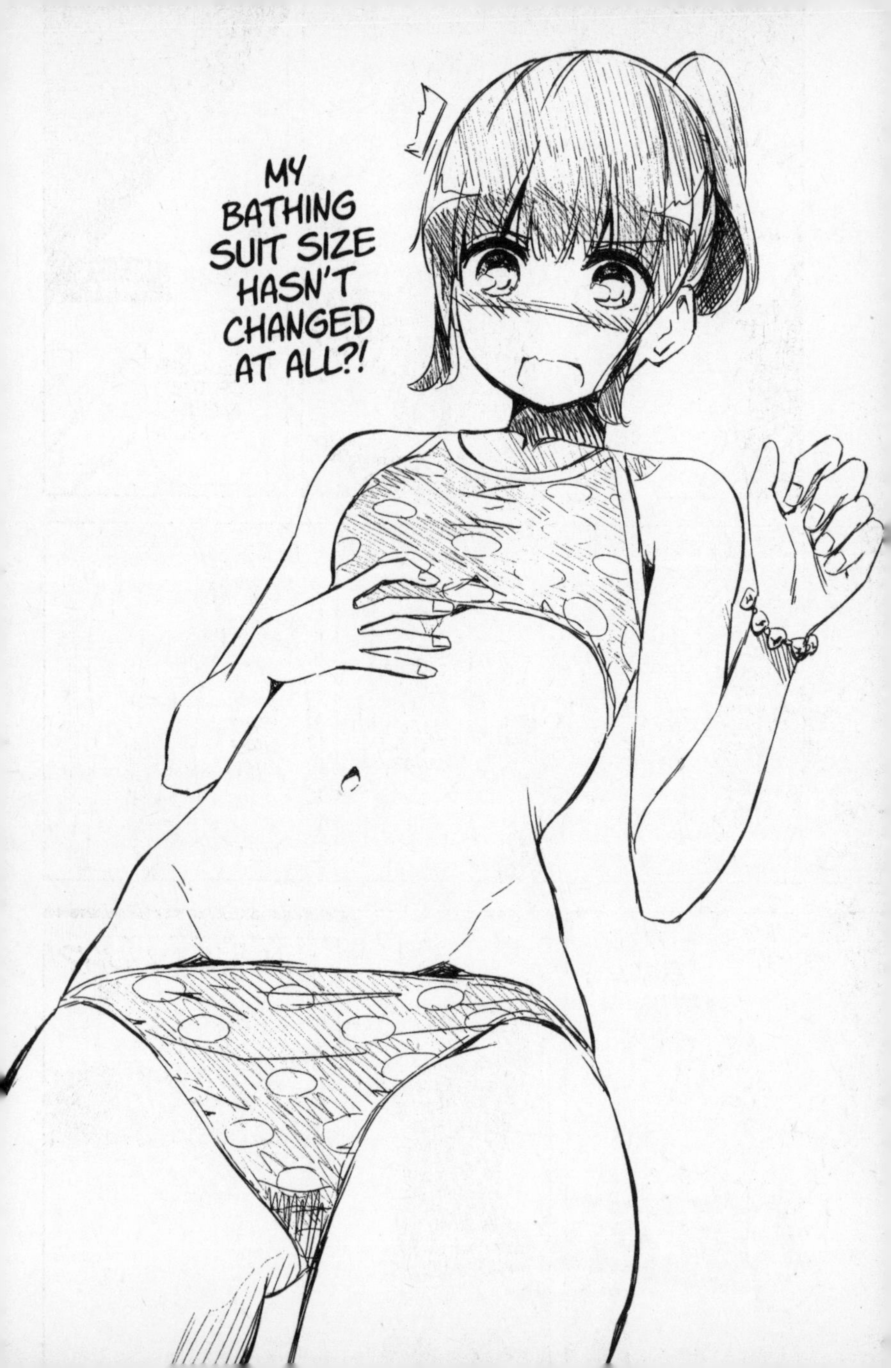
MY BATHING SUIT SIZE HASN'T CHANGED AT ALL?!

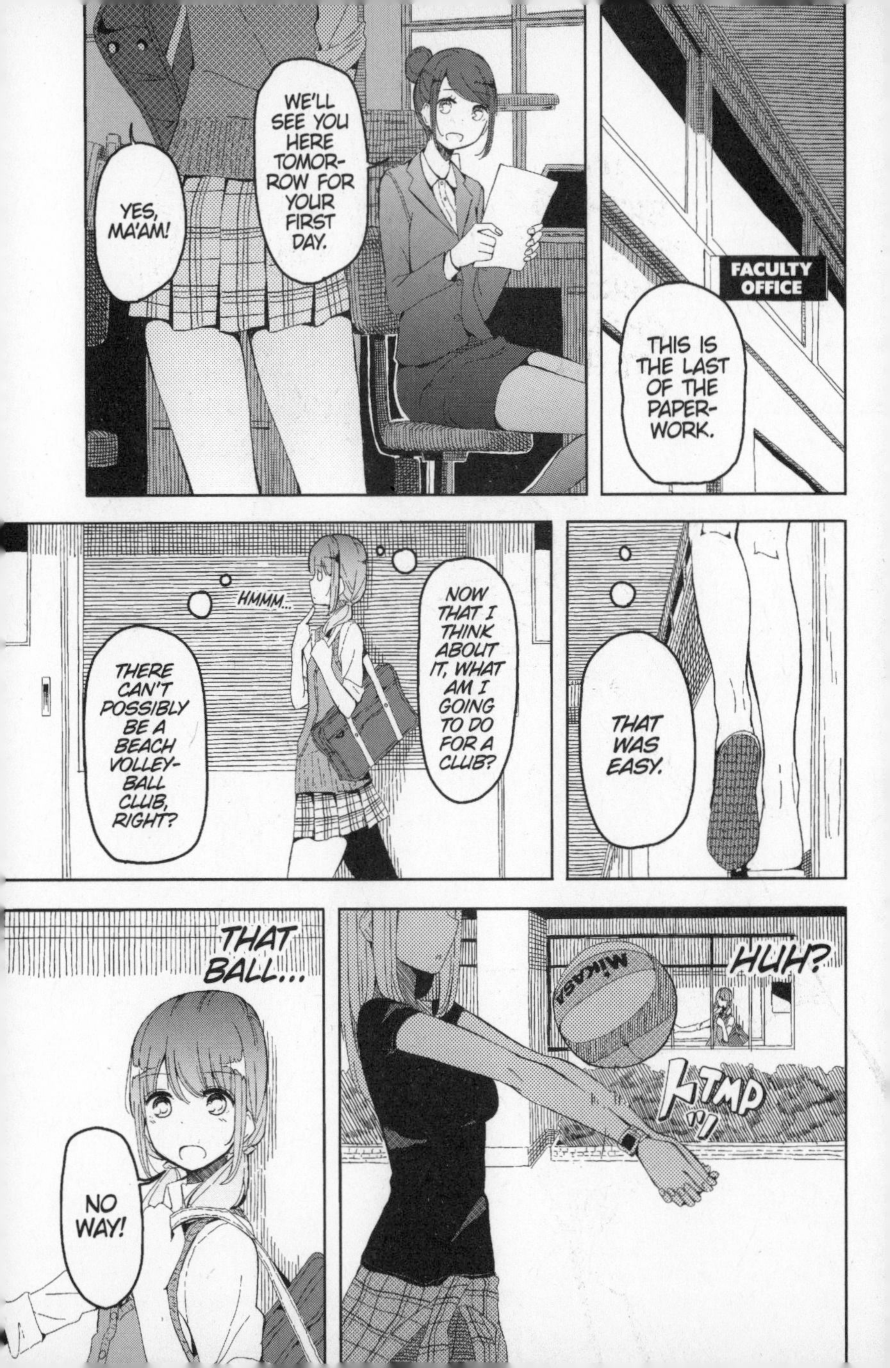
FACULTY OFFICE
THIS IS THE LAST OF THE PAPER-WORK.
WE'LL SEE YOU HERE TOMOR-ROW FOR YOUR FIRST DAY.
YES, MA'AM!
THAT WAS EASY.
NOW THAT I THINK ABOUT IT, WHAT AM I GOING TO DO FOR A CLUB?
HMMM...
THERE CAN'T POSSIBLY BE A BEACH VOLLEY-BALL CLUB, RIGHT?
HUH?
MIKASA
KTMP
THAT BALL...
NO WAY!

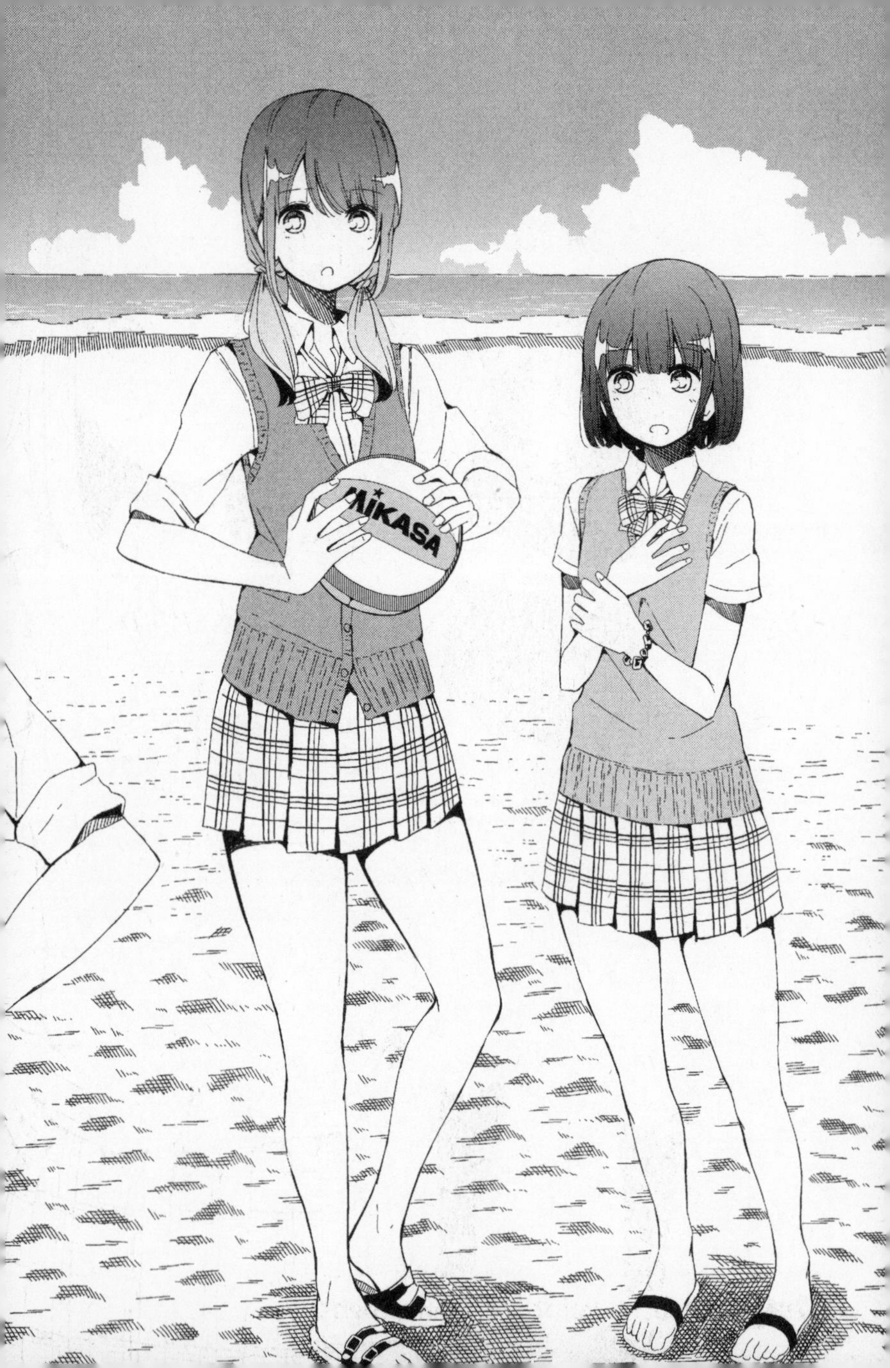

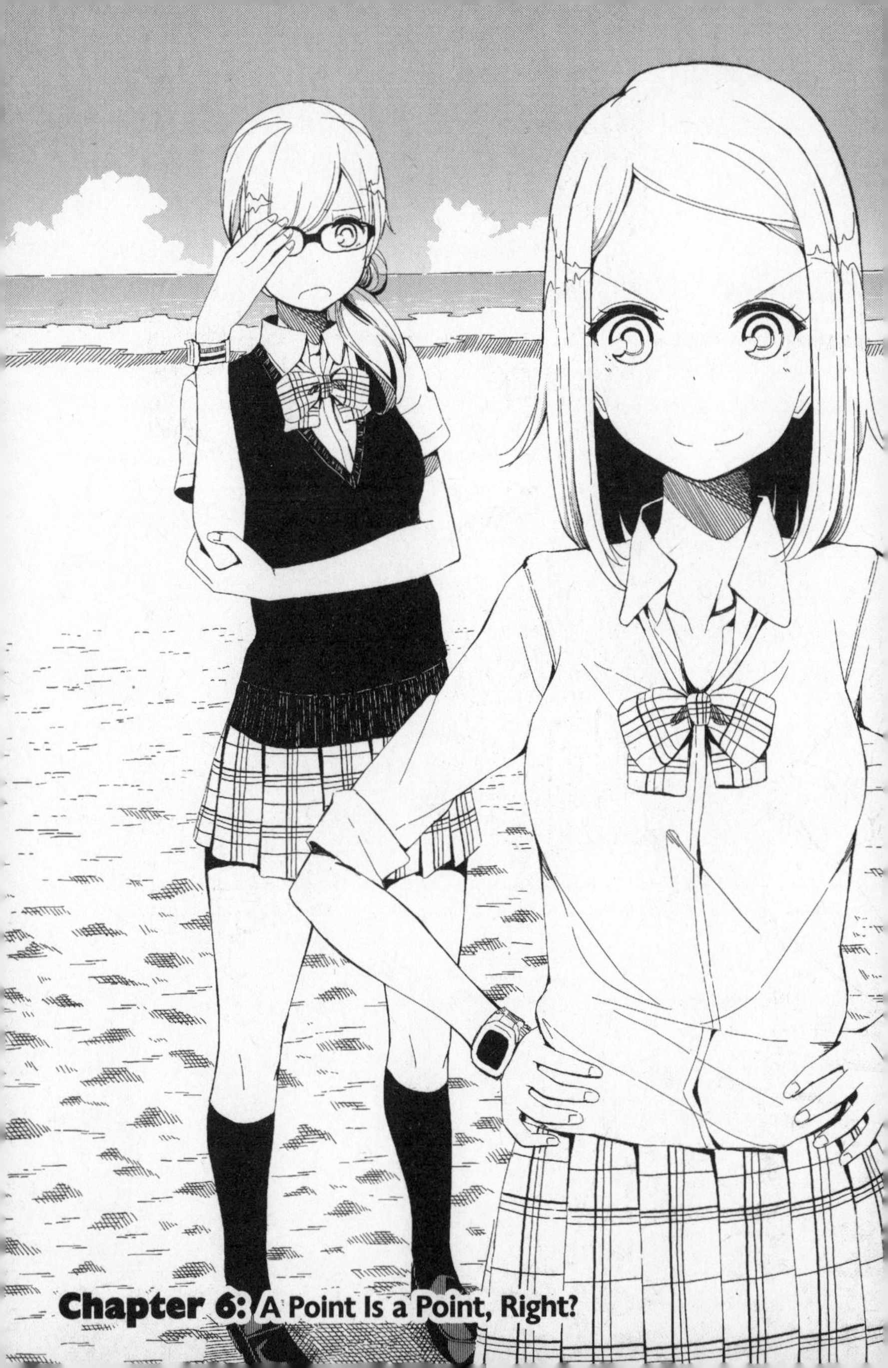

Chapter 6: A Point Is a Point, Right?

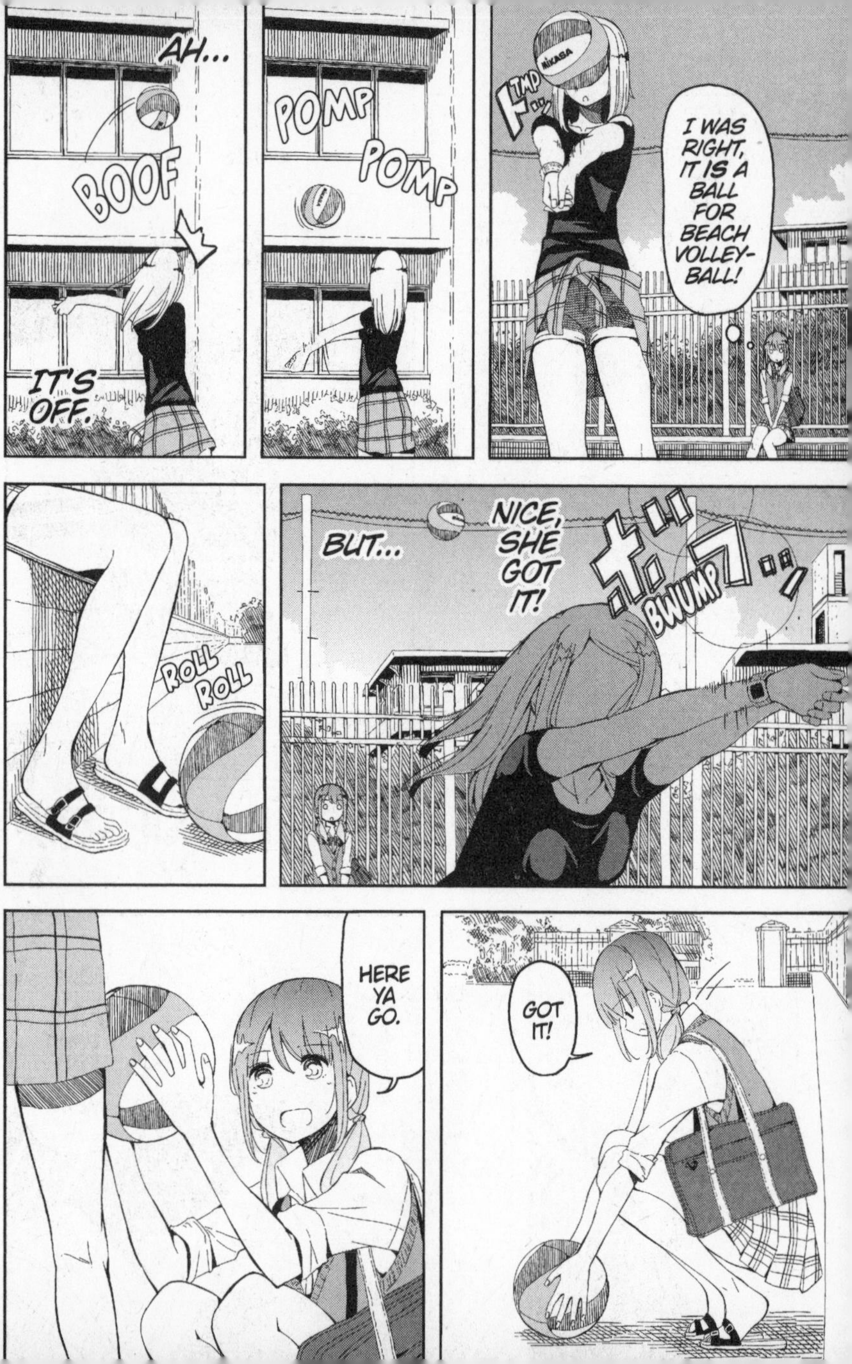
TMP
MIKASA
I WAS RIGHT, IT IS A BALL FOR BEACH VOLLEY-BALL!
POMP
POMP
AH...
BOOF
IT'S OFF.
BWUMP
NICE, SHE GOT IT!
BUT...
ROLL ROLL
GOT IT!
HERE YA GO.

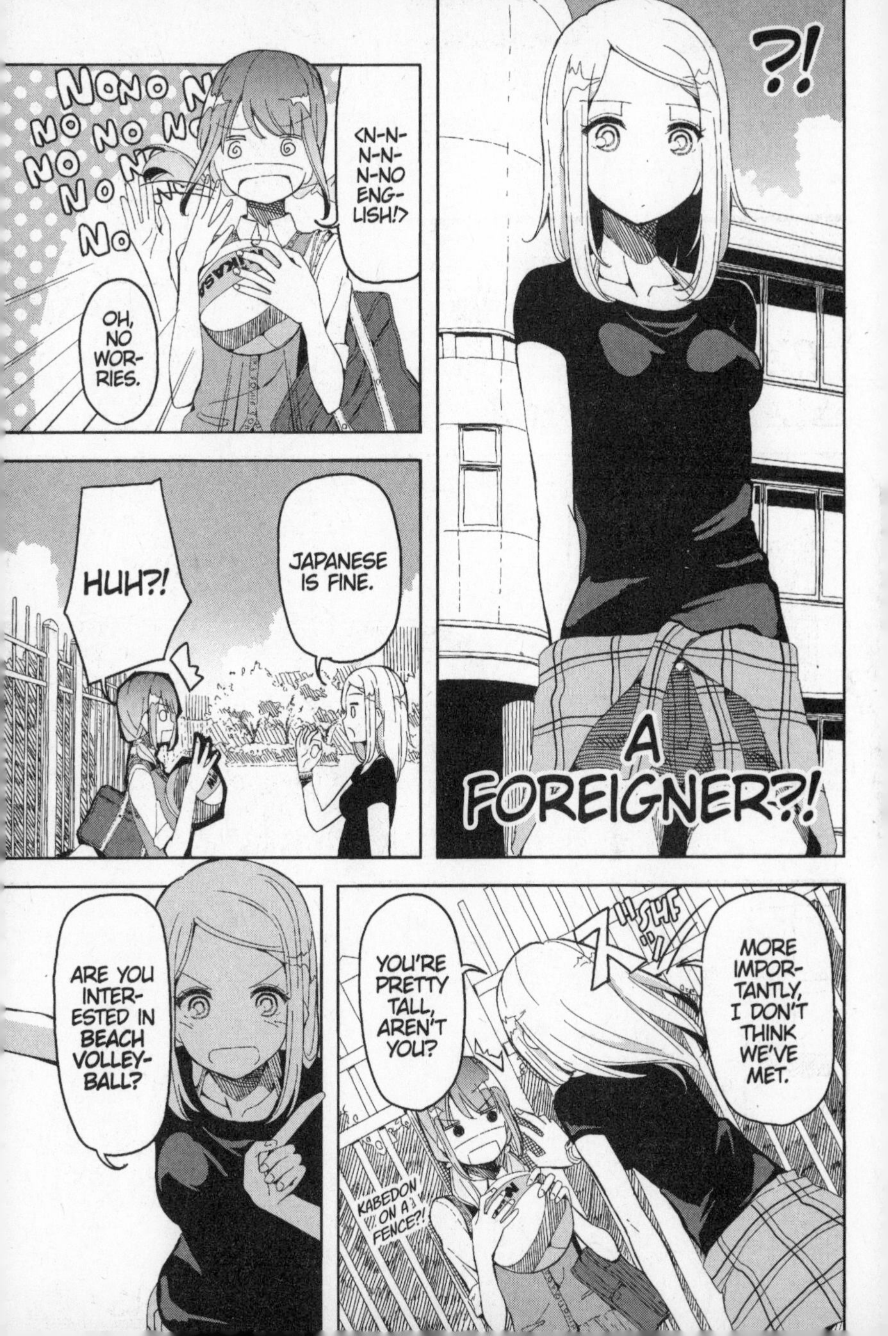
?!
A FOREIGNER?!
<N-N-N-N-NO ENGLISH!>
NO NO NO NO NO NO NO NO NO NO
OH, NO WORRIES.
JAPANESE IS FINE.
HUH?!
MORE IMPORTANTLY, I DON'T THINK WE'VE MET.
YOU'RE PRETTY TALL, AREN'T YOU?
KABEDON ON A FENCE?!
ARE YOU INTERESTED IN BEACH VOLLEYBALL?

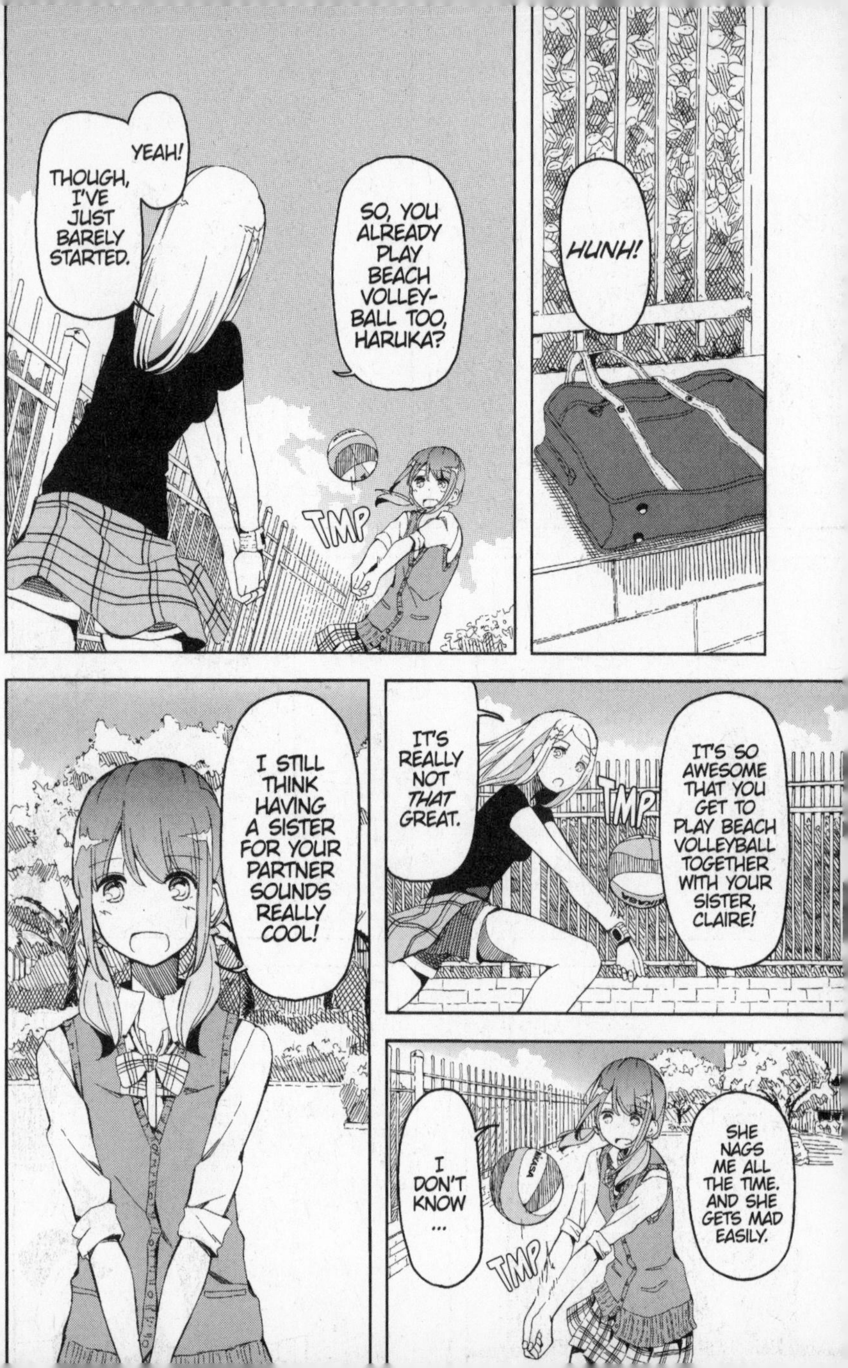
HUNH!
SO, YOU ALREADY PLAY BEACH VOLLEY-BALL TOO, HARUKA?
YEAH! THOUGH, I'VE JUST BARELY STARTED.
TMP
IT'S SO AWESOME THAT YOU GET TO PLAY BEACH VOLLEYBALL TOGETHER WITH YOUR SISTER, CLAIRE!
IT'S REALLY NOT *THAT* GREAT.
TMP
SHE NAGS ME ALL THE TIME. AND SHE GETS MAD EASILY.
I DON'T KNOW ...
TMP
I STILL THINK HAVING A SISTER FOR YOUR PARTNER SOUNDS REALLY COOL!

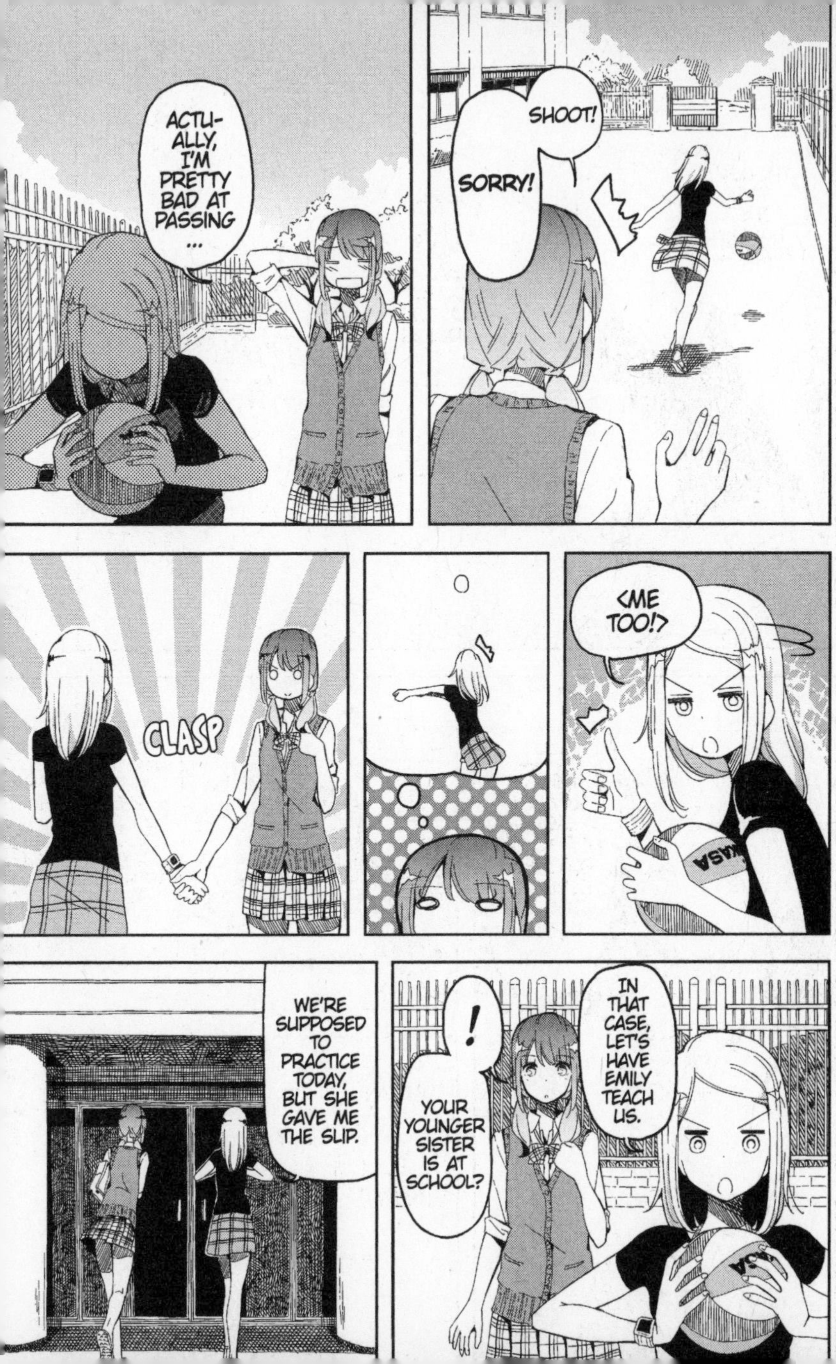
SHOOT!
SORRY!
ACTU-ALLY, I'M PRETTY BAD AT PASSING...
<ME TOO!>
CLASP
IN THAT CASE, LET'S HAVE EMILY TEACH US.
!
YOUR YOUNGER SISTER IS AT SCHOOL?
WE'RE SUPPOSED TO PRACTICE TODAY, BUT SHE GAVE ME THE SLIP.

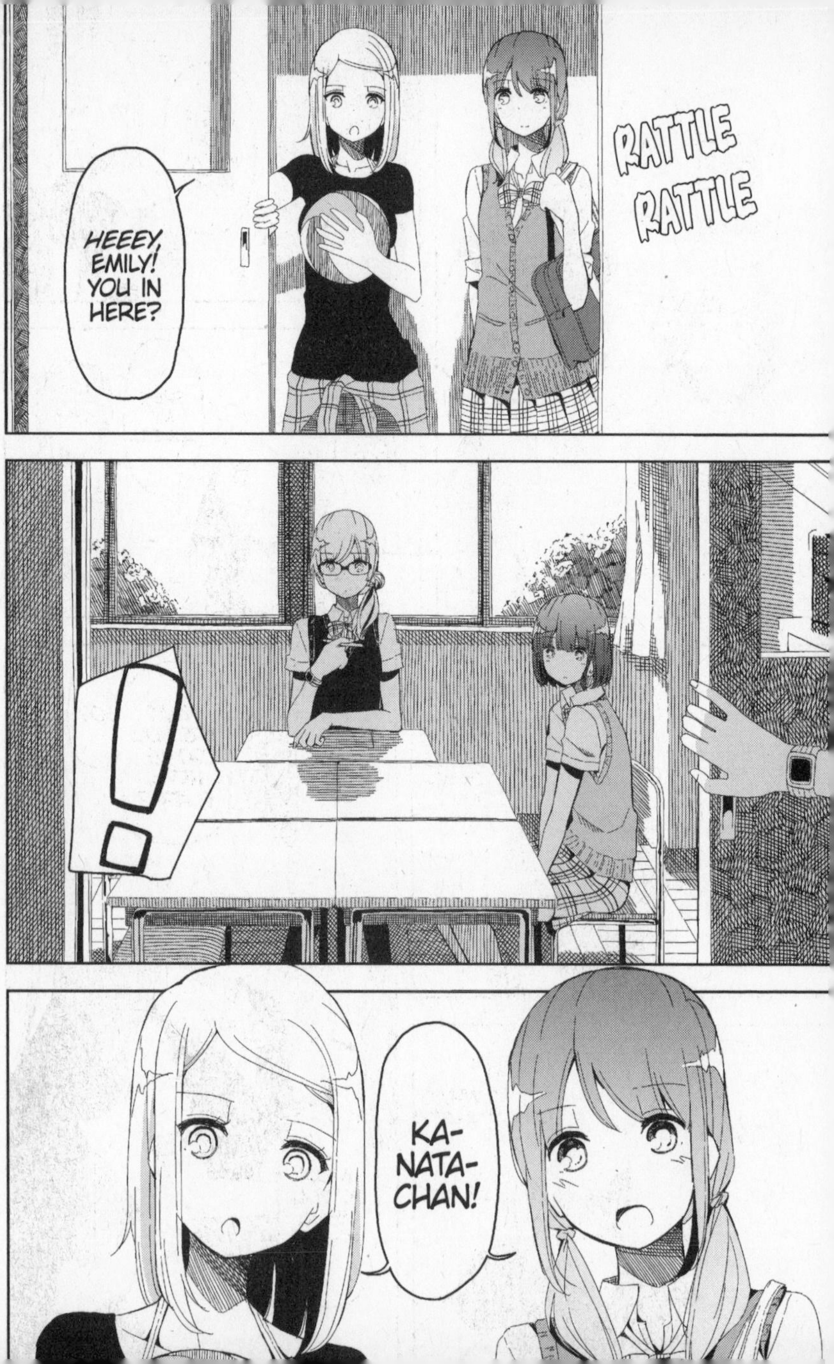
RATTLE RATTLE
HEEEY, EMILY! YOU IN HERE?
!
KA-NATA-CHAN!

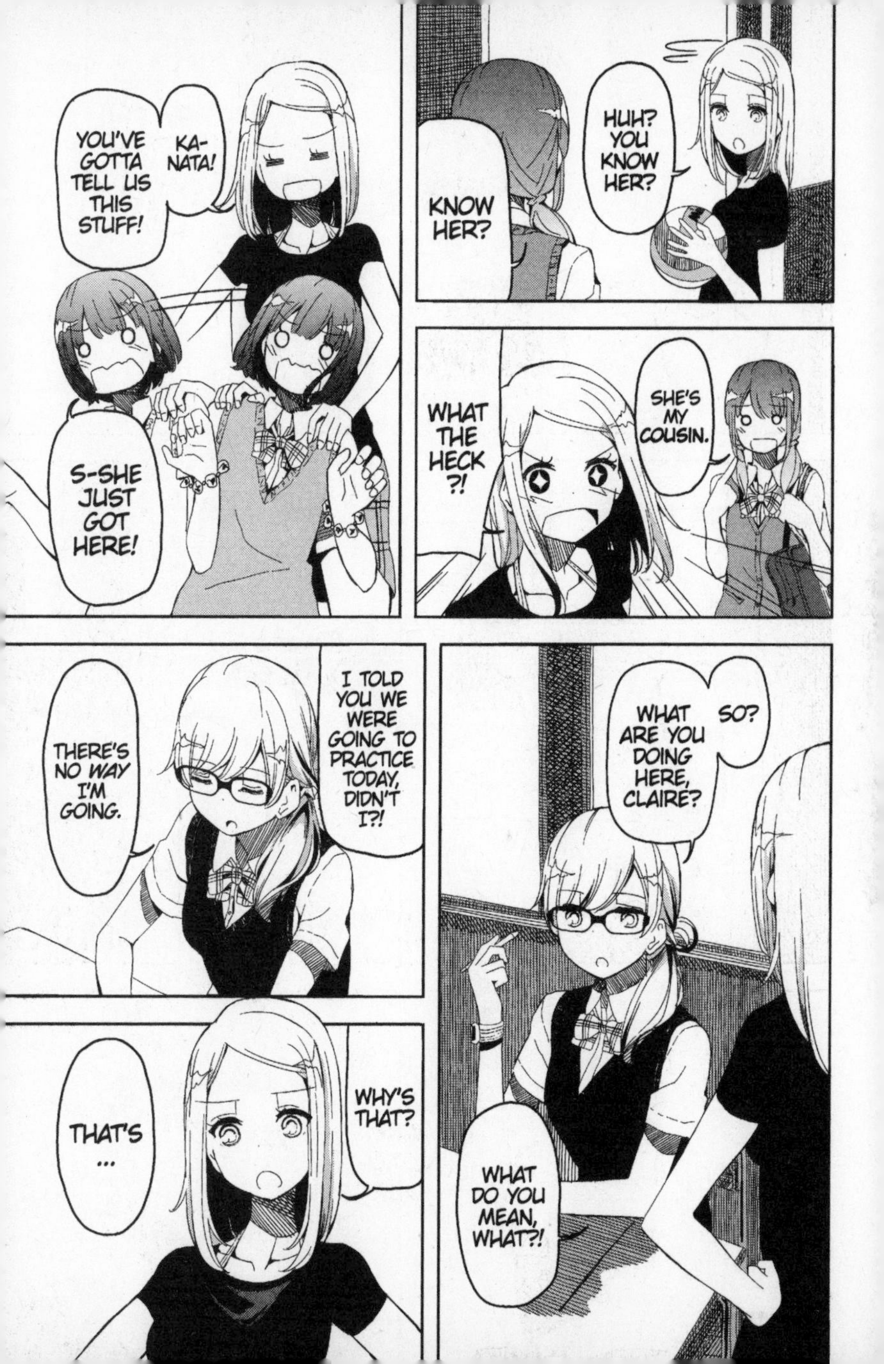
HUH? YOU KNOW HER?
KNOW HER?
SHE'S MY COUSIN.
WHAT THE HECK ?!
KA-NATA!
YOU'VE GOTTA TELL US THIS STUFF!
S-SHE JUST GOT HERE!
SO?
WHAT ARE YOU DOING HERE, CLAIRE?
WHAT DO YOU MEAN, WHAT?!
I TOLD YOU WE WERE GOING TO PRACTICE TODAY, DIDN'T I?!
THERE'S NO *WAY* I'M GOING.
WHY'S THAT?
THAT'S ...

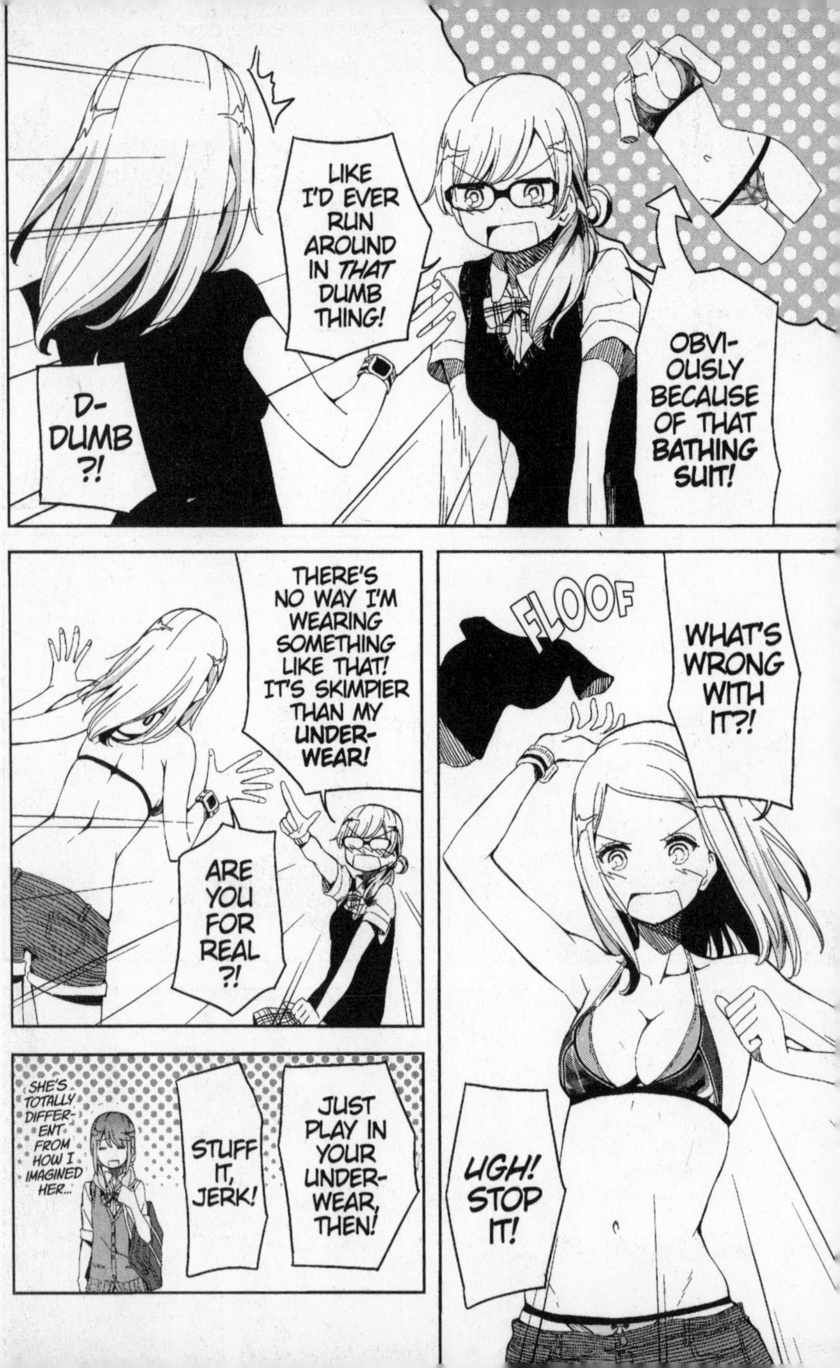
OBVIOUSLY BECAUSE OF THAT BATHING SUIT!
LIKE I'D EVER RUN AROUND IN *THAT* DUMB THING!
D-DUMB?!
FLOOF
WHAT'S WRONG WITH IT?!
UGH! STOP IT!
THERE'S NO WAY I'M WEARING SOMETHING LIKE THAT! IT'S SKIMPIER THAN MY UNDERWEAR!
ARE YOU FOR REAL?!
JUST PLAY IN YOUR UNDERWEAR, THEN!
STUFF IT, JERK!
SHE'S TOTALLY DIFFERENT FROM HOW I IMAGINED HER...

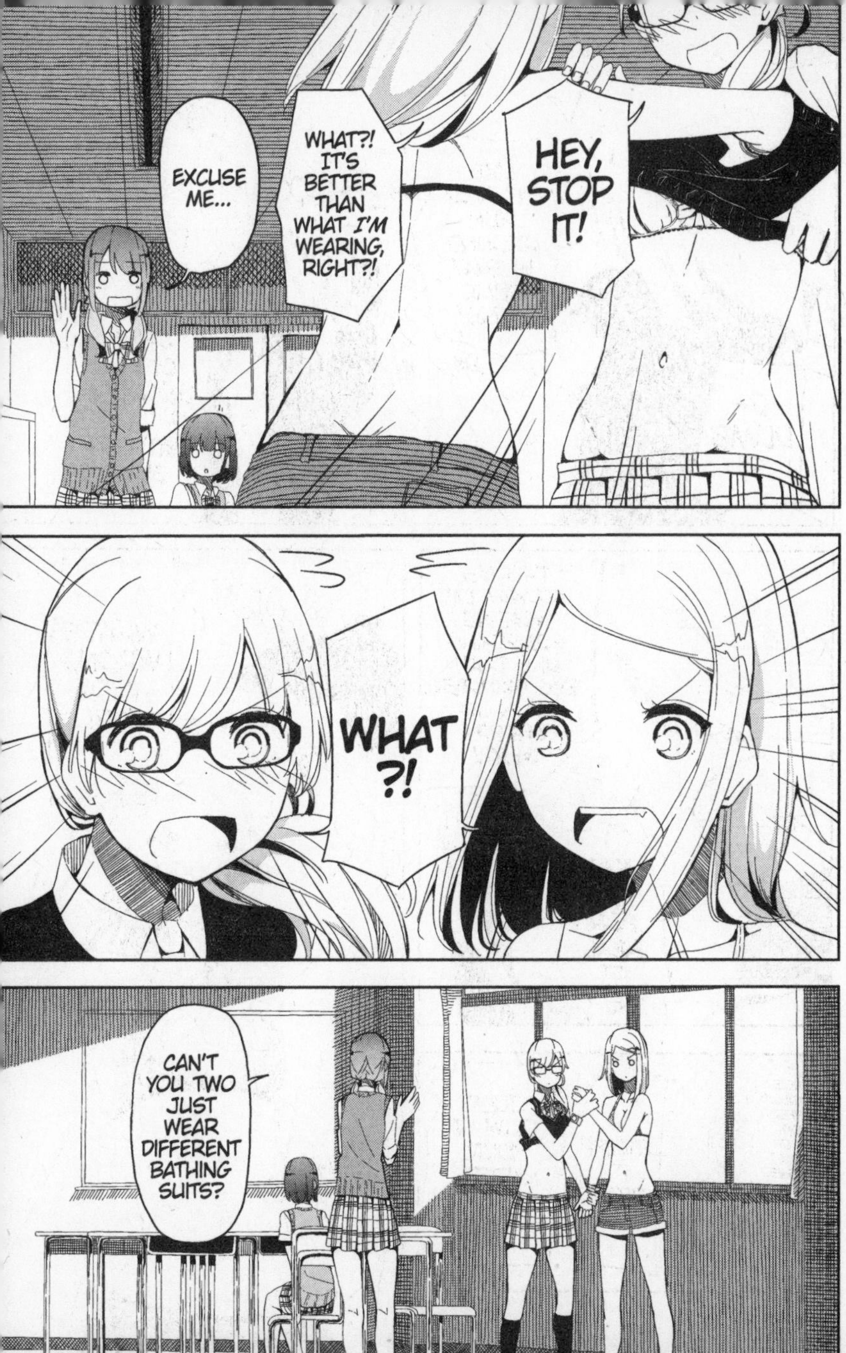
HEY, STOP IT!
WHAT?! IT'S BETTER THAN WHAT *I'M* WEARING, RIGHT?!
EXCUSE ME...
WHAT ?!
CAN'T YOU TWO JUST WEAR DIFFERENT BATHING SUITS?

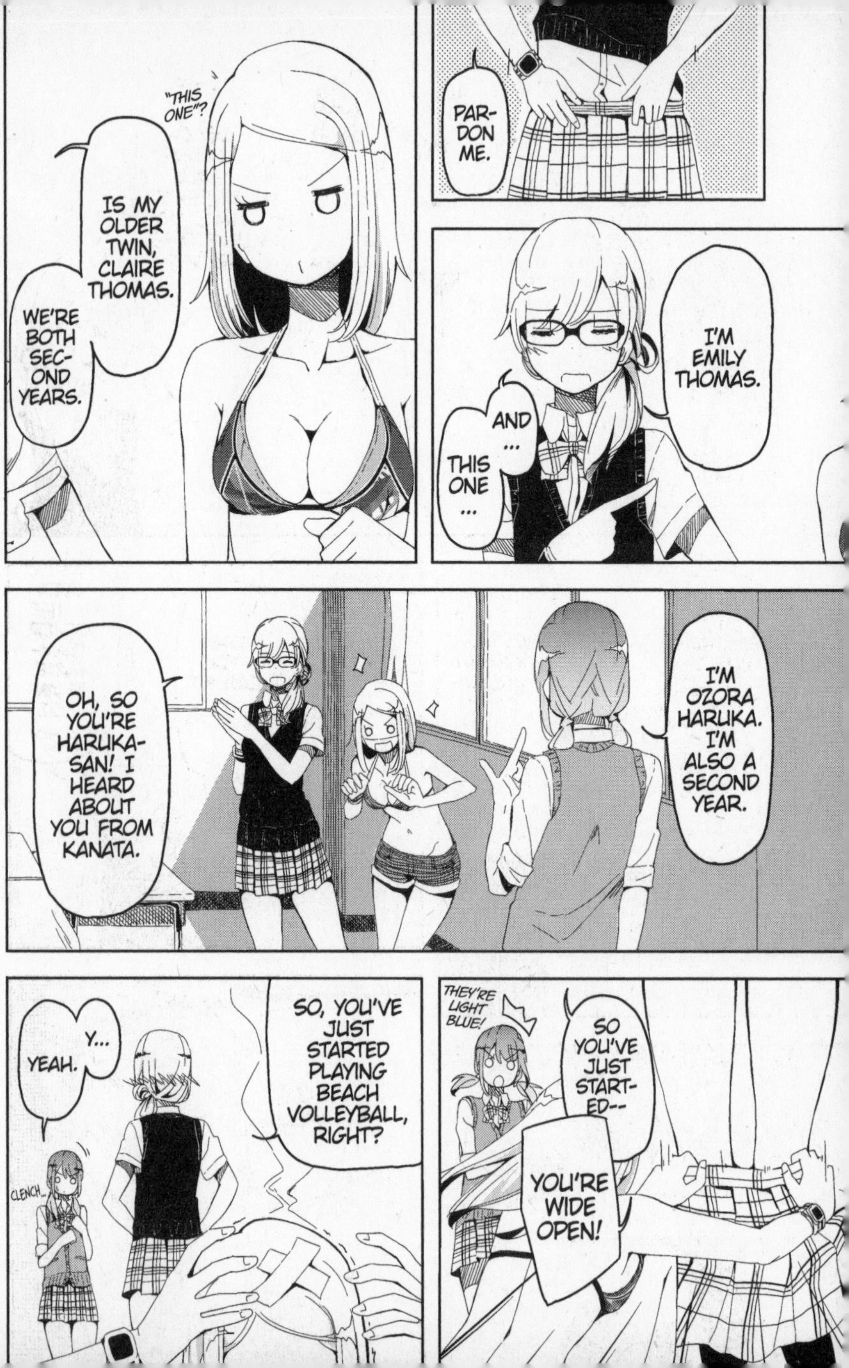
PAR-
DON
ME.
I'M
EMILY
THOMAS.
AND
...
THIS
ONE
...
"THIS
ONE"?
IS MY
OLDER
TWIN,
CLAIRE
THOMAS.
WE'RE
BOTH
SEC-
OND
YEARS.
I'M
OZORA
HARUKA.
I'M
ALSO A
SECOND
YEAR.
OH, SO
YOU'RE
HARUKA-
SAN! I
HEARD
ABOUT
YOU FROM
KANATA.
SO
YOU'VE
JUST
START-
ED--
YOU'RE
WIDE
OPEN!
THEY'RE
LIGHT
BLUE!
SO, YOU'VE
JUST
STARTED
PLAYING
BEACH
VOLLEYBALL,
RIGHT?
Y...
YEAH.
CLENCH...

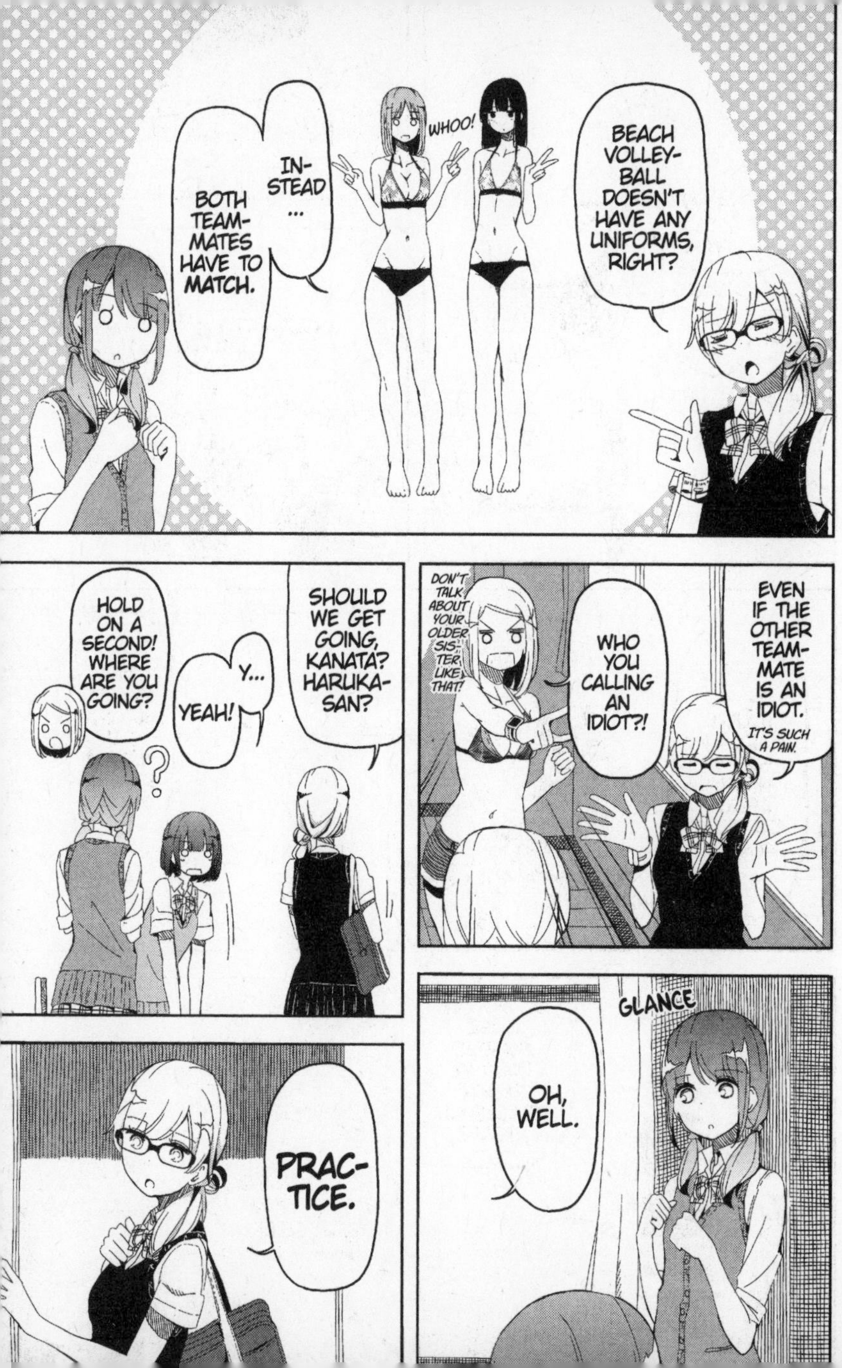
BEACH VOLLEY-BALL DOESN'T HAVE ANY UNIFORMS, RIGHT?
WHOO!
IN-STEAD ...
BOTH TEAM-MATES HAVE TO MATCH.
EVEN IF THE OTHER TEAM-MATE IS AN IDIOT.
IT'S SUCH A PAIN.
WHO YOU CALLING AN IDIOT?!
DON'T TALK ABOUT YOUR OLDER SIS-TER LIKE THAT!
SHOULD WE GET GOING, KANATA? HARUKA-SAN?
Y...
YEAH!
HOLD ON A SECOND! WHERE ARE YOU GOING?
GLANCE
OH, WELL.
PRAC-TICE.

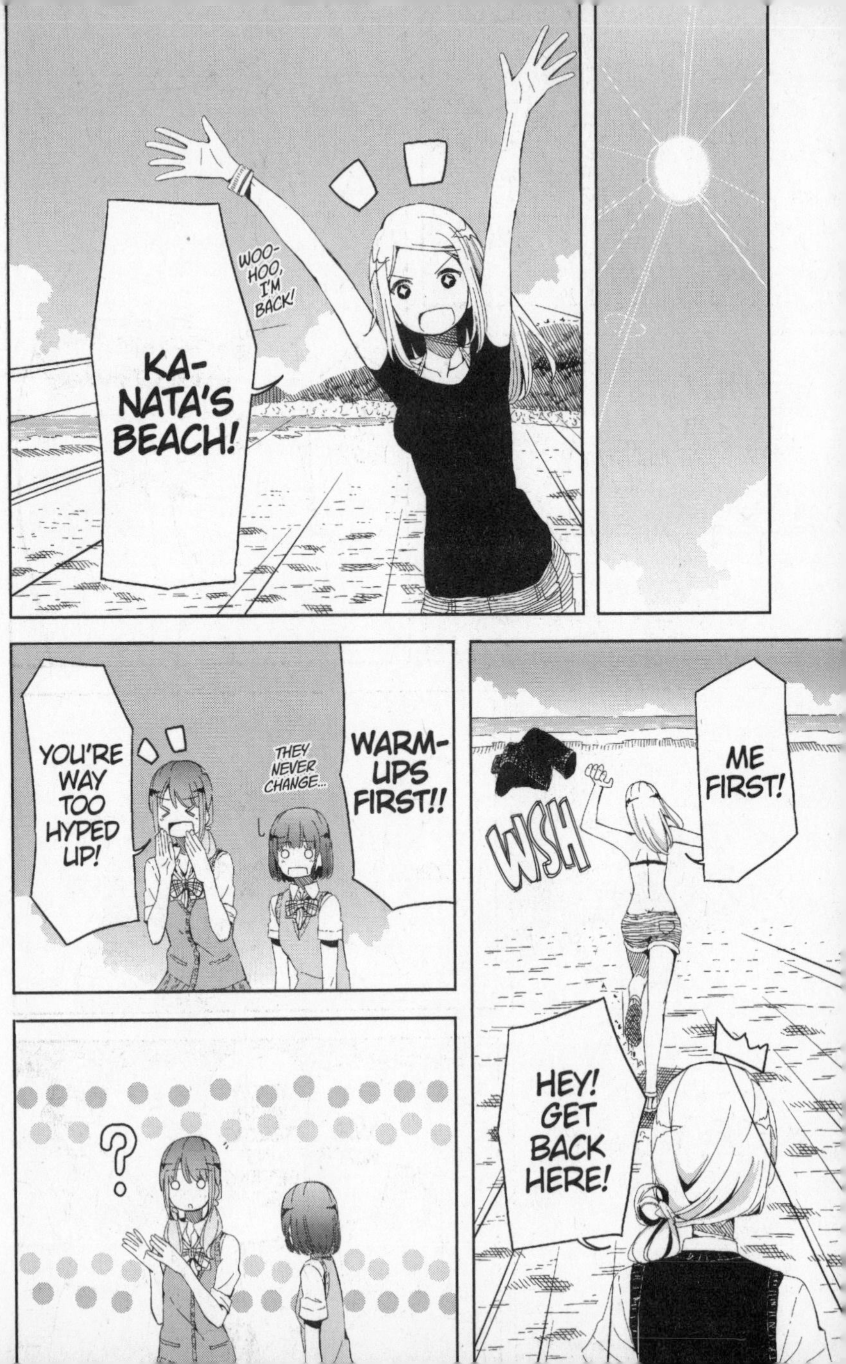
WOO-HOO, I'M BACK!
KA-NATA'S BEACH!
ME FIRST!
WSH
HEY! GET BACK HERE!
WARM-UPS FIRST!!
THEY NEVER CHANGE...
YOU'RE WAY TOO HYPED UP!
?

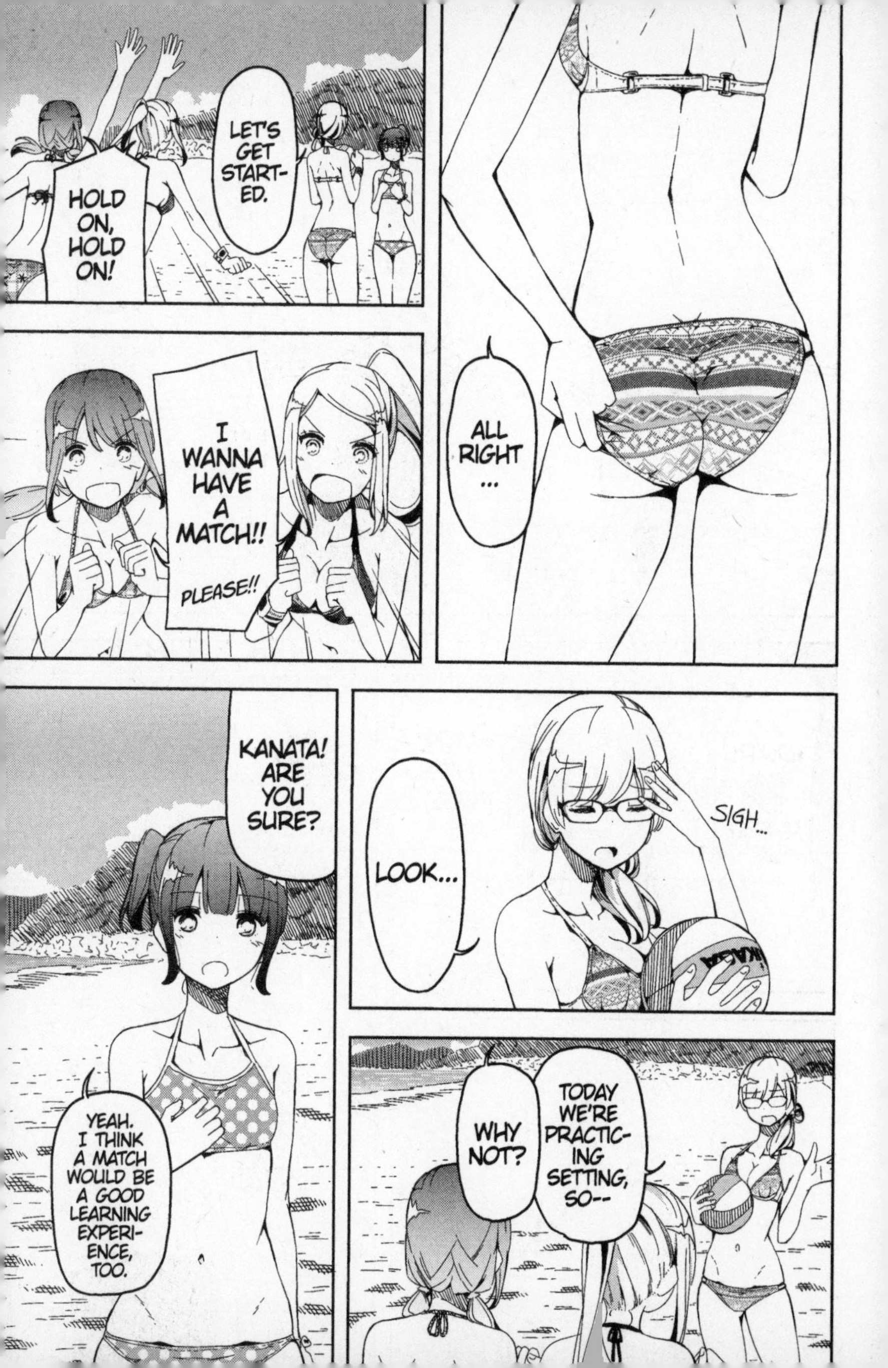
ALL RIGHT...
LET'S GET STARTED.
HOLD ON, HOLD ON!
I WANNA HAVE A MATCH!!
PLEASE!!
SIGH...
LOOK...
TODAY WE'RE PRACTICING SETTING, SO--
WHY NOT?
KANATA! ARE YOU SURE?
YEAH. I THINK A MATCH WOULD BE A GOOD LEARNING EXPERIENCE, TOO.

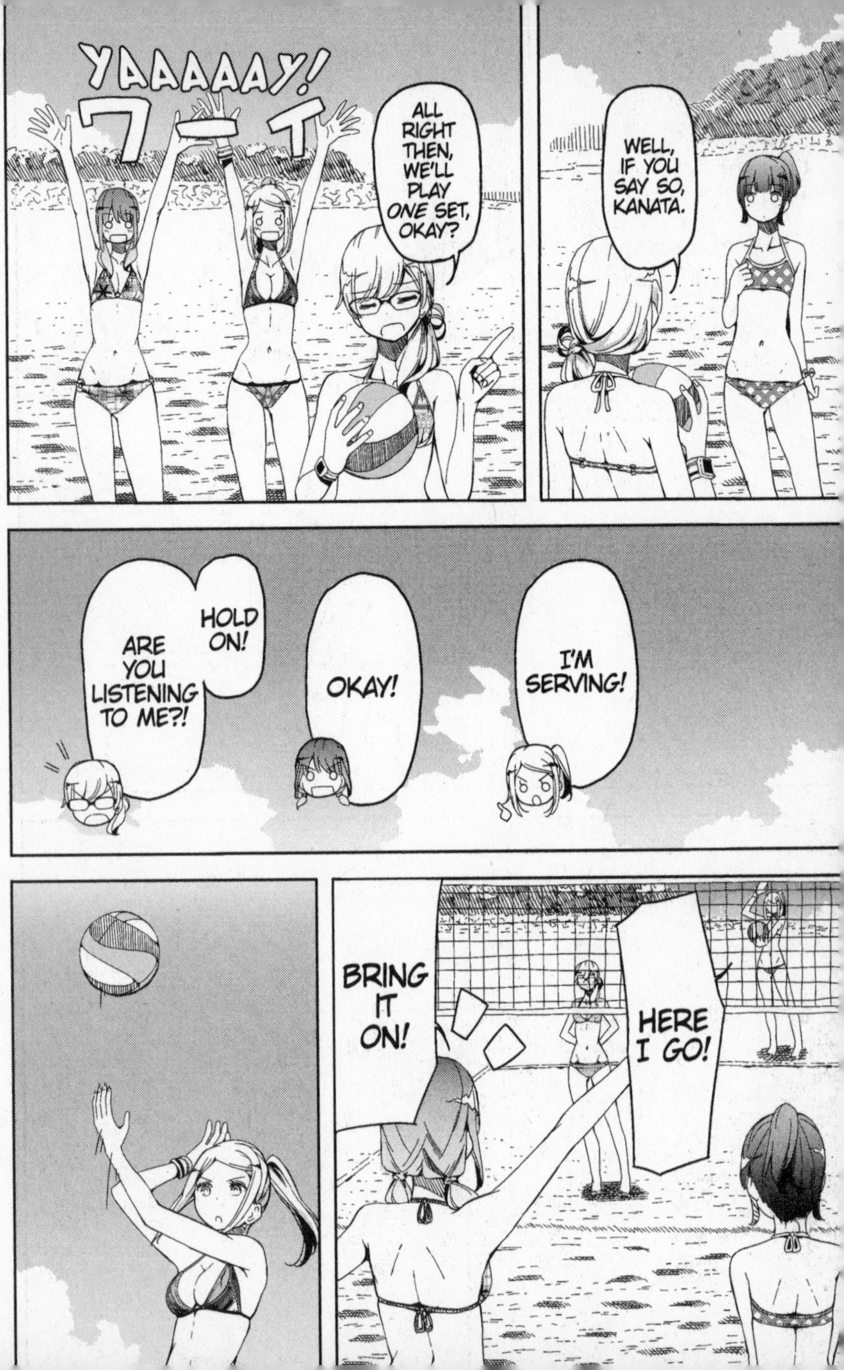
WELL, IF YOU SAY SO, KANATA.
ALL RIGHT THEN, WE'LL PLAY *ONE SET*, OKAY?
YAAAAAY!
ワーイ
I'M SERVING!
OKAY!
HOLD ON!
ARE YOU LISTENING TO ME?!
HERE I GO!
BRING IT ON!

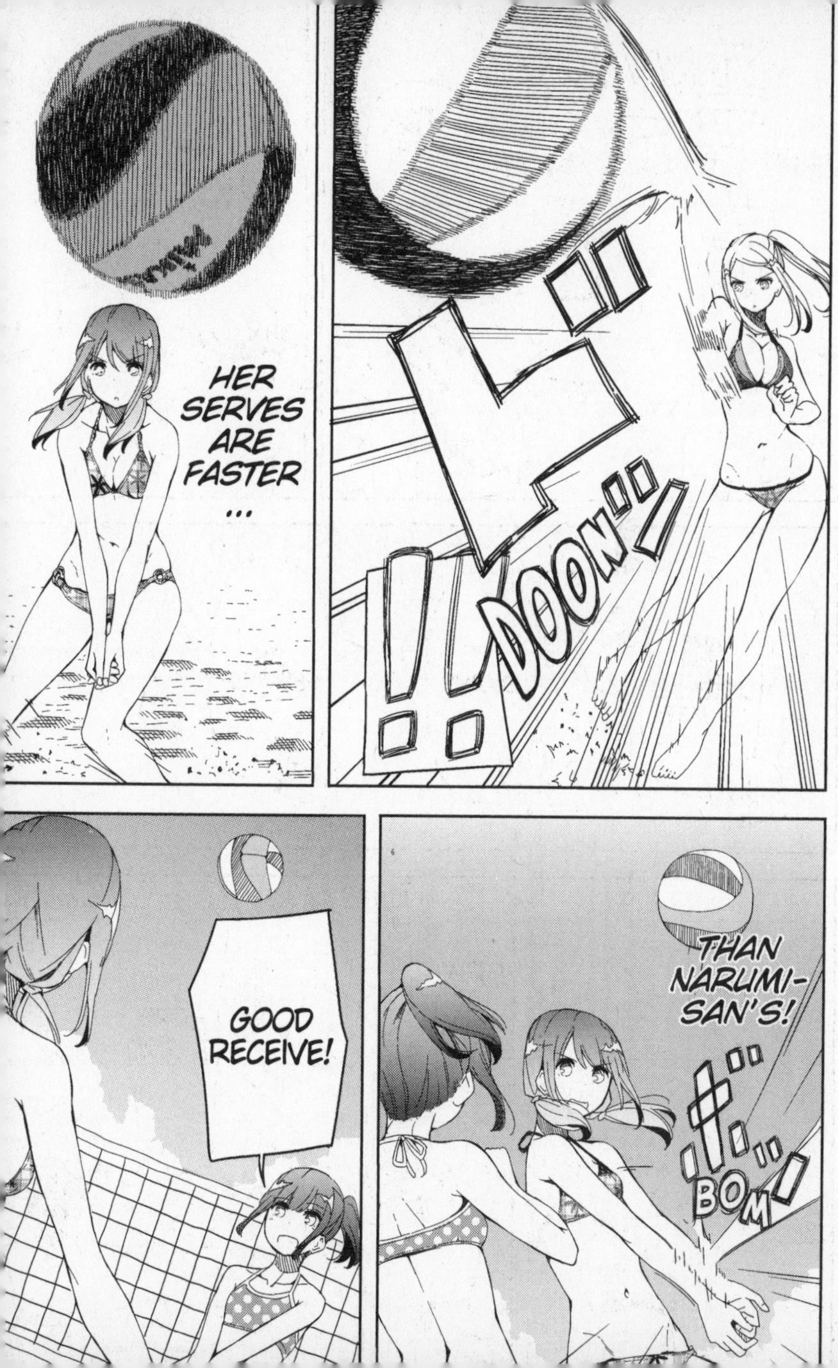
DOON!!
HER SERVES ARE FASTER ...
THAN NARUMI-SAN'S!
BOM
GOOD RECEIVE!

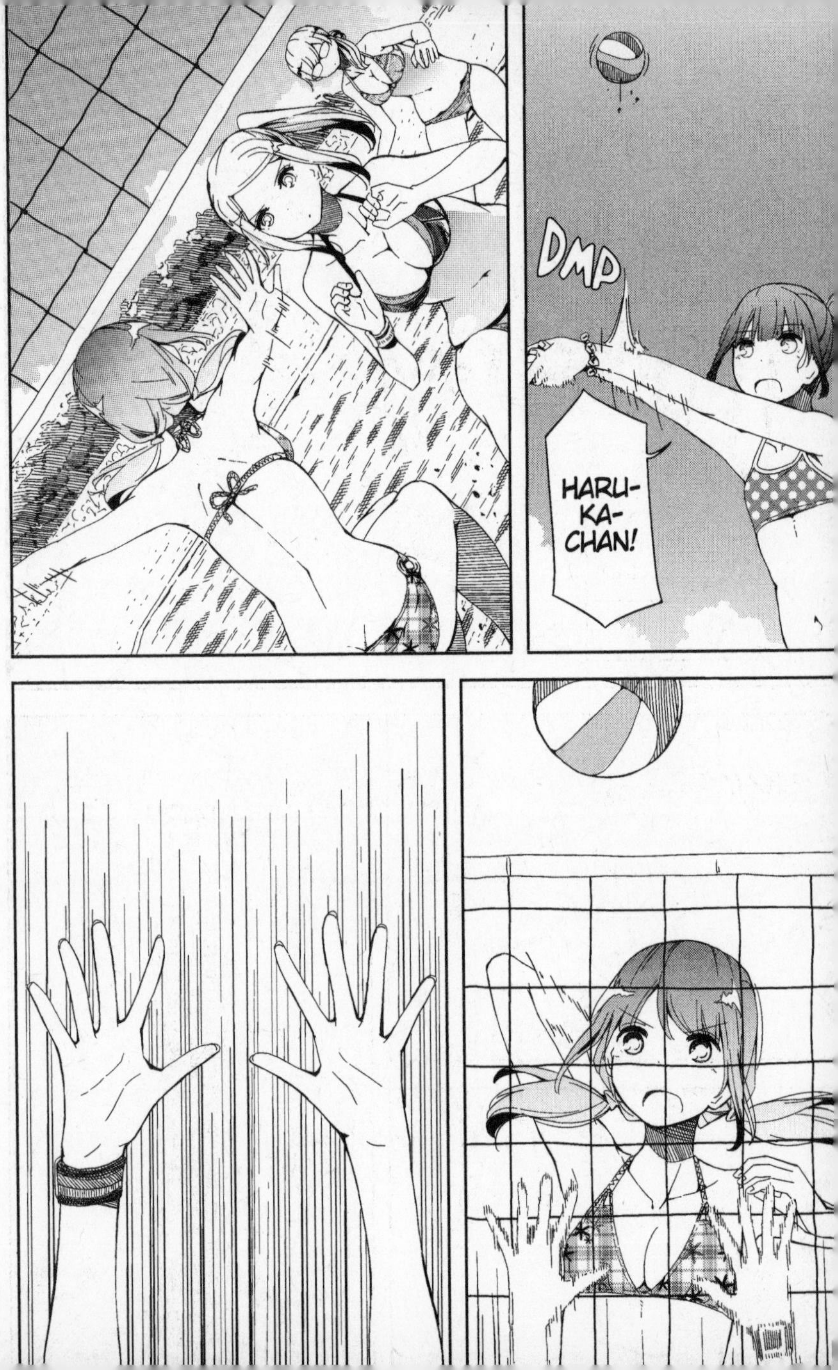
DMP
HARU-KA-CHAN!

BWACK

Haru-kana	Eclair
0	1

WAH?!

SLAP

YEAH, GIRL!

ARGH!!

YAHOO!

IT'S OKAY! NEXT ONE!!

DARN IT!

ALL RIGHT !!

N-NEXT TIME YOU DO THAT I'M NOT GOING TO LET YOU OFF SO EASY, GOT IT?!

OKAY, OKAY!

I'VE GOT IT!

STOP!

I'LL GET US ANO-THER...

DMP

POINT!

NOO-OOO!!

DUMB-ASS!!

Haru-kana	Eclair
1	1

HUH?!

IT'S OUT OF BOUNDS!

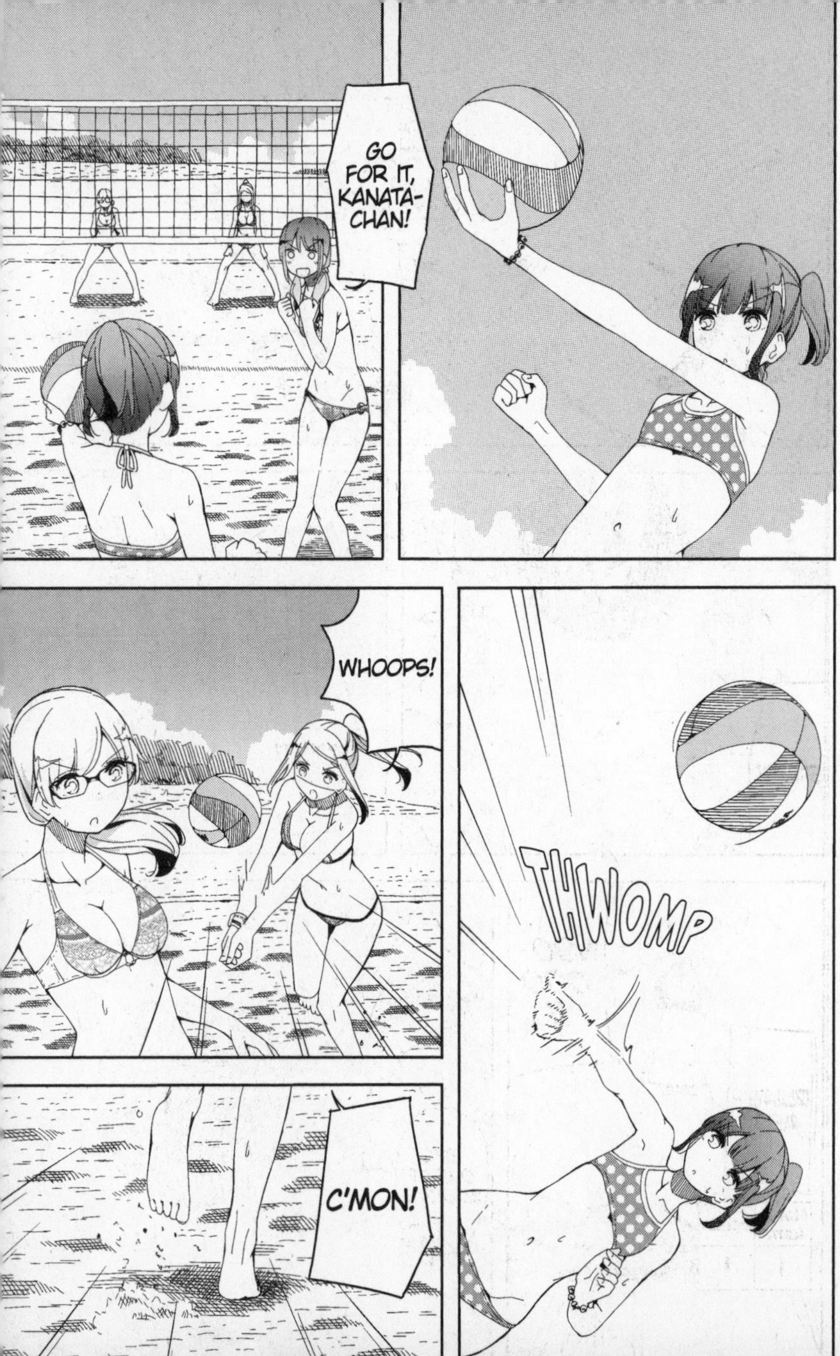
GO FOR IT, KANATA-CHAN!
THWOMP
WHOOPS!
C'MON!

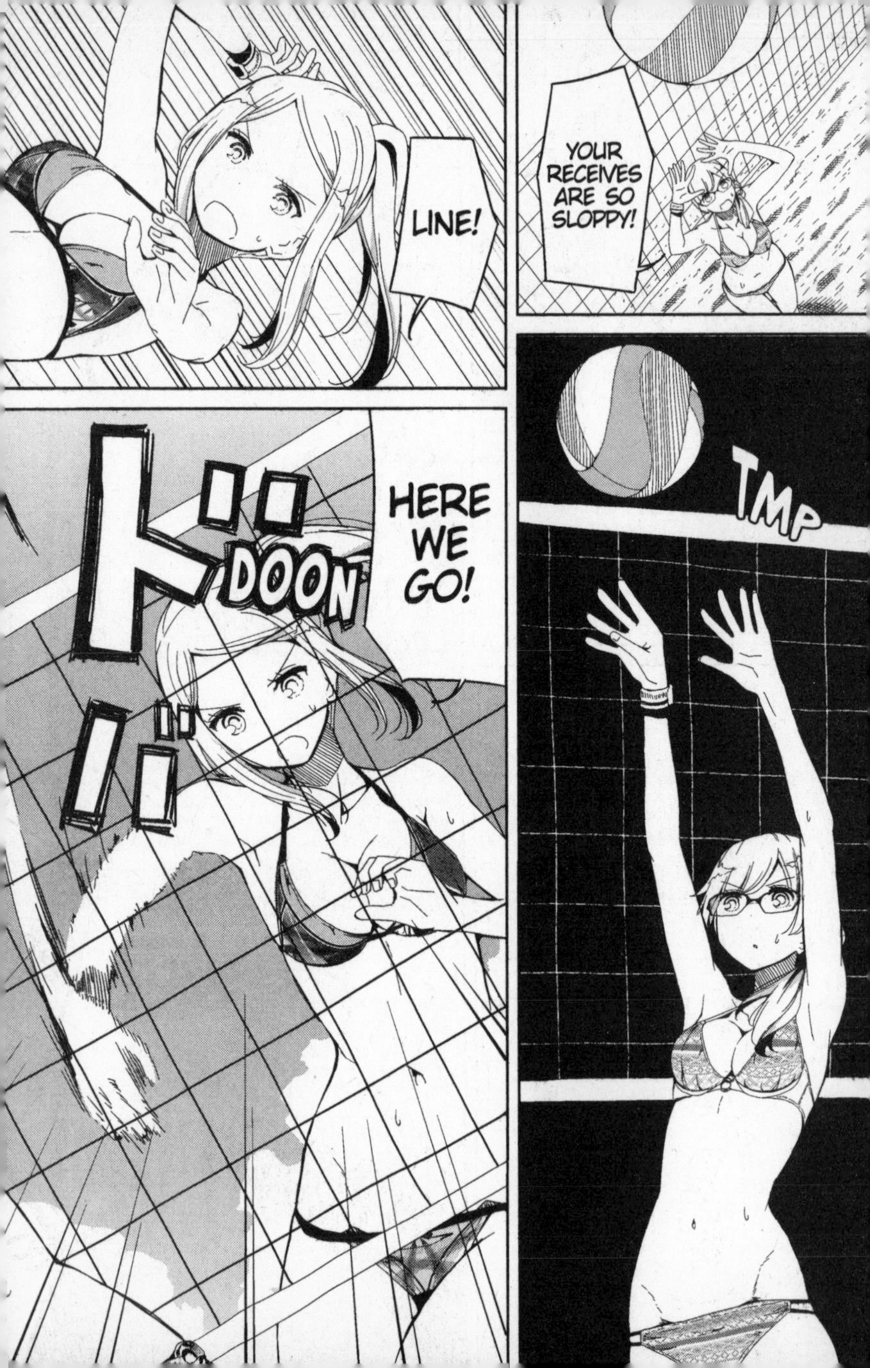
YOUR RECEIVES ARE SO SLOPPY!
LINE!
TMP
HERE WE GO!
DOON

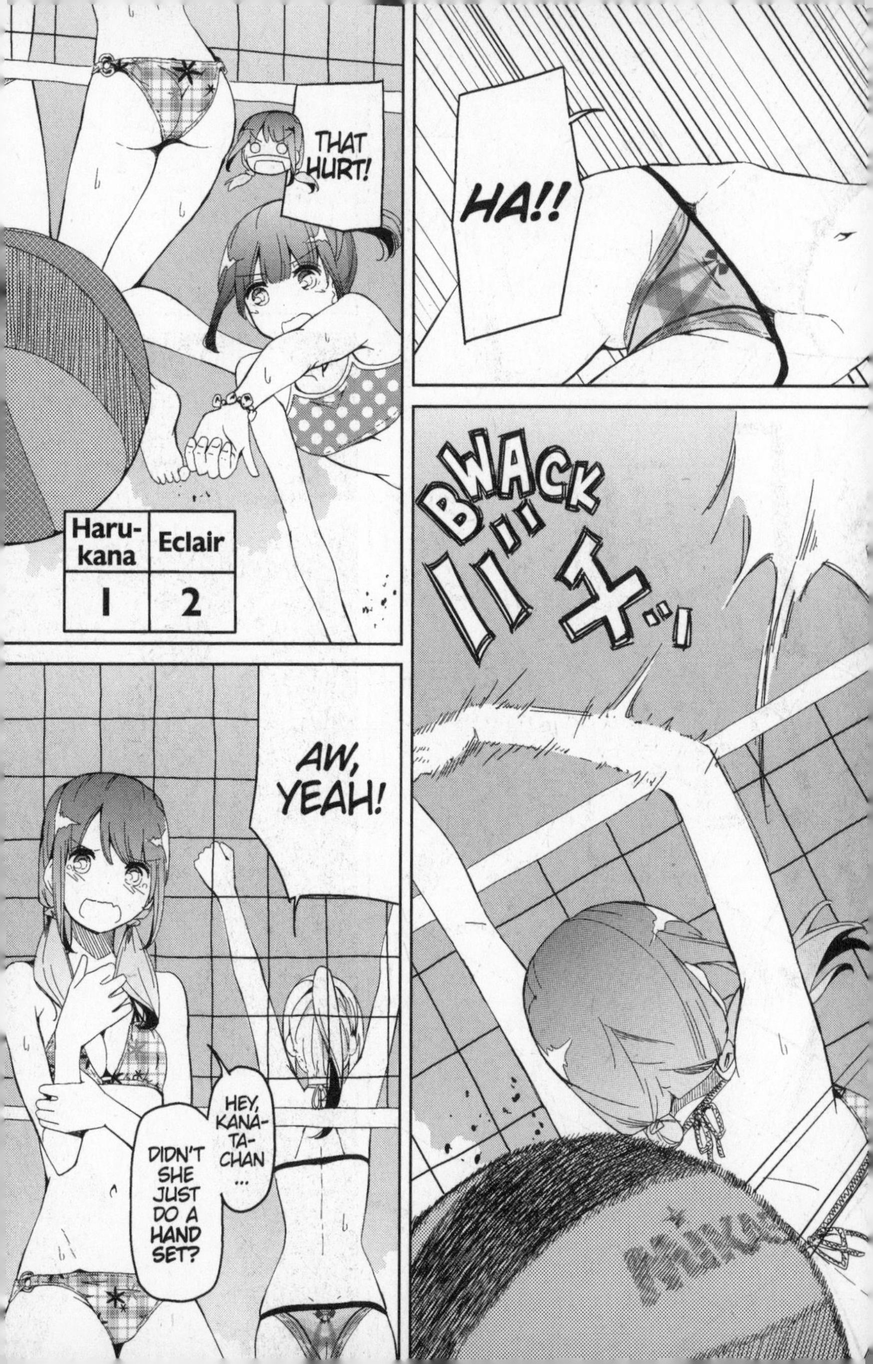HA!!
BWACK
THAT HURT!
Haru-kana 1
Eclair 2
AW, YEAH!
HEY, KANA-TA-CHAN...
DIDN'T SHE JUST DO A HAND SET?

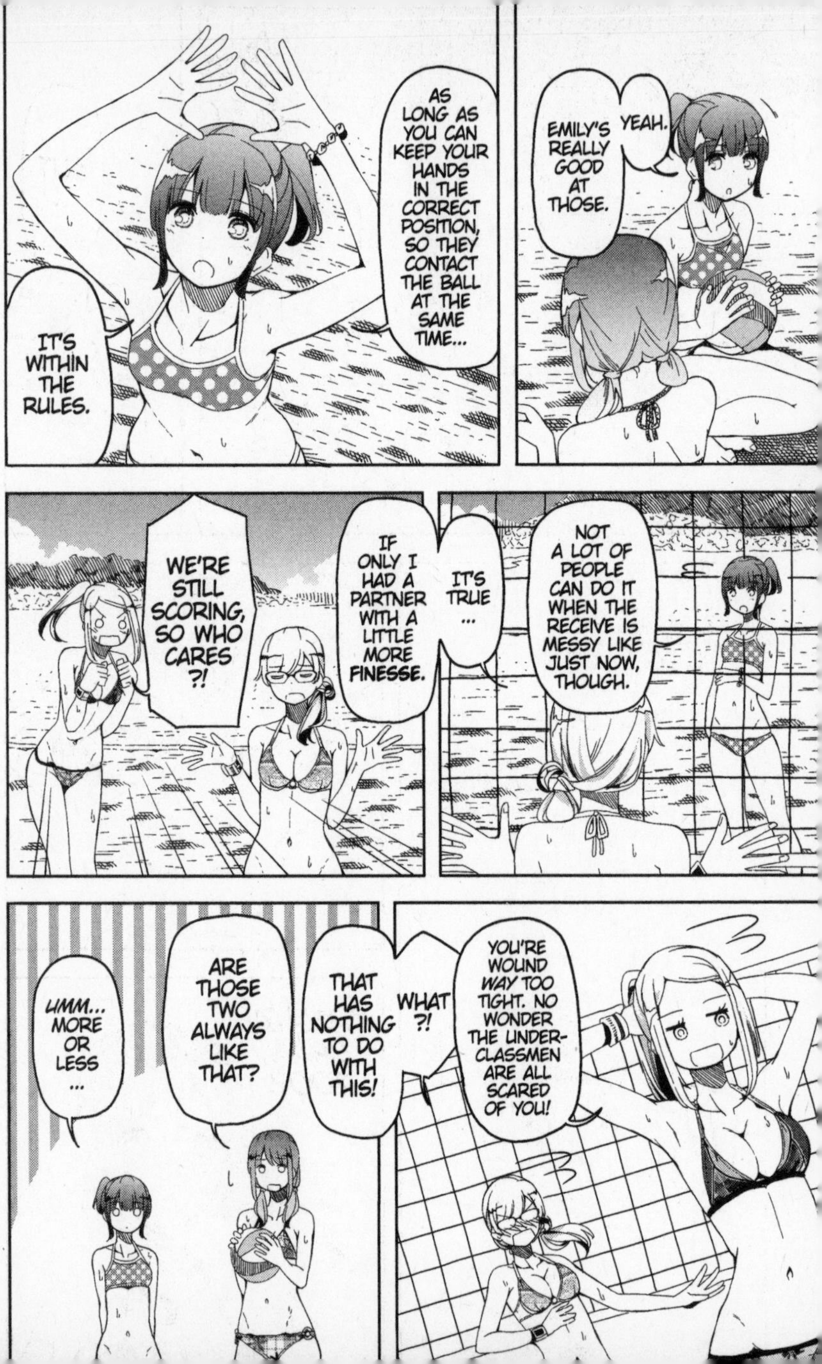
YEAH.
EMILY'S REALLY GOOD AT THOSE.
AS LONG AS YOU CAN KEEP YOUR HANDS IN THE CORRECT POSITION, SO THEY CONTACT THE BALL AT THE SAME TIME...
IT'S WITHIN THE RULES.
NOT A LOT OF PEOPLE CAN DO IT WHEN THE RECEIVE IS MESSY LIKE JUST NOW, THOUGH.
IT'S TRUE ...
IF ONLY I HAD A PARTNER WITH A LITTLE MORE FINESSE.
WE'RE STILL SCORING, SO WHO CARES ?!
YOU'RE WOUND WAY TOO TIGHT. NO WONDER THE UNDER-CLASSMEN ARE ALL SCARED OF YOU!
WHAT ?!
THAT HAS NOTHING TO DO WITH THIS!
ARE THOSE TWO ALWAYS LIKE THAT?
UMM... MORE OR LESS ...

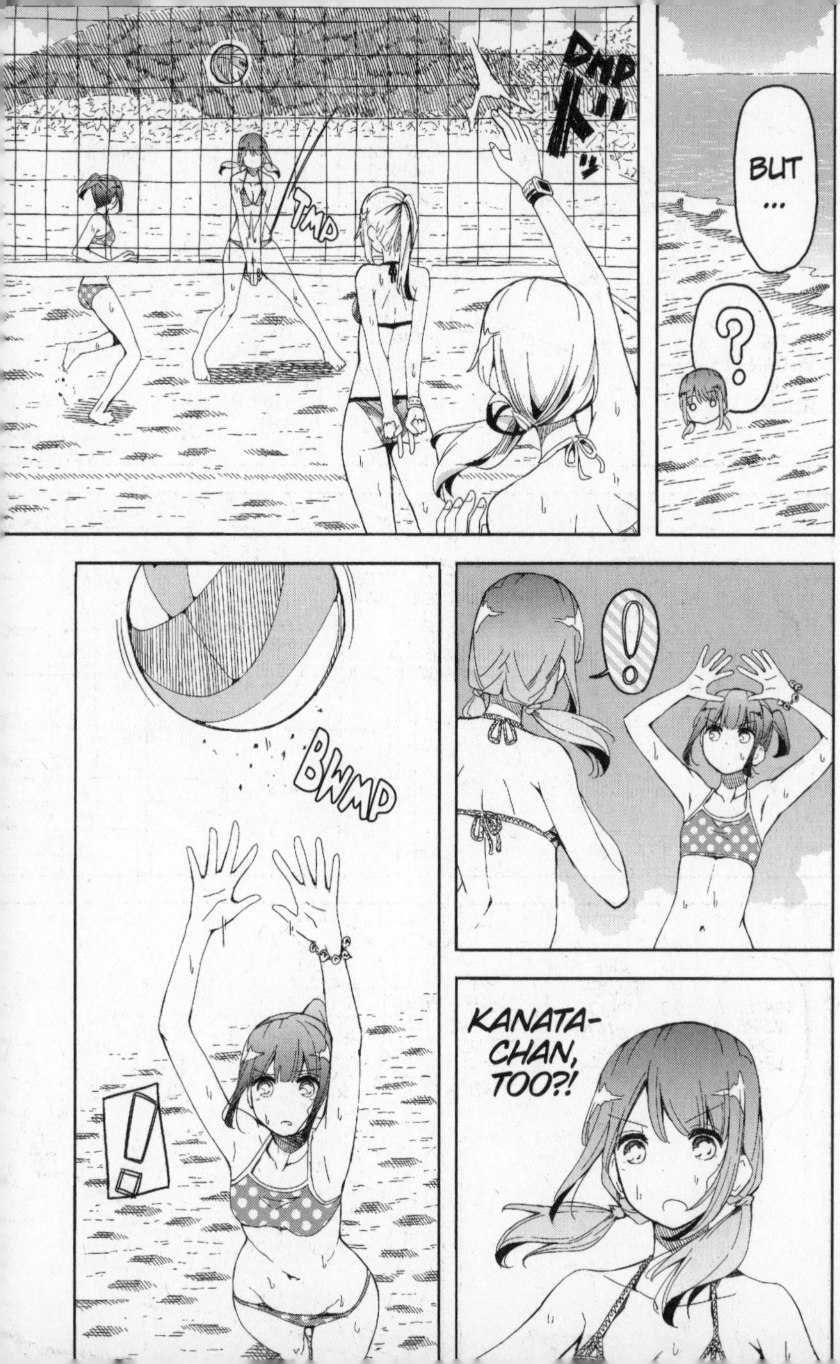

BUT ...
?
DMP
ドッ
TMP
!
KANATA-CHAN, TOO?!
BWMP
!

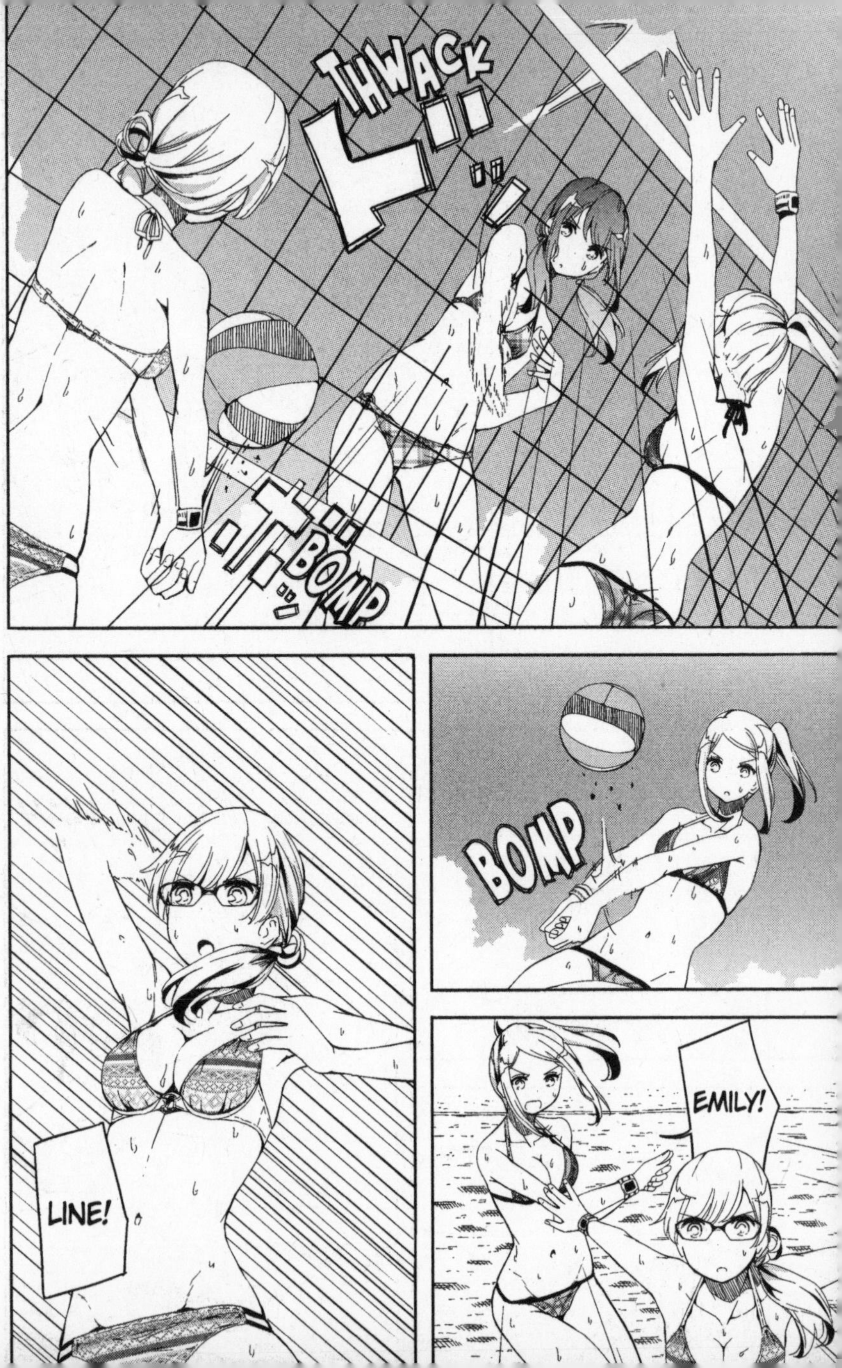
THWACK
BOMP
BOMP
EMILY!
LINE!

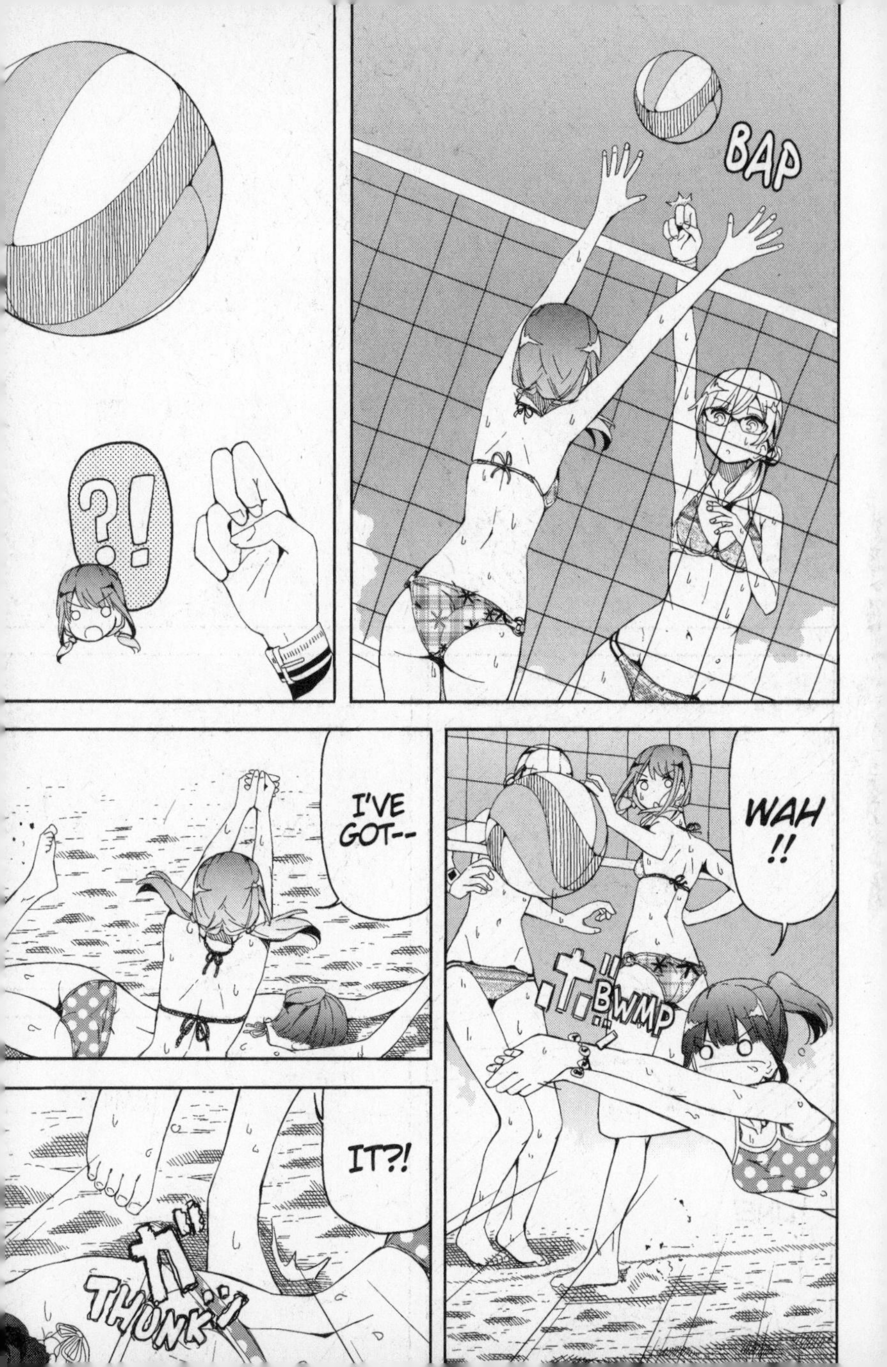
BAP
?!
WAH !!
BWMP
I'VE GOT--
IT?!
THUNK

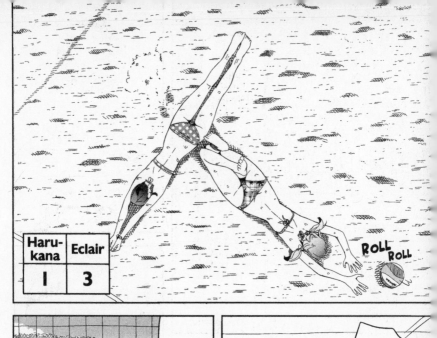

Haru-kana	Eclair
1	3

ROLL ROLL

YOUR HANDS WERE TOO OUT OF SYNC AND YOU GAVE THE BALL TOO MUCH SPIN.

WHAT? REALLY?

WATCH CLOSELY.

THIS GAME HAS TOO MANY RULES!

CAN YOU LET GO OF ME?

I'M OKAY, REALLY...

I'M SO SORRY, KANATA-CHAN!

ARE YOU HURT?!

KANATA, THAT SET WOULD HAVE BEEN A FAULT.

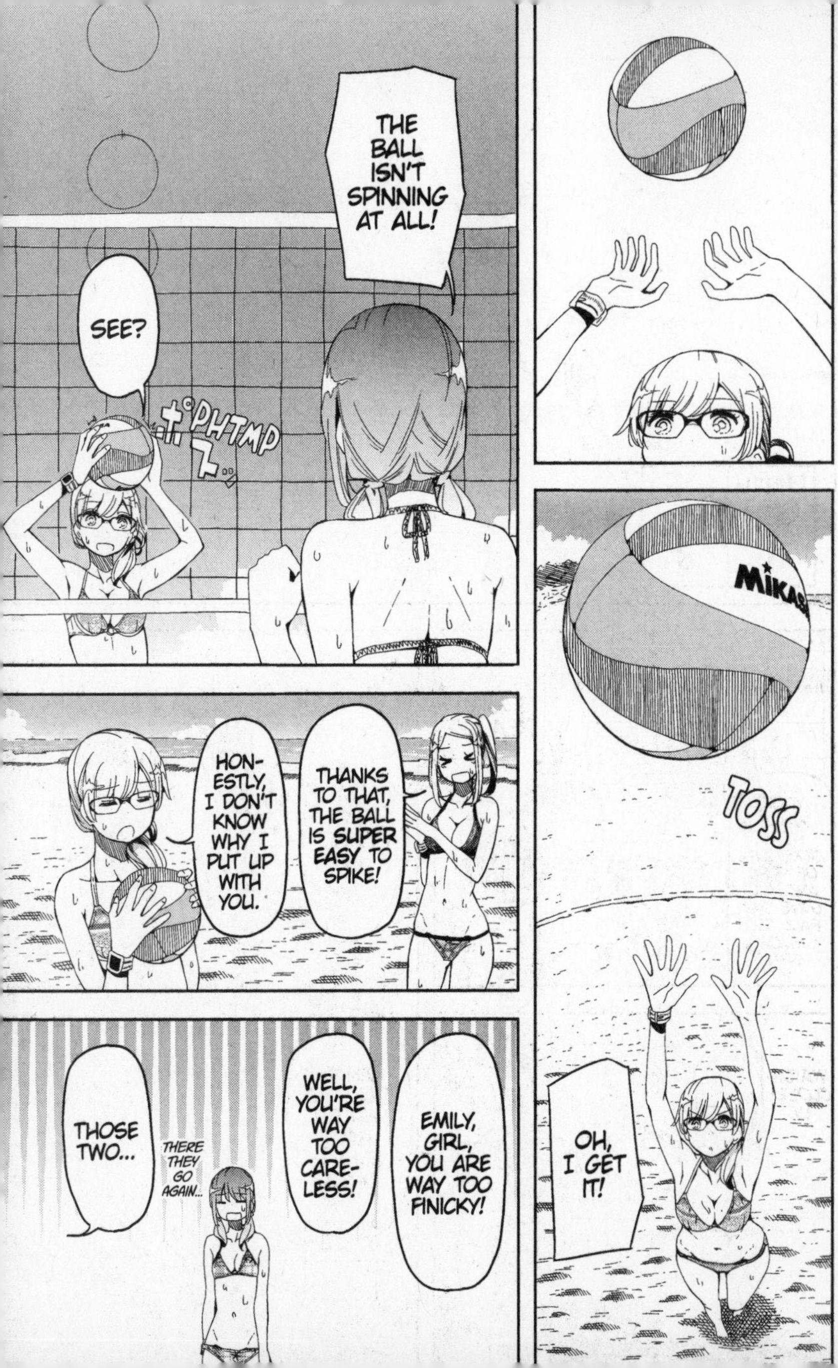
MIKASA
TOSS
OH, I GET IT!
THE BALL ISN'T SPINNING AT ALL!
SEE?
PHTMP
THANKS TO THAT, THE BALL IS SUPER EASY TO SPIKE!
HON-ESTLY, I DON'T KNOW WHY I PUT UP WITH YOU.
EMILY, GIRL, YOU ARE WAY TOO FINICKY!
WELL, YOU'RE WAY TOO CARE-LESS!
THERE THEY GO AGAIN...
THOSE TWO...

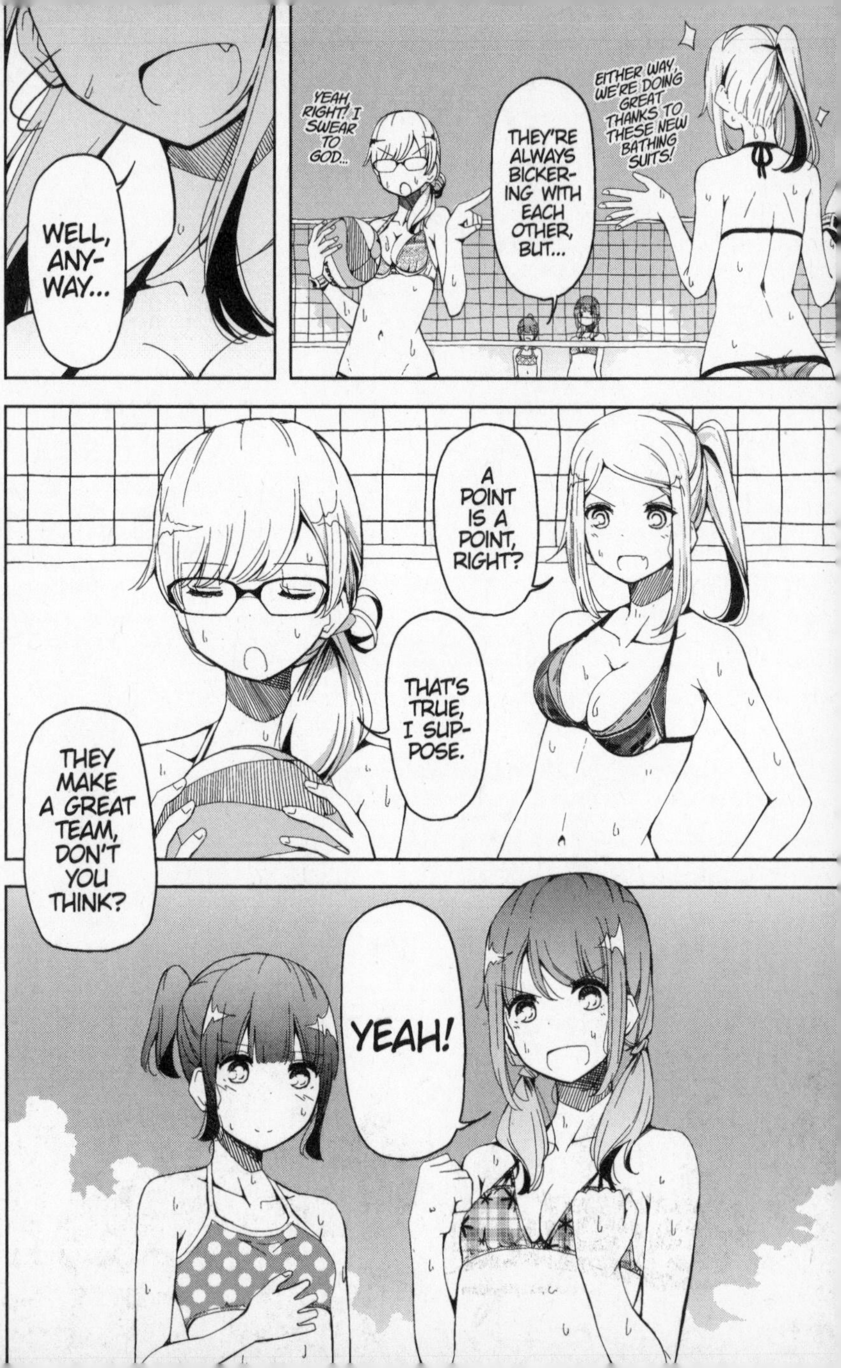
EITHER WAY, WE'RE DOING GREAT THANKS TO THESE NEW BATHING SUITS!
THEY'RE ALWAYS BICKER-ING WITH EACH OTHER, BUT...
YEAH, RIGHT! I SWEAR TO GOD...
WELL, ANY-WAY...
A POINT IS A POINT, RIGHT?
THAT'S TRUE, I SUP-POSE.
THEY MAKE A GREAT TEAM, DON'T YOU THINK?
YEAH!

Harukana★Receive

Presented by Nyoijizai

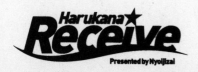

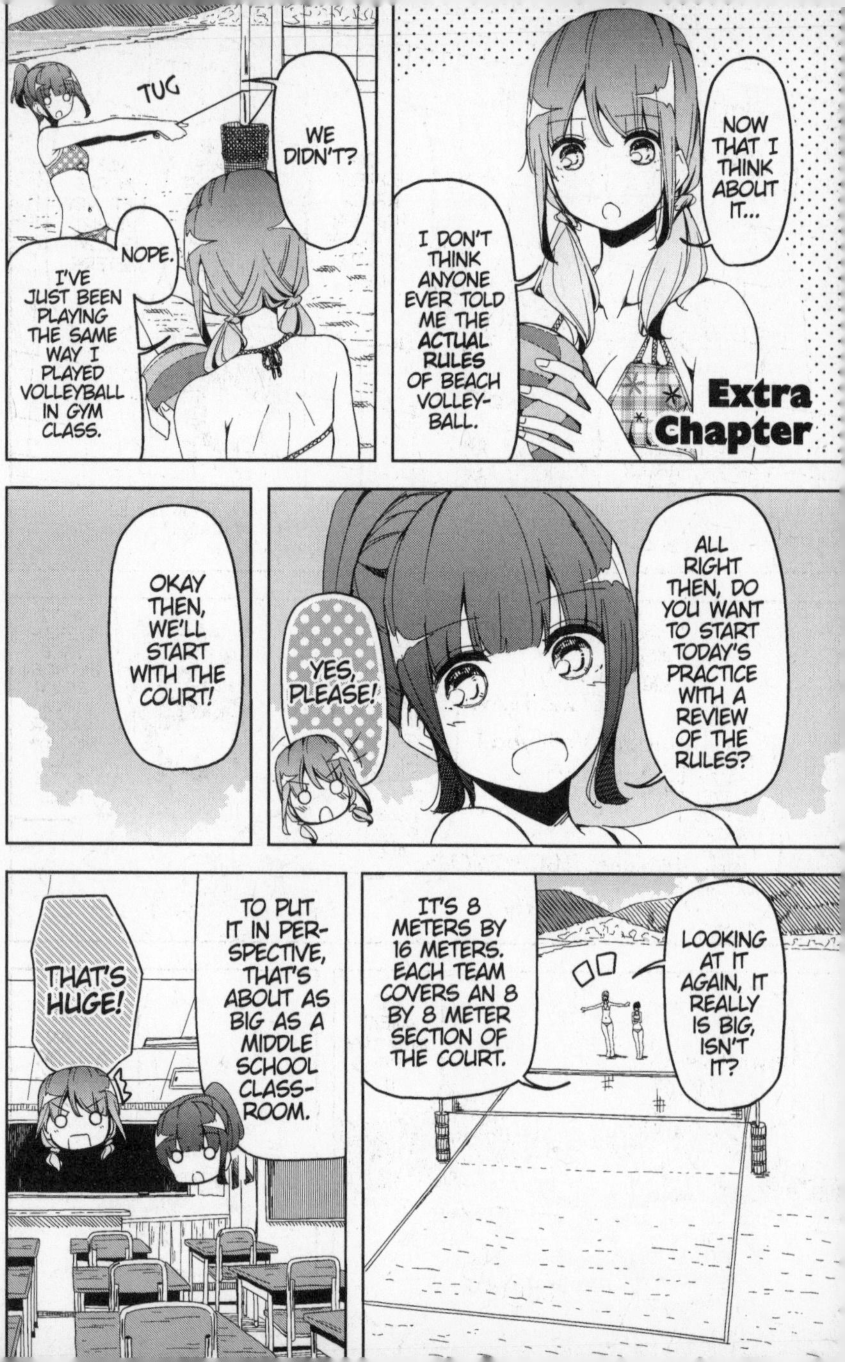
Extra Chapter
NOW THAT I THINK ABOUT IT...
I DON'T THINK ANYONE EVER TOLD ME THE ACTUAL RULES OF BEACH VOLLEY-BALL.
WE DIDN'T?
TUG
NOPE.
I'VE JUST BEEN PLAYING THE SAME WAY I PLAYED VOLLEYBALL IN GYM CLASS.
ALL RIGHT THEN, DO YOU WANT TO START TODAY'S PRACTICE WITH A REVIEW OF THE RULES?
YES, PLEASE!
OKAY THEN, WE'LL START WITH THE COURT!
LOOKING AT IT AGAIN, IT REALLY IS BIG, ISN'T IT?
IT'S 8 METERS BY 16 METERS. EACH TEAM COVERS AN 8 BY 8 METER SECTION OF THE COURT.
TO PUT IT IN PER-SPECTIVE, THAT'S ABOUT AS BIG AS A MIDDLE SCHOOL CLASS-ROOM.
THAT'S HUGE!

NEXT IS THE NET. NET HEIGHT IS 2.24 METERS...

THE SAME HEIGHT AS AN INDOOR VOLLEY-BALL NET.

I CAN BARELY REACH THE TOP, SO THAT'S PRETTY HIGH!

I'VE GOT MIXED FEELINGS ABOUT THAT...

MY CONFLICTED FEMININE HEART...!

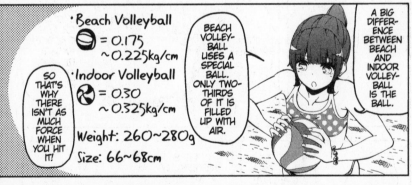

A BIG DIFFER-ENCE BETWEEN BEACH AND INDOOR VOLLEY-BALL IS THE BALL.

BEACH VOLLEY-BALL USES A SPECIAL BALL. ONLY TWO-THIRDS OF IT IS FILLED UP WITH AIR.

·Beach Volleyball
= 0.175 ~0.225kg/cm

·Indoor Volleyball
= 0.30 ~0.325kg/cm

Weight: 260~280g
Size: 66~68cm

SO THAT'S WHY THERE ISN'T AS MUCH FORCE WHEN YOU HIT IT!

THIS IS AN INDOOR VOLLEY-BALL.

GO AHEAD AND TRY HITTING IT.

RIGHT!

BOMP

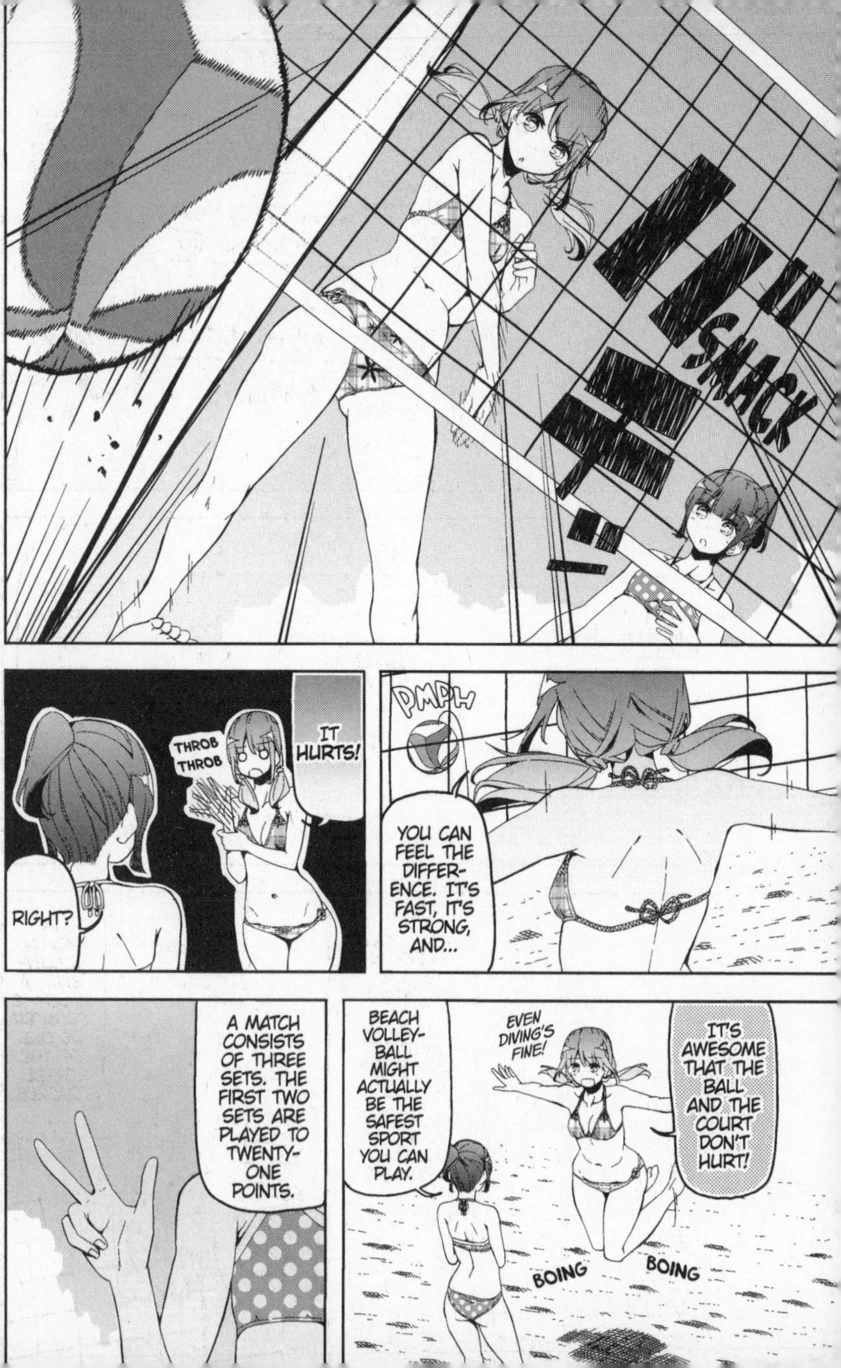
SMACK
PMPH
YOU CAN FEEL THE DIFFERENCE. IT'S FAST, IT'S STRONG, AND...
IT HURTS!
THROB THROB
RIGHT?
IT'S AWESOME THAT THE BALL AND THE COURT DON'T HURT!
EVEN DIVING'S FINE!
BEACH VOLLEYBALL MIGHT ACTUALLY BE THE SAFEST SPORT YOU CAN PLAY.
BOING BOING
A MATCH CONSISTS OF THREE SETS. THE FIRST TWO SETS ARE PLAYED TO TWENTY-ONE POINTS.

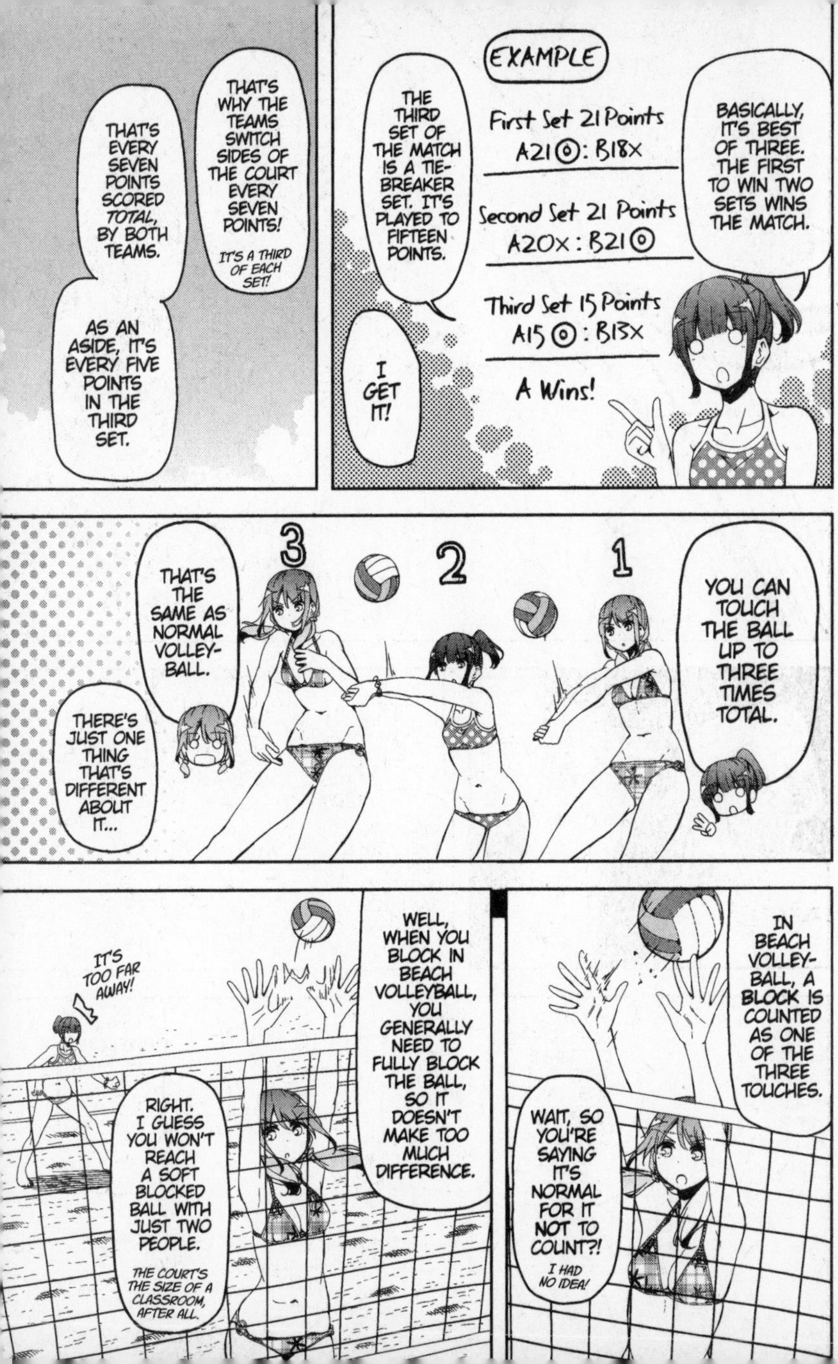
BASICALLY, IT'S BEST OF THREE. THE FIRST TO WIN TWO SETS WINS THE MATCH.
EXAMPLE
First Set 21 Points
A21 ◎ : B18 ×
Second Set 21 Points
A20 × : B21 ◎
Third Set 15 Points
A15 ◎ : B13 ×
A Wins!
THE THIRD SET OF THE MATCH IS A TIE-BREAKER SET. IT'S PLAYED TO FIFTEEN POINTS.
I GET IT!
THAT'S WHY THE TEAMS SWITCH SIDES OF THE COURT EVERY SEVEN POINTS!
IT'S A THIRD OF EACH SET!
THAT'S EVERY SEVEN POINTS SCORED TOTAL, BY BOTH TEAMS.
AS AN ASIDE, IT'S EVERY FIVE POINTS IN THE THIRD SET.
YOU CAN TOUCH THE BALL UP TO THREE TIMES TOTAL.
1
2
3
THAT'S THE SAME AS NORMAL VOLLEYBALL.
THERE'S JUST ONE THING THAT'S DIFFERENT ABOUT IT...
IN BEACH VOLLEYBALL, A BLOCK IS COUNTED AS ONE OF THE THREE TOUCHES.
WAIT, SO YOU'RE SAYING IT'S NORMAL FOR IT NOT TO COUNT?!
I HAD NO IDEA!
WELL, WHEN YOU BLOCK IN BEACH VOLLEYBALL, YOU GENERALLY NEED TO FULLY BLOCK THE BALL, SO IT DOESN'T MAKE TOO MUCH DIFFERENCE.
IT'S TOO FAR AWAY!
RIGHT. I GUESS YOU WON'T REACH A SOFT BLOCKED BALL WITH JUST TWO PEOPLE.
THE COURT'S THE SIZE OF A CLASSROOM, AFTER ALL.

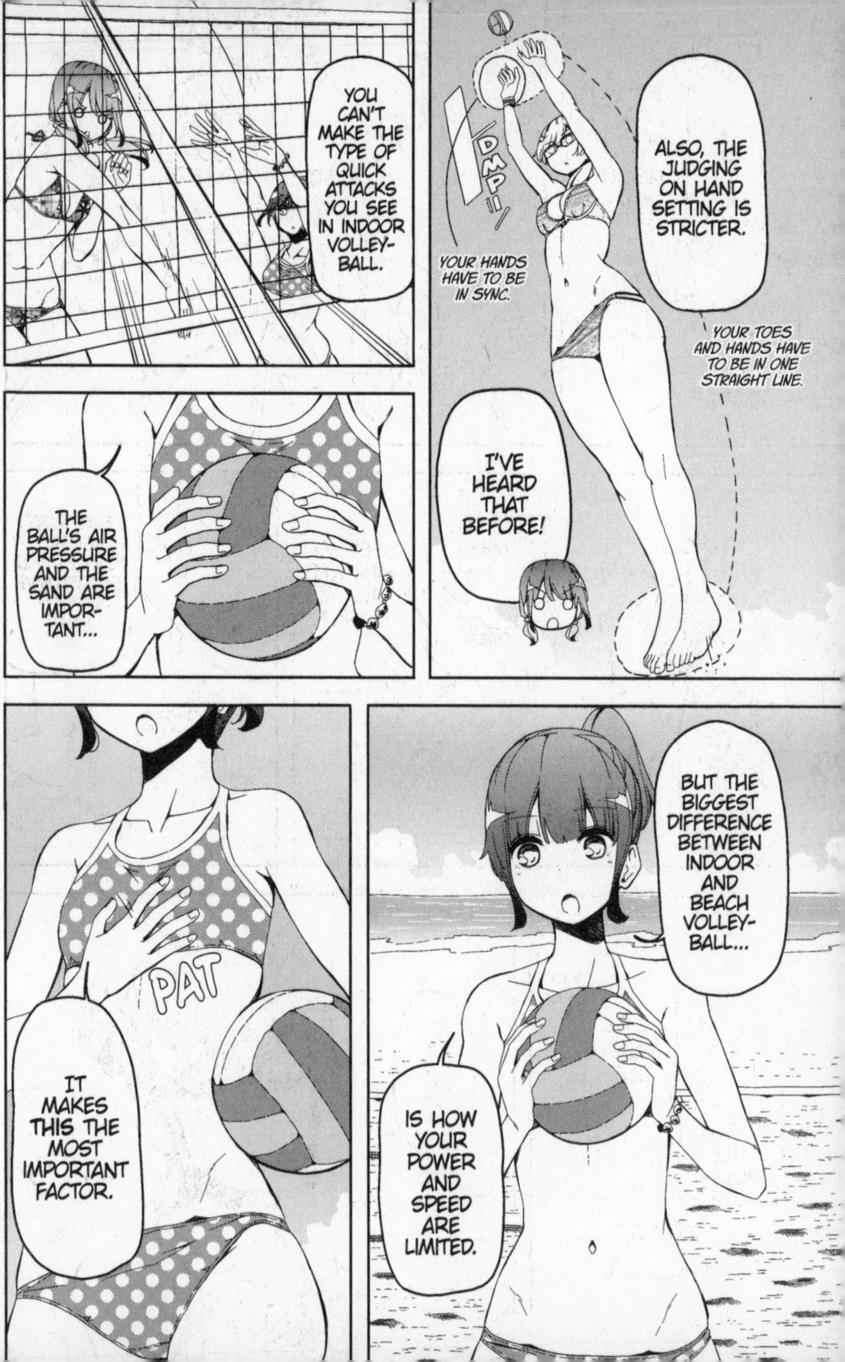
ALSO, THE JUDGING ON HAND SETTING IS STRICTER.
DMP!!
YOUR HANDS HAVE TO BE IN SYNC.
YOUR TOES AND HANDS HAVE TO BE IN ONE STRAIGHT LINE.
I'VE HEARD THAT BEFORE!
YOU CAN'T MAKE THE TYPE OF QUICK ATTACKS YOU SEE IN INDOOR VOLLEY-BALL.
THE BALL'S AIR PRESSURE AND THE SAND ARE IMPOR-TANT...
BUT THE BIGGEST DIFFERENCE BETWEEN INDOOR AND BEACH VOLLEY-BALL...
IS HOW YOUR POWER AND SPEED ARE LIMITED.
PAT
IT MAKES THIS THE MOST IMPORTANT FACTOR.

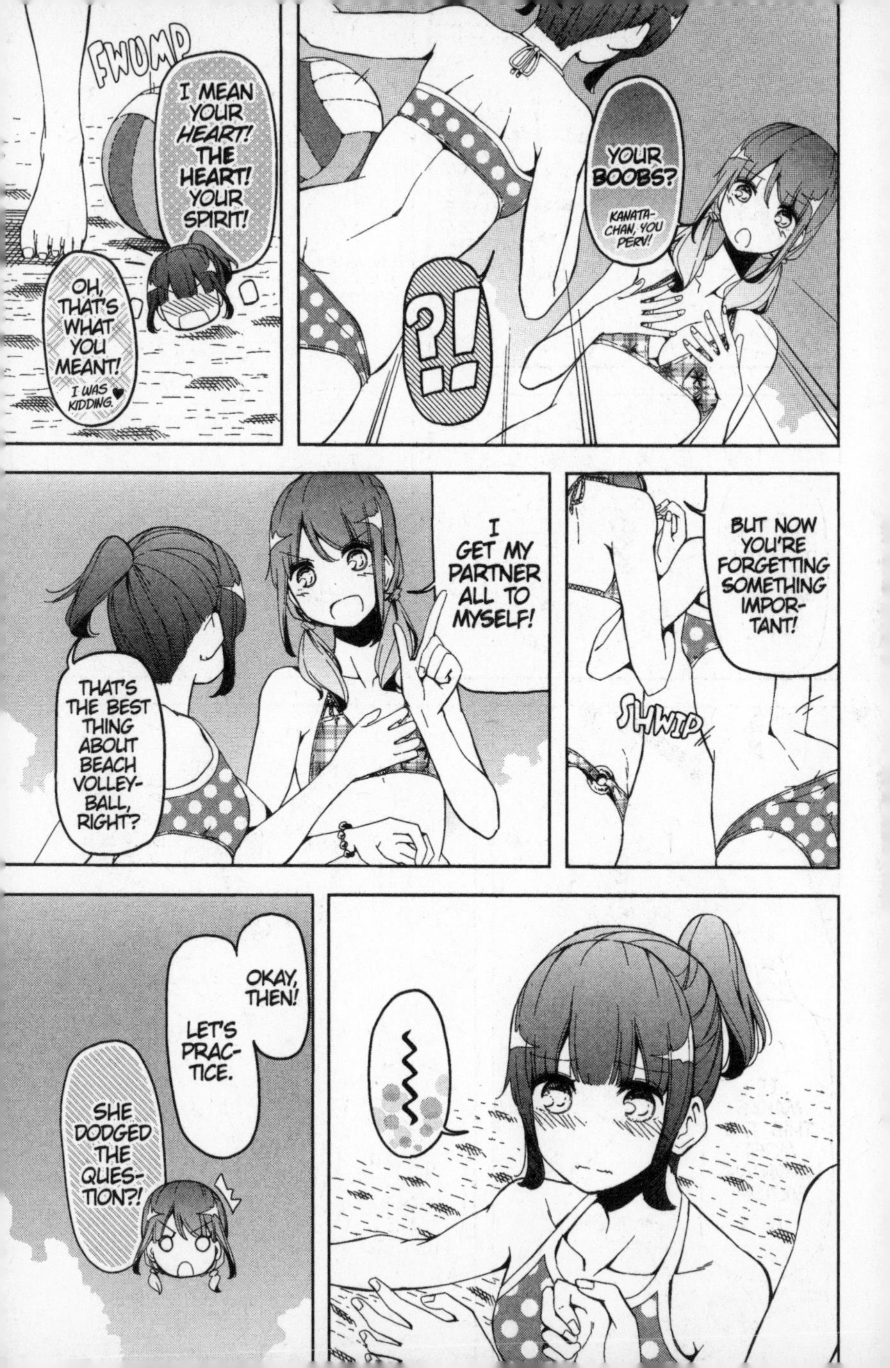
YOUR BOOBS?
KANATA-CHAN, YOU PERV!
?!
FWUMP
I MEAN YOUR HEART! THE HEART! YOUR SPIRIT!
OH, THAT'S WHAT YOU MEANT!
I WAS KIDDING.
BUT NOW YOU'RE FORGETTING SOMETHING IMPORTANT!
SHWIP
I GET MY PARTNER ALL TO MYSELF!
THAT'S THE BEST THING ABOUT BEACH VOLLEYBALL, RIGHT?
OKAY, THEN!
LET'S PRACTICE.
SHE DODGED THE QUESTION?!

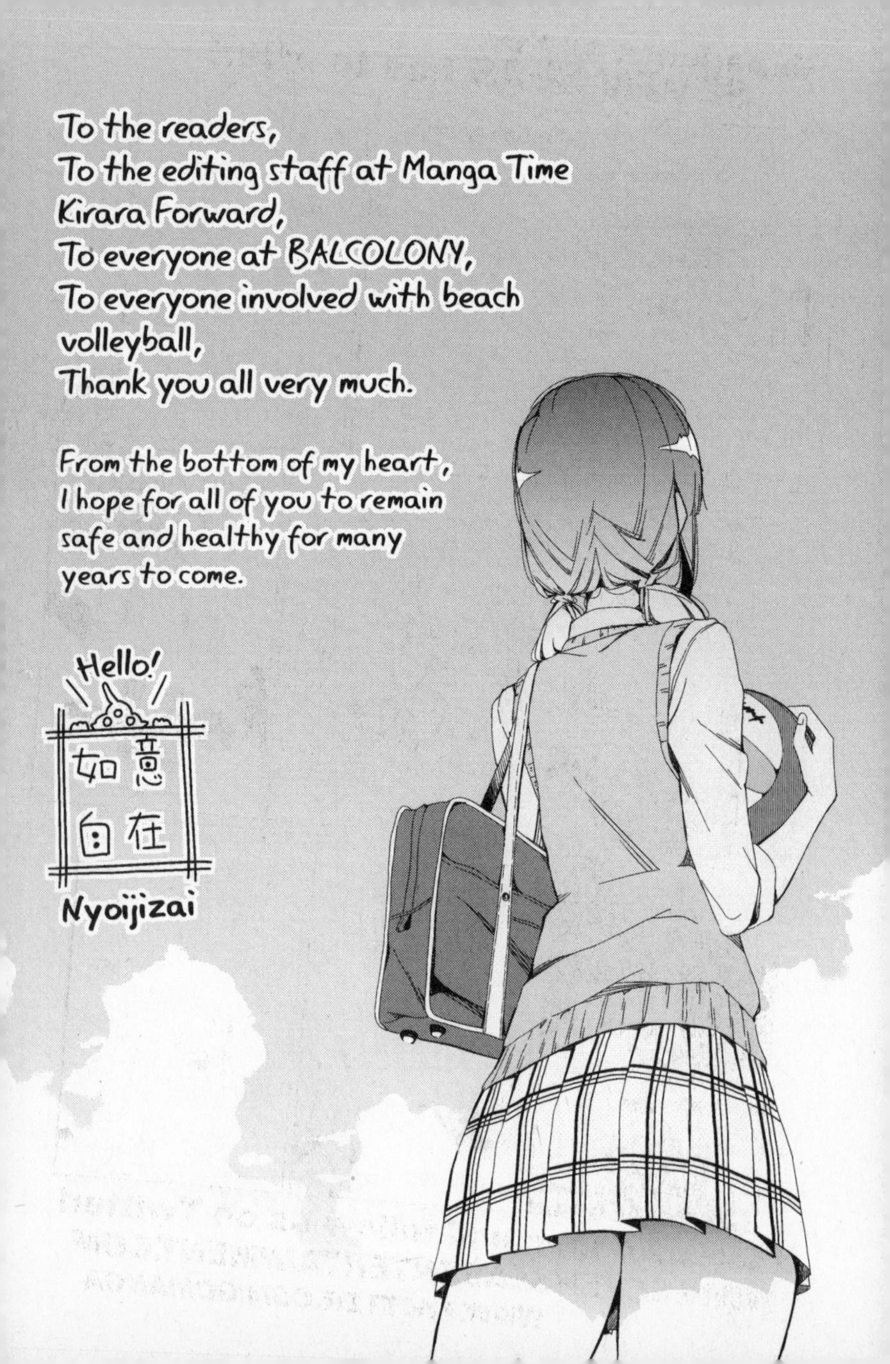
To the readers,
To the editing staff at Manga Time Kirara Forward,
To everyone at BALCOLONY,
To everyone involved with beach volleyball,
Thank you all very much.
From the bottom of my heart, I hope for all of you to remain safe and healthy for many years to come.
Hello!
如意自在
Nyoijizai

SEVEN SEAS ENTERTAINMENT PRESENTS

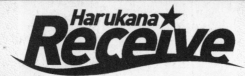

Harukana Receive

VOLUME 1

story and art by NYOI JIZAI

TRANSLATION
David Musto
Amanda Haley

ADAPTATION
Claudie Summers

LETTERING AND RETOUCH
Ray Steeves

COVER DESIGN
KC Fabellon

PROOFREADER
Shanti Whitesides
Stephanie Cohen

ASSISTANT EDITOR
Shannon Fay
Jenn Grunigen

PRODUCTION ASSISTANT
CK Russell

PRODUCTION MANAGER
Lissa Pattillo

EDITOR-IN-CHIEF
Adam Arnold

PUBLISHER
Jason DeAngelis

HARUKANA RECEIVE VOL. 1

First published in 2016 by Houbunsha Co., LTD. Tokyo, Japan.
English translation rights arranged with Houbunsha Co., TLD.

ISBN: 978-1-626929-05-0

Printed in Canada

First Printing: July 2018

10 9 8 7 6 5 4 3 2 1

FOLLOW US ONLINE: ***www.sevenseasentertainment.com***

READING DIRECTIONS

This book reads from ***right to left***, Japanese style. If this is your first time reading manga, you start reading from the top right panel on each page and take it from there. If you get lost, just follow the numbered diagram here. It may seem backwards at first, but you'll get the hang of it! Have fun!!

1
2
3
4
5
6
7
8
9

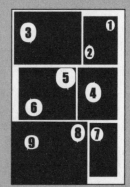

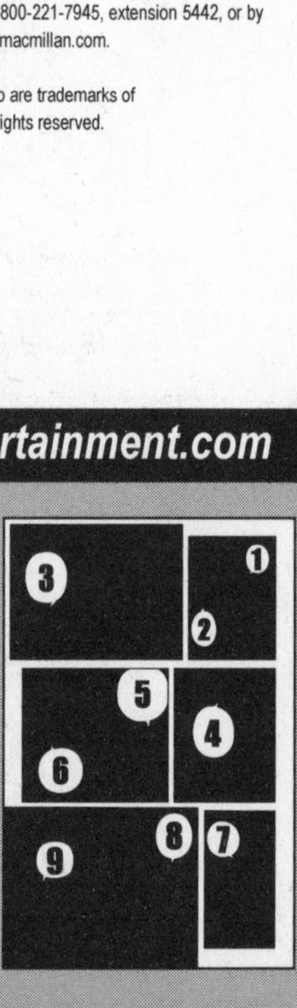